Publisher's Note

The book descriptions we ask booksellers to display prominently warn that this is an historic book with numerous typos or missing text; it is not indexed or illustrated.

The book was created using optical character recognition software. The software is 99 percent accurate if the book is in good condition. However, we do understand that even one percent can be an annoying number of typos! And sometimes all or part of a page may be missing from our copy of the book. Or the paper may be so discolored from age that it is difficult to read. We apologize and gratefully acknowledge Google's assistance.

After we re-typeset and design a book, the page numbers change so the old index and table of contents no longer work. Therefore, we often remove them.

Our books sell so few copies that you would have to pay hundreds of dollars to cover the cost of our proof reading and fixing the typos, missing text and index. Instead we usually let our customers download a free copy of the original typo-free scanned book. Simply enter the barcode number from the back cover of the paperback in the Free Book form at www.general-books.net. You may also qualify for a free trial membership in our book club to download up to four books for free. Simply enter the barcode number from the back cover onto the membership form on our home page. The book club entitles you to select from more than a million books at no additional charge. Simply enter the title or subject onto the search form to find the books.

If you have any questions, could you please be so kind as to consult our Frequently Asked Questions page at www.general-books.net/faqs.cfm? You are also welcome to contact us there.

General Books LLC™, Memphis, USA, 2012.

-:-   -:-   -:-   -:-   -:-   -:-   -:-   -:-

PART III OF THE PUBLICATIONS OF AN AMERICAN ARCHAEOLOGICAL EXPEDITION TO SYRIA i899-1900 GREEK AND LATIN INSCRIPTIONS PART III OF THE PUBLICATIONS OF AN AMERICAN ARCHAEOLOGICAL EXPEDITION TO SYRIA IN 1899-1900 » UNDER THE PATRONAGE OF V. EVERIT MACY, -CLARENCE M. HYDE, B. TALBOT B. HYDE, AND I. N. PHELPS STOKES « 8reek AND LATIN INSCRIPTIONS BY

WILLIAM KELLY PRENTICE, PH.D. Copyright, 1908, by The Century Co. *Published April, rgo8*

The Devinne Press GREEK AND LATIN INSCRIPTIONS CONTENTS

PREFACE TO PART III HE inscriptions published in this volume belong to four different regions, which are treated in Chapters n, in, iv, and v, respectively. The first region lies east of the great bend of the Orontes River and west of the modern city of Haleb (Aleppo): its most northern point is Kal'at Sim'an, which is about opposite the center of the Bahr il-Abyad or Lake of Antioch: towards the south it reaches almost to the 30th parallel of latitude. This region includes three mountain ranges, the Djebel il-A'la, the Djebel Barisha and the Djebel Halakah. Of these, the first two are parallel ranges of nearly equal length, running nearly due north and south, the Djebel il-A'la on the west, the Djebel Barisha on the east of a narrow, irregular valley. At its northern end the Djebel Barisha turns towards the northeast, until it ends abruptly in the deep gorge which separates it from the Djebel Halakah, and through which runs an ancient Roman road. The Djebel Halakah, or *Ring Mountain,* stretches from this pass towards the northeast, and encloses the plain in which Sermeda and Dana are situated: the northeastern part of this ring of mountains includes the Djebel Shekh Berekat and the Djebel Sim'an. The inscriptions of this region are dated according to the era of Antioch, which began in October of the year 49 B.c.

The second region lies almost immediately south of the first. It is the region of the Djebel Riha, at the foot of the eastern slope of which, not far south of its center, lies the modern city of Ma'arrit in-Nu'man. With it, however, has been included also Kal'at il-Mudik, the ancient Apamea. These inscriptions, with the exception of those from Ruweha, Ktellata. and Riha, are dated according to the Seleucid era, which began in October, 312 B.C. The three towns just mentioned are on the northeastern slope of the mountain; they seem to have employed the era of Antioch.

These two regions together comprise the first district discussed by Mr. Butler in Part II of these publications under the name of Northern Central Syria. Properly this district extends as far northward as the modern carriage road from Iskenderun (Alexandretta) to Haleb (Aleppo), which, after traversing the Bailan Pass and reaching a point about opposite to Kal'at Sim'an, makes a wide bend to the north in order to avoid these mountains. The northern end of the district, however, was not visited by this expedition, but was explored in the Spring of 1905 by an expedition sent out by Princeton University. The whole of this district has a certain unity with respect both to its natural conditions and to its architectural remains. The hills are of white limestone, and are now almost bare: it is evident, however, that in former times they were to a large extent covered with soil, and capable of a high degree of cultivation. In them are to be found the ruins of from two to three hundred ancient towns, which flourished between the middle of the first and the middle of the seventh century after Christ. The character of their beautiful buildings, constructed of the splendid material furnished by the hills themselves, attests the luxury and refinement of the ancient inhabitants.

The third region includes, first, Selemiyeh and Kinnesrin. The former of these is situated about twenty miles southeast of Hama: the latter, now sometimes called il-'Is, is a small village on the site of the ancient Chalcis, at the northern end of the marsh called il-Matkh and about twenty miles southwest of Haleb. Secondly, the Djebel il-Hass, a long range which lies east of il-Matkh and south of the lake called isSabkhah. Thirdly, the Djebel Shbet, a smaller mountain which lies southeast of the Djebel il-Hass. The inscriptions from this region are dated according to the Seleucid era, and most of them belong to the sixth century after Christ. The region of the Djebel il-Hass and the Djebel Shbet differs from the first two regions in that its mountains are of a black basalt, which forms a striking contrast to the white limestone of the regions farther west. The ruins also show a difference, both in methods of construction and in style of ornamentation, as great as the difference in the materials of which they are constructed.1 With the inscriptions from this district I have also

'See Part II, Chapter vm.

included eighteen others from Ba'albek, Tell Nebi Mindo, Hama, Ma'arrit in-Nu'man, Khan Sebil, Isriyeh, Palmyra, the "Khan il-Abyad" on the route from

Palmyra to Damascus, and Dmer.

The fourth region is that of the Djebel Hauran, or Djebel id-Druz, the mountain range lying southeast of Damascus and east of the Sea of Tiberias. No attempt was made by this expedition to explore thoroughly any part of this region, which many travelers have visited. But about a hundred Greek and Latin inscriptions2 were copied here, and these are given below. Some of these inscriptions are dated by the name of the emperor or governor under whose administration the monument was erected, some according to the so-called era of Bosra which is reckoned from March, 105 A.d., some according to various local eras.

A description of these regions and maps of the country will be found in Part I of these publications.

In the arrangement of the inscriptions the itinerary of this expedition has been followed as far as seemed practical: but such changes have been made as were necessary to secure a continuous progression. Thus in the first region, the arrangement of the towns begins with Benabil, a village near the northern end of the Djebel il-A'la, proceeds southward through this mountain range, crosses to 'Arshin at the southern end of the Djebel Barisha, passes northward through this second range and finally turning toward the northeast traverses the Djebel Halakah to Kal'at Sim'an. In the second district the order of towns begins at the south, with Kal'at il-Mudik, and passes northward through the Djebel Riha to its northern extremity. In the third district the order begins with Selemiyeh and Kinnesrin, then passes through the Djebel il-Hass and the Djebel Shbet from northwest to southeast, and lastly includes the nine other towns mentioned above. In the fourth district the order passes down the eastern side of the Ledja from Sawara il-Kebireh to Tarba and Mushennef, thence westward through Shehba, Kanawat and Suweda to Zor'ah.

Within the several localities the dated inscriptions have been placed first, in chronological order, and after them the undated inscriptions. But it seemed im-

practicable to carry out this plan strictly, because some of the undated inscriptions belong obviously to an earlier period than any of the dated ones, while others were so closely inscriptions, Nos. 356-438.

associated with dated inscriptions that to separate them seemed foolish. The departure from a simple plan, however, has involved the editor of this volume in certain inconsistencies; and some undated inscriptions, which doubtless belong to an earlier period, have been placed with the rest at the end of the collections from their respective towns. Moreover, there are some inscriptions which now, after the lapse of several years, this editor would gladly transfer to some other place in their series; but, inasmuch as the other members of the expedition, in referring to the Greek inscriptions, were obliged to use the numbers which had been assigned already, it was impossible to make any change in the original order of arrangement.

In preparing this volume I have endeavored to present a complete collection of the Greek and Latin inscriptions of the Djebel Riha, the Djebel il-A'la, the Djebel Barisha and of that part of the Djebel Halakah which is on the northern and western sides of the Plain of Dana, so far as these inscriptions had been published already or were discovered by this expedition without excavation. I have also included herewith the inscriptions of the Djebel Shekh Berekat and those published by Waddington from Katura, Refadeh and Dcr Sim'an. On my second visit to Syria in 1905, I found a number of inscriptions in the Djebel Riha which I had not seen before, a larger number in the Djebel Barisha, particularly at Dar Kita where ten new inscriptions were discovered, and about a hundred between Katura and the road from Iskenderun to Haleb, which properly belong with those from the Djebel Halakah. To each of the inscriptions in Chapters 11 and in a separate number has been given, irrespective of whether it was reported by this expedition or not. No attempt has been made to publish here a complete collection of the inscriptions found in the other regions mentioned (Chapters iv and v), but only those are given which were reported by this expedition, together with a few others which have some special connection with these or which throw light on some inscription or monument discussed in these publications. Inscriptions of this sort are distinguished by a letter added to the number of the inscription immediately preceding, as for example, No. 336 a, Nos. 364 a-d, etc.

In cases where an inscription presented here has been published by others, I have not thought it necessary to quote the variant readings, except when my own seemed to me uncertain and the variant readings might make possible a better rendering of the text. But I have endeavored in every case to give references to the other editions' of these inscriptions. In view of the large number of publications in which inscriptions appear, and the limitations of our American libraries, this has not always been possible for me. In particular I regret exceedingly that I have not seen the "Inventaire des inscriptions asiatiques chretiennes" by M. Cumont in the *Melanges d'Archeologie de I' Ecolefrangaise de Rome*, xv, pp. 245-299, and M. Sejourne's article in the *Revue Biblique* for 1898. I regret also that the copies of certain of the following inscriptions made by M. Gosche, Belgian Consul at Aleppo, about the year 1700, and published by M. Seymour de Ricci in the *Revue Archeologique,* Sept.-Oct. 1907, p. 281 ff., did not reach me in time to be of service in my own publication. M. Gosche's copy of No. 100 is especially important, inasmuch as this inscription appears to have been intact when seen by him: this earliest copy, however, confirms the restorations proposed below. Also for No. 98 M. Gosche has preserved the date 235-236 A.d. If there are others whose writings I have overlooked, I beg them to believe that in ignorance I did it, and not through failure to appreciate their scholarly work. A list of abbreviations used in referring to various publications will be found at the end of this volume.

In editing the text of these inscriptions I have made such emendations and restorations as seemed to me certain. In so doing I have employed the usual signs: the square brackets, , enclose letters, originally carved, but now lost; the round brackets, ( ), signify that letters included between them either were not originally carved, but are necessary to complete the words intended, or that these letters, while originally carved, have been misread. Reference to the epigraphical text, which is given in each instance, will make immediately apparent the significance of these brackets in each special case. Lastly, the angular brackets,), have been used to distinguish letters which were carved upon the stone by mistake, and are not necessary for the proper rendering of the inscription. Other emendations or restorations, which seemed to me uncertain, I have presented in the commentaries to the several inscriptions.

Much difficulty has been experienced in the rendering of proper names. A large number of the names in these inscriptions are undoubtedly Semitic in their origin, although they appear here in Greek forms. Some of these are to be found in the Greek literature, and they have come to have a traditional rendering with regard to the breathing of the initial vowels and to the accent. I have generally followed this traditional rendering; in some cases, however, especially where the name has had no Greek tradition, I have omitted the breathing and accent altogether.

Lastly, I wish to express my thanks, first of all, to the four gentlemen by whose generosity this expedition was equipped and supported, and secondly, to the other members of this expedition for the continued assistance which they have rendered to me, especially Dr. Littmann, by whose advice I have profited throughout the whole preparation of this book, and who supplied almost all the information published here with regard to the Semitic forms of proper names. I hold in grateful recollection Professor Friedrich Blass and Professor Wilhelm Dittenberger: to them and to Professor Carl Robert I am deeply indebted for their teaching and personal influence during my student life in Halle, as well as for the suggestions which are acknowledged in the commentaries to several of the inscriptions. To Professor Clermont-Ganneau I would express my appreciation of the friendly interest which he has taken in these publications, for the suggestions which he has made to me personally on several matters, and for the guidance and inspiration which I have had from the long series of articles by this master of Syrian epigraphy. Lastly, I wish to acknowledge my indebtedness to the late Professor Mortimer Lamson Earle and to Professor James C. Egbert of Columbia University, of whom the former contributed valuable suggestions concerning the inscription of the bath at Serdjilla, and the latter kindly consented to advise me with regard to the Latin inscriptions in this volume.

William Kelly Prentice.

Princeton University, December, 1907.

GREEK AND LATIN INSCRIPTIONS FROM NORTHERN CENTRAL SYRIA, PALMYRA AND THE REGION OF THE HAURAN GREEK AND LATIN INSCRIPTIONS FROM NORTHERN CENTRAL SYRIA, PALMYRA AND THE REGION OF THE HAURAN CHAPTER I THE CHARACTER AND PURPOSE OF THE INSCRIPTIONS OF NORTHERN CENTRAL SYRIA

THE Greek and Latin inscriptions from Northern Central Syria, collected by this expedition, fall chronologically into two distinct groups, the one ranging in date from about 60 A.d. to the year 250, the other from 324 to 609 A.d. Of two hundred and eighty-three inscriptions from this region more than one hundred are definitely dated: most of the others can be assigned with reasonable certainty to one or other of the two periods mentioned, either by the contents of the inscriptions themselves, or by the character of the buildings and monuments on which they are carved, or by the forms of the letters. This last criterion, however, is by no means so decisive as might be expected. Numbers 100-108 a, from the Djebel Sh£kh Berekat, for example, together with numbers 8 and 48, all of which belong to the first or second century after Christ, present nearly all the characteristic forms which occur until near the end of the fifth century. Only for the sixth century, beginning with about 480 A.d., there appears to have been a new style of writing, which I have not found earlier in these inscriptions, though the older styles still continued in use. This later style comprises such forms as A, which in these inscriptions appears first in 550 A.d., and again in 554, 567, 588, and 609, M found in inscriptions of 480 and 635 A.d., and X in inscriptions of 483, 536, 554, 567, 570 and 588 A.d. A few other forms, occurring less frequently, seem also to be of comparatively late usage in this country, such as A, 473 A.d., A, 473 and ¥, 635 (Ba'albek): also (= A), 537, and Oo(= B), 480 and 537. 3

In the second place, the inscriptions of the earlier period relate, in the main, to temples and images of the pagan gods, or to tombs and sepulchral monuments:1 the inscriptions of the later period are found upon nearly every sort of monument and building, but chiefly upon tombs, churches and private houses. It may be, however, that some of the undated inscriptions on dwelling houses, such, for example, as Nos. 10 and 114, belong to the earlier group.

Thirdly, no single one of these inscriptions, which can be assigned with certainty to the earlier period, contains the name of God, or a Christian symbol of any sort, or any reference to the Christian religion. The later inscriptions, on the other hand, are predominantly Christian in character.

The monuments and buildings belonging to the earlier period, which are described by Mr. Butler in Part II of these publications, show that between the middle of the first and the middle of the third century after Christ, at least in certain localities of this region, there were persons of wealth and distinction living in no small degree of refinement and luxury. To choose but a few examples out of many, no handsomer building has been discovered in this region than the temple at Burdj Bakirha,2 no finer rock-hewn tomb than that built for

Sosandros at Bshindelaya.,3 no handsomer sepulchral monuments than those at Benabil, at 'Amud Sermeda and at Kefr Ruma.4 Dated inscriptions of this period were found at the following places: Bshindelaya, Kefr Finsheh, Burdj Bakirha, Bakirha, Babiska, 'Amud Sermeda, Dana, Djebel Shekh Berekat, Katura, Kal'at il-Mudik, Kefr Ambil, Khirbit Hass and Ma'arrit Betar; and these may be taken as examples of the early centers of this Greco-Roman-Aramaic civilization. A second journey which I had an opportunity to make into this country in the Spring of 1905 convinced me that, in general, the earliest settlements in this region are those farthest north, and that on the slopes of the Djebel Shekh Berekat and in the country which lies about Refadeh and Katura, and still farther north about Kefr Nabu and Brad, are the oldest settlements of which remains are still preserved. In these localities groups of buildings were found of a type which seemed to me earlier than those of the dated buildings which belong to the latter half of the fourth century.

There is little in these earlier inscriptions to show either the character of the people, their manner of living, or their form of government. The few names given in the inscriptions are predominantly Greek, such as NeiKarcup Mevia-Kov (Nos. 100 and 101), KpaTeas 'AvSpoveLKov (Nos. 104 and 105), or Roman, e.g., Ai/uixxio? 'Pyeu'os (No. 112), or Greek with Roman nomina and praenomina prefixed, e.g., Ti. ΚΧ. Oixokxtj?, son of Ti. ΚΧ. twravhpo; (No. 8): a few others, however, are of Semitic origin, e.g., XaX/JiW, Mαpiav, MaXiW, 'Apajoio?, Kcua(ju)o5, A/n/3as, Bapov/n/u,os, and a feminine Knrapow. An inscription5 found at Kal'at il-Mudik, the ancient Apamea, shows that this city was 1 There are of course a few others, such, for example, as 2 Inscription No. 48.

Nos. 74 and 127, referring to public, highways, No. 126, re-:i Inscription No. 8. Part II, p. 60 ferring to some public work, No. 125, referring to a statue 4 Inscriptions Nos. 2, 87 and 173. Part II, p. 59 ff.

of an emperor, etc. 5 Inscription No. 126. especially favored by one of the Antonines. An inscription1 of Trajan and another of Septimius Severus2 were also found at this place: certain other inscriptions3 show that a part, at least, of the Second Parthian Legion and a squadron of Roman cavalry, the Ala Britannica.were stationed here at one-time. Aimillios Regeinos, whose tomb at Katura is dated 195A.D.,4 was a *fior)dbs Kopvucovkap'uav vnarLKov*, i. e., *adjutor officii comiculariorum consnlaris*. The inscription on the living rock near Kasr il-Benat shows that a road was built here under the emperor Marcus Aurelius.

The ancient religion lingered on in this region certainly through the first and second centuries. The names of Zeus, Helios, Selene, Eros, Nike, and Agathe Tyche5 appear in the inscriptions, also a god Selamanes, who has been identified with the Assyrian Shalmanu. Representations of certain gods appear also among the few sculptures of the region, chiefly those of the gods of the sun and moon, the former with rays about the head, the latter with a crescent either above the head or back of the neck, the horns of the crescent rising on either side of the head. One Manlaios son of Antas6 calls himself a priest, without mentioning his god. At least three pagan temples are still preserved in part.7 One at Silfaya8 is without any inscription, and seems to have been rebuilt and put to another use at some later time. A second is the beautiful temple of Zeus Bomos at Burdj Bakirha.9 The gateway in the wall of the temenos, within which the temple is situated, bears an inscription10 which includes the date 161 A. d. The dimensions of this temple and its various parts show that this building, unlike the others in this region, was planned according to the Roman units of measure, and this fact suggests that this temple was erected by architects sent from the West. Before the temple, towards the East, are the remains of an ancient altar hewn from the living rock. And the name of the god indicates that this altar was an ancient "high-place," where the old Aramaean inhabitants worshipped a local god, who doubtless had no proper name, but was called simply the ba'al, i.e., the god of that place. To this god, in the Roman time, was built, perhaps by order of the emperor, a splendid temple. But the god remained still, as before, without a proper name; for the builders of the temenos gateway called him simply Zeus Bayids, or *Zeus-Altar.* Perhaps they were using these Greek words in a Semitic fashion, and meant simply the *ba'al-of-the-ancient-altar:* or perhaps to them the altar itself had become idol as well as altar, and hence they may have used the common noun *altar* as a proper name, feeling that some other name besides Zeus, or Ba'al, was needed in so formal an inscription.

Much the same phenomenon appears in connection with the third temple of which 1 Inscription No. 125. 7 The remains of other pagan temples also in the northern 2 Inscription No. 127. part of this region were found by the Princeton Archeologi 3 Inscriptions Nos. 128-134 inclusive. cal Expedition in the Spring of 1905.

4 Inscription No. 112. 8 See Part II, p. 71. 5 In most cases these are the Greek names assigned to Ori-9 See Part II, p. 66 ff. ental deities. 10 Inscription No. 48. 6 Inscription No. 86, dated in the year 112 A.d.

I have spoken, that of the Djebel Shekh Berekaf Of the temple itself only a few fragments and broken columns are now visible, and in fact even these fragments may prove to have belonged to the colonnade within the temenos wall, in which case there may have been no temple in the common sense. But the walls of the great temenos remain, in which and in the fragments of which nine inscriptions have been found, showing that this temenos was erected in the latter half of the first and the beginning of the second century after Christ, to the gods called Zeus Madbachos and Selamanes. Madbachos is but a Greek form for the Syriac word *madhbakh: altar,* and hence has precisely the same significance as the name Bw/aos at the other sanctuary. The other god has been identified with Shalmanu. In the center of

the temenos there appears to have been an ancient altar, as at Burdj Bakirha, and a seat of ancient Semitic pagan worship. The strange thing here is, as I have said elsewhere,2 that the local god was obliged, eventually, to share his honors with a naturalized foreigner.

These are but a few remains of ancient paganism, in view of the many ruins which this region still preserves. But doubtless the fierce fanaticism, for which the " Christians" of the diocese of Antioch were noted during the three centuries of their unrestricted power, sufficiently accounts for the complete obliteration of the monuments of the ancient faith. One may even wonder how it was that the temple at Burdj Bakirha was spared. Tradition has it that the temple was once used as a convent of nuns, and holes in the inside of the cella walls, as if for the beams to support the floor of a second story, seem to confirm the belief of the modern natives, who still give to the building the name *Kasr il-Bendt: the Castle of the Maidens.* If so, then this temple was preserved for the same reason as that other, the temple at Silfaya, both having been converted from their original use. The sanctuary on the Djebel Shekh Berekat was perhaps too hard of access to make its site desirable, save to those for whom the place was hallowed by its pagan associations. A single stone found on the summit of the mountain3 contains a cross, and a few letters which undoubtedly were part of a Christian inscription. But this is now the only visible mark of Christian occupation, and may have been brought from elsewhere. From its present condition one would judge that the mountain top had been deserted, and that its buildings had fallen into ruins, through the lapse of time; and in fact we learn from Theodoretus that the mountain top was " shunned as a place of devils." I have no doubt also that not a few churches in this region have utilized in their building the sites, and in part perhaps the foundations and even walls, of other pagan temples, as seems to have been the case at Babiska, as M. de Vogue believes to have been the case at Khirbit Hass, and as certainly was

the case in the Church of St. George at Zor'ah.5 And doubtless many other monuments of paganism, which could not be otherwise used, were destroyed, when Christianity was sanctioned by the state. There may well have been many more seats of pagan worship, and monuments of pagan art, in this region, during the first three centuries of the Christian era, than the extant ruins would indicate. On the other hand the fact that, among the inscriptions of the earlier period, not one shows any single trace of Christianity, certainly does not prove that there were not many Christians in this country at that time: it only proves, what is of course natural enough in itself, that on the. buildings and monuments Christianity was not openly acknowledged.

It is not strange that no inscriptions dated between 250 and 324 A.d. were found.1 These were troublous times, which began with the persecutions of the Christians under Decius and the great plague in nearly all parts of the empire under Gallus, included the defeat of the Romans under Valerian at Edessa and the raids of Sapor, the internal disruptions of the empire under Gallienus and the wars against many aspirants to the imperial throne, the restitution of the empire in the East by Aurelian, the defeat of Zenobia near Antioch and again near Horns, wars against the Parthians under Probus and under Carus, the reorganization of the empire under Diocletian and a general persecution of the Christians, the wars of Maxentius and Constantine, and later of Licinius and Constantine, and finally ended with the complete triumph of Constantine and the legitimation of Christianity. It is not strange therefore that the impulse to build new pagan monuments was lacking, when paganism was certainly moribund. On the other hand it is not strange that Christians did not begin to inscribe their monuments and buildings in such a period of persecution and of war. But the fact that not even tomb inscriptions of this time were found indicates, I think, that the private wealth of these communities was already in the hands of Christians.

With the year 323, however, when Constantine the Great became the sole ruler of the world, when Christianity was recognized by the government and favored above paganism, this region entered upon a new era. Beginning with 324 A.d. thirty dated inscriptions of the fourth century were found, thirty-eight of the fifth and twentynine of the sixth. Of these only one, the inscription of the tomb of Abedrapsas at Frikya, dated in the year 324, is distinctly pagan: almost all the others are distinctly Christian in character. Yet there is no reason to think that there was any change in the population, or in the conditions of life, in this region at this time. The names remain of the same types, except perhaps that purely Roman or Greek names occur less frequently than in the earliest inscriptions, particularly in those from the neighborhood of Katura. Nor could I see that there was any change, which might have taken place at this time, in the style of architecture or the types of buildings, as if the control of affairs, prosperity and building activity passed at this time to a different class of society. The single exception to this statement is that, of course, from the fourth century2 1 A few inscriptions of this period were found by the ex-but this date is most uncertain. The church at Babiska is pedition of 1905. dated 401 A.d. (Nos. 67 ff.; Part II, p. 131 ff.). Doubtless 2 The earliest dated church of this region is perhaps at churches were built before this. In 1905 a church was found Ba'udeh and may be as old as 336 A.d. (Inscr. No. 72); at Faiirtin, dated 373 A.d. on, churches and ecclesiastical buildings, of various sorts and in constantly increasing number and variety, were erected; but the oldest of those found by this expedition date from the very end of the fourth century. The change, therefore, which took place at this time seems to have involved only the practice of inscribing the monuments: up to this time apparently only the pagans had carved inscriptions upon their buildings: after this time the Christians did so. But if the development of the country was gradual, it is strange that we should find nearly as many dat-

ed inscriptions of the last three-quarters of the fourth century as of the fifth century, and even more than of the sixth. One reason may be that in the fourth century, when Christians began to place inscriptions upon the buildings which they erected, they also placed similar inscriptions on buildings which had been erected previously, but which had been without inscriptions during the pagan regime. If so, then the age of the inscriptions does not necessarily determine the age of the buildings which bear them, and, although no dated inscription earlier than the second quarter of the fourth century was found on any private house, and although most of the inscriptions on private houses are "Christian," yet many of these houses, even when so inscribed, may be as old as the third century after Christ, or even older. Moreover, since more than half of all the inscriptions are undated, it is impossible to make any accurate estimate of the number of inscriptions belonging to any particular century.

Practically all of the inscriptions of the later period, 324-609 A.d., are, as I have said already, "Christian" in their general characteristics. Many of these inscriptions, in my opinion, reflect the church service of the age.1 The best example of this is the following inscription, No. 6 below, which was found in the ruins at Bshindelinteh, in the mountain country immediately east of Antioch: "Ayios 6 ®eos, ayios 'Ir(x)v/os. ayios 'A$dva.Toi, (o-)Ta(v)/3o0(el)s Si'ias, r/f-qrov 17/Aas/ *Holy God, Jioly Mighty One, holy Immortal One, crucified for us, have mercy upon us.* This is the famous "trisagion,"

"Ayios o @eds, dyios ,(ryyp6i, dyios A#di/aTos, iker)rov i/xa?, together with the phrase 6 oTav/3cu#eis

St' /ias, inserted by the heretic Peter the Fuller, bishop of Antioch, about the year 470 A.d. The insertion of this phrase was a part of a fierce ecclesiastical controversy. The orthodox churchmen of the fifth century, believing that such formulae of worship should apply to the Trinity, interpreted the threefold invocation of the trisagion as referring successively to the three Persons of the

Godhead, and considered the subject of the verb *ikerjaov* to be the Trinity thus invoked. On the other hand, the sect of the monophysites, which was strongly represented in Antioch at this time, applied the whole invocation to the one God, and Peter, in inserting the words *"crucified for its,"* made the trisagion a distinctly monophysite formula, asserting that God was crucified.

This matter is discussed at greater length in a paper read before the American Philological Association in July, 1902. *Transactions Am. Philol. Ass.,* Vol. xxxm, p. 81 ff.

The trisagion, or *hymnns trisagius,* is to be distinguished from the *hymnus tersanctus,* or "triumphal hymn." The latter is one of the earliest hymns of the Christian Church, and had a place also in the Jewish ritual. The trisagion is not properly a hymn, but a short invocation, often thrice repeated, and is found in most of the Eastern liturgies, as, for example, in the Alexandrine liturgy, called the "Liturgy of St. Mark," in the so-called "Liturgy of St. James," and in the Syriac liturgies:1 it is not found, however, in the so-called "Liturgy of St. Clement." It was usually employed in the service after the "little entrance," and before the lections, as Iobios, a monk of the sixth century, States concerning it:2 d.p.a T5 *Trpbs* To 8vcri.a(TTtjpLOv daievai Tous *lepels 6 ipoijidTri;* dvcadev avafioa ro'Ayios 6 ©cos *Kt.* I believe that this inscription indicates that the church at Bshindelinteh belonged to the Jacobite sect, and this conclusion is strengthened by the fact that the trisagion, with a variant form of the monophysite clause added at the end, was found at Selemiyeh.3 I believe also that an inscription at Khanasir4 contained the monophysite version of the trisagion, and certainly the inscription reported by Egmondand Heyman from near Antioch.5

Not less interesting, in some ways, is an inscription found at Hass, on a mausoleum which dates probably from the fifth century:6 EvX-oy/xeVos 6 *ipx6p. evo; iv 6v6p.a.Ti Kvpiov©eos Ku/dios Kol intyavev r)p.lv: Blessed (is) he that cometh in (the) name of (the) Lord. God (is the) Lord, and hath shown tis light.* This is taken ultimately from Psalm cxvii, 26 and 27. But Psalms cxv-cxviii, to quote from Mr. Warren,7 "formed the second part of the Hallel, and were sung by every Jewish family or company at the conclusion of the Paschal Supper": they are generally supposed to have constituted "the hymn recorded to have been sung by our Saviour and His disciples after the institution and reception of the first Christian Eucharist." Almost the same words as those in this inscription occur in the *"Apostolic Constitutions"* vii, 26: *evoyqp.evos 6 ipXop.tvo; iv 6v6p,ari, Kvpiov.* ©cos Kupios 6 eVi£ai'eis 17ju.1i' *iv (rapid.* The first part also OCCUTS in the so-called "Liturgy of St. James"8 as a part of the *hymnus tersanctus,* or "triumphal hymn," of which I have already spoken, and which is said by Mr. Warren9 to have "formed a part of every known ancient liturgy. " It also forms a part of the Jewish *Kedusha.10*

Another liturgical passage occurs in several inscriptions, one found at WadI Marthun11 and the others at il-Barah.12 All these are undated. The first two are over 1 See C. A. Swainson, *The Greek Liturgies,* 1884, p. 12 n. 3, tary that it is not possible to say with certainty whether they pp. 14, 226, 383. include the heretical phrase or not.

2 Photius, *Bibliotheca,* Cod. 222 (edition of Bekker, 1824, 8 Waddington No. 2661 a, and No. 167 below. See also p. 191 A, 38ff). Part *U* P-160 ff „.T 7F. E. Warren, *The Liturgy and Ritual of the Ante-Nicene* 3 No. 295. ' *J* 22 *Church,* 1897, p. 33.

'322' 8 Swainson, p. 268.

5 *C. I. G.* 8918. Nos. 8916 and 8917 in the *Corpus* con-9p. 171. tain the trisagion without the addition: these inscriptions, 10Warren, p. 215. however, are not from Syria. Nos. 11, 205 and 312 in the n No. 213. present collection contain the trisagion, but are so fragmen-12 Nos. 196 and 197 a = Waddington No. 2647. doorways which apparently led to private dwellings, while the third is on a windowlintel. The first and third are fragmentary: the second is as follows: *Aoga iv wjuorois ©edJ, Kal im yy; eip-*

ijinj, iv avdpornois euSoKia; *Glory to God in the) highest, and on earth Peace, good will among men.* This passage is taken from Luke ii, 14, and is especially interesting in view of the dispute as to the reading cuSoxia or vSoaa?. It also occurs in the "Liturgy of St. James"1 to be repeated three times, and in the Coptic liturgy.2 The *Gloria Patri,* or "Lesser Doxology," is found in several inscriptions, one of which is in an underground rockhewn tomb at Kokanaya, dated in the month Loos, 369 A.D.3 The whole inscription is as follows: Euo-e£i & X/ioTiaiai. Ao£a *Uarpl Kal* Ttw Ku 'Aytw *Tlvevp.aTL.* vetou? £«/, *p,r)vl Adov K%';* *For Eusebius a Christian. Glory to the) Father, and to the) Son, and to the) Holy Spirit. In the) month of Loos, on the) 27th day), of the) year 417.* Another inscription, published in part by M. l'abbe Chabot, after a copy by M. Poche,4 contains the fuller form of this doxology. It is on the lintel of a ruined and half-buried building, probably a tomb, at il-Khanasir: Adfa *Uarpl Kal Olov Kal 'AyCov HvevpaTos (vvv) Kal* d(ei) Ka(l) e(i)s Tovs *al(i)va;. 'Apijv.* These words are followed by another line, which probably contains the date and the builder's name, but which I have been unable as yet to decipher. The *Gloria Patri* occurs in the "Liturgy of St. James," and in the Coptic liturgy. 5

In one inscription, found at Hass,6 on a lintel ornamented with an almost classic egg-and-dart moulding, the *Gloria Patri* is followed by the words *ISxrov Kvpie rbv XaoV aov: Lord save thy people.* The passage is undoubtedly taken from Psalm xxvii, 9; but it also occurs in the "Liturgy of St. James,"7 and near the beginning of the "Liturgy of St. Basil":8 in the latter case these words are immediately preceded by what is practically the equivalent of the *Gloria Patri:* on *irpeirei crot iraaa* Sofa, *npr) Kal irpoTKvvT)ri;, Tw Uarpi, Kal (kt.).*

Another inscription, found by M. de Vogue at il-Barah,9 contains the sentence K(vpio)? *iroip.ev(i) p,e, Kal ouSeV poi vo-Teptj(r(ei): The Lord is my shepherd, and nothing shall I lack.* These words are taken from Psalm xxii,

1: they occur also in the "Liturgy of St. James."10

Each of these six passages which I have thus far described is to be found, in precisely the same form, in one or more of the extant liturgies: all are to be found in the so-called " Liturgy of St. James." While three of them are from the Psalms, one is from the Gospel of Luke, and two arc not contained in the Bible at all. Hence they are not simply quotations from the Psalter, and they show that at least some of these Syrian inscriptions contain fragments of the ritual employed in the churches of this 1 Swainson, p. 254. 6 No. 156. 2 Swainson, p. 395. 7 Swainson, p. 230 f. 3 No. 34. 8 Swainson, p. 76: compare pp. 77 and 86. 4 *Journal Asiatique,* 1901, p. 442 = No. 321 9 Waddington No. 26so = No. 200. below. 10 Swainson, p. 314. 5 Swainson, p. 215 ff., and 226: compare also pp. 16, 76, 220 and 373. region between the third and the seventh centuries. They suggest that this ritual resembled either the "Liturgy of St. James" or the "Liturgy of St. Basil," in their present form, more closely than any other of the liturgies which remain to us. They suggest also that inscriptions may furnish some new and independent evidence as to which of the various manuscripts represent most nearly the original form of the liturgies which they contain. For example, of the four manuscripts of the "Liturgy of St. James," only the *Codex Rossanensis* and the *Codex Parisimis* No. 2509 contain the passage: Kupios *noifiaivu /xe* Ktx.

There are some fifty other texts among these inscriptions, which have much the same general character. None of these, however, has an exact parallel in the extant forms of the "liturgies "; but they are not, on this account, without importance in this connection. For it must be remembered that, with the exception of the few brief paragraphs in the *"Didache of the Apostles"* which is thought to date from the second century, and the remains of the liturgy in the *"Apostolic Constitutions"* we have no liturgy whose present form is known to be older than the eighth century: the Barberini codex, containing the liturgies called by the names of St. Basil, of St. Chrysostom, and of "The Presanctified," dates from the eighth or ninth century; a fragment in the University Library at Messina, containing a portion of the "Liturgy of St. James," is dated 960; while all the rest are from the twelfth century or later. And these manuscripts do not represent a fixed tradition, like so many copies of various literary productions. This is proved by the wide divergences between the different manuscripts purporting to contain the same liturgy. But each manuscript appears to represent that form of the given liturgy or liturgies known and in use at the time and. place at which the manuscript itself originated.1 None of our manuscripts of any liturgy therefore necessarily represent the liturgy used in the churches of Northern Syria between the third and the seventh centuries. That there was a liturgy, however, at that time, and indeed as early as the second century— perhaps from the very beginning of the Christian religion — is abundantly proved by the "Didache of the Apostles" and by the writings of Church Fathers such as Clement of Rome and Origen. Moreover, those passages, which the Greek versions and the Syriac versions of the " Liturgy of St. James" have in common, make it probable, as Sir William Palmer has pointed out,2 that certain portions of this liturgy were in existence, and were probably in use, in Northern Syria before the schism which took place not long after the Council of Chalcedon in 451 A.d. It follows that the absence of the text of an inscription from the extant liturgies does not prove that this text was not contained in a liturgy at all. On the contrary, a liturgy, fragments of which are found in inscriptions of the fourth, fifth and sixth centuries, is much older than the present form of most, perhaps of all, of the traditional liturgies.

1 See Swainson, *Greek Liturgies,* Introduction, pp. xxvii-xxxi.
2 *Origines Liturgicae,* 1845, Vol. I, p. 27 ff.

Some of these liturgical inscriptions, while they do not reflect the traditional

liturgies directly, are so similar in sense and in phraseology to certain extant passages, that it may be possible to determine the part of the service in which they probably belonged. The most interesting inscriptions of this sort in the present collection are the two following. The first is painted on the wall of a rock-hewn tomb in Shnan:1

The four letters BYMr, placed after each line except the last two, have numerical values whose sum is 2443: this is the sum of the numerical values of the letters of the refrain, 'tyo-ovs o Xpeiords. It is possible that these letters have also some other significance, as, for example, *B(oijdt),* T(os) *M(ovo)y(ars)*:2 *Help, Only-Begotten Son.* The other lines, exclusive of the refrain, begin with the letters A, r, A, E and z respectively, and are arranged in the alphabetical order of these letters:3 the refrain itself, which appears first as the second line, when written as a cryptogram begins with B, and thus completes the alphabetic sequence of initial letters from A through z. It seems to me improbable that such verses, containing no direct reference to the dead, were composed specially for an interior wall of a tomb. The third verse may be compared with a passage in the " Eighteen Benedictions " of the Jewish ritual, sec. 14b:4 "The branch of David Thy servant speedily cause to flourish," etc. But the rest, as far as concerns the thought, resembles in no small degree the hymn which, according to Dr. Neale, is indicated by the words 'o *povoyevrj? Tios xal* Adyos in the Alexandrine liturgy:5 'o *p.ovo yevr/s* Tios *Kox* Adyos *Tov* HeoC *adavaros virdpcjv,* KaraSefd/ievos Sid *rr/v r/fierepav crurrqpLav crapKwdrjvat, K rrjs* dyi'as *deoroKov /cat denrapdevov* Mannas, *aTpeTTT(o; ivavdpu)injo-a;,* crravptodeis Tc, Xpicrre 6 Beds, *Oavdrco ddvarov* naTtjcras, cfs *Stv* 777s dyias TpidSos, *crvvco£a£6fievo; rat TlarpX nai Tw dyua Uvevp-aTi, o-Sxrov* iias. The same hymn is referred to in the " Liturgy of St. James."6

The other inscription to which I have referred is from the "Tomb of Eusebios and Antoninos" in Hass:7 1 No. 254.

frain, dont le graveur aura omis le second vers, commencant 2 See below, p. 24, and Inscription No. 254. par la lettre B." 3 M.S. Petrides, in "*Echos d'Orient"* for May, 1904, p. 185, 4 Warren, *Liturgy and Ritual of the Ante-Nicene Church,* in a review of my paper published in the *Trans. Am. Philol.* pp. 213 and 243.
Ass., 1902, p. 81 ff., first called my attention to this fact: "Le 5 Swainson, p. 12. reste me semble etre le debut d'un alphabet rythmique a re-"Swainson, p. 220 f. 7 No. 170. to be a kind of abbreviated creed. It may be compared, however, with such passages in the liturgies as the following, from the-Alexandrine liturgy:1 Efs *Uarr/p* aytos, efs Tlos ayios, *ev Uvevp.a ayiov,* cis *ivonqra Uvevp-aTOS ayCov. p.rjv.* Similar passages OCCUT in the

"Liturgy of St. Basil,"2 the " Liturgy of St. Chrysostom,"3 the "Liturgy of St. James,'4 the " Liturgy of the Presanctified,"5 and in the lectures of Cyril of Jerusalem to the newly baptized.6 The Bakirha inscription contains, after the formula given above, the words /3or0ija-(Lf) rows *fov/3ovp,euow; airov: He shall help them that fear him,* while in the latest of the inscriptions from Dar Kita the formula is followed by the word *fior)6-q* or /3ot7#t7s. Texts such as these occur frequently, e.g., at Djuwaniyeh:7 Efs Be6s *Kal 6*

X/aioTo? *avrov;* at the same place, dated 398 A.D.: 8 Efs Oe6s *fiovos 6 fiorjOwu irdcriv* T019 *(fi(ov riv avrovf);* and at the same place again, dated 374 A.D.:9 Efs *@ecis 6 (iwrqdwv* Tous *fw3ov1* 10 *p.evov; avrov. A* similar text is curiously combined with others in one of the oldest of all dated Christian inscriptions in Syria, found by Waddington on the lintel of a doorway at

Katura: it is dated 336 A.D.:11 ®(eo)v *Xprja-re, fiorfdi.* Efs ©eos *p,6vo;.* "E/fTicrev ©dXacrts. "Ocra Xeyis, £iXe, K£ crol rd Si7rXa. "Erous ewt'. EiaeXde, Xpiar)e; *Christ of God, help lis)!*
There is) one God only. Thalasis built this). Whatsoeierthou say est, friend, may that be) unto thee also, twofold/

In the year 385. Enter, O Christ/ The words *elo-eXde,* X/jiotc, recall a passage which occurs in the "Liturgy of St. Basil,"12 and in the "Liturgy of St. Chrysostom":13 ripdo-es, Ku/nc *'l-qaov Xpicrre,... Kal i0e eis To ayidcrai* 17/ieis/ *Give heed, Lord Jesus Christ,... and come unto the sanctifying of us.*
Another sentence, very common in certain localities—I found it, for example, on the lintels of three houses in il-Barah14 — is the following: Ku/(io?) c/wXdfry rrjv io-o86v o-ov Kal Tt)i i£o§ov, dvo rov vvv Kal ecu? T5v aXoiv-tuv. '*Afir/v: The Tord shall preserve thy coming in and thy) going out, from this time forth) andfor evermore. Amen.* The same is found also in an inscription at Taltita, dated 570 A.d.15 The text is taken, originally, from Psalm cxx, 8: it may be compared, however, with a passage at the end of the "Clementine" liturgy:16 Tous Oikovs *avrotv (fvaov,* rds eicrdSous *avrtov Kal* rets efdSovs *fpovp-qoov.* Compare also the following sentence from Chrysostom's account of the service in his day:17 *TrapaKaXe-crwfJiev... Xva evkoyrjaj)* rds etcdSovs *avr&v Kal* rds e'fdSovs *trdvra rov fiiov avrSiv.*

A tomb at Ruweha, in the form of a temple distyle in antis, bears the following inscription:18 Efs Beos /xdvos *6 $or)9(a)v).* '*Tirep* crcoTT/pi'as *Kal p,vijp.(rf;) rSv t,6vrov.* '*Aveveaxrev* Bd-crcriu.as Kal Ma0/Ja/8ed, erous yXv'.- *(There is) one God only that giveth aid. For the safety and remembrance of the living. Bassimas and Mathbabea renewed this tomb) in the year* 1 Swainson, p. 66.
2 Swainson, p. 86. 1 Swainson, p. 94. 4 Swainson, p. 310. 5 Swainson, p. 98. u Swainson, p. 210. 7 No. 24. See also No. 27. 8 No. 22. 9 No. 21. 10 See, however, below, p. 22 f. and the commentary to No. 25.
"No. 116.
12 Swainson, p. 86. 13 Swainson, p. 93. ,4Nos. 192-194.
15 No. 12. 16 Brightman, *Liturgies Eastern and Western,* 1896, p. 27. 17 Swainson, p. 218. Compare also the "Alexandrine Liturgy," Swainson, p. 32. But see below, p. 24 f. 18 No. 263,

dated 384-5 *A.d. 433.* This recalls such oft-repeated passages in the liturgies as, for example, in the
"Liturgy of St. James ' I1 Ert 8e *Kal inep oarrr)pia; Ka.1 dfeo-ew; dfiapTi-wv* Toj *irpoo'eveyKavri d8efu r)p.(ov. Kal inep fivrjfj.rj; Tcjv ocriwv vaTe'pav r)p.av Kal dBefwv, eiTroip.ev tra.vre.%* eVrevois. In the inscription, I believe that the words *Twv ,6vtwv* refer to those living the life beyond the grave, as in the prayer for the dead in this same liturgy:2 '*ekci aurous dv6.Tra.wrov iv topo. t,0)VTwv, iv* /3acrieta *ovpavwv, ...* eis Kokrrovs 'ASpaa/A, Ktx.

Perhaps I should also mention in this connection, for the sake of completeness, such simple phrases as '*o «rl ndmwv ©eo'?,* and *Wr/kovia.* The first of these is found in an inscription at Frikya,3 and again on the lintel of the citadel at Khanasir.4 It recalls Romans ix, 5, or Ephesians iv, 6; but similar phrases are found in the Liturgies.5 The latter, found on two lintels of the same house at Khirbit Hass,6 is one of the commonest liturgical formulae.

Lastly, there are two Syriac inscriptions from this region, which were communicated to me by Dr. Littmann, and which may be mentioned in this connection. They are, first:7 *Deliver me, O Lord, from the evil man,* and secondly:,, *Let God arise and let all his enemies be scattered.* The first text is derived from Psalm cxxxix, 1: '*E£eo£ p. e, Kvpie, eg dvdpamov irovrjpov, Kt.;* but the passage may also be compared with the following, from the " *Didache ofthe Apostles* 'V9 *Mvrjo-drfTi, Kvpie,* Ttjs *iKKrjcria: aov Toc pvaaadai avrrjv drrb iravrbs irovqpov.* Compare also, from the Alexandrine liturgy:10 *udo-av rrovqpwv dvOpcaTTwv iTri/3ovr)V iKOt)ijov df r)fiov, 6* ©eds, *Kal dirb* rrjs ayi'as *crov KaOoiKrj; Kal dirooToiKrj; (kKkr)o-La:,* and from the "Liturgy of St. James":11 *Kvpie ... pvaai raids dirb Tov irovrjpov, Kal dnb Toiv ipywv avrov.* The second text is derived from Psalm lxvii, 2: '*vao-rrjTO) 6* ®eds, *Kal Siao-Kopma-OriToxTav oi i0poi avrov, Kt.* The same thought, in somewhat different words, occurs repeatedly in the various Alexandrine liturgies, e.g.:12

'*Egeyepdr/Ti, Kvpie, Kal Siao- KopTT-LO-dr/TCJO-av 01 i6poi aov.* 1 have not attempted to make a comparison between the texts furnished by these inscriptions and what remains to us of the Jewish ritual of the early Christian centuries. But two inscriptions resemble closely those portions of that ritual which are quoted, for purposes of comparison, by Mr. Warren in his book on the *Liturgy and Ritual of the Ante-Nicene Church,* to which I have already referred. One of these is from il-Barah:13 *Tevono, Kvpie, To ekeos crov ifi r)p.a; Kaddrrep r)irioap.ev iirl ae ; Let thy mercy, O Lord, be upon us, according as we hope in thee.* This is derived from Psalm xxxii, 22: it is also contained in the "Eighteen Benedictions," or the "Prayer '*Shemonah Esrah* '" of the Jewish ritual, sec. 13:14 "On us bestow, O Lord our God, Thy mercy; give ample reward to all who trust in Thy name in sincerity, make our portion with them

'Swainson, p. 312., 6 Nos. 183 f. 11 Swainson, p. 306 ff.
2 Swainson, p. 300. 7 Part IV, Syriac No. 19. Compare 12 Swainson, p. 20. Compare also pp. 3No. 251. also No. 268 below. 17, 23 and 46 f. 4 No. 318. "Part IV, Syriac No. 19 f. 13 No. 202. 5 For example, in the "Liturgy of St. 9Swainson, p. xlix. u Warren, p. 210. James," Swainson, pp. 244 and 268. 10 Swainson, p. 4. for ever, and let us not be ashamed, for we trust in Thee." There is something similar, but not identical, in the "Liturgy of St. Basil";1 and in the "Liturgy of St. James."2 The second is from a ruined house at Djuwaniyeh:3 Kv/hos /WtXevci ets *iai-va: The Lord is king for ever.* Psalm xxviii, 10, contains the words: Katfiel-rai Ku'pios /Sao-iXevs *eh Tov alu)va.* Compare with this the following passage from the "*Kedusha*": "And in Thy Holy Word it is written, thus saying: 'The Lord shall reign for ever and ever, Thy God, O Zion, from generation to generation.'" Compare also the "*Didache of the Apostles*" sec. 14, and the "*Apostolic Constitutions,*" vii, 30,5 the "Liturgy of St. James,"6 and the Alexandrine liturgy.7

Besides these texts already discussed,8 there are other inscriptions containing passages, directly quoted from the Bible, which must have been familiar to all Christians of that time, but which I have not found in any of the extant Greek "Liturgies." Most of these are from the region with which the present discussion is specially concerned: a few, however, are from the region farther east. First, passages quoted from the Psalter:

Psalm iv, 8 f.: on a large dwelling house in il-Barah: No. 198.

Psalm xxiii, i:9 on two tombs in Der Sambil: Nos. 228 and 229.

Psalm xxx, 1:10 on a displaced lintel in Khanasir: No. 327.

Psalm xxxiii, 9,11 and perhaps also verse 23, are reflected, though not literally quoted, on a lintel in Dana: No. 261.

Psalm xlv, 8 and 12:12 on the fragments of a lintel, probably of a dwelling house, in il-Barah, and again on another lintel in Dana: Nos. 199 and 260.

Psalm 1, 1: on a sarcophagus in Midjleyya: No. 207.13

Psalm lix, 4: on a mausoleum in Hass: No. 166.

Psalm lxiv, 10: on the same mausoleum: No. 166.

Psalm xc, 1 f: painted on the lintel of a large dwelling in Ruweha: No. 267. A part of the same passage is contained in the inscription on a sarcophagus at Midjleyya, No. 207, and on a lintel in Mektebeh, No. 315: also in the two Syriac inscriptions mentioned above.14

Psalm xc, 9 and 10: on another sarcophagus at Midjleyya: No. 208.

Psalm xcii, 5: on the lintel of a church at Der Sim'an: No. 124.

10 The same inscription includes a quotation from Ps. cxvii, 6: see below. 11 Compare also Psalm lxxxiii, 13. The first part of Psalm xxxiii, 9, occurs in the "Liturgies," apparently as the beginning of a hymn, the rest of which is omitted in the manuscripts: see, e.g., Swainson, p. 316 f., etc. 12 A part of these verses, however, the words *Kvpu w Swvayutuv,* occur not infrequently in the " Liturgies," e.g., Swainson, pp. 282, 306 and 89. lsThe same inscription

includes Psalm xc, 1. 14 Part IV of these publications, Syriac Nos. 19 and 20.

Psalm cxii, 7: on a lintel of a dwelling at il-Barah: No. 201. Above this quotation is written: xpioro? *ael Viks.. n«ms,* cXiris, *ayairij.-Christ ever conquers. Faith, hope, love!* The last three words recall a passage in the "Liturgy of the Presanctified":1 *BefSaLuxrov Olvtovs iv rrj irixrra-aTrjpov iv* e'A.7HoV *rekeiaxrov iv ayairrj.*

Psalm cxvii, 6: on a lintel in Khanasir: No. 327.2

Psalm cxvii, 20:3 on a lintel of a church at Mu'allak: No. 332.

Psalm cxxi, 7: on a fragment of a displaced lintel at Dana: No. 259.

Secondly, there is one inscription which contains a quotation from Ecclesiastes i, 2: on a tomb at Der Sambil: No. 230.

Thirdly, from the New Testament:

Matthew xvi, 18: on a church lintel at Mu'allak: No. 332. Matthew xxii, 31 f. :4 on a house lintel at Selemiyeh: No. 296. Luke xxiii, 42; on two lintels, probably of dwelling-houses, in Selemiyeh: Nos. 284 and 293.

Romans viii, 31: found frequently in these and other Syrian inscriptions: I found it in Delloza, for example, three times on lintels of houses: No. 221 ff. In the Delloza inscriptions the words, El Oeos *imkp* n's *Ko.6' rp.uv: If God befor us who can be) against?is,* are followed in one case by the letters XMr, in the other two cases by Ad£a avrw *iravTore: Glory to him forever.*

But the fact that some of these inscriptions contain passages from the Psalter, or from the liturgy, or from some other part of the church service, does not explain why they were carved on the buildings. Moreover there are many inscriptions which obviously have nothing to do with customary forms of worship. Thirdly I do not consider that, in discussing the reason for these inscriptions, it is possible to dissociate them from the many symbols, most of them Christian symbols, crosses and the like, which abound in the same region.

Doubtless after the formal triumph of Christianity, the Christians took pride in

proclaiming their religion in this way. Perhaps also the open profession of Christianity in this period gave greater security of possession to householders. Perhaps in some cases there was a genuine desire to hold the cross before men's eyes, and to propagate religion by these pious words. Probably these inscriptions and symbols oftentimes were merely ornamental, and matters of the fashion of the age, much like the mottoes which some people still hang upon their walls. But I believe that the main reason was a superstitious one, and that the purpose was to bring good luck, but especially to avert evil, i.e., evil spirits. Certainly the name of God has always been, and is now,

'Swainson, p. 96. 3 See above, p. 9. This verse is very frequent on 4 Compare also Mark xii, 26 f., 2 Includes also Psalm xxx,i. lintels of Syrian churches, e.g.,Waddington, i960,1995 and Luke xx, 37 f.

and 2413 a: *C. I. G.* 8930-8934 inclusive. in the East, the most potent charm against evil: so also, in the "Christian" period, the name and symbols of the Christ. Hence such symbols, and phrases containing the names of God or Christ, were carved or scratched or painted everywhere, even on the interior walls of stables, wine-presses and shops: hence also the commonest place for such carving was the lintel or some part of the frame of a door or window, not only because this is the most natural place for ornament of any sort, but also because, as is well known, evil spirits, however ethereal, do not penetrate solid walls, but, like the rest of us, enter by the door or perhaps through the window.1

A special form of ornamentation occurs on Syrian lintels with the greatest frequency, a form for which, in these publications, the name *disk* has been employed. These "disks" are not always circular; some are simple squares, some formed by two squares crossed, some are hexagons or octagons. They measure from six inches to two feet across, and formed a convenient frame for symbols of every sort. Most of them contain the cross in some form or other, + or %

, All), the name of God, or of Christ, Emmanuel, or the like. Some, however, contain no Christian symbols whatever, and recall rather certain of the emblems of ancient pagan gods. Common among these non-Christian disks are circles filled with curved lines raying from the centers, suggesting whirling spheres: also stars of five, six or eight points. M. Schlumberger, in an article in the *Revue des Etudes Grecques,* Vol. v. (1892), p. 87, quotes a brief passage from Alexander of Tralles, *QepaurevTiKd,* x., c. i, which gives the following prescription for an amulet to be used as a preventative of colic, the cause of which was thought, by Alexander at least, to be the bile: "Take an iron finger-ring," he says, "and make the ring an octagon, and so write upon it evye, *lov xV' v fo/ avSaXdsare Ifyrci,"* i.e., *Flee, oh bile, the lark pursues thee.* Evidently the Shape of the amulet had something to do with its effectiveness. Another amulet, now in the Cabinet des Medailles de France,2 contains the words *'Avaxpt, xoXe,* To * fftov* o-e Siokci, i.e., *jWx«iy« xvi)* T0 *9e?v* o-e Siw/ cet. I do not feel certain whether To *delov* means *7he Deity* or *sulphur;* but in either case the bile (or something else) is directed to withdraw. Now this second amulet is in the form of an eight-pointed star, and it seems to me quite possible that some of the "disks" on the Syrian lintels, such for example as the octagons and the eight-pointed stars, may have had their origin in the same superstitions as these amulets. It is possible that other disks had their origin in symbols of pagan religion, and perhaps they were used, in very ancient times, to protect dwellings against evil spirits and to attract the powers of good.3

Certainly there is evidence that the custom of inscribing door-frames in some way is older than the Christian religion. One of the commonest formulae on lintels in Syria is the phrase Els @os /aovos; *There is one God only.* On my first visit to 1 See below, inscription No. 44 and commentary. 3 Compare, for example, the use of the so-called " Seal of 2 Published by Lenormant in the *Revue Archeologique,* Solomon," two tri-

angles crossed so as to form a six-pointed 1846, p. 510. Both these amulets belong probably to the figure. See Lidzbarski, *Ephemeris,* II, 1906, p. 145. first half of the sixth century.

Syria I found it, in one form or another, in thirty-three inscriptions:1 it is to be found in all collections of similar inscriptions.2 Speaking of this phrase, M. ClermontGanneau, in the *Quarterly Statements of the Palestine Exploration Fund,* 1882, p. 26,3 says: "The Christian character of this formula is clearly demonstrated." "It is probably of Jewish origin, and must have sprung from the well-known verse (the fourth) in the sixth chapter of Deuteronomy, which contains the word inNHliT, *Jehovah,* rendered in the Septuagint by *Kvpios Efs,* and which precedes the dissertation on the Commandments."5 "It is, properly speaking, the axiom of monotheism, besides which it plays an important part in the Jewish liturgy." "It is worthy of remark that this formula is generally found inscribed above the entrance doors, as ordained in the ninth verse (with regard to the Commandments, of which it is, so to say, the preamble), 'And thou shalt write them on the posts of thy house, and on thy gates.'" In fact the Efs @o? has been found on monuments distinctively Jewish or at least Jewish-Christian.6

But whatever is the origin of this custom, the character of many of these inscriptions as formulae to avert evil is shown clearly by the following examples, some of which are still unpublished: all of them are from lintels. First, from Der Sambil, dating probably from the fifth century p. c: XMrY X(piaro)v To *Vlkos.* 4evye *tarava; Ch(rist) born) of) M(ary). Christ's the victory. Flee, Satan!* Secondly, from Herakeh, 524 A. D.: +'0 *Secm6Tri;-qfioiu 'l(r)o-ov); X(pio-r6);,* 6 Ttds, 6 Aoyos *T(ov)* 0(eo)u, *ipddSt /faroiKci fir)hev la-LTco Kolkov: Our Lord Jesus Christ, the Son, the Word of God, dwells here: let no evil enter.* The next, from Pdjaz,9 is really in the form of a prayer to God, and hence does not properly belong with the others: its purpose, however, is the same, and it helps to explain the meaning of

those which follow. It is in eleven hexameters, of which I quote the fifth, sixth and seventh: *Xpiorb; aa£ci(ioi vo-Cirripova. XPa Ko/u'£«-TovvtKd ov rpopeopt KaKoppeKTOLO p-q)ava; Saipovos* ou8' *avSpbs o-Tvyepbv Kcu adco-piov op pa; Christ, ever living, bears his) hand that-frees-from-ill: therefore I fear not the) machinations of evilworking demon, nor the hateful and lawless eye of man* (i.e., the evil eye). Another, found at North Dana,10 is in two fragments, both somewhat mutilated: its date is 550 A.d. With the inscription are three small disks, each containing a cross: ToC *a-Tavpov 7ra/(d)jTos, eVtfpos ov* Kano-vo-i; *JVhere the cross is present, the) enemy shall not prevail.* Much the same thought is contained in an inscription from Sabba', dated 1 For example, Nos. 14, 16, 21, 22, 24, 25, etc.

2 E.g.,C./.6:.8945,9iS4,etc. Cf.also 8946. SeealsoChabot's index of Waddington's publication, and note 4 below. 3 See also Clermont-Ganneau: *Recueil,* i,p. i69f.,anda/*ports sur une Mission en Palestineet en/%/«;«(1881),p. 2 iff. 4 By the examples cited from Waddington, Nos. 2066, 2689, 2682, 2704, 2562 1, 2451, 2262, 2057, 2053 b, 1918. 5 Verses 4-9 of the sixth chapter of Deuteronomy, in Hebrew, were found carved on the lintel of adoorwayin Palmyra, and on the jambs verses 14 and 15 of the seventh chapter. Mittwoch, in *Beitrage zur Assyriologie,* iv, 1902, p. 203 ff 6 See Schick in *Quarterly Statements P. E. F.,* 1887, p. 55. Clermont-Ganneau: *Recueil,* 1,p. 170. Also No. 25, below. 7 On these letters see below, p. 23. 8 Compare the inscription painted on the wall of a shop in Pompeii: O *rov* Aios irais *Kowivukos* 'h/ooks v#a&u icaToocct, *Ht)8v dfTfuuxia Kukov.* Kaibel: *Epigrammata Graeca,* No. 1138. 9 Published in part by Dr. Hans Lucas, *Byzantinische Zeitschrift,* xiv, 1905, p. 51, No. 80, from a copy furnished by Freiherr von Oppenheim. 10 No. 91 below. 546 A.d. , which however is so badly mutilated that nearly half of each of the three lines has been lost. In the center of the lintel were two, perhaps originally three,

disks, each containing a cross. My restoration of the text is as follows: t'Erous *rjvoi, privb; Hepiriov(f)--'. Tov Oikov Tovtov* Ku/jios 8ia£tAa£ei*rrjv lcr _oc)ov Kox rrv iijoo'ovy* (t)o(w) *crravpov yap npoKipepov oi'crxvr;i 6fdapb; fiao-Kavo;In the) year 85 S =* jyftf *A.d.) in the) month Peritins ?). Of this house the) Lord shall guard the entrance and the exit; for the cross being set before, no malignant eye shall prevail against it)* The last line is of course most uncertain: the words *crravpov yap TTpom,p.4vov,* however, are preserved here, and were found again on the fragments of a lintel at il-Anderin, which also contain a disk with a cross: + *Xravpov irpoKip.evov... ov KarCcrxvcrti ....* Lastly, a broken lintel from 'Odjeh2 contains a disk with a cross in relief, and the words: 'E en. *rifl irekecrdr.* 'T7r(o)/a/j.e *irpbs injwx"tv rwv ivOdhe Kar_oiKovvrav* ?: *"In the year J06 =394 A.D.) this building) was finished. I am set for the peace of those that dwell here."* I believe that the verb refers to the sculptured cross as its subject, and that the inscription is in all respects comparable to that on the golden bell found at Rome, and published by Bruzza in the *AnnalideWInstitute,* 1875, p. 50 ff.:3 Tot? *oppao-iv vnoreraypai; "lam set against eyes."* Obviously the bell was a charm against the evil eye.

Now it may appear to some that, while these few examples which I have quoted are perhaps magical in character, the many other inscriptions which contain quotations from the Psalms, or combinations of quotations, such as *"Lord, save thy people, and bless thine inheritance"* words which appear also in the ancient Greek "liturgies," or such phrases as *"Lord Jesus Christ, help so and so"* are genuine expressions of piety. But many of these same phrases and quotations appear in the magic formulae preserved in the literature and on amulets. And the most characteristic part of it all is the incomprehensible commingling of paganism, Judaism and Christianity in these formulae. M. Schlumberger, in a very interesting article in the *Re%ue des Etudes Grecques,* v, 1892, p. 93, quotes a number of examples of such formulae from the *Geoponica,* a work dedicated to Porphyrogenetus (Constantine VII, 911-959). First a prescription to prevent wine from turning sour: "Write upon the casks, or upon an apple which you will then throw into the wine, these divine words *Qtla ypdppara*) from Psalm xxxiii, 9 (xxxiv, 8): *O taste and see that the Lord is good."* Second, a prescription for enabling one to drink a great deal of wine without becoming intoxicated: "Repeat, when taking the first drink, this verse from Homer: *But upon them, from the heights of Ida, wise Zeus has thundered."* Third, a prescription to keep away snakes from a dove-cot: "Write the word '*ASdp. Adam)* on the four corners of the cot. " Fourth, to secure a miraculous catch of fish: "Write on shell the words 'law *2aPaa0.A Lord of 'Sabaoth,* and throw it in the water." 1 Cf. Matthew xvi, 18, which is quoted in an inscription (No. 4 'IuL = rpi'p = (*Yahwe) Adonai=yc* the Septuagint) 332) on the lintel of a church in Mu'allak, dated 606 A.d. *Kvpios.* 'Iau *2a/Sai0* appears also on amulets, e.g., *R. E. G., 2 Byzantinische Zeitschrift,* xiv, p. 46, No. 63 v, p. 82 f. See Deissmann: *Bibchludien,* p. 1 ff. Also 3 Also in *Inscriptions Graecae,* xiv, No. 2409, 5. Heitmuller, //// *Namen Jesu: Forsch. 3. Rel. it. Lit.,* 1, 2.

One of the most remarkable of the amulets is that published in the *C. I. G. ,* iv, No. 9065. One side bears the figure of Christ upon the cross, with the Mother of Jesus, St. John and others: beside the figures is written: *'l(r)o-ov); X(pio-Tos). u(dTe)p,* «s (tov irap a rid 17 fi 1 To *ir(vv)fj.d p.ov.* 'H *p.Lrqp-6 vov; aov: Jesus Christ. Father, into thy hands I commend my spirit7 Behold) thy mother/ Behold) thy son I* The reverse bears, in hexameter verses, the legend: *Pevy drf* eVcs *f/a8wjs, 8oop,yjxave, jevye* ratora, *fevy' air' ip.av fieXccw, "0l, Hvp,.. . X/3tor6 s dvai; Kekerc* ere £euyeZ v, ei 9 Xer/aa *dakdacrr) Kt. Flee from my heart, thou mischief-maker, flee quickly, flee from my limbs, Snake, Fire!... Christ (the) king bids thee flee, into (the) depths of (the) sea, etc.* The words *Flee, thou mischief-maker,* recall the inscription of the house at Der Sambil, with its *Flee, Satan.* Another amulet from Constantinople, published by M. Schlumberger in *R.E.G.,* v (1892), p.77, bears about the rim of the obverse the legend: tcv-ye *p.ep.uTip.evi, Slokl* o-e 6 ayycXos Apa1 /(=#cot) *OipieX-tfrevye p,tcrovp.vr)f)'; Flee, hated (phlglie) 7 he angelArchaph (or Arlapli),pursues thee, and Uriel! Flee, hateful!* The rest of this face of the amulet is described by M. Schlumberger as follows: "In the field, unfortunately badly corroded, appear the three magi, with hats on their heads: behind them a tree: they are presenting themselves before the Virgin who is seated upon a throne, and holding the Child Jesus.... Back of the figure of the Virgin are the words Xpioros *Viks.,* followed by certain letters now illegible. Below are the words *yE,ppavov, @co's."* The names of archangels, especially the name ofMichael, are found repeatedly on lintels in Syria, particularly in il-Anderin and its neighborhood: the names of Michael and Gabriel appear on the lintel of one of the doors of the great church at Kalb Lauzeh. These two names, Michael and Gabriel, are found together on amulets from Beirut and elsewhere.2 Michael appears with Solomon in the inscription of a very singular amulet,3 the text of which is as follows: Sia'/o? *Zdevro* eVi *Tov p,ydov %oopavos Kol MixatjXov Tov dyyikov, fir) dpao0ai Trjs fopovo-r);; Covenant which they made under the great Solomon and Michael the angel, not to touch the bearer.* The words *Xptoro? vad: Christ co/u/uers,* on the Constantinople amulet, occur frequently on the buildings, for example at Der Sim'an, il-Barah and Serdjilla.4 Sometimes other, but equivalent, expressions are used in the inscriptions, such as tNtxae.-5 *(In this cross) conquer,* To *o-riploiv Tovto Vlko.;6 This sign conquers, Xpio-rov To Vikos;7 Christ's is the victory.* The meaning of these phrases is made clear by the amulets containing such formulae as El? @e69 6 *Vikw To. /ca/ca.-8 One God who conquers the evil.* Certainly there can be no doubt that the amulets refer to the overcoming of evil spirits, or in general the powers of evil. The name '*Ep.p,avovyj* also, which appears on the Constantinople amulet, is found similarly 1 Compare another amulet found at Smyrna, and published in the 3 Schlumberger, 1. c, p. 87. same article by Schlumberger, p. 76: *&evyc fxe/uai/xin, Apat 6 ay*-4 Nos. 124, 201 and 219. *ytAos re &oict.* Both of these are thought by M. Schlumberger to 5 No. 210.

be somewhat later than the second half of the third century A.n. 6 No. 255. 2 Schlumberger, in *R. E.* 67., v, p. 83 ff. Also Perdrizet, in 7 No. 234. *R. E. G.,* xvi (1903), p. 46. f., where these names are joined 8 Schlumberger, *R. E. G.,* v, p. 80 f. with those of Uriel and Raphael. (From Beirut.) on lintels, once joined with Xptoros *Viks.,* as on the amulet:1 it is found again in the disk on the lintel of the citadel of Khanasir.2

But the most significant of all these amulets, in this connection, is one in the Metropolitan Museum. It is described as a small object not unlike a thick nail, with a hole through it near one end, doubtless for the cord by which it was hung about someone's neck. The four sides bear an inscription which was published first by Dr. Isaac Hall in 1894,3 and discussed by Professor T. F. Wright in the following year.4 I have not yet been able to see the amulet myself; but I believe it should be read as follows: 'o a *Tolkcov iv /3or)0iq T(ov) 'Txpia-T(ov), ftoyjOi.,* ayio? *Kvpios, 'lovXidva),* r5 *8oi5A(a) crov, Tw fopo(vv)Ti; He that dwelleth in the help of the Most High, he//, holy Lord, Julianos, thy servant, the bearer.* The words *6 Koltoikcov iv fior)6La rod 'tlotov* are quoted directly from the Septuagint, Psalm xc, 1. But they were also found painted on the lintel of a house in Ruweha:8 they occur in an inscription found at Horns, and published by M. Lammens in the Musee Beige, 1901, p. 291, No. 64. The rest of the inscription on the amulet, */Jo'fli, ayios Kvpios, 'lovidv(p,* Tu SouX(a)) *aov,* Tw *fopo(vv)Ti,* excepting of course the words Tw *fopovmi: the bearer,* which are appropriate only to an amulet, is the very commonest of all the formulae which appear upon the house-lintels. Numerous variations, equivalent in

meaning, may be found in almost every collection of post-classical inscriptions, especially of course of those from Syria. On my first visit there I found /Soifflei or *fioijd-qo-ov* some twenty times, and almost always on lintels, generally of houses, for example */3o&l* Kupic; *Help, Lord, Kv(pie) Xpvare fiorjOi;* Lord Christ, help, Kupie 777? Sofis *fioSiaov ip.lv iravras;* Lord of Glory, help 11s all, Xpiari fioidi; Christ, help, 'Io-ou Xpr/ore *ffajd&;* Jesus Christ, help, Iij(crov)s *fiorjdi;* Jesus, help, not to mention the phrase Kwp(te) *(Sorjdi, T(t)v)* lo-ohov; Lord, help the entrance? which I take to be the equivalent of the very common Kv/ho? *jvda* (or Kv/aie *fvXxijov)* TT/v daohov *aov* Kcu *r-qv egoSov;7 The Lord shall guard* (or Lord, guard) *thy coming in and thy going out.* This list also excludes the very common formulae in which the Kvpe *fiorjOu* is combined with the *Ei? ©eo? p.6voi,* as, for example, Efs ©eos *p-ovos, 6 /80179uv TTaa-iv; One God alone who aideth all/8* It also excludes those inscriptions in which various saints are invoked with some form of the verb *fto-qdelv,* as t "Ayie *Hpyi fioijdeo-ov: Saint Sergius, help!* In somewhat more than half the cases there is added, either with or without TM *Sova o-ov thy servant),* the name of the person (or persons) by whom aid is sought, just as in the case of the amulet. On my second visit to Syria I found, as before, many of these *fiotjOei* inscriptions, and among them the following, which has certain refinements which deserve special mention. It is from a house-lintel, still in 1 No. 219: *Hixi±avovy.,* XMr *Xpurrbs vuca.* Syr. Inscr. 19, 20). The whole of the Ruw£ha inscription -'No. 318. Also in the inscriptions of "The Princeton is as follows: "He that dwelleth in the help of the Most

Arch. Exp. in 1905," not yet published. *High shall abide in the shelter of the God of Heaven. He 3 Journal Am. Oriental Society,* Vol. xvi, *Appendix,* p.cxv. *shall say unto the Lord: Thou art my protector and my ref 4 Quarterly Statements P. E. F.,* 1895, p. 124 ff. *uge, my God: I will trustin him." 5 Wad.* 2672; No. 267 below. The same words

were also 8 Inscr. No. 184, from Khirbit Hass. found, curiously enough, on a broken sarcophagus at Midj-7 Psalms exx, 8. See Inscr. No. 12, etc. leyya (No. 207), and in. two Syriac inscriptions (Part IV, 8 Inscr. No. 22, from Djuwaniyeh.

situ, in the ruined town now called Mir'ayeh, near Kerratin it-Tudjdjar (i. e., *"Tarutia of the Merchants"):*1 XMrneixeYC + Akohkypibtwattay

It is characteristic of magic lore that it belongs to the initiated only: its formulae, therefore, are not always to be understood by the ordinary wayfarer. Hence such formulae, or words of supernatural power, were sometimes expressed in the form of cryptograms, which were comprehensible only to the initiated—and of course to spirits. It was peculiarly easy to devise such cryptograms in Greek, because the letters of the Greek alphabet were used also as numerical signs: A=i, B = 2, 1=10, P = ioo, etc. Consequently it was always possible, in Greek, to represent any group of letters, whose numerical value equalled a certain sum, by another group of letters whose numerical values equalled the same sum. This matter has been discussed by a number of scholars, last of all, I think, by M. Perdrizet in an article entitled *"Isopsephie"* in the *Revue des Etudes Grecques."2* So, for example, in the following inscription, which seems to be a prayer addressed to God or Christ: £Xe' *iLvrjo-dtjrn Tov Bovov (tov,* M. Perdrizet has pointed out that *f* = 535 = 20 (i.e., K') + 400 *(v)* + 100 *(p)* + 10 (i') + 5 (c'). The inscription, therefore, is to be read: *Kvpte vrjad-qTi Tov Sovxov O-ov: Lord, remember thy servant.* It has been generally recognized that the number of the beast in Revelations xiii., 18, has a similar explanation. The same method has been applied in composing the inscription on. the Mir'ayeh lintel. The first group of letters, XMT, appears very frequently on Syrian lintels, and has been much discussed. M. de Vogu6, de Rossi and others have believed that these letters signify x(/iords), *M(ixatj),* r(a/8/)«?X): Christ, Michael, Gabriel. But in my opinion this explanation is unsatisfactory, because of the context in which these letters sometimes appear. For example, in an inscription upon a rock-hewn tomb at Hass:3 Efs ©cds, XMr./ xwos, it is obviously impossible to read: *There is one God, Christ, Michael, Gabriel, alone.* Waddington, on the other hand, proposed to read these letters x(/«rrov) (6 Ac) M(api'as) *yevvr)0):* *Christ, born of Mary,* and this reading is confirmed by an inscription discovered by Waddington on a house in Refadeh:4 *f'lr)o-(ov);* 6 Na£wp&)S, 6 ac Ma/u'a? *yevvedfc,* 6 T(io)s *Tov @(eo)u, vda KaTOLKi, Kt.; Jesus of Nazareth, who was bom of Mary, the Son of God, dwells here,* etc. At the same time, as M. Perdrizet suggests, these letters may also have a cryptogrammic significance, such, for example, as that proposed by Perdrizet himself: XMr = 643 = I (a) + 3 (y) + 5 (e') + IO (1') + 70 (o) + 200 (r) + 70 (o') + 9 &) + 5 (e) + 70(0') + 200(0-') =Ayeios 6 0eds *Holy (is) God.* These words form the beginning of the "trisagion," which I have discussed above: if they were used as a magic formula they may properly be compared with the words'Ayio? Kupios on the amulet of the Metropolitan Museum.1 They also recall the words of an amulet published by Froehner in *Philologus,* Supplementband v, p. 42 ff., and again by M. Schlumberger in *R. E. G.,* 1892, p. 91: both these editors give the text as follows: tAyios, aytos, ayios, K(upi)e *tafiawd, 6 ar)pr); (?), 6 oipavos.* It takes, however, a very slight emendation to read *irX-qp* for the incomprehensible 6 ar/ps. We have then the familiar *Holy, holy, holy, Lord of Sabaoth,heaven is full of thee).* The same words appear with some variations on other amulets published by Perdrizet in an article called *XfoayU 2okop.wvo;* (Solomon's Seal), in the *Revue ties Etudes Grecques,* 1903, p. 42 ff. I have found the same words on house-lintels, for example at il-Berdoneh, it-Taiyibeh and il-'Anz.

The second group of letters in the Mir'ayeh inscription is M9: it is well known that He = 99 = 1 («') +4o(/) +8(V) +5o("') = *'Afnjv.-Amen?*

The third group is the very familiar IX9YC, letters which, as initials, signify

'1(770-01)9) X(pio-Tos), @(eoG) T(ids), *l,oTijp): Jesus Christ, the Son of God, our Savior,* and which together form the Greek word *XyBvs: fish,* and suggested to the early Christians the use of a fish as a symbol of their faith. Perhaps these letters also have some occult significance; but if so, it is unknown to me.

The next group is AKOH. This, of course, is the Greek word *a.Korj. hearing;* but the letters obviously have some other meaning. Now AKOH = a'(i) + K'(2o) + O'(7o) + T'(8) =99= 1 («') + 4o(/a') + 8(1?') + Sv') = *AMV-*The letters AKOH, therefore, have the same cryptic significance as H0.

The obscurity of the remainder of this inscription is secured partly by abbreviation: it may be read *Kvpi(e) (2(oj)dei.) T5 8(ouW) (a-ov) Uav(a): Lord, help thy servant Paulos.* Of this phrase, *fiorjdu Tu otlva, T5 Sovkw o-ov,* I have already spoken:3 it is significant in this connection, I think, that such phrases are on Byzantine seals also, for example, t *K(vpi)e fiorjOeL Tw tw 8ouw AiXta.- Lord, help thy servant A ilias,* or *BeoroKe, fioijjBei T& Sov'xw a-ov.-5 Mother of God, help thy servant.* At the same time, the method of abbreviation on the Mir'ayeh lintel is striking, and suggests that there may be some hidden meaning in these letters after all. If the *iota subscript* in *T$* be included, then the sum of the numerical values of the letters Kvpi /3. Toh 8. riau. equals 1227 = 'itjo-ogs 6 Na£eupcuo?.-6 *Jesus of Nazareth.*

I have already spoken of the cryptogram involved in the inscription in the tomb at Shnan,7 where a refrain, 'itjo-ogs 6 Xpeio-rd?.-*Jesus the Christ,* is written out in full, but is also expressed at the end of each line in the form BYMr = 2443 = 10(1') +8(V) + 200(0-') + 70 *(o)* + 400 *(v)* +200 *(r')* + 70 *(o)* + 600 *(x')* + IOO *(p)* + 5 *(e')* + IO *(l)* + 200 *(o-')* + 300 *(t)* + 70 *(©')* + 200 *(cr')* = '1170-01)5 6 Xpeiords. There is one other cryptogram among the inscriptions

P. 22, above. 4 Schlumberger, in *R. E. G.,* vn, 1894, p. 323 ff.

2 See, for example, Clermont-Ganneau:

Recuril (VArcheol. 3 Ibid., p. 330: this seal belongs to the 8th or 9th century. *Orient.,* vi, p. 8i ff. Also G. Horner: *The Coptic Version* "John xix, 19. *of the New Testament,* 1905, Vol. Ill, p. xlv. "See above, p. 12. 3 Page 2 2 above.

published here, and this, I think, is the most important of all. It is on a lintel at Serdjilla,1 over the outer doorway of a passage leading to a group of small buildings adjoining the church and probably used as dwellings by the clergy. The lintel is a large block with a smooth face and bears simply the letters HNA. The letters are large, well cut and perfectly preserved: there is nothing else upon the lintel. The numerical value of these letters is 8051, and this is the sum of the numerical values of the letters which compose a verse from Psalms,2 very common on lintels especially in this region, in the form Kupios *(favXdijri Tt)v* eicroSoV *rov Kcli Tt)v* IfoSoV *rov, airo vvv Kol* ecus *aitovtov afitjv; The Lord shall preserve thy coming in and thy going out, from now even for evermore: amen.* It seems to me clear that, when this verse was written so, as a cryptogram, it was not intended either as an expression of piety, or for the edification of the men who passed beneath the lintel, but that it was regarded as a formula with magic power to avert the evil spirits which might otherwise enter here. And if Such a verse was used on lintels solely as a magic charm, there is good reason to suspect that most of the so-called Christian inscriptions, especially those on the lintels of dwellinghouses, had the same character and purpose. If so, then they did not differ essentially from that other common formula, which I believe belonged originally to the pagan time, and which is frequently met with on house-lintels, *"Oa-a Xeyeis, fake, Ko.1* o-ol *To. Si7ra."What thou say est, friend, may that be to thee also, twofold"* — i. e., *"Ifthou blesses t this house and its inmates, may thy blessings return upon thee, and if thou cursest, may thy curses return upon thee, doubled,"* except that this pagan formula was addressed to men, and intended to avert their curses or invite their blessings; while the so-called Christian formulae were addressed primarily to the evil spirits. Superstition is at least nearly as old as man, and we ourselves are not free from it when, from other motives than politeness, we refrain from crossing a funeral procession, or from passing under a ladder, or from playing against the grain of the table. But it tends somewhat to disillusionment to discover how much of pure superstition there was, in what at first sight seems to be the genuine expression of sincere piety on the part of the Syrian Christians in the fifth and sixth centuries.

1 Inscr. No. 220. 2 Psalms exx, 8. See above, p. 14. for *jvka£r)*, is found on two lintels in the neighboring town 3 The form *tvkdiir)*, which I believe to be for *jvd$u*, not il-Barah, Inscrs. Nos. 192 and 193. Compare also No. 194. CHAPTER II INSCRIPTIONS OF THE DJEBEL IL-A«LA, DJEBEL

BARISHA AND DJEBEL HALAKAH

1. Benabil. Fragment. On a fragment of a moulded block, lying upon the ground. Copy of the editor.

Such devout phrases are very common in the Syrian inscriptions. See below,

Nos. 3, 26, 31, 32, etc. Compare also the inscriptions quoted from Waddington's collection in Chabot's *Index,* Xii, s. v. *fiorjdei.* Similar phrases abound in Thammudene, Safaitic, Kufic and Arabic inscriptions as well. See Part IV, p. no. Doubtless the primary intention of these inscriptions was to call down blessings and avert evil from the building. See Chapter 1, p. 17 ff. and p. 22.
2. Benabil. Rock-hewn Tomb. Over the doorway, within the vestibule of a large tomb hewn in the living rock, immediately below a bi-columnar monument. See Part II, p. 62. This monument stands about two hundred yards southeast of the village of Benabil, on the opposite side of the wadi: the doorway of the tomb is about fifteen feet northeast of the northeast corner of the monument. Seven other rock-hewn tombs are in the immediate vicinity.
The monument obviously faced the town, and on the west side of the single remaining column is a small dovetail plate in relief; I was unable, however,

to find any trace of an inscription, either on this plate or on the base of the monument. Similar plates, without trace of any inscription, are frequent on Syrian monuments, and some at least of these are so well preserved that it is quite certain that no letters were ever carved upon them. Possibly such plates had become a purely conventional form of ornament: possibly they were intended to bear inscriptions to be carved at some later time: I think, however, that often inscriptions may have been painted upon them. Such a plate, without trace of letters now, was found also at the back of the large sarcophagus, marked E in the plan, opposite the entrance.
26
Plan of the tomb of Inscr. 2. Scale T:2000
The inscription was carved above the doorway of the central hall (c): I was, however, unable to read more than five letters. These letters are of handsome form and doubtless belong to the second cei... s Eu... century A.d. Copy of the editor. PY *pvl* 3. Bettir. House. Lintel of a large and handsome, though plain, house. The space occupied by the inscription measures 2.90 m. in length. The letters are slightly over 6 cm. in height. Copy of the editor.

I. + KYXPYBOHem-ANeiKOYITOYrKE-TOYCEniBAPrOCKYIKOZ t
2-THXNITAj
The Y after XP is probably due to false analogy with Kv(pic): the sign after Bapi0c seems to be an abbreviation for /ecu.1 The latter part of the inscription is very perplexing. It is perhaps possible that Bapycw and Kuiko? should be read as genitives depending on eVi.-they seem, however, to be nominatives, perhaps treated as indeclinable. The last word looks like Ttjx""?/ but I think TiX"""at was intended. Probably the author of this inscription fell between the two phrases: Bapyos *Kol Kv(p)ko,* Texn-ai, and eVl (or better Sta) *Bapyov Kcd Kv(p)kov, rvnS)v.* But it is also possible that the second line was originally longer, and that one or more names preceded njxwas, which may then have been a nominative singular: I found no trace, however, of any

letters before this word.
The names themselves are as perplexing as their syntax. Perhaps we should read B£p(i)o5 and Kui(fr)os, names which would be familiar enough in the Latin forms *Varius* and *Quintus.* I am not inclined to believe, however, that these are Roman names. Dr. Littmann tells me that, while no Syriac name equivalent to Bapyos is known, it recalls the Syriac noun *barkd: flash, lightning,* which is doubtless akin to the wellknown Phoenician name *Barkas.* In 1905 a young Syrian from the village of Herakeh told me that his real name was *'fsa,* but that his friends called him *Bavkn:* and as a matter of fact he was, for a native of Herakeh, unusually alive. The name Bapyos occurs also in an inscription from Cyzicus (C. /. G. 3683), and in another found at Rome (C. /. G. 9789). In Kvikos, as Dr. Littmann has suggested to me, perhaps some shorter form of the name Kv/naKds is hidden: if so Ku(p)i»cos or Ku(,/)kos should be restored in the text. In Syriac there are various forms of this common name, such as *Knryaka, Knrika,* etc.: perhaps also *Kirk Beza,* the name of a modern village on an ancient site very near Bettir, may be akin. The Greek form Ki/ptcuco's is common enough.2 In 1905 I found at il-Anderin mention of one *lrefavo; KvpiKov.* Doubtless the name is 1 Cf. No. 61 below.
2 C. I. G. 3990 f., 8652 = Wad. 2412 m. ,882 2, 8866 and 9174. In 1905 I found at Abu
Hamiyeh the name Kvpia»coC, and at Zabbudeh *iwl KvpjiaKov.*
derived from *KvpiaKos,* with special reference to 17 *KvpiaKrj,* sc. cpa.-*The Lord's day,* and was given to a child born on Sunday. Syriac names with the same significance are discussed in Part IV, p. 44. Doubtless the name Sci/fanou, which I found at Kfellusin, has the same meaning, and the similar names given in Pape: Sa/3/3aTiai/d?, Sa/J/SaTixd?, etc. Accepting therefore, though not without some hesitation, Bapyos and Kv(/)ko9, I should read as follows: + Ku(pie) *Xpv(oTe) ficnjdi. Mrj(vb;) aavdiKov i, Tov yKf'* crows, *inl* Bapyos (*Kcli f)* Ku(p)/cos (?), + *TTjvZrat. Lord Christ,*

lulp (us). On the) ioth of (the) month Xanthikos, of the J2jrd year, Bargos and Kyrkos, builders. (April, 475 A.D.)

In these inscriptions the Tcxvtj? seems to have been a builder or contractor, who was perhaps also the architect or designer of the houses which he built: the word seems to be synonymous with oi/coSdpos. See the list of such workmen given by Mr. Butler in Part II, p. 426.

4. Kalb Lauzeh. Church. The first part of the inscription is in a concave medallion, in the ornamentation immediately above the keystone of the apse arch of the church. The keystone contains a bust, which is not shown in M. de Vogue's drawing: probably it was a bust of the Christ; but it is now much defaced. The medallion above is divided into segments by the usual monogram, +, both monogram and letters standing out in relief from the concave field. In the left upper segment is the Greek letter *alpha,* while in the right upper segment there appears to be a Syriac *ale/.* In M. de Vogue's drawing, which was followed by Waddington, this second letter has the form of a Syriac *mini,* although it was not recognized as such by M. de Vogue himself; but this drawing is incorrect in this particular, for a part of the monogram was mistaken for a part of the character at the right. Copy of the editor, squeeze and photographs. Published by M. de Vogue, *S. C,* p. 138 and pi. 129, 2. Wad. 2685. See also Part II, p. 221 ff.

Af K. 'Hcrous) Xpiord?: A.-f *A Jesus Christ.*

With regard to the second part of the inscription, M. de Vogue says: 'Talv6ole centrale porte le monogramme du Christ avec les mots A. n. Xpio-rds. Au-dessous regnait une longue inscription qui est aujourd'hui illisible." I overlooked this inscription entirely. Apparently it was carved on the topmost band of the mouldings of the keystone of the arch and upon the voussoir adjoining on the right, as shown by M. de Vogue in plate 129, 2, where the following letters are given: WrENDC TEA. Tt is of course impossible to say what this may have been; but it

suggests the word *p.ovoyevij;* so often applied to Christ. Possibly this part of the inscription was something like this: fteov *vlos* /xofjcoyeffr/)?, *ytwj)6d;... Oitly-begottot son of God, boyn ....*

Inscr. 4. From a squeeze and photographs. Scale 1:10.
5. Kalb Lauzeh. Church. On the lintel of the central doorway in the south side of the same church: this was the main entrance on this side.1 The first nine letters, with a cross at the beginning, are distinct: the rest have crumbled away. These nine letters measure 39 cm. in length and are 4 cm. high: they are nearly in the center of the lintel. Below the inscription is a disk" containing the-f, and on each side of the disk are the remains of what seem to be the two busts reported by M. de Vogue. Copy of the editor, squeeze and photograph.

Published by M. de Vogiic, *S. C,* p. 136.

The names of the archangels Michael and Gabriel are found together in other inscriptions, sometimes joined with the names of Christ, the jfPffijffifjfBsfjSfl Mother-of-God, the apostles, or other saints, as, for example, inScr. 5. Cast from a squeeze, in *C. I. G.* 8694, 8695, 8756, 8765 and 8792/' I do not be-+ M'x, raft'X.t lieve, however, that either these or the present inscription throw t *Michael, Gabriel,* t any light, as M. de Vogue suggests, upon the vexed question of the letters XMl-.4 6. Bshindelinteh. Church (?). On a lintel in situ, apparently of a church. In the center of the inscription is a large cross. Copy of Dr. Littmann.

tAriOC O 9 OCAriOCl_AVPOC AriOCA9ANA TOC TAOPOGOC A I HM AC H A _ HCOVN HMAC + Ayio? *6* Bed?, ayios 'I cr()u/3os, ayios 'A#cuaTos, o-Ta(v)po#(el)s Si' *rjfias,* 17Xe-*qaov rjfias.* + *Holy God, holy Mighty One, holy Immortal Onef crucified for us, have mercy upon us.*

This, as I have said in Chapter 1, p. 8 f, is the famous "trisagion"5 "Ayios 6 Bed?, ayios 'Io-u/ad?, ayios *da.va.TOi, iXerjcrov* ijjuas, together with the clause *o o-TavpcjOeU* Si' iaas, inserted by the heretic Peter the Fuller (Petros "Cnapheus," Petrus "Fullo"), bishop of

Antioch, about the year 470 A.u. The insertion of these words was part of a fierce ecclesiastical controversy. The orthodox churchmen of the fifth century, believing that such formulae of worship should apply to the Trinity, interpreted the threefold invocation as referring successively to the three Persons of the Godhead, and considered the subject of the verb *tkeqo-ov* to be the Trinity thus invoked. On the other hand, the sect of the monophysites, which was strongly represented in Antioch at this time, applied the whole invocation to the one God, and Peter, in inserting the words *"crucified for us,"* made the trisagion a distinctly monophysite formula, asserting that God was crucified.

There is some uncertainty as to the age of the trisagion; but the traditional story of its origin is too edifying to pass over lightly. According to John of Damascus, a writer of the eighth century, and Nicephorus Callistus, of the fourteenth, it seems that in the time of Theodosius the Younger, when Proclus was bishop of Constantinople, 1 See Part II, p. 224. 4 See above, p. 23.
2 Part II, p. 33, No. 24. 5 See Swainson, *The Greek Liturgies,-p.* 12 n. 3, 3 See also Dussaud et Macler, *Voyage Archeo-* pp. 14, 226 and 383. *logique,* 1901, p. 206, No. 99. i.e., between 434 and 446 A.d., there were violent earthquakes, occasioning innumerable disasters on land and sea, great loss of life, and a general panic, so that the people of Constantinople held public services, making supplication unto God to avert their total destruction. And while they were praying, "a child was taken up from among them, and so was taught, by the teaching of the angels in some way, the thrice holy hymn: *'Holy God, holy Mighty One, holy Immortal One, have mercy upon us.'* And when the child returned and told what it had been taught, the whole multitude sang the hymn, and thus the calamity was stayed." 1 But the child died, according to one account. Some say, however, that the hymn was taught by the angels to Proclus himself, and that it was a Combination of Psalm xli, 3: *ehtyqoev 77 i/a»x? pov 717365 Tov Oeov, rbv ioxvp6v, Tov Iwma,* with

the hymnus tersanctus (also called the "seraphic" or the "triumphal hymn"), which was composed from Isaiah vi, 3: "Ayios, ayios, ayios, Kv/nos *2a/3aad, irrfpT)s 6 oipavbs Ko.1* 17 *yrj* Ttjs Sos rov.[2] Others again believed that the hymn was older than Proclus. Nicephorus[3] says: "the hymnus trisagius, as it appears, was handed down through the church of Christ from the time of the apostles, at least as it seems to me." In the next sentence the story is told of the child who learned the hymn from the angels in the time of Proclus; but evidently this author would have us believe that the attempt on the part of some at that time to attribute suffering to the "Divinity of the Only-Begotten" was the Cause of the earthquakes: *Tivwv Tr/vLKavTa nddos rjj BiorrjTL Tov, Movoytvovs npooa.ine.lv l-rvipovvroiv, of.iop.SiVT i£cucri(ov X"PLV "To.v8-rjp. ov Teovpevr)*-Xmijs: also thattheangels taught, not a new hymn, but the hymn without the heterodox addition: d7rA. ws *ovroi Tov rpi.oa.yiov vp.vov,-Tpoo6rjKr)s dvv.* Now according to his own statement at the beginning of this same chapter, and also in xv, 28, this addition to the trisagion was made by Petros Cnapheus some twenty years after the death of Proclus. So that Nicephorus seems to be trying to reconcile a supposition of his own, for which he has no proof to offer, with the general belief that the hymn originated in the time of Proclus. Somewhat better evidence is to be found in the anonymous life of Basil the Great. The author of this biography, who may have been Amphilocius Iconiensis, and who in any case appears to have lived at least as early as the time of Proclus, says in chapter iv, p. 55,[4] that once on a public occasion Basil[5] led the people in this hymn. But the first certain record of the trisagion is in the acts of the council of Chalcedon, at the end of the first session. This council was held in 451, five years after the death of Proclus. After the trial and sentence of Dioscorus and his associates, the bishops of Illyria wished clemency to be shown to the condemned; but the bishops of the East exclaimed that the judgment was just, and began to shout

the trisagion, and such phrases as 'Nicephorus Callistus, *Historia Eccl.,* xiv, 46; John of *Hist. Eccl.,* xvm, 51.

Damascus, *Expositio Fidei Orthodoxae,* m, io, and *Epistola* 4 Migne, *Patrologia Graeca,* Vol. xxix, p. cccxii, 1, C; *ad Iordanem de hymno trisagio. Acta Sanctorum,* Junii III, p. 432.

'-Jobius, fl. 530 (?), in Photius, *Bibliotheca,* cod. 222, p. 5 Lived about 329-379 A.d. 191 b 5 ff.

"Long life to the council!" "Long life to the emperors I" "Christ hath put down Dioscorus!" etc., evidently wishing to drown out by their noise the suggestion of their opponents.

Whatever may be the true date of the trisagion itself, there is a general agreement as to the origin of the heretical phrase added to it and contained in the Bshindelinteh inscription: this phrase is ascribed, as I have said, to Peter the Fuller, a cleric of somewhat unsavory reputation, who became bishop of Antioch. Theodorus Lector, a writer of the sixth century, in his *Ecclesiastical History,* i, 20, says: "When Martyrius held the episcopate of the church of Antioch, Zeno, the magister militum, who had married Ariadne, the daughter of the emperor Leo, came to Antioch. In his company was a certain Peter, who was called 'Fullo,' a presbyter of the church of St. Bassa the Martyr, which is in Chalcedon. And, coveting the throne of that city (Antioch), he persuaded Zeno to join with him in his undertaking. Then, giving money to some of the sect of Apollinarius, he stirred up countless tumults against the faith and against Martyrius the bishop, anathematizing those who did not say that God was crucified. In doing so he brought the people to faction, and in the trisagion Peter added the phrase '6 (rravpcodeU 81 rj/ xas.'" The "*Libellus Synodicus*" adds that Peter called a "vile council" to establish his addition to the "hymn."[1]

The first accession of Peter to the episcopal throne of Antioch, about the year 470, affords, therefore, a definite limit to the age of this inscription. And it is, of course, possible that the new formula was carried at once to the little town in the hill country where the in-

scription was found. But this is unlikely. Furthermore, it is unlikely that a formula, whose orthodoxy was still a subject of fierce dispute, should be accepted by the country people, unless it were in deference to an authority which seemed to them both complete and permanent. But Peter's position in his diocese was never secure. For the first two years he was involved in a constant struggle with his rival, the orthodox Martyrius, who was supported by the emperor Leo. In 471, Martyrius having given up the fight, Peter was banished by order of the emperor, and succeeded by Julian. Under Basiliscus, in 475, Peter was restored to power, and again enforced his addition to the trisagion; but he was compelled to retire again on the fall of Basiliscus two years later. One of his successors, Calandio, bishop of Antioch 481-485, not only refused communion to all who would not anathematize Peter, but, in order to neutralize the heretical implication of Peter's innovation, introduced in the trisagion, before Peter's phrase, the words *O Christ, our King.*[2] In 485 Peter was again restored to his bishopric, and remained in office until his death, about 488. But in the very year of this last restoration both he and Acacius, bishop of Constantinople, who had supported him, were condemned and anathematized by a synod of bishops held at 1 *M. uxpav TroLr)frdfi.(vo; jvvo&ov irpoo-OriK-qv Tov Tpuraylov, 6 crrav-'-KaXavStoiv* 8e Tu *Kvtupti avriir-paTTOiv, Tout tKCtvon irpoo-drjpiaOtlt St' r/pMs, KcuvoToptti* 6 *diwiosSacrosancta Concilia,* ed. Kuk *irpoo-vr 'iBti T5 Tpio-uyim To Xpiort BcuriAeC.*-Nicephorus Labbe, 1671, iv, p. 1009; ed. Mansi, vn, p. 872. Callistus, xv, 28.

Rome, and were discredited in many churches even in the East.[1] Now it is evident that, even in the time of Calandio, the trisagion with its heretical addition was current at least in the city of Antioch itself. But it is not probable that a small country community, in a period of such uncertainty and disturbance, should have chosen, except under compulsion, to have carved, in permanent form and in a place most likely to attract attention, a formula so much in dispute and so generally condemned by the authorities of both church and state.

Not long afterward, however, when Severus was bishop of Antioch, from 512 to 519, the monophysites became dominant in all this region, and enforced with violence the acceptance of their dogmas. This Severus, who was regarded as the true founder of the organized monophysite sect, was a monk who, for his dissolute habits or his heterodox views, or for both, had been driven out from at least one monastery—some say from several—and had come at last to Constantinople, where he joined with Timotheus, afterward bishop of that city (511-517), and others in a determined war upon the orthodox faith. The emperor Anastasius himself (491-518) declared in favor of the monophysites, and undertook to reduce the orthodox bishops to submission, or to dispossess them of their sees. Through all this movement Peter's addition to the trisagion was the watchword and warcry of the party, and crowds of heretic monks, clergy, and laity, incited by the emperor and his coadjutors, together with the rabble which was hired for the purpose in various cities, singing the new version of the old formula, started the riots which preceded the downfall of recalcitrant prelates. Flavian, the bishop of Antioch,2 and Elias, bishop of Jerusalem, were among the first to be attacked. They were compelled to reject the decrees of the council of Chalcedon, and to anathematize all who accepted these decrees. In Antioch the disturbances were greatly increased by the rival parties of monks who, pouring in from the Syrian mountains, united with the opposing factions in the city.3 At Constantinople mobs in two of the principal churches, "in singing the trisagion added the words ' *JVho wast crucified for us,* ' so that the orthodox of necessity drove them out with blows."4 The emperor, then, and his party began to make war openly upon the bishop Macedonius, loading him with insult and abuse, until a large number of the people rose in his defense with the cry: "Now is the time for martyrdom: let us not desert our father!"5 In the riots which ensued, houses were burned and many lives were lost: finally the emperor himself was frightened and prepared for flight. 6 Theophanes tells much the same story in another place, p. 136, as if it were a second occurrence, adding that Timotheus gave orders to all the churches to sing the trisagion with the addition: that some did this through fear; but that the orthodox monks went about chanting another hymn, and 1 See "*Sacrosancta. Concilia*" ed. Labbe, iv, pp. 1123-4 'J'aAAoires *iv Kvpuucrj To Tpurayvov irpoo-criOovv To 6 o-ravpui* l 1 2 7; ed. Mansi, VII, p. 1137 ff. St' *r/pa. 's, Uhtti* Tous *6p0o86$ovi i$ avdyKr)pTa Trkrrytav avrovs* 2 I.e., Flavian II of Antioch, 498-512 A.d. e'Axurat. (Theophanes.) 3 Theophanes, *Chronographia,* 131 f. 5 Kuipos *paprvpiov, prj KaruXttyoiptv Tov irai-epa rjp. iLv.* 6 Theophanes.

were greeted with fanatical enthusiasm by the people. Theophanes' account is somewhat confused and not very reliable: the two passages doubtless refer to the same event, and Timotheus, who does not seem to have been bishop at that time, is not likely to have given such an order to the churches. But the main features of the story are corroborated by Evagrius (about 536-594) in a simple, and in the main credible, account, for which he cites as authority a letter written at the time of these events by Severus himself to Sotericus, bishop of Caesarea in Cappadocia, who sympathized with Severus' faction.1 But the emperor's party won: Macedonius was deposed and Timotheus, a rabid monophysite, put in his place. "Then Anastasius the lawless emperor and Timotheus the unholy bishop of Constantinople so ill treated the monks, laity and clerics, who took the side of Macedonius and the synod, that they drove many to take refuge in the Oasis of the Thebaid."2 Soon afterwards, partly through deceit, Flavian was deposed, Severus made bishop of Antioch3 and the acceptance of his authority secured by trickery or by force."

Once installed, and confident in the support of the emperor and the bishop of Constantinople, Severus seems to have entered on a career of violence and intimidation throughout his diocese. In this he had the hearty cooperation of his subordinate, the infamous Peter of Apamea. Among the stories told of their cruelty and oppression in the memorial presented by a body of Eastern monks to Memnas, the orthodox bishop of Constantinople, in 536 is the account of how a company of "Hebrew robbers," employed for this purpose by Severus and Peter, waylaid a band of old men who were traveling to the monastery of St. Simeon, doubtless the great Der Sim'an, not far from the town of this inscription. The pilgrims were killed, and their bodies stripped and left unburied. 5 It is not impossible that at such a time the church at Bshindelinteh had the formula of the triumphant faction carved on its lintel, either to win the favor of those at that time in power, or to protect the community during this reign of terror, or perhaps even in consequence of a direct threat.

Severus's power soon came to an end. In 518 Anastasius died, Justin became emperor, and Severus was deposed: there never was another legitimate monophysite bishop of Antioch. The monophysite formula does not seem to have been forbidden at once, for even the orthodox Ephraem, who was bishop of Antioch from 527 to 545, in a letter to Zenobius of Emesa, defended its use on the ground that those who applied the whole trisagion to Christ alone might without sin add the clause *Who wast crucified for its"* But certainly after the fall of Severus the addition of the words in ques 1 Theophanes, 131-136; Evagrius, *Eccl. Hist.* , m, 44. *if6vevo-e, To. Ovcriao-Tripw. dwrrpeVw, Kai Tcl iepa o-Ktvq w 6p6o* 2 Theophanes, 133. *86£uv xvevW 6 UpotraXos* (i.e., *Tipodios*) (Theophanes, 135).

3 Theophanes, 134. 5 *Sacrosancta Concilia,* ed. Labbe, v, p. 120'; *Sacrorum* 4 *TSv Si Vtt* 'AiTioxeta, *oi piv o-vvairax6evres virrjxOr)crav... Concilioruiil Collectio,* ed. Mansi, VIII, p. 998 f. *nl Si fila. Kai ivdyKri o-vvtOcvro Tois crvvoSiKots 2,eftrjpov, dvadc-8*

Photius, *Bibliotheca,* cod. 228 (ed. Bekker, p. 245 *A, paTurpbv* «x0l"T"/ "A"1 *o-vv6Sov* Kai *Tsv Xonrwv Tuiv tl- prjKoTwv* 43 ff.). Photius, however, in commenting on Ephraim's

Su'o £ixreis 17 *iStoTrp-af* ori *Tov Kvp- wv* (Evagrius, *Eccl. Hist.,* toleration, adds that the other fathers prohibited these words

"'1 33)-Stmjpou *yap Tt/v Kotvomav 7rdVres 01 6p668o£oi Zcpvyov,* altogether (p. 245 B, 20 ff.). *pdXio-ra 01 povaxol, ois pira Trrjdov% aypouaKOV nptopwv woWovi* tion was never compulsory in the Catholic Church, and was soon discontinued in most places. Nicephorus Callistus says:1 "This heresy, which was begun by Cnapheus (i.e., Peter the Fuller) and attained its growth to a great extent from Severus and his followers, not long afterwards was entirely quenched, it having been abolished in the Church of God, and persisting still only among the Armenians, who do not choose to be obedient to the catholic traditions." And as a matter of fact the trisagion with the addition does not occur in any of the traditional liturgies, so far as I have been able to discover, except in the Armenian Church. In the ancient Syriac liturgies which I have been able to examine, viz., through the Latin translations, the trisagion occurs without the addition. The dialogue, however, between "The Jacobite" and "The Melcite," written early in the thirteenth century by David, son of Paul, and published in part by Assemani in the "*Bibliotheca Orientalist* i, p. 518 ff. , proves that in this century the trisagion with the addition was still in use in at least one branch of the Jacobite Church. Assemani also says that in the liturgical books printed in Rome for the Maronites of Syria in his time (the middle of the eighteenth century) the trisagion with the addition occurred. The monophysite clause is also a part of the Arabic version of the trisagion still in use and quoted to me in 1905 from the regular service by the priest of the church of St. Sergius at Sadad, a village about twenty-five miles east of Ras Ba'albek. 2 The Jacobite Church was founded during the reign of Justinian. In the year

535 an effort was made to reconcile the various parties in the church. Justinian the emperor, under the influence of the empress Theodora who favored the monophysites, summoned Severus to Constantinople. For a time it seemed as if the monophysites would recover much of their lost power. But this was prevented by the pope Agapetus, who happened to be in Constantinople at that time on other business: Anthimius, who sided with the monophysite party, was deposed and the strongly orthodox Memnas made bishop of Constantinople. Memnas then called together a synod at which Severus was condemned again, and his doctrines formally repudiated. Not long afterwards Justinian decided to compel all the clergy to conform to the decrees of Chalcedon, or to retire: his decision was actually carried into effect, and many churches in Syria were deprived of their leaders. Certain monophysite bishops, moreover, who had gone to Constantinople to persuade the emperor to reconsider his action or to secure the protection of Theodora, were imprisoned by Justinian's orders. In their imprisonment they ordained James Baradaeus, of Edessa, who had been called to the city by the empress in the interests of the monophysite faith. James was ordained nominally bishop of Edessa, but virtually as a metropolitan with oecumenical authority. Mounted on fast camels supplied by friendly Arab princes, he traveled through the Flast, reorganizing the monophysite sect, and establishing an independent church. He is said 1 xvni, 51. 2 It is interesting to note in this connection that the people of Sadad still reckon their years according to the Seleucid era, beginning with 312 B.C. by some to have ordained 80,000, by others, 100,000 clergy, including 89 bishops and two patriarchs. Among these was Sergius,»who was ordained bishop of Antioch: this was, however, only a titular see, as monophysite prelates could no longer reside in that city. Sergius is regarded as the second or the third bishop of Antioch in the line of this Jacobite succession, of which the Jacobites themselves considered Severus to have

been the first. I believe, therefore, as I have said, that the church at Bshindelinteh belonged to the Jacobite denomination, which was formally organized in the time of Justinian, about 535, but which some of the Jacobites considered to have begun with Severus, about 515 A.d.1 7. MA'SARTEH. On the lintel of a plain doorway in a ruined wall. The inscription is in two parts, A and B, between which are three disks. Each part consists of five lines; but, inasmuch as the corresponding lines in the two parts are not opposite each other, I believe that each part is to be read by itself, though the second may be the continuation of the first. The letters are now almost illegible, and I have been unable to decipher the text with any certitude. The letters which I read are given below. Copy of the editor, squeeze and photograph.

This may be read as follows:

X(/3«rr)e, 6 @(o)s, *Oh Christ, our) God,* d *vaTTav* cr *ov rtjv nr-bring thou to rest the soul X»* 'kvtvvlov irepio8(ew f Antonios (the) pcrio Tov),* (/ecu) *Bapah- wpLov deutes, and of Baradonios Tr- petvfliwepov), xal (fhe) presbyter, and of all , r those... TTOVTUtV TO) y...*

The words *avatravaov Tt)v nxw Ktk.* seem to have belonged to the service for the dead, among the early Christians as in the modern Greek Church. See the very interesting article on this subject by M. A. Dumont, in *B. C. H.* 1877, P-321 "*Fragment de rOffice Funebre de I'Eglise Grecqite, sur une inscription d'Fgypte.*" See also below, No. 170. This part of the service recalls the well known verse in Revelations xiv, 13: *"And I heard a voice from heaven saying unto me, IVrite, Blessed are the dead which die in the Lord from henceforth: Yea, saith the Spirit, that they may rest from their labours; and their works do follow them."* Also Matthew xi, 28: *"Come unto me, all ye that labor and are heavy laden, and I will give you rest. "*

A *periodeutes* was a visiting presbyter, a sort of ecclesiastical inspector ("bischoflicher Kirchenvisitator"), who seems to have had a rank intermediate between that of an eVio-KOTTo? or *bishop,* and that of a *wpea-vrepos* or *presbyter.3* Church buildings were sometimes erected under the direction of these officials, as may be seen, for example, from 1 See also Chapter 1, p. 8 f. p. 176, apropos of the trilingual inscription from Zebed.

2 Professor Sachau, in *Monatsber. Berl. Akad.,* 1881, (See below, No. 336 a.) 3 See A. du Cange: *Glossarium.*

C /. *G.* 8822 I1 ©cow *irpovotq.* eirl row cvXa/Scorarou *TtpunTontp&T* f _/8*vripov* Kc ir6/3ioSeurow ©coktmt-tou *Iktutqi)* To *epyov Tovto* /ce eVl Tow eua/3eoTaTou SiaKoVov e *oiKovopov KvpiaKov.* See also No. 288 below. Probably the lintel under discussion belonged to a church building of some sort, perhaps even a mortuary chapel. 8. Bshindelaya. Tomb Of Klaudios Sosandros, 134 A.d. On the facade of a rock-hewn tomb, beside which stands a monumental shaft, about two hundred yards southwest of the modern village. The tomb is excavated in one side of a rectangular well, measuring about 12 x 23 feet, and sunk in the living rock to a depth of about 8 feet: the entrance to this well, or forecourt, was by a flight of stairs cut in the rock, on the opposite side from the tomb. The front of the tomb consists of a portico of two piers and two pilasters, all cut from the living rock: above the piers runs a two-banded architrave, which bears the inscription, and above that a frieze of bucrania and garlands.2

This inscription is in two lines, of which the first measures 6.60 m. in length, the letters averaging 12 cm. in height: the lower line is 3.25 m. long, and its letters about 8 cm. high. The letters in both lines are well formed, regular and deeply cut; but in some places, especially in the second line, the stone is so badly weathered that the letters have entirely disappeared. Copy of the editor, squeeze and photograph.

Published by Waddington, No. 2684.

TI KA tIAOKAHC TI KA CUJCANAPON TONΠATPAAYTOYICAIKA KITTAPOYN-THNMHTPA Y TOYC6B NHMHCXAPIN 6TOYC BTTP MHNOC AYCTPOY C ANAPC

In thefirst line Waddington read MHT6PA ACKAIMNHMHCXAPIN,from

which he then restored *pyyripa* euo-e/fcf as Ku *pvrjp.T);* x-pw-But the space from the beginning of the letter which should follow MHTPA to the beginning of the N of Mnhmhc measures 1.37 m. , and would admit of 16 letters, not 13. (The first 16 letters preceding measure 1.29 m. in length, the second 16 measure 1.32, the third 1.49.) Furthermore, while in the 5th and 7th places after MHTPA an Y and an are quite distinct, and in the 6th and 8th places there are traces of C and B, yet before the Y an o is evident, not , as in Waddington's reconstruction. Traces also of YT before the OY are visible, as I have indicated in the epigraphical text, so that I believe the word after MHTPA to be AYTOY. After the CB there are traces of what may have been Ackai, as in Waddington's copy. But these traces are now most indistinct, and the AC follow immediately after the CB, while between AC and KAI is a space of 15 cm., or nearly the space of two letters. So that I propose to restore, between AYTOY and MNHMHCXAPIN, some verb form governing the accusatives *Swo-avBpov* and Rum/sow, such as o-e/3d7tej/os. If this is correct, then probably Waddington's reading of B6IAC, in line 6 of the following inscription, should be emended to BOM6.

The second line is so badly weathered that I have been unable to read more than the date with certainty: for the rest I have adopted Waddington's text.

1 From Abrostola, in Phrygia. 2 Part II, p. 60. M. de Vogiid, 5. *C,* pi. 92 and 92 bis.

Ti(/8c/hos) K(au8ios) *tioKrj;* Tt(/3e/3ioi') K(auSioi/) *SaxravSpov, Tov irarepa avrov,* Kcu KX(avSiai/) *Kiirapovv, Ttjv pyrepa* ajvrou, ere/? dju. ei'os (?), *p,vijp.r);* apiv. "Erous *fitrp, p. t)vb; Avo-Tpov Ki,'.* %dxrav$pe, *Tranjp,* XaPe Tiberios Klaudios-Philocles, reverencing (?) *Tiberios Klaudios Sosandros, his father, and Klaudia Kiparun, his mother, for sake of memory. In the) year 182, on the) 2jth of the) month Dystros. Sosandros, Father, farewell7* (March, 134 A.I.).) 8 a. On the shaft, beside the tomb which bears the foregoing inscription. I did not see

this inscription myself, nor the following one (8 b): nor did I see the figures at the top of the shaft, as shown in M. de Vogue's plate. These two inscriptions, however, were copied by both Waddington and M. de Vogue. The accompanying text is from Waddington, No. 2684 b.

Doubtless, as Waddington says, this inscription is a duplicate of the preceding. But possibly, as I have stated above, the sixth line should be read BOMos.

8 b. On the same shaft as the preceding inscription: see above. The following text is from Waddington, No. 2684 c.

TIKACWCANAPON

Waddington reads this as follows:

KAKITTAPOYNYTTA

Ti. K. *XaKTavBpov,* KX. *Knrapovv... XaiperaL.* XAIPGTAI

Undoubtedly, as Waddington suggests, *Xaiperat* is for *Xa(pere;* but I do not know what can be made of the three uncertain letters before it, YTTA. Perhaps *y)v(v)auca* was meant. In that case the accusatives may have been used here simply because familiar in such inscriptions as o *Selva Tov helva dveaTfoev): such an one set up this statue of) sucJi an one.* There may even have been portrait reliefs of Klaudios Sosandros and Klaudia Kiparun affixed to this shaft, as in the case of the monument described under No. 110. I would therefore read as follows: *To) Tiberios Klaudios Sosandros and) Klaudia Kiparun, (/lis) wife, this monument was erected). Fare ye well I* 9. BSHINDELAYA. PANEL OF

A Balustrade (?). This stone now forms the base of the south end of a Arch containing inscr. No. 9.

pointed arch across a street, about the center of the village (see the accompanying photograph); it appears to be the half of a panel of a balustrade, such as may be seen, for example, in Part II, p. 171 ff. At the left of the present center, enclosed on three sides by mouldings, is a dove-tail plate in relief, on which the inscription is incised across the face, as if the block and hence the plate were made to stand on end. I do not believe that this can have been the case originally: it is most probable that in its original position this plate was horizontal, and, if so, the inscription must have been carved at a later time, when this block was put to some use other than that for which it was first intended. Mr. Butler tells me that torus mouldings were not commonly used for small details in this country during the sixth century, in which the inscription is dated, and that, judged by its mouldings alone, the block should be assigned to the second century after Christ. The plate itself measures 31 x 13 cm. The letters are irregular and not easily legible, so that the reading, given below, is not certain. Copy of the editor, squeeze and photograph. + ’EyeVeTG) Nov/ Lvios rov erovs dp£(afiepov?). + Niirinios was born at the beginning of the 603rdyear. (554 A.D.)

I know of no other Greek inscription like this. But a curious parallel in Arabic was found by Dr. Littmann on the lintel of a khan at Ezra’, and has been translated by him: the name of God! ThamdmaJi (?) b. Ibrahim was bom on Sunday, when twelve nights had passed of the month Shauwdl of the year two hundred and twenty-two!M A similar Arabic inscription, "on a wall of the temple of Isis at Philae, near Assuan," is published in the Corpus Inscript. Arab. No. 515.

My reading of dpg(afievov) seems to me very doubtful; but I have been unable to find any other interpretation of these three letters: of course they may be the date according to another era, or a second date. The P of but I think it is clear from the squeeze that the name 10. Bshindelaya. Lintel Of A House. The inscription is on one of the bands of the ornamental door-cap, which is in relief on the face of the lintel. See Part II, p. 80. Below each end of the cap is a little altar, in relief, and beyond each altar a branch growing out of a globule, also in relief. At the left of the inscription are little figures in relief, 3 cm. high. The first four of these are like the heads of Syrian spades, the 1 Part IV, p. 179 f., Arab. No. 8, dated 837 A.d.

Inscr. 9. From a squeeze, photograph and copy. Scale 1:10.

Novpivios is doubtful enough, is not Nou/iiVios for Nou/xVios. fifth is like such life-preservers as one sometimes sees hanging from the rail of a ship at sea, the sixth is a salamander with conventionalized legs, the seventh like a fiasco of chianti, the eighth a cross. The inscription, which is incised, is.162 m. long by 31/ cm. high: the letters are well formed and regular, and most of them are still distinct. Copy of the editor, squeeze and photograph.

Evidently we have to do here with that double-barrelled wish, found not uncommonly on ancient Syrian houses, especially in the northern districts: its most natural form is 00-a Xeyeis, £i’Xe, Kox vol To. StirXa.-1 IVhat thou sayest, friend, to thee also may that be, twofold. This was addressed to the outsider, who might speak good or evil of the house and its owner, and so bring down blessings or a curse. Here, however, it does not seem to me certain who is addressed. I have thought to find in AT- TOYAINAAPIC a proper name, meant perhaps for Airoivdpt.; = ’A-Trokkivd- pios . if the writer omitted one A, he gave good measure by doubling the second A, and if he omitted the second o he at least compensated by increasing the quantity of the first. If so, and if this name is not to be regarded as indeclinable, then it would seem as if the owner of the house were expressing a wish that the blessings wherewith he had blessed others might return to him like a boomerang. Perhaps he was also addressing to himself a warning to be careful what he said of other people’s houses, his own now being glazed. This interpretation is further borne out by the fact that here the word Ka(X)Ss has been inserted in the formula, and that the verb ei7ras is in the aorist tense.2 On the other hand, Dr. Littmann suggests that this name may have been treated as indeclinable, after the analogy of Syriac names ending in —is. If so, then perhaps we should consider "A-rrovXi- vaapis as genitive, and translate: This is the house) of Apitlinaris: what thou sayest well, etc. I am inclined to the other view, however, and would translate as follows: Apitlinaris, what thou

saidest well, to thee also (may) that (be) But possibly the letters ATTOYAINAAPIC do not form a name at all.

The formula 00-a Xeyas, fie, Kt. is, I believe, the oldest found on private houses in Syria. I believe it was in use in the pre-Christian period, for one of the inscriptions containing it, No. 114 below, is certainly pagan. The examples which I found myself are on houses of the earliest type, and in what appear to be the oldest settlements, 1 See Nos. 114, 116, 186, 235, 262; cf. Nos. 42 and 89; vVaddington, No. 2485, etc. 2 Or is this intended for a gnomic aorist? as, e.g., in both Danas, in Dar Kita and in the region about Katura. The dated examples known to me are all early, e. g., No. 89, dated 324 A.d., and No. 116, 336 A.d.: another example which I found at Dar Kita in 1905 is dated probably 295 A.d., and one at Kharab Shekh Berekat is dated 236 A.d. It is probable, therefore, that the present inscription is not later than the fourth century.

I do not consider that this formula has any connection with the words Ko. 1 av,1 found on tombs and sepulchral monuments. These words seem to mean: thou too farewell, or thou too (shall die): they are perhaps reflected in the cheerful cynicism, addressed apparently by the owner of a tomb unto-himself:2 ddpa-i, tyvxn’ ts dddvwro: Be of good cheer, (my) soul: no one is immortal. Similar expressions in sepulchral inscriptions are well known.

11. Bshindelaya. Fragment of a lintel, found in a stone fence built from the ruins, near the outskirts of the town, where the remains of several villas are still standing. The space, on which the letters are, measures 10 cm. in height. Above this are simple mouldings. The fragment measures, along the top of the letter space, 26 cm., along the bottom 31 cm. The letters are well cut and regular: they are 2J/2-3 cm. high. This fragment was brought back by the expedition as a typical example of the stone of which all the buildings in this region were constructed. Copy of the editor.

At the end of the first line are traces of a B, and at the beginning AriDCwL of the second line are marks which may be parts of a T or an □.

nYTWHKTICB The second complete letter in the second line may be I. It is quite + "Ayio? w Beds possible that we have here another example of the trisagion: tovtw r/KTicrdT) Ayios 6 ©cos, ayios 'Iaxvpos, ayios *Addvaros, Kt.* See above, No. 6. *Holy God .... 12.* Talttta. Lintel, 570 A.d. Stone built into a wall *This was built. ..* about twelve feet high, now supporting a terrace. Evidently the stone was originally a lintel. Its face presents a single plane, without mouldings. Above the inscription is an eight-pointed star in a circle. A large piece has been broken from the lower part of the stone, in the center. The total space originally occupied by the inscription measured 1.90 m. in length, the break in the center.70 m. In consequence of this break some twenty or more letters have been lost. The letters, from 4)4 to 6 cm. high, are clear, but of comparatively late form. Copy of the editor. t KCJ)VAAIITHNICOA JAUU«BINA гTMHX-TOVC t + K(vpio)? *jvd£i rr)v* icroS *ov rov Kal Tt)v o8ov. Mtjj/os Awov ft, ivS. y', T(ov)* 117' *erous. + +* The Lord shall preserve thy' coming in and thy going out. (On the) 2nd of (the) month Loos, indiction 3, in the 618thyear. + (August, 570 A.D.) uat is for £iAaf«, as *io-ohov* for *ela-oSov.* The sign of abbreviation after In A, and the order of the letters which give the date, are noteworthy. The words of the text are taken from Psalm cxx, 8: they were the more familiar to all since they were woven into the ritual of the church service.1 Compare, for example, the following passage at the end of the "Clementine" liturgy:2 Tous *Olkovs avrwv fvafov,* rds «od8ous aw-wv *teal* rds cfoSous (*frpovprjo-ov.* Compare also the following sentence from Chrysostom's account of the service in his day,3 in his *Second Homily on the Second Epistle to the Corinthians: TlapaKaXeaoi/jLev... Iva evXoyyjaj)* ras etcrdSovs *avruv Jccu* ra? *i£6hov; irdvTa Tov fiCov anC)v.* Also the "Alexandrine" liturgy.1 This text is very common on lintels of houses in this country.5 13. Taltita. Pedestal Of A SarcophACXUS, about ten feet high,

a short distance south of the modern village. This monument, which stands alone on one of the highest points of the mountain, commands an extensive view, and is itself visible from a great distance. The sarcophagus, which is unusually large, is placed so that its length lies east and west. The southeast corner of the base IYTONAYEI . *ivrov* Auet- has fallen down, together with much of the facing of the adjoining sides and possibly of the northern side also. On the south side of the sarcophagus there is a dove-tail plate in relief, and another on the west end of the cover: no inscription was found on either plate. A fuller description of the monument is given in Part II, p. 107. The present inscription is on the left stone of the two which now form the third tier below the sarcophagus, on the western side, behind the right arm of the man shown in the accompanying drawing. The letters are large, but not regular in form. Copy of the editor. Obviously this is incomplete. Possibly this block belonged originally to some other monument. Or possibly this inscription was never finished. But it is hardly-probable that so handsome and conspicuous a monument was left without a complete inscription of some sort. The most natural place for an inscription on such a base as this would be in the same tier as the present inscription, but on the south side of the base. Perhaps there was an inscription there, and perhaps it may still be found on 1 See Chapter 1, pp. 14 and 25. 3 Swainson, *Greek Liturgies,* 1884, p. 218. 2Brightman, *Liturgies, Eastern and Western,* Swainson, p. 32. 1896, p. 27. 5Cf. No. 192 ff.

Monument which bears Inscr. 13. Drawn from a weak photograph. the under side of the blocks which have fallen from the monument. Perhaps then the letters on the west side are the ending of an inscription, which began on the south and was continued around the base.

On the other hand, if the letters on the west side are not the ending of a longer inscription, the last four letters

AYE I suggest the *ethnikon AveLpr)v6,* while the first four letters might be read rajiW, or perhaps /8ouXevrdV, for /SovXcvrqV. *Aveipa,* or *Avepia,* the modern Hauwarin, is a town on or near the ancient road from Damascus to Palmyra, situated between Sadad (Danaba), and Nezala (Karyaten).1-*Tavros,* as Dr. Littmann tells me, is a purely Arabic name (Ghauth),2 found in Safai'tic and Nabataean inscriptions, and not likely to be borne by anyone in this region, unless he had migrated hither from the country further south.

14. 'arshin. Tomb, 433 A.d. On the south side of a cover, like that of a sarcophagus, over the top of a rock-hewn tomb, east of the modern village. The tomb consists of a narrow well, like a deep grave in the rock, with a simple arcosolium in each of the long sides, similar to the tomb of Eusebios described in Part II, p. 104.3 The cover has been moved part way to one side, and its acroteria slightly broken. The side of the cover which bears the inscription is 1.88 m. long and 40 cm. high. The letters are 4 cm. high, and not well preserved. Copy of Dr. Littmann. 1. EICBE-DEIICEDXPICTDCAVTDVBUUH-BIMEjANAPDCr-BIUJNL 2. HTICEITINMH-NOCAPTEMlCIDYICTDYAnYETDVr:

In the word after MEIANAPDC the second letter is most uncertain. It may be A or u, or possibly two letters, of which the second one is N. Between B and u it is uncertain whether there was any letter at all.

Els ©eos ce 6 Xpioros avrow-*fiwnjOi.* MewwSpos *r-yS-awof-* (eic)nre(i/) (e) (?) *p-yvbs 'ApTep,Lcriov K, Tov atrv* erovs. *One God and his Christ: help (us)! Meiandros (son) of had (this tomb) made on (the) 20th of (the) month Artcmisios, in the 481styear.* (May, 433 A.D.) *MeCav8pos* is perhaps for *MaiavSpos* or *MeavSpos.* For the second name *Yvfipwv* occurs to me; but I have not ventured to restore this in the text. Els @eos *Kt.* is one of the commonest formulae among these inscriptions. See above, p. 13 f. and 18 f., and below, No. 25. 1 Moritz, *Zur antiken Topographie der Palmyrene,* 1889, p. 76. Blau, in *Z.*

M. G., xv, p. 444. Renan, in *J. Asiat.*, pp. 17 and 23. Sachau, *Reise in Syrien und Mesopotamia* 7e S£rie, xix (1882), p. 12. Clermont-Ganneau, *Etudes,* 1883, p. 54. Ptolemy, 5, 15, 24. 11 (1897), p. 33, No. 55. Dussaud et Macler, *Voyage* 2The name occurs frequently in Waddington, e.g., 2019, *Arch, au Safd,* etc., 1901, p. 177. 2079, 2562 a, h, and i, etc. See also Wetzstein, *Reisebericht,* 3 See also below, No. 34. 15. Kiftin. A Rock-hewn Tomb, about twenty minutes' walk south-southeast of the village of Kiftin. The tomb consists of a ΠΡΟΚΑΟC ΜΑΡΚΟC square chamber, in the rear wall of which, opposite WAOY,,,. the entrance, are two narrow arched openings, *r r* leading into passages 7 feet long by *2/2 feet Proklos. Markos (son) of Olos,* that is, 1-,i 1 _ ,1 1 w v,.,. wide, with a narrow sarcophagus in the rock on
Marcus son of Aulus.1.
each side. The inscriptions are painted in dark green on the rear wall of the square chamber. Copy of the editor.

The name *Proklos* is at the right of the top of the entrance to the passage on the left: the word measures 1.01 m. in length, and the letters are 8 to 16 cm. in height. The name *Markos* is above the entrance to the aisle on the right: it measures 75 cm. in length and 14 cm. in height. The last name is at the right of the same entrance, beginning under the o of Markos: it measures 51 by 11 cm. The letters are of a type found comparatively early in this region: I think the tomb may well date from the second century A.d. 16. Der Seta, House, 412 A.d. On the lintel of a house, in the south center of the town. See Part II, p. 169. Above the inscription is a row of six small disks in relief below the surface, among which, in a row at the bottom, are five little incised figures like the letter o. A few letters have been broken from the right end of the inscription. The length of the remainder is 1.82 ElcεEOCOBOHBuiNnACINETOYCiYHAP-TEMlC m.: the height of the fascia „ „ ,„ ......, Efs @os 6 *RornBSiv naaiv.* Erous *£v',* U,ij(i6s) Apreuio-iou which it occupies is 15 cm., the average height of the letters (*There is) one God, that*

helpeth all. In the) year 460, in the) month n. _,, Artemisios... (May, 412 A. d.) *Sl/2* cm. The letters are not very well formed, but are clear and regular. Copies of Dr. Littmann and the editor.

Published by M. de Vogue: *La Syrie Centrale,* p. 123 and pi. 100.2 Waddington, No. 2678.

On the words Efs ©eos *Kt.* see No. 25 below.

17. Der Seta, Lintel Of North Church. Two fragments lying within the ruined walls of the North Church. Fragment A. Fragment B. These fragments appear to have been 1. oocAm YKAlAriOYT-TNEYtfK/THCeE parts of a lintel, doubtless a lintel of 2. Anc 9EN CTTrAHAYTi one of the portals of this church. Copy of the editor.

Published by Waddington, No. 2679. See also de Vogue, 5. *C,* pi. 116, and Part II, p. 195 f.

1 Compare *C. I. G.* 5587 (Himera), 5855 (Puteoli), and 6987. 2 The lintel shown in M. de Vogue's drawing of this house, however, is not the lintel which bears this inscription.
See Part II, p. 169.

The first extant letter in the second line of Frag, A, and the seventh in the same line of B, may be A, A or A. The fourth letter in this line in A may be X. The sixth in B looks like r. E or C. Between GEN and CTT is space for about seven letters.

Line i. 'Ei ovofiari IlaTpjo? *Kal* Tiou *Kal 'Ayiov Uvevfiaro'i)* /c(ai) r/Js ®e-oroKOu *In name of Father and Son and Holy Spirit and the Mother-of-God.*

The north portal of this church was very high above the level of the ground outside, and could never have been much in use: in Mr. Butler's opinion it could never have been reached from without except by a flight of steps. At some time after the church was completed, this portal was permanently closed with great blocks fitted to the door frame, as may be seen in the photograph published in Part II, p. 195. The lintel itself is broken so that all the part over the doorway is gone, only the parts over the jambs remaining. And I think it is evident that the lintel was broken some time after the doorway was

blocked up, and when the church was destroyed, for otherwise the edges of the break would hardly have been left jagged, as they are now. If so, these fragments may belong to the lintel of the north portal, and the inscription upon them may refer to the blocking up of this doorway. Perhaps, then, the second line may have been something like this: *ot6kov* Manias or otokov *Uapde-vov avepLoOav1 ....*
... e 7t(u)xt7 aur7j, for *avpLadt f) 7Ti5Xij avrr).*
But this reading rests upon so uncertain a basis, that I hesitate even to suggest it here. If, however, these fragments really belonged to the lintel of the north portal, the first letter or two of each line may still be found on that portion of the lintel which remains in situ, over the left jamb. When I was on the spot, I supposed that these fragments belonged to the west portal of the church, for they were found near the west end of the building. On the other hand, this church was evidently at one time a stronghold, as is shown by the walls, twice as thick as the original, closing the eastern end of the ruins. Here, in the baptistery, are to be found also pointed arches of Saracenic type, to support a roof of stone, and a well-built stairway resting upon pointed arches, indicating that the rebuilding was due to the Moslems, a conclusion which is further borne out by the presence of Mohammedan graves near this baptistery and elsewhere in Der Seta, some of which bear Arabic inscriptions,5 dating from 1431 to 1530 A.d. It would be natural to suppose, therefore, that the north portal was blocked up by the Moslems at this time, in which case, of course, the inscription in Greek cannot refer to the closing of the doorway. The words n?s ®(ot6kov (with or without Mapia? or *Uapdevov),* eVl *Tov iravev(f(rp.ov) . .0ev* might also be read at the end of line 1 and the beginning of line 2. With regard to the first line of this inscription, see below, No. 232.

1 Cf. *iycxp(rOr)* 7 *irvt),* Malalas, *Chronogr.,* xv, p. 380, dington as "*martelc.*" Possibly some letters, carved by line 13, ed. Dindorf. mistake, were

erased, and the space then left unoccupied. 2 After GEN there is space for seven letters, accord-3 Published by Dr. Littmann in Part IV, p. 216 f. ing to my calculation. This space is described by Wad 18. Bankusa. In a subterranean chamber hewn in the solid rock. The entrance is through an open dromos, to which steps lead down from the main level. This dromos is now partly filled up with debris. In the left wall of the dromos, as you enter, near the door of the chamber, is a cistern. Over the door of the chamber a circle inclosing a cross has been cut, rudely but deeply: I am not sure, however, that this cross dates from the time when the chamber was originally made.

The chamber itself is about 25 feet square, and 7 feet high. The floor is covered to a depth of a foot or two by the soil which has been washed in. Just inside the doorway, at the left, the top of a circular basin, probably part of the living rock, appears above the soil. In the wall opposite the entrance and near the floor is a broad, shallow niche: the natives said that someone, a stranger to them, dug there and found treasure. At the left of the niche is a kind of closet in the wall, 4 feet wide, 3 feet deep and 6 feet high. In the ceiling of the chamber are sockets, as if for upright posts, and two eyes cut in the rock, as if to suspend ropes or chains. There seems to have been an opening in this ceiling above the circular basin, but, if so, this opening is now completely stopped with stones and earth from above. There was no other opening in the chamber, for

Entrance to the rock-hewn chamber containing Inscr. 18. ljgnt Qr ventilation, except the doorway.

I believe that, at one time at least, this chamber contained a press for oil or wine. Above, the top of the rock was flat. Doubtless there was a building immediately over the chamber; but I could find no traces even of its ground plan. All about, however, are large, plain, square-dressed blocks, which belonged to this or to other buildings in the immediate neighborhood.

The inscription is on the left wall as one enters, near the back of the subterranean chamber: it is incised in a plate, 65 by 67 cm. square, and sunk about a half an inch in the surface of the rock. The bottom of this plate is about three and a half feet above the floor. Below the lower left-hand corner of the inscription is what appears to be a very rude head or face, cut in the rock. The letters, 5 to 7 cm. high, are not very good, but nearly all are perfectly legible. Copy of the editor and squeeze.

Published by Waddington, No. 2680.

Ot itravafiaivovTts 7rcu8s eis rd te' err), £/xy8aifoKrcs ets rd it;', Iva tvvySao-Tawcri 177 Kco/xtj ras—. Inscr. iS. Cast from a squeeze.

I cannot understand this inscription, although I have had many theories about it. The last three letters in the last line are about half as high as the rest, and as the tops of all these letters are on a level, the last three appear to be suspended by their tops. Obviously the last three letters are smaller than the others because otherwise they could not have been written in this line; for after Kco/ at? there is space for only two letters of the larger size. This fact indicates to my mind that the inscription is complete. For the fourth line shows that the carver did not divide his words always by syllables, and, had he intended to write more than we have here, there seems to be no reason why he should crowd the last three letters of the eighth line into the space suitable for two. The inscription, as it is, fills fairly well the plate in which it is contained; but if there had been more to write, a line of small letters might still have found room at the bottom of the plate below the eighth line, or the plate might easily have been enlarged — it is merely a rectangular space sunk in the wall of living rock — or a word or two more might have been carved on the wall beside the plate. Consequently I do not agree with Waddington, when he says of this inscription: "Elle est evidemment incomplete, et cependant il n'y a pas trace d'une autre tablette; il est probable qu'elle n'a jamais ete achev£e."

If the inscription is complete, there are at least two ways of interpreting the last line, which have occurred to me as possible: (1) TAC may be the article, as Waddington regarded it, and may then agree with some object suggested by the figure which is sculptured in the rock immediately below the lower left-hand corner of the inscription. This figure I took to be a human face; but, though I have two squeezes of it, the sculpture was so rude that I am altogether uncertain whether a human face or something else was intended. This would be the most natural use of the verb o-v/A/3ao-7-a£w, as may be seen from a passage in Appian's HistOfia Rotnana, XVI ('e/ a£vxiw 8'), 27: veKpbv o-w/ta iKKop.p. i£6p,evov v7roords rols fyipovcri crwe/ 3aoTa£e To Xeos.

(2) On the other hand 777 may be the adverb, and /(w/Avas may be the object of (rvvfiaaralwo-i. For possibly rviJLacrTLw is used here like a-wKplvm, in the sense of "to Put together as parts of a whole," "to compose," "to make." So in English we might say: "that they may make good soldiers." In modern Arabic the phrase he made a soldier, i.e. , he became a soldier, is common. Perhaps then rvp.ia.o-Tdt,uv was used here in translation of some Aramaic expression. But I have been unable to find any other example of such a use of this verb. Moreover, the use of Kaiifjru, in the sense of fullfledged members of the community as distinguished from the watSe?, seems to me strange. Perhaps, however, the whole clause had its origin in an Aramaic idiom. If so, I should translate the inscription as follows: The boys who enter above, until their fjth year, those who enter belmv, until their 16th, that they may become citizens of this village. Perhaps this was a boys' school. 19. Bankusa. North Church. On the jamb of a doorway in the North Church, situated in the northeastern extremity of the ruins, on the slope of the hill. The northwest corner of the building is in part hewn in the living rock. Mr. Butler considers this to be one of the earliest churches of this region, and thinks CAAJ the building itself may even belong to the pre-Christian period. See Part II, p. 88 f. The inscription is on the western face of the eastern jamb of OA the westernmost of the two doorways on

the south side of the building. N The letters are very badly weathered and almost illegible. Copies of Dr. 1/ A I Littmann and the editor.

AYT

I believe that the stone which bears this inscription was originally a stele IO of some sort, and cut down to make this door-jamb. How much of the inE= scription has been lost I cannot say. Unfortunately no measurements n were taken of the stone or of the letters. And I have been unable to find any clue to the meaning or character of the inscription. 20. Djowaniyeh. Tomb, 340 A.d. On the north side of a sarcophagus resting upon the basement of a built tomb, at the eastern side of the ruins. Originally there were two of these sarcophagi; but the one on the south side has been thrown down and broken. The pieces lie about; but I was not able to find a trace of an inscription on any of the fragments. The two sarcophagi must have been placed side by side, with no intervening space, for the ANTIOXOY south side of the one which is still standing is rough 6TOYC9TTTMHNOC YTTPBPT0 Y B dressed. Above the sarcophagi was a canopy of some sort, which has tumbled into ruins: within the basement are Widvou. "Erou? dm', firf three arcosolia of the usual type, hewn in the rock, Over j/os 'TirepfieptTeov /8'. which are arches. A photograph of this tomb is published in Part II page IIO This is the tomb f) of Antio

T-i c. jrL- j-j-.i chos. In (the) year 180, month lhe first word of the inscription is incised immediately.

Hyperberetaios 2nd. (October, above a dove-tail plate in relief which contains the rest: 34Q A D it measures 61 cm. in length by 7 cm. in height. The plate, exclusive of the dove-tails, measures 1. 05 by 0.56 m.: the letters within the plate are 8 cm. high. All the letters are well formed and regular, and all except the last are perfectly clear still. Copied by Dr. Littmann and the editor. 21. Djowaniyeh. House (?), 374 A.D. On the lintel of a doorway which stands alone in the northwestern part of the town, facing east. This seems to have been the doorway of a large dwelling house.

The inscription is on a dove-tail plate, 1. 14 m. long and 31 cm. high. On either side of this plate is a five-pointed star in a disk, and above the plate a moulded door-cap. The letters are clear, but not very well"formed or regular. Copy of the editor.

I am not perfectly sure that the omission of the N from ju/o? in the second line is not due to an oversight on my own part in making my copy. I am sure, however, that a t was carved both at the end of the first and at the beginning of the second line. The author of this inscription, moreover, had little idea 1. icewcoBujHea)NTOYct of the ti of his llabl as is shown by 2. JWBOYMENOY-CAVTOYMHOIYTTP n , n , n n ,, 3. BPT60YITOVrKYTOYC — P.Jdwv' 9wpou/tewws. TnepepeTjov. 1 he use Ot

Cf ,, « « o v /x, 0 orfdelu with the accusative, however, and the fievovs amov. Mij(v)os 'rnepfiepeTeov phrase Tows £w/3ou/xeVous avrov may be explained as 1, Tov yKv' erous. due to Semitic influence. For in most Semitic Thereis) one God that helpeth them that languages the verb help commonly takes a simple fear him Month Hyperberctaios roth, of accusative while in g riac Oskklau, his fearers, the 4.2 yrd year. (October, 374 A.D.) J J is very common: in most Semitic languages, also, the participle shares both nominal and verbal constructions. On the words of this inscription see below, No. 25. 22. DjOwANfYEH. Tomb, 398 A.d. On the front of a canopy tomb, west of the town and backed up against the hillside. The visible part of the tomb consists of four piers connected by arches supporting a pyramid. The inside of the monument is filled with stones which have rolled down from the hill above, and with earth. It is probable that within the piers was the entrance to a rock-hewn chamber. Tombs surmounted by pyramids seem to have been common in Syria. In some the pyramid was supported on piers, forming a canopy, as here and at Kokanaya:1 elsewhere the pyramid was built up from solid walls, as, for example, at il-Barah. See Part II, p. 109 ff. M. Perdrizet, in an interesting communication to the Institut de Cor-

respondence Hellenique on the subject of the mausoleum at Hermel,2 attributes tomb-pyramids to Egyptian influence: "L 'idee de super poser d tin edifice de plan carrd une pyramide quadrangulaire est d'origine egyptienne. La pyramide avail une destination funeraire. Le ntonu Tomb of Kassianos at Djuwaniyeh. fUent obtcUU par la Superposition lSee No. 36 below. 2B. C. H., xxi (1897), p. 614 f.

d'unePyramide d un mastaba est pareillement un ddifice funeraire. Et les monuments constritits hors dEgypte, d Vimitation des mastabas a toit pyramidal, sont tons des tombeaux. 7els le maiisolee d" Halicamasse et les edifices a toit pyramidal de Palestine, de Syrie, di4frique, quitest interessant de rapprocher du maiisolee" (i.e., the mausoleum at Hermel).

The inscription is on the east side of the northeast pier, immediately below the short moulding, like that of a pilaster cap, which is at the top of the pier, on each side of the corner and below the cornice moulding which forms the base of the pyramid. The first five lines occupy a space 53 cm. long by 28 cm. high: the letters are from 3 to 6 cm. high. The last word is on the stone below, and measures 51 cm. in length by 6 cm. in height. All the letters, especially those of the upper part of the inscription, arc irregular in form and size; but all are perfectly legible. Copied by Dr. Littmann and the editor: squeeze and photographs.

In this inscription H has the strange form k The form M in the third line I believe to be due to the carelessness of the stone-cutter, and to be intended for N, not for M. At the end of the third line, after JI A, there is room for one letter at most. Dr. Littmann read $i'Xois; but 4ik(ovaiv), sc. airov, is more probable. If the author of the inscription really had £i'Xois in mind, this also must have been due to Semitic influence, for in Syriac rahmd, the word used for friends, is the participle of the verb rehem, and properly means loving. Kassianos was doubtless the owner of the tomb. On the words see No. 25 below.

23. Djuwaniyeh. House. On the lintel of a doorway in the second story of a large private house in the eastern part of the town, about 50 feet west of No. 20. This doorway opened on the upper story of a colonnade on the south side of the building, near the west end. In the lower story, which has been buried to perhaps half its height and is therefore fairly well preserved, there are three doorways opening on the colonnade. The capitals of the columns are of various orders and of somewhat bizarre forms; but on the whole the colonnade was unusually handsome, and especially the two remaining plates of the balustrade of the upper story. One of the capitals is grooved, a type very rare in this country: the only other example found by this expedition was in the East Church at Babiska, dated 401 A.d.1 See Part II, p. 176.

The inscription is carved on a rectangular plate in low relief, 30 cm. high and 22 1 Part II, p. 131 ff. Nos. 67 ff. below.

Inscr. 22. Cast from a squeeze.

broad, at the left end of the lintel: at the right end is a Christian monogram. The letters are neither very regular nor very clear. Copy of the editor.

The use of e for at in *iwa* is of course KYpioc common; but the absence of the article seems Baciay Kwpios /WiXofei ei? *ia»va.* to me strange, especially as there was room IIC *The Lord is king forever.* on the plate for three more letters, and these mNA would in fact have improved the general appearance of the inscription: «9 *dSiva,* however, does occur in the Septuagint, and once in the New Testament: it is also found in another inscription published below, No. 74. Possibly the phrase may have been influenced by the Syriac *le 'a/am: forever,* which, in this sense and with *le,* never stands in the *status emfthaticus,* i. e., with the article.

Psalm xxviii, 10, contains these words: *Kadietrax Kvpios ySao-iXcus tU T6v alwva.* Compare with this the following passage from the Jewish *"Kedusha":1 11 And in Thy Holy lVord it is written, thus saying—' The Lord shall reign for ever and ever, Thy God, O Zion,from generation to generation.'"

Also in the "Liturgy of St. James":2 *"Ayios el (BacnXev rcov alcovetv,* Kcu 7700-175 *dyiwowr/s Kupios Kou Sorrjp.*

From the presence of the grooved capital mentioned above, and from a comparison with the other inscriptions of this place, it is probable that this inscription dates from the end of the fourth or the beginning of the fifth century.

24. Djuwaniyeh. Fragment. On a corner-stone, with mouldings on two adjoining sides, found among a few other blocks face up on the ground, a few yards eiceeoCKAloxpiCTOCAYTOY southcast of No-23-The inscription is 1. 04 m. in *Eh* fceos *Koi 6 xPLTTbs amov.* length, the letters 7 cm. high. Copy of the editor. *There is) one God and his Christ.* See the commentary on the next inscription, No. 25. 25. DjOwANiYEH. House. On the lintel of a doorway in the west center of the town, facing north. This was apparently the main entrance of a small and plain dwelling. In the center of the lintel was a disk of some sort. The letters are large, and originally were fairly well cut, the lines being broad and probably shallow: they are now almost completely obliterated by weather and lichen. Copy of the editor. EICBEDC /.X.CTDCAV II ATI AWn A N H. . TDV

Els @05 /cai 6 X/31(tt6s *Olvtov* ka *I* to 'Ayia II(vu) /xa. *(There is) one God and his Christ and the Holy Spirit.*

There is space enough in the first line, between □ c and the disk, for five letters: perhaps, therefore, we should read Eis Beos *novo?, 6 Xpioros avrov, Koi To* "Ayia *Uveva.* I be 1 Warren, p. 215. 2Swainson, p. 270. See also the *"Didache of the Apostles"* sec. 14, the *"Apostolic Constitutions,"* vii, 30 (Swainson, p. li); and the *" Alexandrine Liturgy"* Swainson, p. 7. lieve that the last three letters of the second line belong to the last word in the first line: the same thing occurs elsewhere, for example in No. 233. The final syllable in the adjective 'A-yia is probably due to the influence of the following word *Uvev/ xa.* Or the A here may be for an o, as is

the case not infrequently in these Syrian inscriptions.1 In No. 61 we have To A-yio *Uveva.* This may be regarded simply as an incorrect form of the neuter singular, after the analogy of *T6,tovto,* etc., or it may be thought that the final N was omitted through carelessness. Or is it possible that these words were pronounced, and therefore written here, as one, T6 AyioTreC/Aa?

The formula E?s ®eds; *One God,* is very frequent in these inscriptions, either alone, or with the word /aovos.-*only,* and often with the addition of some such clause as 6 *fio-qdwv iraa-iv: that aideth all.* It occurs in Nos. 16, 21, 22, 33, 96, 116, 152, 155, 248, 263, 278, 280, 302, 340 and 354. Efs 0eos #ceu 6 Xotcn-ds, or 6 Xpioros *airov,* is found in NOS. 14, 24, 26, 27, 35, 58, 78, 95 and 271: Efs ®os Kcli 6 Xouttos *airov Kal To "Xyiov* Ilveryta in Nos. 25, 52, 56, 57, 61, 69, 90, 249 and 250. Similar inscriptions may be found in almost all collections from Syria.2 M. Clermont-Ganneau, speaking of the formula El? 6s *novo?,* says:3 "The Christian character of this formula is clearly demonstrated by these examples" (cited from Waddington, Nos. 2066, 2689, 2682, 2704, 2562 1, 2451, 2262,2057, 2053 b, 1918). "It is probably of Jewish origin, and must have sprung from the well-known verse (the fourth) in the sixth chapter of Deuteronomy,4 which contains the word "inNmrP: *Jehovah,* rendered in the Septuagint by Kvpios Efs, and which precedes the dissertation on the commandments. It is worthy of remark that this formula is generally found inscribed above the entrance doors, as ordained in the ninth verse (with regard to the commandments, of which it is, so to say, the preamble), *lAnd thou shallwrite them on the posts of thy house and 011 thy gates.'"* In fact the El? @eds has been found on monuments distinctively Jewish, or at least Jewish-Christian. Commenting on the inscription from Koloniyeh, first published by Dr. Schick in the *Quarterly Statements* of the Palestine Exploration Fund, 1887, p. 55: Efs ®e6s /ecu 6 Xoio-(t)6? *avrov.* t5s. Zorf. *Mvr)o-0jj Bapox-s,* M. Clermont-Ganneau writes:6 "Nous avons done affaire, selon toute apparence, a un jud£o-chretien. Ce fait prend une signification toute particuliere si on le rapproche de la presence de notre meme formule efs @eds gravee sur le chapiteau bilingue d'Emmaiis, a cote d'une inscription hebraique en caracteres pseudo-archaiques, et aussi sur un des deux chapiteaux que j'ai trouve a Ni'ane avec ce beau plat de bronze cisele ou sont represented, entre autres symboles juifs, le chandelier a sept branches et l'armoire aux rouleaux sacr£s." I believe that all the inscriptions in the present collection which contain even the simplest !See the orthographical index below. Also Clermont-*Palestine et en Phenicie"* (1881), by the same author, where

Ganneau, *Recueil,* m, p. 247. this matter is also discussed (p. 21 ff.).
2 For example, C. I. G. 8945,9154, etc. See also the exam-"It is, properly speaking, the axiom of monotheism, pies from Waddington given by M. Clermont-Ganneau. besides which it plays an important part in the Jewish 3Palestine Exploration Fund, *Quarterly Statements,* 1882, liturgy." Clermont-Ganneau. p. 26. See also *Recueil,* 1, p. 169 f. , and ill, p. 247. I have 5See also above, Chapter 1, pp. 13 f. and 18 f. not been able to consult the *Rapports sur une Mission en 6Recueil ,* p. 170. form of this phrase, Eis 0eds, are Christian, with the possible exception of those from Ruweha and Riha.1 The formula, moreover, is not only common, but also comparatively early. M. Clermont-Ganneau says:2 "Elle se trouve notamment sur des inscriptions datees de l'an 378 et de l'an 483." I have found Eis ®eds in six dated inscriptions earlier than 378, of which one is of the year 326 s and another,4 obviously Christian, of the year 336 A.d. I have found none containing the simpler formula dated later than 412 A.d.: Eis ©cos *Kal* 6 X/hotos auroG, however, was found in an inscription at Sermeda, dated 341 A.D.;5 Eis @e6s *(Kal)* 6 Xpioros avrov *(Kal)* To "Ayio *Hvtvp-a* at Dar Kita, dated 537 A.D.6 This formula may be compared with certain passages in the traditional Greek

liturgies, for example in the Alexandrine liturgy:7 El? *Tiarp* ayios, eis Tlos ayios, *h Uvevfia dyiov,* ets *ivonyra Uvev/jLaTO'i ayiov.* 'Afirjv. Similar passages occur in the " Liturgy of St. Basil," 8 the " Liturgy of St. Chrysostom," 9 the " Liturgy of St. James,"10 the " Liturgy of the Presanctified,"11 and in the lectures of Cyril of Jerusalem to the newly baptized.12 26. Djuwaniyeh. House. On the lintel of a doorway, apparently the entrance to a simple dwelling-house, near No. 25. The first two lines of the inscription occupy the upper third of the stone. The lower part of the lintel has at the left a small oblong plate, with pointed ends instead of the usual dove-tails. This plate contains the second part of the inscription, except the last two letters, which are below the right end: each end contains a simple cross. The rest of the lower part of the lintel is occupied by a variety of Christian symbols. The letters of the first part of the inscription are 5 cm. high: those of the second part, in the plate, are about 8 cm. in height. The letters are regular and of fairly good form; but they are now badly weathered, so that the reading is uncertain. Copy of the editor.

For the accusative with *foT)d4w* see on No. 21. I believe that *'AXtitavhpav* is for 1Nos. 263, 278 and 280. Two of these are dated in the 5 No. 78. years 433 and 434 respectively. The inscriptions of the rest 0 No. 61. This is the only example of this formula which of the Djebel Riha are dated according to the Seleucid era. I have found to be dated later than 483 A.d. If that were so here, these inscriptions must belong to the 'Swainson, p. 66. See also above, p. 13 f. early part of the second century A. d., and are then doubtless 8 Swainson, p. 86.

Jewish rather than Christian. See, however, the commen-9 Swainson, p. 94.
tary to No. 263. 10 Swainson, p. 310. 2Recueil, r, p. 170. 11 Swainson, p. 98. 3See Nos. 338-340. 12 Swainson, p. 210.
No. 11C.
'WeijavSpov, not 'AkegdvSpav. Com-

pare to "Ayta *U(vev)p.a* in No. 25, and *Tovtcl /jLvrifjuav,* etc., in an inscription from Edessa, published by Prof. Sachau in *Z. M. G.,* xxxvi, p. 166, and by M. Clermont-Ganneau in his *Recueil,* in, p. 247. See also Part IV, p. 49 f. Of course it is possible to emend these names so as to read a dative in each case, *&6p.vo* and *Evo-e/3Co(i)* for *A6p.va* and *Evo-efiua, Ma(p)o)(v)q.* and *'AXegdvSp):* the reading is uncertain at best; but the meaning is of course clear. 27. Djuwaniyeh. Tomb. On the cover of a sarcophagus, which stands upon a base on the hill-side south of the town. The sarcophagus itself is perfectly plain, and the base has only a simple cornice; but the cover is more than usually ornaeiceeo iy mental, having four large acroteria, and being carved on top to represent the tiling of a temple roof. This monument is published in Part II, p. 107. The inscription is on the southeast corner of the cover, and occupies a space of 40 by 15 cm. The letters are about cm. in height, shallow, badly carved and unequal in size. Copy of Dr. Littmann.

See the commentary on No. 25. This inscription probably dates from the early part of the fifth century.

28. Djuwaniyeh. Boundary Stone, 554 A.d. Two fragments of a stele, found one on either side of the path to Bzimbeh, across the valley to the east of Djuwaniyeh. These fragments lie about half a mile in a straight line from Djuwaniyeh, nine minutes walk by the path. The first fragment measures 1.21 m. in length,.60 m. in breadth, and.41 m. in thickness: it lay face down, so that the letters were protected. The other fragment measures.79 by.60 by.39 m.: it lay face up, and, in consequence, its inscription is badly weathered. The letters are well formed and regular, and of the sixth century type. Copy of the editor.

The explanation of this inscription will be found in the commentary under No. 29.

29. Djuwaniyeh. Boundary Stone. On a large stele, found about 15 meters south of the church in the southeast corner of the town.1 The stele was standing up-

right, and facing the broken stump of another block of stone which stood 3 or 4 meters west of it, as if the two had once formed the jambs of a wide gateway. In that case the inscription would have been on the inside face of the east jamb, facing the other. But the two blocks were comparatively far apart, and there was no indication that doors were ever hung between them. Possibly they were placed here, in comparatively late times, on either side of an unclosed opening in a rude wall. In any case I doubt whether the inscribed stele is in its original place, although undoubtedly it stood originally in close proximity to this church, and to this church doubtless belonged the sacred lands marked by this stele, by No. 28, and by a series of others now lost. Lack of time prevented any serious excavation, which would have been difficult because of the size and weight of the blocks of

Stele and church at Djuwaniyeh, from the south. Stone which He all about, buried or half buried in the soil. It is quite possible that the lower end of the stele is still in situ, and that it stands on the pavement of an open court south of the church. If so, I should expect it to be some fifteen or twenty yards west of where the upper part was found, and about in line with the western facade of the church shown in Part II, p. 230.

I first photographed the stele as it stood; but this photograph was unfortunately lost: I then had the stone dug out and placed on its back. It measured 194 cm. in length by 56 in breadth and 46 in thickness. The lower end had been sunk in the ground to a depth of 66 cm. The inscription begins 25 cm. from the top of the stone. At the bottom the stone is broken through the 18th line of the inscription, so that only traces of the tops of the first four or five letters of this line remain. It is of course impossible to tell how long the stele was originally, or how much of the inscription has been lost.

When I had finished making a squeeze and copy of the inscription, I had the ground leveled and the stone turned over on its face, in order to protect the inscription, it being 1 See Part

11, p. 229 f.

impossible, with the force at my disposal, to replace the block in the position in which it had been found. I then photographed the stone as it lies at present, the camera box lying on the back of the stele, which shows clearly in the photograph here reproduced. The stone may be recognized easily by any traveler, from its position in relation to the ruins of the church. The letters are 5 to 8 cm. high, somewhat irregular both in size and shape, but most of them still clearly legible. Copy of the editor and squeeze. + Opoi *dcrvia; Tov dyLov Tr-panofidprvp(o;)* *XTefdvov, fioTifjL7)dev(TO;)* *irapd* *Tov yakj)voT(aTov)* *rfp.o)y* *6acriA.eiw9 j. lovoTLviavov Tov aioiviov avyovOtov,* eVi *Tov a.yL(ixr(a.Tov),* /xa/ca/3i-ur(a*Tov*), *a/3i77t(r/c(oTrou)* *fjp.cjv, iraTpidpov Aop.vLvov, Tov iv&o£(ora. Tov) Kop.(rjTO;),* twj *v 0of)(i,eoTd.Ta)v* '*HpaicXeiov 'Av8/3 e' a(f) (/cai)* '*iwdvvov Tr(pecrSvTep(ov),* Limits of the asylum of the holy first martyr Stephanos, by grace of our most serene king Fl(avtus) Justinianus, Semper Augustus, under our most holy and) most blessed archbishop and) patriarch Domninus, our most glorious head, the most God-beloved Hcrakleios, (son) of Andreas, and Joannes (being) presbyters,...

Inscr. 29. Cast from a squeeze.

Asylia (dovUi) is properly *inviolability, or security of person or property against seizure by force.* Right to such security in ancient times was based on treaties, mutual agreements or, within the limits of the several states, on law: this right might be granted to special persons, such as magistrates and *proxenoi*, or even to whole states on the part of other states. The word also signifies the right to afford protection to persons or property, a right which from very early times attached to altars and temples. Such a right was sometimes claimed, and secured by treaties, for the whole territory of a state, as in the case of Teos, whose citizens dedicated their entire land to a god, Dionysus, and claimed thereby "asylia." A temple, or locality, which had this right of sanc-

tuary, was called acnAo?, *da-vXov,* whence the Latin *asylum.* Fugitives, even slaves, who sought refuge here, were secure as long as they remained within the limits of the sacred precinct, and to remove them forcibly was sacrilege. The extent of these "asyla" was sometimes very large, so that refugees could live within them for long periods, as, for example, Pleistoanax is said to have lived in the asylum of Zeus Lykaios at Megalopolis for nineteen years,1 and the asylum of Artemis at Hierocaesarea extended in a radius of two miles from her temple.2 The number of such places of refuge gradually increased. "The Romans at first were not unwilling to allow this, for citizens often found in these places refuge from ill-disposed provincials: when, however, these places became centers and shelters for disorderly people, from which runaway slaves, insolvent debtors and notorious criminals in safety could defy the laws, the emperor Tiberius, in 22 A.d., ordered a revision by the senate of the rights claimed by various states."3 The result of this investigation was a recognition of the right of sanctuary in a limited number of cities, and with express legal restrictions. The right of sanctuary passed, in the Christian period, from the pagan temples to the churches, as may be seen from the passages cited in the article Asylon in PaulyWissowa. So Zosimus, in an account of riots in a town of Scythia in the time of Theodosius I and Valentinian II, the end of the fourth century, says:4 "But those who fled betook themselves to a building held in honor by Christians, considered inviolable." And again a little later, speaking of a certain Eutropius:5 "And he fled, running to the church of the Christians, which had the right of sanctuary from that (time when churches first had this right). But since Gai'nas was insistent, and said that Tribigildus would not otherwise be satisfied unless Eutropius was put out of the way, even contrary to the law passed with regard to the inviolability of churches they seized him, and sent him to Cyprus, under strict guard. " The following story is told by Ioanncs

Malalas of an attempt on the part of the emperor Zeno, at the end of the fifth century, to put to death a prefect of the praetorian guard named Arcadius:6 "And this came to the cars of Zeno, and he commanded that when Arcadius entered the palace he should be killed. But Arcadius, learning of this, when he was summoned by the king, as he was passing from the church, made as though he wished to pray; and descending from his carriage he entered into the great church of Constantinople; and there he remained, and was saved from death."

The stele under discussion, together with No. 28, served to mark the limits to which an asylum of this sort extended, namely the lands belonging to the church of St. Stephen at this place. Evidently both inscriptions have the same date, 554 A.d.: the 1 Thucydides, v, 16. *asyla institui coeperunl."* Reitemeier, in *Comment, /list, in* 2 Memorabantur Perpennae, Isaurici multaque alia impera-*Zos.)* To do-vAov. tVti *hi* Jtoavs 6 *Tatvrfi, Ovk iXXwt avrjo-uv* torum nomina, qui non modo templo sed duobus milibus *cyuv Tov Tpifiiyikhov, tl fir)* EvrpoVios *inTrohtov ylvotro,* rat *7rapa* passuum eandem sanctitatem tribuerant: Tacitus, *Annates, Tov tin* Tu do-uAu *Tuv (KKkyjo-tiov rtOtvra vopov iiapwdo-avrts* III, 62. *avrbv* ets *Ttjv K.v7rpov ixTrip.Trova 'iv, vwb tpvXaicrjv aKpiftrj KaTaarr/* 3 Pauly-Wissowa, *Reakncyclopiidie,* s.v. Asylon. *o-avra.* 4 Zosimus, *Hist.,* IV, 40, 8: *Tov hi awohpavrai* cocero *irapa* 0 Ioannes Malalas, *Chronographia,* xv (ed. Dindorf, p. *Xpio-Ttavuiv Tipwptvov olKoSoprjpa, vopiZ,6pvov* otruXoi'. 39)-Compare also Malalas, xiv, p. 373 Dind.; xvi, 5 Zosimus, v, 18, 2 f.: 6 *hi, hpopaios £7ri Ttv Tgv Xpumavuiv* 396 f.; Zosimus, v, 8, 3; v, 3. 6; Ammianus Marcellinus, *iupTqo-ev inKkrfriav, iovauv t(lutivov* (i.e.," *ex Mo tempore, quo* xxvi, 3, 3; Cassiodorus, *Variae Epist.,* 11, 11.

una cum religione Christiana invecta in rem publicum, etiam forms of the letters are the same, and No. 28 appears to be an abridgment of No. 29. The two stelae are now about half a mile apart, and between the two lies the fertile wadi which is on the eastern side of the town

of Djuwaniyeh: evidently St. Stephen's acres were both broad and rich.

Inscriptions similar to these are to be found under Nos. 298 and 350, and in other collections. Such fulsome titles as are employed here were common enough in Justinian's time: compare, for example, Nos. 305 and 306. On yaXoVaTos see also van Herwerden's *Lexicon Sitppietoriitm* and the appendix to the same. The abbreviation *npp*for *npeafivTepoi,* occurs in No. 2185, *Oeof.* for *0eo£iXeoTaToi* in No. 2497, of Waddington's collection.

30. Kefr Finsheh. Stele, 189 A.d. Base of a broken stele, found beside the modern path east of the town, at the foot of the hill. Doubtless the ancient road was here. A description of this monument is given in Part II, p. 276. The letters are well cut and of regular form, except in the latter half of the second line: they are 5 to 7 cm. high, and the inscribed space 60 by 35 cm. All the letters are perfectly clear. Copies of Dr. Littmann and the editor, and squeeze. 6TOYCZAC MHNOCIANAI KOYBIANTIOXOC

"Erov? £a.x', *ftT)vb;* HavSiKov /8i'. 'avtioxos. *In the year 237, month Xandikos 12th. Antiochos.* (April, 189 A.D.) Inscr. 30.

I suppose Antiochos to be the subject of the sculpture.

31 Kefr Finsheh. Chapel. On a block of stone found lying in the ruins of a chapel, at the western end of the building, at the right of the western entrance. This block is from the south wall of the clearstory: its place was at the west end of the course immediately above the moulding which was above the roof of the colonnade. At the left end is a plate in relief, 42 cm. square, containing the inscription: at the right end of the plate a single dove-tail, and at the right end of the block the terminal volute of a window moulding. It corresponded to the block still in situ at the eastern end of this wall, and shown in the photograph on p. 237 of Part II: this second block bears inscription No. 32.

The chapel is about five minutes' walk northeast of the town. It stood alone, except for one other building, probably an oil-mill, about fifty feet north of it. In

the northeast corner of this other building was a circular stone, which I took to be the bottom of a machine for crushing olives:1 it was 1.90 m. in diameter, and had in the center a socket measuring 25 by 23 by 8 cm. The chapel has been described by Mr.

Jsee on No. 187 below.

Butler in Part II, p. 236 f. Beneath the chancel arch of which he speaks were what seemed to me to be the bases of a kind of balustrade, like a chancel rail. Just west of the arch, in the north wall of the chapel, was a small alcove, 1.70 m. long by 0.54 deep, which may have been the grave of a person in whose memory the chapel was erected.

The letters of the inscription are incised upon the raised plate mentioned above.

They are badly formed and poorly cut: they are also weathered so that many of them could not be read with certainty. Both this and the following inscription seem to be the work of men whose skill in carving letters was as deficient as their knowledge of the forms and syntax of the Greek language. Copy of the editor.

This reading is very uncertain. If the second line is cor .,, ..,,,, tdriMAPiOBoei rect, probably 5/. *Domittits* is meant, although the second t Ar'lAOMHTIBOei syllable of this name is properly short. The *Martyrologiimi Romanum,* under July 5th, gives this item: "In Syria + vW Maa) o(#. natalis sancti Domitii Martyris, qui virtutibus suis multa + AyL(e) &MTL(e) incolis praestat beneficia." One might perhaps think also *Holy Mary, help us) oiDometius:* "Nisibi in Mesopotamia sancti Dometii Mo-*HolyDomitius), help us)* nachi Persae, qui cum duobis discipulis sub Juliano Apostata lapidatus est." 32. Kefr Finsheh. The Same Chapel. On a block in the south wall of the clearstory of the chapel, at the east end, immediately above the string moulding which is above the roof of the diaconicum. At the left end of the block is the terminal volute of a window moulding. The rest of the block is occupied by a plate in relief,.75 m.

long and.52 m. high, ornamented with

a single dove-tail, which is at the left end: see Part II, p. 237. The stone corresponded to that which bears the preceding inscription (No. 31). The letters have much the same forms as those of No. 31, but are more clearly cut and better preserved. Copy of the editor.

Ad&s is obviously for Sd£»js, as *fio &Lo-ov* for *fiorjOr) a-ov*, and *ifiiv* for *rjlv: Trdvra;* should, of course, be *naanv.* 33. Kokanaya. Lintel, 349 A.d. In a dove-tail plate on the lintel of a doorway now incorporated in the wall of a modern enclosure, on the west side of a street running south, near the northwest corner of the town. The doorway itself is closed by a rude wall of rough stone: its lintel, jambs and sill are of single blocks. The plate, exclusive of the dove-tails, measures.84 m. in length by. 242 in breadth. The letters vary from 3 J/2 to 7 cm. in height. Copy of the editor, and squeeze.

It is possible that this date should be read September, 348 A.d. For in this 34. Kokanaya. Tomb, 369 A.d. In a tomb excavated in the solid rock, in an open field a short distance south of the town. Near by are other tombs. This tomb consists of a well sunk perpendicularly into the solid rock, about 7 feet long, 3 feet wide and 6 feet deep. In the wall of rock on either side of the well is a simple arcosolium containing a single sarcophagus, the top of which is about 8 inches above the bottom of the well, and which is about 3 feet deep. At one end of each sarcophagus the rock at the bottom was left somewhat higher, as if to form a kind of pillow for the dead. On the west side of the well this pillow was at the north end of the sarcophagus, on the east side the pillow was at the south end. At each end of the well a boss was left projecting from the rock, doubtless for a step. Upon the top of the well a heavy stone cover, like the cover of a sarcophagus, was laid flaton the solid rock, which

Tomb of Eusebios. Inscr. 34 js now quite bare at this point, and which probably was never covered with soil to any considerable depth. See Part II, p. 104. Tombs of this sort are not uncommon in this region.1

The inscription is carved on the west wall of the well, immediately above and on the right of the arch of the arcosolium. The extreme length of the inscription is 1.47 m. The letters are irregularly, but deeply and clearly, cut: protected from the weather, they are perfectly preserved. The rest of the rock, inside the shaft, is 1 See, for example, No. 14. smooth, and of a dark yellow color; but in the letters I found pieces of what looked like black crayon, as if someone had been crayoning the inscription in recent times. I saw no trace of any inA rSATTATf T i eToCTT scription on the other side. The letters ; NI'AlorKZ j 2 to 6 cm high Copy of the rV'j editor and squeeze.

Inscr. 34. From a squeeze and drawing. Scale i: 20 Published by M. de Vogue, *S. C,* p. 119, pi. 96.

Waddington, No. 2681.

+ *Evaefiut)* t *XpLcmavw.f Aoga Uarpl Kcu Tlw Kcu 'Ayiw TlvevfjLaTi.* vetous *£iv, fiiqvX Awov* K£''. + *For Eusebios + a Christian.-)? Glory to (the) Father and to (the) Son and to (the) Holy Spirit. In (the) year 4.17, in (the) month of Loos, (the) 2jth.* (August, 369 A.n.).

This is one of the earliest inscriptions of Syria which is indisputably Christian. It contains the "Gloria Patri," or " Lesser Doxology," doubtless familiar to all from the Church service. It is found repeatedly in the "Liturgy of St. James."1 Compare also Nos. 156, 321, etc.

When I was at Kokanaya the cover had been moved partly off the top of the well, so that it was possible to descend into this tomb. Perhaps the tomb has been blocked up since then. For while I was working over the inscription, a crowd of natives gathered, and when I reappeared I found them anxious to know what the writing said, and whose tomb this was. I read to them: *Eia-efiup Xpio-nafw,* and then, through one of our men who acted as interpreter, I told them that this was the tomb of a certain Eusebios: that there was a Eusebios who was a very learned and famous man, but that I hardly thought that that was the Eusebios who was buried here. Later on I learned that our dragoman, who had heard what I said, had told the natives

that this was *"Jusuf Bion"* a follower of Mohammed and a very holy man. The villagers said that they would close up the tomb and build a pile of stones above it; that no one should go into it again, for it was evidently a very holy place. One of these same men applied at our camp shortly afterwards to be cured of a pain which he had had in his stomach for the last three years, of the stoop in his back, and of a hard lump, the size of a hen's egg, on the right side of the spine between the shoulder-blades. The dragoman told him that if he would block up that tomb he would undoubtedly be cured. I think that the dragoman was not very superstitious himself; but, like Lucretius, he liked to see trouble from which he himself was free. However, as we left this town on the next day, I do not know whether the tomb was blocked up, or whether the native was cured.

35. Kokanaya. Doorway, 378 A.d. Lintel of a doorway immediately outside of the north gate of the city, on the west side of the gate. The doorway faces east, 1 Swainson, p. 215 ff., 226, etc. See Swainson, pp. 16, 76, 220, 362, 373. and the south end of the lintel rests against the city wall. There is no building im) mediately behind the doorway, but a passage, broader than the doorway itself, on the north side of which are to Inscr. Cast from a squeeze. t .1 r .1.. j 1 be seen the remains of the two-stoned colonnades of a row of buildings which faced towards the city. The space occupied by the inscription measures 1.23 by 0.17 J/2 m. The letters are 3 to 6 cm. high. Copy of the editor, and squeeze.

Published by Waddington, No. 2682.

The name Aa/xas or Aa/xa? is given in Pape: perhaps it may also be found in an inscription from Heit (in the Hauran), published by M. Possey in *B.C.H.,* xxi (1897). 41, No. 8.

36. Kokanaya. Tomh, 384 A.d. On the south side of the pier at the southwest corner of a tomb. This tomb consists of an arched chamber excavated in the living rock, the entrance to which was originally closed by a cover, like that of a sarcophagus, which lay upon it. Above the tomb chamber are eight rec-

tangular piers supporting a pyramidal roof. A part of this roof has fallen in, breaking the cover and choking the entrance with fragments. The rest of the structure is intact. Most of the spaces between the piers, which were originally open, have been closed, probably in comparatively recent times, by walls of loose stones. See Part II, p. 109.

The unusual position of this inscription, which is on the face of a pier, instead of being on the architrave as one would expect, doubtless explains the fact that it was overlooked by MM. Waddington and de Vogue, although a drawing of the tomb is given by the latter, pi. 97. Neither Mr. Butler nor I saw the inscription at first, although both of us examined the tomb, and even when I was told by Dr. Littmann that an inscription was there, I found it only after a careful search. It occupies a space measuring. 55 by.18 m. The letters are 4 cm. high: they are not well formed, and they are now somewhat indistinct; but the reading, I believe, is certain. Copy of the editor.

Pier showing the squeeze upon Inscr. 36.

Possibly this date should be read: September, 383 A.d.1 The phraseology of this inscription is so similar to that of the following, that it suggests some connection between the two. This similarity, however, may be due only to the prevalence of a certain fashion in inscriptions of the same locality. Compare the use of the phrase *Seov SiW/uis* in *C. I. G.* 8909. On the connection between the pyramid and tombstructures, see on No. 22.

37. Kokanaya. House, 431 A.d. Lintel of a house facing south, a little north of the center of the town. Nothing is left of the house itself except the remains of the vestibule. See part II, p. 179. The outer doorway of this vestibule is plain; but the inner, which bears the inscription, is ornamented with a moulded door-cap, on each side of which are Christian symbols. The space occupied by the inscription is 1.62 by 0. 11 m. Copy of the editor.
Published by Waddington, No. 2683.
1.　　　　teeOYKAIXPICTOYAYNAMI-

CANHriPeNMHNOC + ®*eov* /ecu Xpiorou Swa/iis *avyyipev,* 2. AUUOYA-TOY90Y6TOYCAOWNOCTXNITHC　t　s A"ou *a' Tod 6ov' *ous' AoI'os TC" (*The) power of God and Christ erected this house), on the) 1st of (the) month Loos in the tfyth year. Domnos architect.* (August, 431 A.D.)
See the commentary on the preceding inscription.

38. Kokanaya. Fragment, 552 A.d. On a moulding upright, i.e. on end, in a modern wall. Once, in its present position, this stone was a door-post. Now it is only a stone built into the wall of a square yard in front of the colonnade of a well-preserved ancient house. I believe that the stone was originally a lintel, or a part of an architrave. The length of the inscription, from the cross to the end, is. 75 m.

The height of the letters is 4 cm. Copy of MM　t　MnANOINANETOYXE-TOYC the editor.
. / v N n / / x *a* - v ' » I cannot explain the marks which precede + *mrvoi) liav(Tjfx,ov) u, Lvoiktlojvo;)* Ic, *Tov* r r Y' Iron?. the cross. I doubt very much whether they are letters at all. If they are, they must be (*On the) gth of (the) month Panemos, indiction 15,...... of the 600th year.* (552 A.D.) the last letters of a Part of thlS inscription borne by the stone which originally adjoined this one on the left. The stone in that case was probably a part of an architrave. There may be also a letter after the *x* f the date; but I think the mark in the stone at that point is accidental.

39. Kokanaya. House. On the lintel of one of the two doorways in the upper story of a colonnade facing east, in the southwestern part of the town. The house, to which this colonnade belonged, has disappeared, leaving only its front wall and its 1 See on No. 33. colonnade. The colonnade, however, is almost intact, even the stone roof being still in place. But the floor of the upper story has been destroyed, and has fallen in upon the rest of the debris, which fills up the lower story to the caps of its rectangular piers. A view of this house is given in Part II, p. 174 ("House II"). The lintel of each of the doorways in

the upper story contains an ornamental disk. The inscription is above the disk on the lintel of the southernmost doorway, incised on a raised dovetail plate. This plate, exclusive of the dove-tails, is.28 m. long and.09 broad. The letters are from *il/2* to *2/2* cm. high. They were originally good; but now about half of them are almost illegible. Copy of the editor, and squeeze.

I think that probably the author of this inscription meant *% o ®eo?, ekcrjo-ov; God have mercy,* although he probably did not realize how bad his spelling was. In the dove-tail at the right end there appear to be the letters T or TC: I am not sure that these are really letters; but if they are, perhaps they may be read T(ovs) o-(ov): *upo)i) thine awn.1*

Inscr. No. 39. Cast from a squeeze 40. MA'RATA. Fragment found lying in the courtyard of a dwelling. Copy of 41. Bankafur. Altar (?). An oblong stone like a pillar, measuring 2.46 by 0.42 by 0.424 m., found about two hundred meters north of the town, on the highest part of the hill looking off towards the Amanus Mountains. I supposed it to be a boundary stone of some sort, or a guide-post; perhaps even a mile-stone. It has a plain, rectilinear cap and base, the two ends being alike. On the face is an obelisk-like figure in rude relief, vaguely suggesting a gigantic *phallus?* above and on either side of which is the inscription. The squeeze, which may be seen on the stone in the accompanying cut, shows the position of the inscription

Stone containing Inscr. 41.
and the outline of the top of the figure in relief. The letters are 3 to 4 cm. high: the whole monument is badly weathered, and the reading very uncertain. Copies of Dr. Littmann and the editor, and a squeeze.

If this reading is correct, the 1. MAX-OCZHNO 6. KAinA no. monument is not a boundary 2. AUJPOYTONBUJ 7. A I OYf-stone, but an altar. It seems 3. MO-NAN6 THC6 8. n j _ also cicar that this is not the 4. MATUJnp_ 9.--Y beginning of the inscription, 5. PAY TOY and that there must have been one or more lines, on the cap and above the squeeze, which contained the name of the god to whom the altar was erected and the first part of the dedicator's name.1 We may then read at least the following:. .. //.axo? *ZrjvoSwpov Tov fiojfJLbv dvecrTrjaev machos, (soil) of Zenodoros, set up this altar.* Lines 4 ff. suggest at first ju,e(T)a *Tw 77*(a) rjepi avro£i Kol 7ra7r(7r)(&))»cai...; but I cannot reconcile this reading with the squeeze. The letter after M in the fourth line has much the same form as the curious 2 in No. 30, dated 189 A.d, and in fact these two inscriptions are so similar in the character of their script, that I am inclined to believe the present one to be as old as the second half of the second century of the Christian era.

42. Mar Saba, Tomb (?). In a rock-hewn chamber on the east side of the road, a short distance south of Mar Saba. The inscription is on the south wall near the center, and above a niche, in an oblong, rectangular space about half an inch deep, sunk in the living rock. The letters are well formed, and carefully cut to a depth of about a quarter of an inch.

Close to the Greek inscription are two inscriptions in Syriac, published by Dr. Littmann, Part IV, Syriac 4 and 5.2

In the east wall of this chamber, near the southeast corner, is the entrance to another and smaller chamber, more roughly hewn than the outer one. The place has been described in detail by M. de Vogue, p. 128, pi. 113, and by Mr. Butler in Part II, p. 269. In my own opinion at least the outer chamber was originally a tomb, and was afterwards, both in ancient and again in comparatively recent times, used as a press. The inner chamber was doubtless constructed at some time later than the other. Copies of Dr. Littmann and the editor.

Published by Waddington, No. 2686, after a copy of M. de Vogue, but wrongly assigned to " Eschreq " or Ishruk.

This seems to mean: *Thou too (O reader, shalt die!)*, or else: *Thou* KAI CY *too (/areiae/l/)*, as if, in answer to the usual x"Pe ' *farewell*, spoken by Kal *av.* eacn mourner, the dead replied: (x"P«) *tal rv.* These words actually occur in an inscription found at Smyrna by M. Kontoleon, the text of 1 See No. 353 below:

also Nos. 417 a and 421; Wad. 2203 a, 2374, 2413k and n, 2575.
2 Dr. Littmann's drawing, published in Part IV, p. 13, includes the Greek with the Syriac. which is given by him as follows:1 Aa/x7ra8ie *UapOevov Yiclktcdxcov Alclkovov* I xP' xPe Kc" aFranz had already proposed this explanation in *C. I. G.* in, 4565, although he read in this case *Ku* O-u to. 8i7ra, which Waddington reports incorrect.2 The formula *Kal dv* occurs also in the inscription of the tomb of T. Flavius Iulianus at Katura,3and I believe that it belongs properly to funerary inscriptions.4 The formula *Ko.1 rol* rd Sittxs, on the other hand, I believe to be distinct: it is commonly found on dwellinghouses, not in tombs. 5 The only example in a tomb known to me is No. 89, where, however, the inscription has been carved in such a disorderly way that it is impossible to tell whether these words really belong with the rest or not: if they do not, then they may have been written when this chamber was not used as a tomb.

The present inscription is probably pagan, and, like No. 111, may be as old as the second century A.d.: the Syriac graffiti below it, however, belong to the Christian period.

43. Turlaha. Lintel of a good-sized building, part way down the hill towards the southeast from the center of the town. Only the lower half of the walls remains. The building seemed at first to have been a two-story house. But there were no windows in the walls which are still standing, with the possible exception that there may have been a single window at the right of the entrance, where an opening has now been broken through. The whole lintel is 1. 72 m. long, and in the center of the surface on which the inscription is carved there is an ornamental disk, 34 cm. in diameter, dividing the inscription into two parts. The letters were never good, and are now barely legible. Copy of the editor.

The second figure is somewhat uncertain. If the marks now upon the stone are all original, this letter has a highly ornamental form, although all the rest of the letters are plain. The letter may per-

haps be 9, in which case the date would be 443-444 A.D.

44. Bashakuh. House. On the lintel of the front doorway of a small two-story building in the northwest corner of the town. The walls of the building are still intact, up to the roof-line. The lintel has an elaborate door-cap, ornamented with mouldings and a large central disk: the mouldings are all elaborated with various designs, except two, the second and third fasciae from the bottom, on which the inscription is carved.7 Such door-caps are very common throughout Northern Syria, and are peculiar *IB. C. H.* x (r886), p. 453, No. 1. 2 Waddington, No. 2491. Franz compares *C. I. G.* 4457 = No. 89 in the present collection. 3 No. 111 = Waddington, No. 2699. 4 See Waddington, No. 2686, commentary. 5 See above, on No. 10. 6 No. 89 =*C. I. G.* 4457, Waddington, No. 2688. 7 The distortion in the accompanying photograph, which is especially noticeable in the apparent inclination of the jambs, is due to the angle at which the camera was tilted. to the architecture of this region. Each line of the inscription occupies a space about 1.03 by 0.06 m. : the letters are well formed, and of a type common in this neighborhood in the sixth century;1 but they are not nowvery distinct. Copy of the editor, and squeeze.

The form *vlv* is for *vlt, vlo* for *vlai, Xvfieovov* for *ifiecjvov*:2 crvfievov and crvpeve for or)na.Lvov and o-7jff.aLve respectively. Doubtless Lintel containing inscr. 44. the author wished to make a double pun on the words *tifiewvrjs,* 0-17/1 aivav and o-/AcuVecrtfai. The verb *cn)p.atvuv*, from *o-ffia: a sign, a seal*, is used in the sense of *vpayifa; to set a seal upon a thing*, and may refer concretely to the symbolic disk in the center of the lH OHOl KMWHVlYOWEoN &TOjj lintel: the metaphorical use of the fMENoMr«TIONC£HEYlOAV

Verb Was familiar tO all. Compare, Inscr-44-From squeeze and photograph. Scale 1:io.

forexample, *II Corinthians*, 21 f.: tK(tfp.)c 'V TM tvov roG Aop£(?)-rv 0609, 6 Kot trtpayurait.vos tytas, and 01/ T0l/ T0Vo,, Kai a-ve *vlo avrov. Ephesians*

iv, 30: Kcu /a Ai»7mT To v„ *m* s *Lord help loanes (son) of Siweoius the (son) of Dorel (?): Mark Ilvevua To yiov Tov f)eov, ii a iaSpa-,.....,,,.,.... _v,..*
'*Tr (x., seal) for thyself this place, and mark (.e., point out) for its yi-a0r)Teeiswe 'pavd-n-ovTpwaea;.* The *son (Ais way).* sealing of a person or thing also plays a large role in magic. 3 The other use of *a-paivuv,* in *o-vpcve vlo avrov,* is illustrated by *ExodltS* xviii, 20: *or)pavd;* avrots ret? 68ou?.

I cannot explain the name *Aopek* or Aope, and it is quite possible that this reading is incorrect. *Bopex: Borekh* naturally suggests itself; but A seems clear in the squeeze.

45. Bashakuh. Lintel, copied by Dr. Littmann: Idid notseethismonumentmyself.

I cannot read any word here with 1. OYA-N HTOYCI--6TOCYMM-UJ f 2.-ej-AnUJAHNAPIOC-YCUJOCNHHCTABOY-CAN reasonable probability, unless it be the name *'A-rrik7)vdpL0;* for *'ATroWivdpios.* 46. Bashmishli. Baptistery, 536 A.d. Incised on a raised dovetail plate, in the cove of the cornice, above the entrance of a small square building, about the center

'*E.g.*, No. 12. 3See M. Perdrizet's most interesting -Or *Svfucueov.* The name is very common in Syrian inscriptions, especially article, *2,jpayU Soao/ moiw,* in *R. E. G.,* after the middle of the fifth century: cf. Waddington, Nos. 2691, 2693, 2696. I93, Vol. xvi, p. 42 ff. of the town. This-was probably a baptistery: its walls are almost intact, and it is now used as a dwelling. See Part II, p. 239 f., where a photograph of this building is given. The left end of the inscribed plate may be seen at the top of this picture. It is interesting to notice also that neither this plate nor the window below it is on center with the doorway. Copy of Dr. Littmann.

This reading is very uncertain. Compare, however, Wad. 1878:1 'El *Tov* dyuorarou *'iwdwov iirio-K6tTov)-q/ji-cov Kt.* In particular the second name seems to me doubtful. It may be tTOYCTT©TTI there is some connection between the Ioannes TOYN OT Mtf of the present inscription and Ioannes the

' UAN T!ANN/ *periodeutes* mentioned in an inscription found + Brow e7r cVt T0V (ay)ior(aTw) by Sig. P. Martinori in the mosaic floor of a 0(TM)MTM (or eW W")) chapel in the western part of Der Sim'an:-L J L J w r *a Tt-u -» o* s »t' + *In the year 585, under our most holy bishop*

Me*raorTi* K (upi)e *Tov evKapeo-raTov Trepiooevrov, Iwav-"* ,x/-j' » *Ioannes (son) of Ioannes.* (536-537 A. D.).

I/ou AABAKlxlN, /cai *iravTbiv To)v OMMpepovTwv avrov.*

But unfortunately the second name here also is obscure. Of course 'W? is a very common name: it is contained, for example, in Nos. 29, 62, 75, 336a and 437a, all of which belong to the sixth century, but afford no certain grounds for identification.4 47. Bashmishli. Lintel over the entrance to the courtyard of a modern dwelling, on the west side of the main street of the village. Mr. Butler believes that this stone is in situ, and that it was originally the lintel of the entrance to the courtyard of an ancient house. It is without mouldings, but in the center there is a handsome ornamental disk in relief, above which the inscription is incised. At each side, on a separate block, there is a moulded corbel. Copy of the editor.

Dr. Littmann has suggested to me that possibly this name should be read W, for BOANlANAMAECIOYTOYAXE-TOYCt *'Avivaa,* i.e., Hanmnaa, a Syriac name which *r..* t Ku'(pie) *Boi-nda)* ANI-ANA. M(w6s) (A)e is not uncommon. It occurs, for example, in *, »,*
'*r' criou, Tov crou?.* T Bakirha.5 There are various other names de-+ *Lordhdp Anidua (?) /n ihg mon(h DeHos (?) rived from the root pn, hann): to be gracious, of the year 601.* t (June, 553 A.d.) such as Hannan, Hannina, etc.

48. Burdj Bakirha. Temenos Pyi On, 161 A.d. On a gateway, standing alone about fifty feet southwest of the southwest corner of the ruins of a very beautiful tem 1 Found at Abila ("A/SiAa *Xva-aviov),* a short distance north-3 The first two letters of this word, in Sig. Martinori's copy, west of Damascus. Dated

564 A.d. Published also by P. are so placed that they occupy the space of three letters: Germer Durand in *Revue Biblique,* 1900, p. 93. Cf. 438. possibly a letter has been omitted between 'Iuxurov and the 2 Found and copied by Sig. Martinori on March 14th, 1880, following B. and very kindly communicated by him in a letter to me of 4 See also the commentary on No. 62.

Nov. 22nd, 1903: the inscription is in a dove-tail plate, in 5Part IV, Syr. 10. front of the site of the altar. pie. The gateway consists of three great blocks of stone, two forming the jambs and resting upon the solid rock. The lintel is ornamented with simple mouldings, the lower bands of which bear the inscription. See Part II, p. 66 ff.

The space occupied by the first line measures 2.08 x.07 m., that of the second 1.95 x.07, of the third 1.85 x.07 m. The letters are 31/2 to 4 cm. high, well formed and that several hours were required to scrape them out so that they could be read. Copy of the editor, and squeeze.

The crux of this inscription is in the strange wording of the third line: AT-TOTTOlKIOYM6I90Y. M. Clermont-Ganneau and Professor Dittenberger both proposed to me to read *fuo-Oov,* and the latter suggested that the word *ênoÎKiov* might be used here in the sense of *estate, à-n-b* eVoi/aou *mo-dov; from the returns of their estate.* But MeieoY appears in the squeeze to be certain.1 On the other hand, M. Clermont-Ganneau, in a letter of September 7th, 1902, kindly gave me the following opinion: "Il y a, pourtant, un point qui me paraît être hors de doute, étant donnée la répétition du mot ô-ovç, répétition qui n'est pas le résultat d'un accident ou d'une faute...: c'est que nous avons nécessairement affaire à deux dates. La seconde, 0r'=2O9, est, selon toute apparence, vu la région, à calculer d'après l'ère d'Antioche, soit 160 j.c... . Ce point acquis, il s'agirait de déterminer la première date, qui se rapporte évidemment à une ère locale; on peut même, je crois, préciser dans ce sens, à une ère ayant pour point de départ l'érection en colonie romaine (eVoi/aa) de la ville antique où s'élevait le sanctuaire de Zeus Bômos. C'est dans ce sens précis que j'inclinerais à prendre l'adjectif dérivé *I-koikiov*. Mais c'est ici que commencent les difficultés. On voudrait trouver, dans le groupe suivant, MIOOY, quelque mot ayant une signification analogue à celle de Ktio-iç; mais je ne vois rien qui convienne. Il faudrait, en outre, admettre qu'à la fin de ligne 2, après erovçjl y avait une ou deux lettres numérales qui ont disparu; car, en général, dans ces formules, les lettres numérales suivent immédiatement le mot èrouç et précèdent les mots que peuvent déterminer celui-ci. Cependant, si l'on admettait une infraction à cette dernière règle, on pourrait supposer, à la grande rigueur: erouç *à-n-b i-n-oLKiov* /x'= 'l'an 40 de la colonization,' ce qui ferait remonter l'érection en colonie à 120 j.c, c'est-à-dire sous le règne de Hadrien, ce qui serait historiquement vraisemblable. Dans ce cas, il ne manquerait rien après erovç— Mais, alors, on se heurte à de nouvelles difficultés; il faudrait considérer *i-n-oïkÎov* comme le génitif d'un substantif." I believe that a clue to the explanation of this phrase is to be found in the epitaphs of certain Syrians from this neighborhood, who died abroad. For example, *C. I. L.* v, 1M. Clermont-Ganneau later suggested the possibility of *jjLt(rp)ov.* p. Io6l, No. 8728: *Aip.* Ma/ceSoi'ios *A/3/3il3a., dnb Ittoiklov Fevveov, opwv 'Airap,ea)v, evda KaraKnai.* Or the following, *C. I. L.* V, No. 8730: 'Ev0aSe /caraKtTe *Avp.* Maptai'os, vtos Ma/Dcocrtiw, drro *itroLKLov* SeicXa, wpwi' 'A7ra/xeW, /C0/117S Su/n'as.1 Evidently then the *inotKLov* Se/cXa was a village (kw/xt/) in Syria. The word seems to be a diminutive from *ivoutia,* which sometimes has the meaning of *colony colonia):* here, however, I believe it to have the same significance as *Koltoiklol,2* i.e. , *a hamlet,* which was counted a dependency of some larger borough. Moreover, the phrase *dwb eVoua'ou,* in the examples quoted, is followed immediately by a proper name of some kind. Consequently I believe that in the letters MIOOY we have to do with such a proper

name as *Yeweov* and 2eXa, and that the *'ettocklov Mei9ov* was a settlement of some sort, probably in the immediate neighborhood of the ancient town whose ruins are now called Bakirha. Only I do not feel sure whether in *Metdov* is found the genitive of the hamlet's name, M«0os or *MuOov,* or the genitive of the name of some man, Metflas or M«0os, to whom the hamlet actually belonged.3 Furthermore, the phrase *dnb eVot/aou—,* in the other instances, qualifies the Persons mentioned, as: *Avp.* MctKeSoVtos *dnb iiroiKiov Ytvveov,* on *Avp.* Maptai6s *dnb inoiKiov* Se/cXa. I believe it is so here, and, in spite of the contrary opinion of so eminent a scholar as M. Clermont-Ganneau, I believe that the first erovs should be expunged. After the analogy of the other examples, we should expect the words *d-nb iirotKLov MeMov* to follow *MapUovos.* Perhaps the stone-cutter overlooked these at first and then, realizing his mistake, added them in the third line, repeating the word crows. Or possibly the first two lines originally constituted the whole inscription, and the third line may then have been added as an afterthought, the first erovs being perhaps concealed by plaster which has now disappeared. If this latter explanation is the true one, one would suppose that the second line originally ended in erous *da* ; but I could find no trace of these numerals. I propose, therefore, to read the present inscription as follows:

Ait Ba/xa *p,eyda* Cvtjkog) *At-towmvios* /cat ATroXXodVrjs *Koi* XaX/3tW, *01 Mapicovos, Tov irvXwva dvecrTrjcrav* erovs — *dvb Ittoiklov Meidov* — erovs Oct, YopTriatov. To great Zeus-Altar, (the) hearer-of-prayer, Apollonios and Apollophanes and Chalbion, the (sons) of Marion, from the village of Meithos, set up this gateway, in (the) year *2op, Gorpiaios.* (September, 161 A.D.)

The name Zeus Bw/ios is obviously the Greek equivalent of the half Syriac name Zeus MasQaxos found on the Djebel Shekh Berekat, the very equivalent in fact supplied by conjecture alone in the article by M. Clermont-Ganneau on the inscriptions of this latter sanctu-

ary.4 Not, I think, that the same god was worshipped in these two places; but 1 See Mordtmann, "*Zur Topographic des nordlkhen Syriens* S. Reinach in *Ji. E. G.* Ill, p. 52. See Foucartin *B. C. H. aus griechischen Inschriften,"* in *Z. D. M. G.* , Vol. XLi (1887), ix, p. 395. p. 302 ff. Compare also *C. I. G.* 9875, which Mordt-3Compare the other similar names in the inscriptions mann reads: "EvfldSe *Kxti Avp«rG* 071-6 e7rouc(Zbu) 'ASSdvwi' r»s quoted in Mordtmann's article referred to in note 1. Svputs. Kirchhoff, however, reads: Avp. *"Traumas K(anrys) i£tndes d'Arche'ologic* CV/V«/V7/,,li (1895-7), p.49,11. 2: "'x 'ASSdiw. rapprochement de Ma8/3axos et du syriaque *madbah, 'autel';* 2 "Karoocm, qui parait synonyme de *aw/xif, vicus,* designe quoique Ton ne voie pas bien comment ce mot aurait pu deune bourgade qui faisait partie d'une cite; *k* laquelle elle venir un vocable divin: un Ztus Bco/xds, une sorte de betyle?" payait des impots et dont elle acceptait la juridiction." See below, Inscriptions 100-108a, and in particular p. 125.

in each case there was a god of an ancient altar, who had no other name than simply the god, the ba'al, of this place. See below, p. 126. In this connection, M. Clermont-Ganneau has made me another very valuable suggestion: "Le toponyme Bakirha a une forme intdressante; il semble devoir se ddcomposer en Ba. = contraction de Bait *house)* + Kirha; le second Element rappelle d'une facon frappante la nnip, Krhh, moabite, oil le roi Mesa' avait elev6 son autel a Kamoch."1

The temple at Bakirha is one of the few remaining buildings in this region which belong to the pagan time. It differs from all the others measured by this expedition in that its dimensions are reckoned exactly by the Roman foot of 29.6 cm. These dimensions, moreover, agree, as Mr. Butler tells me, with the established rules of the Roman architects, given by Vitruvius. And, finally, this building in its entire form and ornamentation is a very fair example of the best style of the period to which its inscription assigns it. The other buildin-

gs whose ruins, more or less well preserved, abound here, show, according to
Mr. Butler's testimony, not only a different system of measures and different proportions, but also an essentially different ornamentation. These other buildings are for the most part of the
Christian period: their style and pecu-
liarities may be seen clearly in the famous book by M. de Vogu6, *La Syrie
Centrale,* and in Part 11 of these publications. The templeof Bakirha, on the
other hand, is genuinely Roman, and it
is even possible that it was erected by
order of the imperial government, and
by architects sent thither from the West.
49. Bakirha. Elevated Sarcophagi. Fragment of a moulded block belonging to
a sepulchral monument, on the hillside,
northwest of the town. The remains of
this monument now consist of a large
sarcophagus resting upon two slabs of
stone set up on edge, and about it the ruins of a large base. I think there is no
doubt that there was originally another
sarcophagus, and that the two stood together on the same base. This sort of
monument is not uncommon in this region. Compare, for example, Nos. 13,
20,27, etc.: see also also Part II, p. 107
f. A pair of sarcophagi together on one
base, as here, stood originally at
Djuwaniyeh (No. 20) and at Khirbit
Faris (Part II, p. 108): in both these cases the sarcophagi, whether used themselves as tombs or not, were monuments
above tomb-chambers, partly built and
so forming an elevated base for the sarcophagi, and partly excavated in the
rock. The ruins of this monument show
it to have been simple, handsome, and
evidently of comparatively early date:
I should judge that it belongs approximately to the same period as the temple
at Burdj Bakirha (No. 48), which stands
on the top of the same hill. Most of the
earlier tombs, however, seem to have
been rock-hewn, and no elevated sarcophagus found by this 1 The same
scholar has also suggested that possibly
the mountain called *Kopvfr/* as opos...
Ko»oci&« */ufiovfuyc* knoll on which the
Bakirha temple stands, and not the *o-fia,*
a description which suits the Dj. Sh£kh
Berekat

Djebel Shekh Berekat, was the *Kttpwfnj*
mentioned by perfectly, but does not apply at all to the site of Burdj Bakirha.

Theodoretus (Migne, p. 1150). For
Burdj Bakirha stands It may even be
that the Dj. Shekh Berekat itself is the
at the northern end of the Djebel Barisha = *fid + rishd,* head referred to in
this name Barisha, *House-of-the-Head.*
the Syriac word for *head.* But Theodoretus describes the See p. 123 f. below.
expedition is dated earlier than the
fourth century. The block containing the
inscription lies in the pile at the lower
side of the sarcophagus. The letters are
large, and well formed. Copy of the editor.

The nameZe/8ewa (genitive?) occurs
in an inscription from Djilin (Hauran),
published by M. Fossey in the *B.C.//.,*
xxi (1897), p. 41. *Afaepane* is probably
for *afaeparrcu,1* and is found on other
sepulchral monuments: see No. 112.

1. 2. *This is the grave) of Apolinarios
and* Q fiAKIRHA. HOUSE, 384 or 391 A.
D. On the *Zebinos his)* son: *it is sacred
to their q &* ' door_frame) standing
alone, and *memory).* buried to within
two feet of the bottom of the lintel.

It is in the western part of the town,
not far to the east of No. 51. Facing the
inscription, at a distance of perhaps 15
feet, is the square-cut entrance to a cave
in the rock. The lintel measures 195 x
73 x 52 cm.: in the center it has an ornamental disk containing Christian symbols, which breaks into the first line of
the inscription. The letters are good and
clear, but not deep, nor of the same size:
they vary in height from 4 to *"jyi* cm.
The total length of the first line, including the space occupied by the bottom
of the disk, is 120 cm. The second line
runs along the very bottom of the stone:
it measures 157 x 6 cm. I could find no
trace of any other letters than those giv-
en below. Copy of the editor.

The first figure in the number of the
year is uncertain and may be G, in
which case the date is 391 A.d. The
name Mt/caXos occurs in an inscription
on a vase at Athens, *C. /. G.* 8517.
Mikkcixos is found in two inscriptions
from Egypt, *C. /. G.* 4716 d23 and d27.
Dr. Littmann has suggested to me that

Amkcdv may be a proper name also:
names such as *Priest, Bishop,* etc., occur in the ancient East as well as in the
modern West.

nr. v

Inscr. 50. From a drawing and photograph. Scale i: 20.

Aulkwv eVotercv, erovs /8X1/,
AprepecTLov K, Mi/caXo?.

*A deacon made this), in the year 4.32,
Artemisius
20th, by name) Mikalos.* (May, 384 A.
D.)

51. Bakirha. Cloister Gate, 491 Or 501
A.d. Lintel of the gateway into a cloister
court, in the western part of the town.
The gateway faces eastward: within, on
the right and forming one side of the
court, are the ruins of a church: on the
left, in the southeast corner of the court,
is a baptistery. The remaining sides of
the court are occupied by what appear
to have been the dwellings of the clergy.
See Part II, p. 191 *i.,* particularly p. 192,
where a photograph of this gateway is
reproduced. Above 1Or is this possibly
afupuTt, 2nd plu. subj. pres.: *Respect
their resting place?* the frame moulden-
gs of the lintel, which bear the inscription and are shown in the accompanying
cut, is a tall cavetto door-cap, on which
are carved upright, stiff and somewhat
conventionalized acanthus leaves, and a
central disk. The inscription, which was
copied by the editor, is in three or four
separate parts, described under A, B, c,
and D respectively.

PfdlKANOi6TPWH»AiACVffl:Z
LiiNHTTPECB A" The space occupied by
w' this inscription measures 221 x 9 cm.
The first twenty-six letters are 5 cm.
high: they

Inscr. 51. From a copy and photograph. Scale i: 20. are irregular, and
mOst of them are not clear. Between
these and the last eight letters there is
a blank space of 26 cm., sufficient for
four or five letters more. The last letters
are 5 to 6 cm. high, and of a different
form. Between the last letter and the
cross which follows the inscription is a
space sufficient for one, possibly two,
letters.

+ Mtjivos) Ai'o(u) 8', *Ka(t) IvS.* te',
(e)rous *pf',* (S)ia Su/i. *amj' npecr/*

3(vTepov) +.

Perhaps we should read *iv8. 1, Ctovs (v)j:* perhaps also the beginning of this line may be actually *iir)(vbs)* Ato(v) *(e)tKacriv* (for *eucoatv, elKoory), (iv)h. Kt. + Month Dios 4th* (or *20th) and indiction 15* (or *10), in the) year 54.0* (or *550), by Symeon, presbyter, -f* (November, 491 or 501 A.D.)

B. Measures 34 x 4 cm.: the letters are well formed and clear.

'En Ta-afiiv: under Hysamin (?). There are no letters on the stone after the N. c. Measures 67 x 5 cm.: the letters are irregular, but clear.

Kou Sv/xewfs BepXov: and Symeon (son) of Berlos (?), or *v/xecovr) ZfiepXov.*

BepXos, if this name is correctly read, may be akin to the Syriac *bcrulci* (Targumic *blrld*), the Greek *(SrjpvWos, beryl.* i). Measures 1.59 by o. 10 m.: the letters are irregular, but clear. After the letter P, in the same fascia, there may possibly be an 6, very much cramped and indistinct: in the turn of the second fascia there may possibly be an U).

t 'Eyw, Su/iewi'rjs, vlbs Mapa_va (?): /, *Symeon, son of Maronas (7).*

The name Maron or Maronas occurs in Nos. 26 and 336. Also in Part IV, Syriac 7 (and perhaps in Syriac 22). Compare also *Mara,* in No. 336 a, and MaptW, in No. 48.

The date, 491 or 501 A.d., is the date of this gateway: doubtless there was a church there then, and probably earlier; but Mr. Butler considers that the present church and baptistery should properly be classed among the sixth century buildings. It is possible therefore that the present church is later than the gateway which leads to it. At the same time, the later elements in the church arc chiefly the exterior decorations of the east end, and this end then may have been rebuilt in the sixth century. See Part II, p. 191 f.

1 For the genitive Sv/itoSvov, or a dative Svfitoivij with Sta (?). Neither alternative is satisfactory. 52. BAKIRHA. Church. On the lintel of a doorway in the church which stands on the north side of the court described under No. 51: this doorway is in the south wall of the church, near the west end. In the interior, about the middle of the nave and in the line of the north row of columns, were the remains of a stone bench, which had a back and was fairly comfortable. The lintel is ornamented with simple mouldings, three fasciae of which bear the inscription; but the ends of the uppermost fascia and part of the first line of the inscription were cut off, when holes were made in the lintel, as if to support the double-pitched roof Of a little Doorway of Inscr. 52 porch before the door. See Part II, p. 190 ff. Copy of the editor, and a squeeze.

I suppose that the stone-cutter may have carved TTN6YMATI instead of 17NYMA because of his familiarity with Ad£a. .. *UvevfiaTi.* Certainly this inscription closely resembles the formula in Nos. 21, 22, etc., and we should expect *Uve-va 6 fior)9S)v.* But perhaps the author really intended the interrogative «. Could he have meant *rl /3or)0Tjoei): what else) shall help,* Or *rl (8c!) fio-qdrjo-e (= f$07)9rjcra.i) Kt.) what need is there) to help them that fear him?* Or perhaps he had in mind some such phrase as this: *ri nonqdrjo-erai* Tovs *fofiovfievow; avrov.* Compare Psalms lv, 12: *C. I. G.* 8909. On the syntax of Tous £o/3oiyteVot/s *avrov,* see the commentary to No. 21.

53. Bakirha. Church Lintel, 546 A.d. Over the west portal of the East Church. The lintel, with respect to its mouldings, is similar to those of the early part of the fifth century: compare, for example, the lintel which bears No. 57. The dimensions and proportions of the ground plan, moreover, are those of early fifth century churches. About the lintel, however, is a hood-mould of much later date, and the west facade as a whole, together with the ornamentation of the exterior of the east wall, is characteristic of the sixth century. Obviously the church has been rebuilt: the

Inscr. 52.

From a squeeze, copy and photograph. Scale 1: 30.

Doorway of inscr. 53. which was the higher, has been mu tilated, and of the first two words only the very bottoms remain. The date given in the Syriac is not absolutely certain, but appears to be the same as that of the Greek. See Part IV, Syriac 10 (p. 28 ff.).

The Greek inscription is on the lowest band of the mouldings, at the bottom of the lintel proper. This fascia is 1.82 m. long by *8l/2* cm. wide: the letters are 4 to 5 cm. high. The letters are all fairly well formed, and were all clearly cut: those at the beginning are still perfectly clear; but those towards the end are somewhat weathered: one or two letters have been lost from the extreme end, through the crumbling away of the stone. Copy of the editor, and squeeze.

Inscr. 53. Cast from a squeeze.

+ "etous o»', *ftr)(vb;) Ar)rCov ift, iyd(v)To 6 Ttvov: f In (the) year 595, on (the) 12th of (the) month Desios, this gatezvay was (tnade).* (June, 546 A.D.) The use of *iyevero* in this sense is common in Syria. Compare, for example, Wad. 2080, 2089, 2189, 2691, etc.; also No. 288 below; John i, 3 and 10. It seems to me clear that the lintel was made in the fifth century. The inscriptions, therefore, were added later, and doubtless when the church was rebuilt. Consequently, the date of the rebuilding is the date given by the inscriptions. The objection to this view is that the Syriac inscription has been mutilated, and apparently in the fitting on of the present hood-mould. Then either, when the church was being rebuilt, the Syriac inscription was carved before the hood-mould was in place, and when the latter was applied it was found necessary to alter the top of the lintel, it being impossible to change the hoodmould without destroying the pattern; or else the church was rebuilt a second time, after 546 A.d., and the hood-mould, at least in its present state, belongs to the last rebuilding. These questions are discussed in Part II and Part IV, 11. cc.

54. Khirbit Tezin. Church, 585 A.d. On the lintel of the west doorway of the church. See Part II, p. 214 f. The lintel is unusually handsome: it has a heavy ovolo cap, ornamented with a deeply carved rinceau. At the top of the ovolo is a single narrow band, 2.32)4 by o. 10 m., which bears the main inscription, A. The letters are 6 cm. high, and are deep,

clear and regular. Copy of the editor. Inscr. 54. Cast from a squeeze.

A. t EKTICeHWOIKOCOYTOCMALUW th ff T rAX ETOYC +

+ 'qktutot) d oucos ouro5 *fi(rjvl) Aww, iv(8). yy', T(ov) y' erous* +. + *This house was built in (the) month Loos, indiction J, of the 633rdyear* -p. (August, 585 A. D.)

All these letters are certain, with the possible exception of the INH. Possibly also there was one letter more after these and before rr; but it looks more as if the stonecutter had begun to carve some letter there, but, finding a slight flaw in the stone, had discontinued his work and begun a little farther along.

The second inscription (b) is on the lowest band of the moulding of this same lintel, at the right of the central disk. At the left of this disk the band has crumbled off entirely. On the right three letters and a part of a fourth may still be seen: the traces of other letters remain only in yellowish discolorations on the crumbled face of the stone. The lintel, which is of a limestone originally white, has weathered on the surface to a rusty yellow. When the surface crumbles off, the stone appears whitish again, and against this white the yellow streaks can be seen where the weathering entered deeper into the stone along the lines of the original letters.

B. 0X1/ ICEN «ctio-«/. 55. Kasr Ibliso. Church. Above the central one of three windows, above the door in the south wall of the church, and about twenty feet from the ground. The letters are 5 to 6 cm. high, and badly weathered. Copy of the editor.

Possibly there were other letters below the rwNr-Ne-TTPM,,,. _ .... left end 01 this line. On a second visit in 1905 ye'ly(«reli/ *iin Ilp* ...(?) _.,,., I was unable to read anything further, even with the help of a ladder and of a telescope. Perhaps, however, with a longer ladder than mine the inscription could be deciphered.

56. Dar Kita. Gateway Of Church Court, 431 A.d. Across the end of a little street1 running northward, in the northern part of the town, stands a simple gateway, whose lintel bears the follow-

ing inscription. Only the frame of the gateway is now standing. This gateway leads into an open court, like that described under No. 51. Inside the court, on the right, against the wall in which the gateway is, stands a large stone sarcophagus. On the left is a baptistery, its apse projecting almost to the line of the entrance to the court. The north side of the court, opposite the gateway, is formed by the south side of the Church of Paul and Moses. Part II, p. 137 ff.: the back of the gateway is shown in the upper photograph on p. 139. The first line of I. 2.

3 the inscription measures i.624 m., and the letters are 5 to 6 cm. high: the fascia which contains this line measures 1.74 m. x *8y2* cm. The second and third lines are carved on another fascia, which measures 1.56 m. x 9 cm. The second line measures 1.51 m. in length, including a space of 14 cm. after the letters HON, where there seems to have been a flaw in the stone when it was carved. The third line is 50 cm. long. The letters are perfectly legible. Copy of the editor. % See No. 25 and commentary. 57. Dar Kita. Church Of Paul And Moses, 418 A.d. On the lintel of the easternmost of the two doorways in the south side of the Church of Paul and Moses,2 opening on the court described above (see No. 56). Part II, p. 137 f. The first line of the inscription occupies a space of 218 x 6 cm.: the inscription itself is 200 cm. 1 Marked *A* in the drawing. 2 Marked *B* in the drawing. in length, and the letters 4 cm. high. The space of the second line is 201 *x/2* x 11 cm., the letters 3 to 4J/2 cm. high. In length, the measurements of this second line are as follows: before the first letter, 22, the first letter to the break, 99, the break to H, 24, H through the date, 74, after the date, 2 cm. Most of the letters are deep and clear; but they are irregular, and not always well formed. Copied by Dr. Littmann and the editor.

The date is certain. The name, with which the second line begins, is commonly written in Greek *Mwvo-fjs;* it appears, however, as *Movo-rjs* in *C. I. G.* 4668 and 8947 c (Pape). In Hebrew it is

Inscr. 57. Cast from a squeeze: the letters are marked with charcoal.

1. + Efs ©ec9 *Kal* 6 Xpicrro? *avrov Kal To "Kyiov Wvevfia. ixV* riauXw *Kal* 2. *Movo-fj-*AtdSajpo; *npecr/3(vTepo;)-*Kupos Tcvtrq5 *fjLrjvbs Aoov* e/c', *Tov igv'* (Irovs).

+ *(There is) one God and his Christ and the Holy Spirit. A vow to Paul and Moses: Diodorospresbyter: Kyros architect: (the) 2jth of (the) month Loos, in the 466th (year).* (August, 418 A.d.)

moshe; but in Syriac it was pronounced *mushe* at all times, even during the period when *0* and *u* were distinguished. The form *Moivo-rjs,* I believe, is due to a misguided attempt at etymology on the part of Egyptian Jews (cf. the Coptic Moot: *water).* See Nos. 56, 58, and the notes on No. 63. 58. Dar Kita. Baptistery,1 515-516 (?) A.d.2 On the lintel of the doorway, on the north side of the baptistery belonging to the Church of Paul and Moses, described above under No. 56. Part II, p. 138 ff.: this doorway is shown at the extreme left of the photograph on p. 140. The first line, exclusive of the cross, is 1.34 m. long. In 1 Marked *C* in the plan on p. 76.-Dated by me originally 422 A.d., and so reported in Part II, pp. 138 and 187 f. I now believe this date to be incorrect, Doorway of Inscr. 57.

the second line the first eight letters are about 30 cm. in length, after which follows a space, 54 cm. long, sufficient for about fifteen letters: the remaining part of the inscription, including the cross at the end, is 45 cm. long. The letters are badly weathered and obscured by lichen: they vary in height from 22 to 3 cm., but, although small, were originally well formed. Copy of the editor, and a squeeze of the lower line. 1. teiC9OC-KAIoXPICTOCWTOVHUJHeiCONTOVKOC-MOV 2. 6TOVCi?.Y NTIOXOCKCN +

I believe that the first line is certain. In the second line, the first figure of the date may be A. In 1899 I read it O, and believed that there was nothing between it and the following y. Consequently I dated the inscription at that time 421-22 A.u. On my visit in 1905, however, I satisfied myself that the first letter is precisely like the A in *AeaCov* of No. 61, and that a 2 follows, before the Y: this reading is also confirmed by my squeeze. Altogether the letters are very similar to those of No. 61 and other sixth century inscriptions,1 especially with regard to the unusual form of B in */3orj0Lo-ovt* line 1. Moreover, as Mr. Butler informs me, the base-mould about the building, and the impost moulding on both the exterior and interior of the apse, indicate a later date for this baptistery than the first quarter of the fifth century. The third figure of the date might perhaps be X; but 8£x' = 664 = 615-616 A. D. is later than the latest known date in this region. Consequently, since the traces of this letter are very faint and uncertain, I believe S££', 564 = 515-516 A.d., should be read. The date, however, must necessarily remain doubtful. The lacuna following the date was doubtless filled by the name and day of the month, which would easily include fourteen letters, e. g., */x-qpos bvorpov* at'. After this 'A»r«xos seems fairly certain. Then KICN, whatever this may mean. I tried again in 1905 to read either *Zktlo-cv* or *iirourev,* but was unable to do so, and the squeeze seems to forbid either of these readings. After the K there may be CIC or The last seems certain: after this IY is quite possible.

+ Eis Weos *Kcu* 6 Xpioros *avrov-fio-jyjdicrov Tov Kocrfiov.* Erous ' 'atuxos($) KCN t: + *There is) one God and his Christ: help thou the world. In (the) year 564(1) Antiochos bnilt(l) (this baptistery).* +

I suppose that *Tov Koo-ov* is for T5 *Koo-pw,* and that the mistake is due to the confusion between *d* and *it* among the Syriac-speaking inhabitants.

59. DAR KiTA. Colonnade, 436 A.d. On the face of a rectangular pier, near the middle of a colonnade, in the northwest corner of the town, and about 200 feet west of the Church of Paul and Moses. See Part II, p. 155. The inscription is incised 1 Nos. 60, 71, etc. 1. TOCATTY 2. MENOC?A 3. AlKOYAl *(The) 14th of (the) month Xandicus, in (the) year 4. 84..* (April, 436 A. D.) in an incised dove-tail plate, which is 40 cm. long

by 23 high. The letters are rough and weathered, but perfectly legible. Copy of the editor.

The line over the letters?A was probably substituted for the N which was omitted for lack of room in this line.

60. Dar Kita. Tower, 551 A.n. On the east side of the street which leads to the Church of Paul and Moses, a short distance from the gate mentioned above under No. 56. The inscription is on the lintel of a building now in ruins, whose ground plan is nearly, if not exactly, a square, and which seems to have been at least three stories in height.1 High upon the front wall is a stone, resting on two brackets, and having a hole in its center directly over the entrance to the building.

The face of the lintel measures 181 by 58 cm., and is perfectly smooth, except for the single line of incised letters along the bottom of the stone, and above that, in the center, an ornament carved in relief, which appears to be a conventionalized wreath crossed by a palm branch, or a tree with a circle behind it. The stone is cracked and broken at the bottom in one place, so that five or six letters of the inscription have been lost. The letters are 5 cm. high: the first twenty-six letters measure 102, the break 21, and the remaining fourteen letters 50 cm. They are badly aligned and of different types, but are still legible. Copy of the editor, and squeeze.

Towers are common in Syria: some *gif'f" jf*

Inscr. 60. From a squeeze and copy. Scale I: 20.

of them are six stories high. See Part II, pages 125, 128 f., 153, 156 and 254. Some were watch-towers, some perhaps merely tall houses. Some are in close proximity to, and apparently in connection with, churches and other religious buildings, and possibly these may have been the dwellings of monks or nuns, as, for example, that of Kasr il-Benat (Part II, p. 156). Some of these towers have no windows in the lower stories, a fact which suggests that perhaps in these cases the highest story alone was used. Such a tower may have been occupied by a solitary saint, who, thus

raised above the world, lived more conveniently, though perhaps no less piously, than those who persisted in exposing themselves on columns, and who, being nearer heaven than his fellow townsmen, was thought better able to call down blessings. For this service such an intercessor would naturally be fed by the community, and perhaps the stone with the large hole through it, which, in the tower of the present inscription, as in other similar towers, projects from above over the entrance, may have had something to do with the raising of con 1 Marked *D,* in the drawing on p. 76. tributions by means of a small basket and rope. An inscription found at "El-BordjAzaoui," and dated 495-496 A.d., seems to me to throw some light on the question of the USe of these towers:1 *K. vp(i)e jvkat;ov Tov irvpyov Tovtov (kcu) Tov Oikovvtov iv* avrw; *fj)rd guard this tower and him that dwells in it.* The singular, Him *that dwells in it,* is significant. 61. Dar Kita. Church Of St. Sergius, 537 A.d. On the lintel of the west portal of the Church of St. Sergius, in the eastern part of the town. Part II, p. 202 f. The inscription is on the broad lowest fascia of the frame mouldings of the doorway shown on p. 203 of Part II. This fascia is 1.60 m. long by 16 cm. broad: the letters are 3 to 5 cm. high. Copies of Dr. Littmann and the editor: also a squeeze. jlcefcoc/oXpifjocj-j-o roTTNeVHaol,e

Inscr. 61. From a squeeze and copy. Scale i: 10.

1. Efs 0eos *(ko.1)* 6 *XpioTO;* (/ecu) *ToAyio(v) Tlvevpa. Bor/dt).* 2. *Mir)(vb;)* Aecri'ou, *iv8. et, Tov eirf* erot/9. ToO *aylov Xepyiov. (There is) one God and the Christ and the Holy Spirit. Help (us)! In (the) month Desios, indiction 15, of the 585th year. (The Church) of St. Sergius.* (June, 537 A.U.) See the commentary on No. 25. The forms of the letters in this inscription are noteworthy, especially the forms of B and A.2 On my second visit, in 1905, I concluded that there was no letter between *fiorjdr)* and the cross at the end of the first line: previously I had read *f8or)dt)o-(ov).* 62. Dar KiTA. Baptistery, 567 A.d. On the lintel of the baptis-

tery, adjoining the Church of St. Sergius (see No. 61), in the eastern part of the town. Part II, p. 202: the doorway of the baptistery may be seen behind the figure of Dr. Post. The lintel is 1.82 m. long, and has, above the frame mouldings, an ornamental doorcap: the inscription is on the space, 1732 cm. wide, between the door-cap and the frame mouldings, as in the case of the Syriac inscription at Babiska (Part IV, Syr. 10). The whole face of the stone is badly weathered and covered with lichen. The letters, though small, were originally fairly well made. Copy of the editor, and a squeeze of the last part of the inscription.

1. t ANHN609HHnYAHn ITOV VCB/H MN-BACIA' IOVCT INOV/TAriOTnANAE: 2. TACIOWnfeNADr/IU-JANNH/CEPriOVAAANXBAXXOY PA-MAYCrP T E IX To 3. INA'ie

Much of the second line, and the figures of the indiction number, are very uncertain. Four of the letters have above them smaller letters as, for example, in *C. I. L.*, v, No. 8730. These are as follows: in the first line, over the T after *'lovorivov*, X; over the following T and n, an A in both cases; over the second T in line 2, apparently an *IB. C. H.*, 1902, p. 195. 2Compare No. 58.

Lj. After this last letter follows , and then v, in combination with which there may be a A, an A, or possibly P: then follows □, or ττ, or n, then *VI*, or possibly rY. The name lUJANNH, however, seems certain. This is followed by a sign which occurs twice in line I: in the first case as a sign of abbreviation, in the second evidently for *Kol*: in this third case it seems to be a punctuation mark. *Xepyiov* and B«xxou are als clear; but between A and the following A there may be I. The first figure of the date looks more like r than like E: the second figure might equally well be A or O. But the date is determined with reasonable certainty by the Emperor, and by the indiction number. I believe that lUJANNH can be only a dative, and in that case must be in a different construction from the names that follow. The words which precede are very perplexing; but I think it is possible to read U7r(6) Tw *evXoyrco) 'Iwdwrj*, although

this use of *vv-6* with a dative is singular. I propose, therefore, with some hesitation, the following reading: + 'Avqveoffr) 17 *Ttvt) irrl Tov* evcrecoTaTov) *qfi(a)v* /8acriX.(eiws) *,ovcrrLvov, kox) Tov dyiord(Tov) ira(rpidpyov) 'Avaaracriov, im(b) Tu evoy(r)Ta) 'icjavirg, %cpyiov, Advov, Baov, Pa/xXu? Tlpcrf3vrepoiv),* T(ou) ei' er(ou?), *ivh. u. This door was renewed under our most pious king Iustinos, and the most holy patriarch Anastasios, under the blessed* (?) *Ioanncs, Sergios, Danos, Bachchos, Rhamlys being presbyters* (?), *in the 615th year, indiction 15.* (566-567 A.I).)

Justin II became emperor on the death of his uncle Justinian, in November, 565, and reigned until 578 A.d. Anastasios, called Sinaitikos, was made patriarch of Antioch about 559: he was banished by Justin in 570, but restored in 593: he died in 599. Ioannes is of course a very common name: this particular Ioannes seems to have held some office intermediate between the patriarch and the presbyters; and possibly he was the periodeutes.1 Of the four other names two at least, together with Ioannes, appear in a Syriac inscription dated nineteen years earlier than this one, and found at Babiska, distant about twenty minutes from Dar Kita. In this case also Ioannes is distinguished from the rest. The Babiska inscription, Part IV, Syr. 15 (p. 33 ff.), is translated by Dr. Littmann as follows: *"In my days the brothers Sargon and Theodore and Bakkhos purchased the gardens, t and I, the brother Yohdnnd, son of Zakkai, built and finished."* The date is given in inscription Syr. 14: *"God b/ess us / There"* was bni/t this stoa in the year *five lutndred and ninety and six, according to the era of Antioch* Now *Sargon* or *Sergon* is the Syriac hypochoristikon of *Sergius, Yohdnnd* the Syriac form of *Ioannes*. It is possible then that the persons mentioned in these two inscriptions are the same. But the relation of *Yohdnnd* to the others, the character of the *"stoa"* at Babiska, and the meaning of the term" *brothers,"* are not clear.

63. DARKiTA. House, 485 A.D. On a lintel, apparently that of the entrance to

a simple dwelling-house, on the south side of a street in the eastern part of the town, near the Church of St. Sergius. The lintel is ornamented with a trapezoidal door 1See commentary to No. 46. On *periodeutes* sec commentary to No. 7. cap, two fasciae of which bear the inscription; the upper one of these measures 1.47 m. by *7y2* cm., the lower 1. 42 m. by 84 cm. The letters, 4 to 6 cm. high, are incised: they are rather rude and irregular in form. The whole face of the stone is badly weathered and covered with lichen. Copy of the editor. 1. tIC0OCKAIOXPICTOCATOYCTH 2. on Y AON B A CI OYfINA'hTO YT A$ + Ef? ®eo? Kal 6 XpioTos *a(v)rov.* "ectttj + *There is one God and his Christ. This door6 Trvkbv fjL7)(vbs)* Atcriou *y IvS. rf, Tow ykf' way was set up on the) jrd of (the) month Desios,* (crovs). *indiction 8, of the 533rdyear.* (June, 485 A.D.) Beside the doorway which bears this inscription, is another with an inscribed lintel, which I discovered in 1899, but was unable, at that time, to decipher: the building, to which this doorway gave entrance, has been destroyed. Its inscription is as follows:

Eis 0605 *Kal 6* XptoTO? *Ovtov.* Eor(i7) *6 rrvkbv fj.7)vl A(oov K/3', ivS. (rj'f), Tov yf' erov?/ There is one God and his Christ. This doorway was set tip on the 22nd of the) month Lobs, indiction 8, of the 533rd year.* (August, 485). A similar inscription, on the outer doorway of a vestibule on the opposite side of the same street, was found in 1905: it is dated May, 462 A.d. Besides these two, eight other new inscriptions have been found in Dar kita, and will appear in the publications of the Princeton Archaeological Expedition, where it is hoped to present a plan of this very interesting town. Of the new inscriptions, one is from a cloister immediately west of the Church of Paul and Moses (Nos. 56-58), and is dated, probably, July, 456 A.d. Two others, dated between 339 and 354 A.d., mention Fl. Eusebios, son of Kyrilis (?), the builder of an "agora." Another, of which the date has been destroyed, refers to a certain Eusebios, an architect (tcxttjs). Still another, dated September, 452, gives the name of an architect Symones.

64. Babiska. Fragments, 143 A.d. Two moulded blocks lying in a heap of ruins at the north side of the north pilaster of the apse in the East Church. See Part II, p. 132. Above the inscription is a series of right-lined mouldings, which is continued around the left end of "a" and the right end of "b," and along the back of each. The block which contains A measures 124 cm. in length; but the other is broken at its left end, so that the greatest dimension of this block at present is nowhere more than 90 cm.: both blocks measure 76 or 77 cm. across the top, and 41 cm. in height. Now 41.25 cm. make one cubit, according to the standard of measure employed in the construction of the temenos of Zeus Madbachos on the Djebel Shekh Berekat, which belongs approximately to the same period (see below, Nos. 100 to 108 a). This cubit, however, differs both from the Roman cubit used in the building of the temple and temenos of Zeus Bomos at Burdj Bakirha (No. 48), and also from the cubit used by the architects of this region in the Christian period (see Part II, p. 36). These two blocks may have formed together the cap of a pier in a temple which preceded the church built on this site, or else the cap of a pedestal. I think, moreover, that my measurement of 124 cm. must have been taken along the bottom of the stone, so that this represents the length of the block exclusive of the overhanging mouldings. Probably the width of the block was 55 cm., or 2 feet (ancient measure), and the difference between this and the 76 or 77 cm. of width at the top represents twice the depth of this overhang, which was then of a cubit = 10.32 cm., or 2/5 of a foot= 11 cm. The measurements of Fragment A are as follows: In the first line, at the beginning, a space amounting to about 15 cm. has been clipped off: the remaining twenty letters measure 105cm. in length, and are followed by a space of 3 cm. at the end: total 123/2 cm. In the second line, a space of 8 cm.; eight letters, 33 cm.; a space of 6 cm.; six letters, 26 cm.; a space of 9 cm.; eight letters, 34 cm.: total 116 cm. The lower right-

hand corner of this stone is slightly broken. The measurements of Fragment B are as follows: In the first line, at the beginning, a space of 4 cm.; the first letter, 4 cm.; a space of 19I/2 cm., from which the letters have disappeared; sixteen letters, 51 cm.: total y8fe cm. The twenty-three letters of the second line measure 83 cm. in length. The letters of both inscriptions are 4)4-5 cm. in height. Squeeze, and copies of the editor.

Fragment A. Fragment B.

Line I. TOYCA?PMHNO CTTA N HMOY
ΓΑ CYBABACB AP6XBHAO

Line 2. ANTWNIOC H PWAHC AA-
CIANAP OCB6P N I Kl A N OC AA I ANA
POY

It is uncertain how long the second of these two blocks may have been originally. But the two inscriptions seem to fit together, so that I am inclined to believe that the two blocks are pieces of the same stone, and that little has been lost from either. For, supposing that the original stone was 5 cubits, or 206.25 cm. long at the bottom, then only 4.25 cm. are lacking from the first and 7.25 cm. from the second line. This deficiency may be accounted for by an unmeasured space between the end of the inscription and the end of the second block. Placed together, these inscriptions read as follows: 1. vetovs ?/', /u-vos *TlavrjfjLov,* _A SuySa/Sas, BapexXos, 2. *'AvrdHvios,* *'HpaJsrjs,* AXefavSpos, Bepj/i/«aios *'Ae£dvhpov. In (the) year ipr, in (the) month Panemos Sybabas, Barechbelos, Antonios, Herodes, Alexandras, (and) Bernikianos (son) of Alexandros.* (July, 143 A.D.)

The name *Sybabas* perhaps reflects the Syriac noun *shebdba = neighbor:* the name *Barechbelos* is doubtless the Syriac *Barr)ekhbel = Bel-has-blessed.* After the word *Uamj/j.ov* it would be perfectly possible to restore Ati Bup?. If these words were originally part of the inscription, then the meaning is doubtless that the six men, whose names are given, erected in 143 A.d. this pier, or this pedestal (and in the latter case doubtless also a statue), to the glory of Zeus Bomos, doubtless the god of the high place at Burdj Bakirha, distant

about half an hour's walk.1 If so, then the god's name was probably erased, intentionally, by the Christians, when a church was built, apparently on the site, and out of the materials, of an older temple. This Alexandros and his son Bernikianos are perhaps indentical with the owners of the handsome bicolumnar monument at Sermeda,2 although the date of the monument is several years earlier than that of the present inscription.

65. Babiska. House Lintel. On the lintel of a doorway in the northern part of the town, and facing northward. Only the frame of the doorway is standing: it appears to have belonged to a private house.

At each end of the lintel is an ornamental disk, the disk on the left containingaplain cross. Between the disks isa trapezoidal door-cap, consisting of two plain bands, each of which is about 10 cm. high, beneath a shallow cavetto. The lower band contains the first line of the inscription. Below the door-cap is a space, 9 cm. high, which contains the second line. The whole lintel is 2.52 m. long and 49 cm. high. The first six letters are considerably larger than the others: they measure 31x5 cm., the next fourteen letters 52 x 3. The second line is 85 cm. long, and the letters vary from 3 to 4 cm. in height. Copy of the editor.

I TOYC Y MHNCTTANH Moyetk 2. AY PANTIOXOCZ OHCTOY6 TTOI6C6

"Brows v, fiJvo; Uamjfiov /3k', A.vp. In (the) year 4.00, (the) 22nd of (the) month Panewos, Anr(elios)

Ai/rioo? Zoiarov iiroUtre. Antiochos, (son) of Zoestos, made (this). (July, 352 A.D.) 66. Babiska. Lintel. On the lintel of a door-frame in situ, facing south in a ruined wall in the northern part of the town, not far southwest of No. 65: it seems to have belonged to a private house. The first, third and fourth quarters of the lintel are filled with rather clumsy designs, formed by shallow incised lines, and including various Christian symbols. The main part of the inscription occupies the second quarter of the stone; but in the first quarter, above the upper cross and the disk, and 1 See No. 48. 2 No. 87.

Door-frame, and lintel which bears Inscr. 65 in line with the first word in the second quarter, are letters, now almost illegible, which I read Xp(aaoc. Below this same disk is written gj. The first word measures 58 x 7 cm.: the other two words together 25 x 10 cm. The letters of the main part of the inscription are large, 5 to 7 cm. high, and most of them are of good form, C being always well rounded. They are, however, shallow and weathered, and were completely obscured by lichen: all the lines were marked out with a dark crayon before the accompanying photograph was taken. A few of the letters are formed by double lines, which give to these letters the appearance of being carved in relief: similar letters are found elsewhere, for example in No. 72. In the last quarter of the stone, at the bottom of the square, there are three or more letters, which I took to be the Syriac shin, semkat, bet, or shin, semkat, resh, but which I now believe to be yod, alaf, kof, waw, bet: *Ydkub,* for *Ya'kub)* Copy of the editor, photographs and a squeeze.

Xe / I'xx o 5 *TafSpavov,* EucreJsi? *TexyLrqs, Kai i/is,* erovs £Xu', ju. 7j(x)v6s *gZavSiKov 'laKovfios,* vtos (XepiXXou).

Cherillos, (son) of Gabronas, Ettscbis (the architect, and Athcnis (erected this building) in (the) year 437, (the)jth of (the) month Xandikos: (also) Iakubos, son (of Cherillos). (April, 389 A.D.) The letters of the main part of the inscription are so placed that the five lines make a solid parallelogram. And I believe that the X at the end of the fourth line was added merely to complete the symmetrical arrangement without breaking the syllable -*VOS.* Gabronas is doubtless the Syriac name *Gabrona.* Eusebios, an architect, is mentioned in an inscription of approximately the same date, found in the neighboring town of Dar Kita.[2] In Dar Kita. also there is the following, somewhat enigmatical, inscription:[2]

Efs @eos /ecu *XpLcrre, fBor)0b; yevov t. Kv(Te/3i(o, vlov* Ku/dixtj?, *dyopas Tt)v Kt'ktt(v erovs rTTT r/yo paaev,* 77?/ e«ncrev crw Bew, *Uav7)p,(ov)* X'. I suppose this to mean: *Otic God*

and Christ, be (the) he/per of Flavios Eusebios, son of Kyrills, the builder (or founder) of the market: in the) year 388 he bought (the ground), in jg8 he built (it), with God's (help), on Panenws joth (i.e., July, 350 A.d.). 11 am indebted to Dr. Littmann for this reading and explanation.
[2] Found by the Princeton Archaeological Expedition in 1905.

Lintel of Inscr. 66. Letters darkened with colored chalk.

67. Babiska. East Church. On a large lintel lying upside down in a pile of ruins in the court at the south side of the East Church. Evidently this was the lintel of the eastern doorway in the south wall of the church. See Part II, p. 131 ff. The first line of the inscription is 2. 04 m. in length, the letters *l/2* to 5 cm. high. The last letter is carved below the two preceding letters, where the moulding is turned downward to be continued along the jamb. The second line is 1. 90 m. long, the letters 4 to 64 cm. high. The letters are well formed, especially in the lower line, but are badly weathered in some places. Copy of the editor. 1. 6TOYC GMY MHNOC A (JU OY B MAP-KIANOC KYPIC TX 2. XPICTOC BOG-+ Y CB IC AIAKONOC-TTTTT

"etov? *Ofiv, fj.r)vb; Aatov /?' Map/aafos Kvpis, In (the) year 4.4.9, (the) 2nd of (the) month Loos. T(e)x(viTrf;).* Xpioro? *fio(r))96;.* + Evcre/3i?, *81a-Markianos Kyris(ivas the)architect. Christ (the) helper. Kovo;, e iroi7)re.* + *Eusebis, deacon, made (this).* (August, 401 A.D.)

It is quite possible that Kvpis is here a title, and not a proper name, as if we should say *Sir Markianos,* or *Markianos, Gentleman,* etc. This use of the word was common under the Byzantine empire: it appears also in No. 87. On the other hand, an inscription found in 1905 seems to indicate that Kvpis was a name. This second inscription is upon a lintel fallen from a doorway in the passage along the south side of the baptistery (?) adjoining the East Church, shown in the plan on p. 131, and discussed on p. 133 f., of Part II, a few feet east of the door in the south wall of the baptistery. The inscription is

in three lines, parts of which are quite illegible: it is as follows: 1. "etovs Tjxh', p,evb; Ylaveji.ov .
2. E15 0eo 6 *ioedov* 17/Aa?, cai *w* X/aioros *avrov-dfiev.* + 3. M. Kupis, 7r pecrj/Svrcpos, *ineoccrev. In (the) year 438, in (the) month Pa nemos, . One God that helpeth us, and his Christ: amen I -f-M(arkianos?) Kyris, presbyter, made (this).* (August, 390 A.D.) If this is so, perhaps this Markianos Kyris is the same as the Kyris or Kyrios who was the architect of the church at Kasr il-Benat,[2] and perhaps also the same as Kyros, the architect of the Church of Paul and Moses at Dar Kita. [3] On the other hand, one might read *MapKiavbs (kol) Kvpts,* T()x(p«"u): *Markianos and) Kyris (were the) architects.* 68. Babiska. East Church. On a small lintel lying upside down in the ruins 6TOVC BNV f tne East Church, just inside the west wall. The lintel _, probably measured about a meter and a half in length, and

Erous *pvv 1 J ...*

doubtless belonged to a window in this church. The date *In(the)year452.* (403-404A.D.) ig spaced from the word *&ovs* by about 6 cm. The letters are 5 to *6l/2* cm. high, and perfectly legible. Copy of the editor. the Princeton Archaeological Expedition. 2 Inscr. No. 76: see also Part II, p. 140 ff, 3 No. 57. Part II, p. 137 f. 69. Babiska. East Church. On an otherwise plain block, built into a wall which appears to be the west wall of the East Church, in the course next below the string moulding, about 15 feet from the ground". This wall is shown in the lower photograph in Part II, p. 132. The inscription is on the west face of the block, but is placed upside down. Probably this wall fell, and was rebuilt at a later time when this inscription had lost its original importance. The stone measures 115 x 53 cm. The inscription runs the full length of the block: the top of the first line *is 4l/2* cm. from the original top of the stone, and the bottom of the second line 37 cm. from the original bottom. The letters are 6 cm. high, and are badly weathered. Copy of the editor. 1. Y AripNnNYMA--OIHCACTA__ 2. TujKT!CANTIrNTO/NYTO

Efs Beos *Kal* 6 Xpioros *avrov* /c(a)i To "Aytov *Uvevfia*, 6 7roii?o-as TA Tc3 KTta-avTt. 'Eyevero (tov) *$vv* Ctous *There is one God and his Christ and the) Holy Spirit, who made the give help?) to the builder. This) was built) in the) year 456.* (407-408 A.D.) 70. Babiska. East Church. On the lintel of a square door-frame, set close against the back of an archway, at the entrance of the court on the north side of the East Church. Directly across this court from the entrance are the ruins of a small, but very handsome, building, perhaps a baptistery. See Part II, p. 135. The lintel is so framed by the arch that both ends are hidden, and the date of the inscription can be seen only by looking between the stones. Evidently the present arrangement is not the one for which the lintel was designed originally. Possibly the square doorframe, originally in some other place, may have been moved here in order to close the entrance more effectively, perhaps when this court with its surrounding buildings was used, as other similar collections of buildings were used, as a fort. Possibly, on the other hand, the square doorframe may have been the original entrance to the court, built some seventy-five years after the church was finished: in that case the archway, and the present west wall of the church with which the arch is continuous, must have been built at some time later still.

The inscription is 2.26)4 m. long, the letters 4 cm. high, excepting o, which is sometimes not more than 24 cm. in height. Some of the letters show traces of red pigment. The first half of the inscription and the last six letters are well formed and clear, but the other letters are cramped and rather uncouth. Copy of the editor.

t

NONoMATIKViVXVTHAIoeHeiTTPoCoy-iC6TTITOVYAAB

HoCoYTTPcWYTTPH'ToYGKcp + 'Ei *bv6fia.Ti* K(vpio)v '1(t)(to)v X(piTTo)v eYXid el *irpocrotyis*, eVi *Tov eva./ 3eoTa,Tov) Mocreov, irp(e)cr(l3vTpov), p.(T)vb;) 'TTr()p(epeTaCov), Tov 0Kf '* (crows). + *In the) name of the) Lord Jesus Christ the vision* (?) *was completed,*

under the most provident Moseos, presbyter, in the) month Hyperberetaios, in the year) $2p. (October, 480 A.D.) I do not understand the meaning of *irpoaotyK;.* Properly the word signifies *appearance;* or *a sight,* or *a vision.* Possibly someone, in consequence of a vision, erected this doorway, so that the vision was thereby fulfilled. Or perhaps the *sight* referred to is the view, which this doorway frames, of the court, and especially of the building opposite to the entrance. If so, then the present inscription gives, approximately, the date of the "baptistery," with its very beautiful doorway.

71. Babiska. Church Oh St. Serou S. On the lintel of the west portal of the Church of St. Sergius, in the western part of the town. See Part II, p. 216 ff. Copied by Dr. Littmann and the

'lttt jt ' 'ir % eitor Squeeze and photograph.

;'MS?M£m The last word at the right end of this drawing is not quite correct: it should be zpPYN or ZAPYA. Inscr. 71. From a squeeze, photograph and copy. Scale i: 20. This is the latest date which, + "Ayce %yt) f$or,dtroV. lipase rr,u KaP7Tofop(tau) SO far aS 1 am aware-haS been *lokopovtia TMv Zopw* (or *Zapvk*). t ¥etous *rjvx-*+ discovered in a Greek inscription _, of this immediate region. For + *Holy Sergius help (us)! Receive the offering of Solomonidas, of the (tribe?) of Zoryn* (or *Zaryt) In (the) year 658.* the phraseology, Compare, for (609-610 A.d.) example, Wad. 2500.

72. Ba'udeh. Church. On the lintel of the south door of a church, in the southern part of the town, a short distance north of the wadi. The lintel is ornamented with plain mouldings of an early period. The lowest band contains the inscription, which is upside down, and begins at the right end of the moulding. The end of the inscription is 71 cm. from the end of the fascia, the whole of which measures 166 by 8 cm. The letters are 5 to 6 cm. high, and eight of them are formed by double lines, about the outside of which the stone has been cut back somewhat, to give the letters the appearance of being carved in relief,

as in No. 33. Copied by Dr. Littmann and the editor.

Squeeze and photograph. Doorway of inscr. 72.

It is possible that the author of this inscription intended to write: etou? T«t' «-ou?. *Year 385 year* (336-337 A.d.), as in No. 303 (dated 379-380 A.d.). But I believe that these letters are to be read as follows: ¥etous *rerpdrov In the 700 and) fourth year.* The word *rerpdrov,* then, is for *rerdpTov.* The same method of writing the date was em ployed in the neighboring town of Dar Klta:1 Miyvi *Uave(p,)ov* Inscr. 72. From a squeeze, photo, *T n m.t j r* graph and drawing. Scale 1:20.

7r(e)/u,7jrc, *rov Teraprov $; In the month Pa nemos, 5th day, of the500 and) fourth year,* i.e., July, 456 A.d. Also, at the same place:1 Mvos) *prep-Lo-Lov Tov* Se/carou *iTvTaKO(Tia(TTov* Ctous. (*The) Jth of the) month Artemisios, in the five-hundredth and) tenth year,* i.e., May, 462 A.d.

In the present case, if the era of Antioch was employed, as in all the other inscriptions of this region, the date is 655 A.d. And it is, of course, perfectly possible that, even after the middle of the seventh century, such a date was carved on a lintel which had long been standing. The doorway itself, however, as its mo ldings show, belongs to the end of the fourth century. It is later than a tomb doorway at Kfer, near Tell 'Akibrin,2 dated 360 A.d., perhaps later than the lintel of the church at Fafirtin,2 dated 372 A.d. On the other hand, it is older than the doorway of the church at Ksedjbeh, dated 414 A.d.,3 or that of the Church of Paul and Moses at Dar Kita, dated 418 A.d.4 Moreover this method of carving the letters,5 which is unusual, is found at Babiska, fifteen minutes walk away, in an inscription dated 389 A.d.6 And lastly, this unusual method of writing the date is found, as I have said, in this neighborhood and in inscriptions of about the same period, namely 456 A.d. and 462. I have not found any other examples. I believe therefore that the present inscription was written by someone more familiar with the era employed in the districts south and east of this, the socalled Seleucid era. If so, then the date given by this inscription 15392-393 A.d., which agrees perfectly with the period to which the doorway, in view of its style and mouldings, would be assigned.

It is most curious that the inscription was carved upside down and beginning with the right end of the lintel. Exactly the same phenomenon is found on the lintel of a house at Surkanya,7dated 406-407 A.d. Perhaps in these cases the stone-cutter, being more accustomed to reading Syriac from right to left than to carving Greek from left to right, reversed his copy and began at the wrong end of the stone. Perhaps also, in the present instance, the original inscription was so composed as to fill the whole space across the lintel; but when it was discovered how bad a job the workman was making, the work was stopped and the inscription left incomplete, the letters, perhaps, 1 Inscriptions found by the Princeton Archaeologi-5Dr. Littmann informs me that a similar method was employed cal Expedition in 1905. in carving many of the South Arabian inscriptions.

-'Princeton Archaeological Expedition, 1905. 6 No. 66. 3 No. 73 below. 7 Princeton Arch. Exped., 1905. In Nos. 82 and 210 of the 4 No. 57. present collection, the Greek letters are right side up, but are actually written from right to left. See Part IV, p. 7. being filled up with plaster, on which the complete inscription may have been painted —from left to right. Of course the plaster would long since have disappeared. 73. Ks£djbeh. Church. On the lintel of the eastern of the two doors in the south wall of a large church in the southeastern part of the town. See Part II, p. 135 f. The lintel of the present inscription is shown in the lower photograph on p. 136. On the jamb of the other doorway is a Syriac inscription published in Part IV, p. 39 f. The present inscription, including the cross, is 2.04 m. in length, and the letters 3 cm. high: they are clear, well-formed and regular, and almost all are perfectly legible. Copy of the editor.

Published by Berggren: //. Enrop. et Orient., II., p. 180. C.I. G. 8615.

Bizzos is doubtless the Syriac Biza or Bizza. A convent of Mar *Saint)* BTza. is mentioned several times in the *Syndoctica*, where lists of prelates from this region are given.1 M. ClermontGanneau2 quotes two inscriptions, from the Jewish cemetery at Jaffa, which refer to a family of Bizzos, e.g., *Mvr)p,(e)lov Twv Bi'££ov. 'EvddSe* K()it(u

Pe/3eK/ca 17 *prTi)p Mdvvov. Eiprjin). Uw&.* See also No. 265 f. below.

74. The following inscriptions, Nos. 74 and 75, are cut in the solid rock beside the ancient road, half a mile east of Kasr il-Benat. See Part II, p. 57 ff. The road at this point runs east and west. On the north side, about 4 feet above and 4 feet back from the present road, is a level place about 4 feet square, where traces of deep ruts of wagon wheels are to be seen, indicating that this was the original level of the ancient road. In the upright wall of rock at the back of this, and 38 cm. above it, a plate, 64 cm. high by 58 cm. wide, is sunk, 1 or 2 cm. deep, in which is inscription No. 75. A little above this again is a similar plate, 44 cm. high and 47 cm. wide, containing the inscription under discussion. The letters are 4 to 6 cm. high, and between the lowest line and the bottom of the plate is a space, 1 Wright: *Catalogue,* p. 706 ff. -*Recueil,* vi, p. 187 f. Inscriptions 74 and 75.

12 or 13 cm. high, which was left blank. A large cross, however, 11 cm. high and 7 cm. broad, has been carved, rather rudely, in this empty space near the center. The letters are well formed, and of a type common in the second century. The same type appears in No. 48, but badly executed. Some of the letters, however, are much weathered. Copy of the editor.

Published by M. Uspensky, *u Archaeological Monuments of Syria,"* p. 109. M. Chapot, in *B. C. H.* XXVI. P-17. 5 f

M. Uspensky's reading of this inscription is AIWNATO KPATO NOCOY; M. Chapot gives Eis *aitova To Kparos Tov Kvpiov fjpwv* ?— — —. I

Perhaps between the fourth 2 and fifth lines a line has been 3 omitted by

the stone-carver 4 from the original text, namely *c* VANTUJNINO: such an addition would have caused the last line of the inscription to fill the empty space at the bottom of the plate, where the cross was inserted, evidently at a much later time. Obviously the date of this inscription falls between 161 and 180 A.u.

Such expressions as «S *alcova To KpaTOS,* or the more USlial *irokXa. To. err* (sc. e"? *Tov /Sao-iXews),* or *7roXXd err),* were common forms of salutation. Similar salutations are still current in Turkish and Arabic.

75. Cut on the solid rock beside the ancient road, half a mile east of Kasr il-Benat, in the lower and larger of the two plates described under No. 74. The letters are 4 to *6y2* cm. high, and of a totally different character from those of the preceding inscription. Copied by Mr. Garrett and the editor.

Published by Berggren, *'It. Europ. ct Orient.,* II, p. 180. *C. I. G.* 8650. Uspensky, *A. M.* p. 109 ff. Chapot, in Inscription 75.

V. 1. In line 2, Uspensky, Chapot and Garrett all read- XOY. But A in this inscription has always the form A, so that it is easily mistaken for X: I believe that my reading is correct. In line 7, after OPOOHC, Berggren and Chapot read XX, Garrett /fx: Uspensky gives *6po0()ri(ov).* The first of the two letters in question seemed to me either 1 with a line across as a sign of abbreviation, or P: the second X or Y or some symbol unknown to me: in 1905, however, I read above this second character a small 0). In line 8 Uspensky read the date cx': all the other copies, however, give £X' as certain.

+ Kara *KeXev&Lv Iavov* (?), *rov iv$o£(ora.Tov) Kotjto1;) rrjs ew, hia 'Iwdvvov,* (row) *ap.TTp(ora.Tov) KaPKeWap(iov) Tov Knrpof3apa&e, eVtTj To 6pod4ri(ov) a(pa;) Bllkwv, lv8. rov £x' erv -J-By order of Paulos, the most glorious Prefect of the East, through Joannes, (the) most illustrious Chancellor of Kaprobarade, the boundary of (the) country of (the) Bizikoi was fixed (at this point), indiction 7, in the 637th year. (588-589 A.D.)*

The 637th year of the era of Antioch began on the first of September or the first of October, 588; the 7th year of the indiction series on the first of September of that year. The date of this inscription, therefore, falls between September first, 588, and September first, 589 A.d. According to Evagrius, *Eccl. Hist.*, vi, 7, quoted by M. Chapot, Asterios was Prefect of the East in 588, and was succeeded by a certain Ioanncs. But according to Evagrius' account, Asterios was deposed in June, 588, or earlier. How long afterwards Ioannes served in this office is not stated: Evagrius merely remarks that Ioannes was incompetent. Uspensky supplies A£tdxov, a name which is mentioned by Zosimus, v, 4 (ed. of Bekker, p. 251, 10). Possibly Paulos, if my reading is correct, may have been appointed *Conies Orientis* some time during the year 589.

The name *KairpofiapaSe* is interesting. Obviously *Kanpo-*and *xanep* are the Greek forms for the Semitic *kefr* =*village,* and are found in other ancient Greek names of Syrian towns.1 *Barad* is an Aramaic word meaning *hail: Kawpo/3apa.8,* therefore, *Hailtawn.* There are ruins of a large and handsome city of this period, not far north of Kal'at Sim'an, which are still called Brad by the modern natives: perhaps the chancellor of that city was sent as an arbitrator to fix this boundary line in 589 A.d. The form *Ka-rrpofiapabe* is singular, and I should be tempted to read *Kairpofiapa.8e(av).* M. Uspensky, on the other hand, cites a seal, which he reads as follows: *Kvpie* /3oi?0ei *K(Dvaravriv(f Trpeo-fUvrepat Kcli Kovovkxtjo-co)* Tw BapaSe. The inscription of the seal, however, is full of abbreviations, and between the A and the of Ba/mSc is what appears to me like a sign of abbreviation.

Perhaps the *Bl£lkoc* may have been the people of the convent of Mar вТza, an important monastery somewhere in the region of Antioch.2 76. Kasr Il-benat. Church. On a circular medallion on a capital of a column now lying in the ruins within the apse. See Part II, p. 140 ff. The capital seems to

'E.g., *Ku(ixrp) Ka7rpcu4'a/3u&uW, C. I. G.* 9893, and *Kairtp Na/Jot,* found

by the Princeton Arch. Exped. in 1905. 2 See Wright, *Catalogue,* p. 706 ff. have belonged to the first column from the apse, on the south side of the nave, medallion is 27 cm. in diameter, the letters 3 cm. high. Copy of the editor. Published by M. Chapot, in *B. C. H.* xxvi, p. 173.

The

Inscr. 76. From a copy and photograph. Scale 1:10.

X(picrTe) /So170i Kupiw T*eyi/Crg. Ey£a(levos ervfev* Tov *avrov* £ apVr os, *tfijal8l(ov)* eV (u/k'si. + *Oh Christ help Kyrios the) architect! In fulfillment of a voiv he built this church): the same (man) having died, (his) tomb (is) in (the) apse.* Capital, in the church at Kasr il-Benat, bearing Inscr. 76.

I take aXioW to be a diminutive of t/»aXts, in the sense of an arcosolium. The word data's is so used in No. 110.

Mr. Butler believes this church to be of the same date as the East Church at Babiska and the Church of Paul and Moses at Dar Kita, which were built in the early part of the fifth century. And it is quite possible that Kvpios, the architect mentioned in the present inscription, is the same as Kvpi9, the architect of the Babiska church, and кОро?, the architect of the Dar Kita church. If so, the name in the inscription of the latter should doubtless be amended to Kvp(t)os.

77. The following inscription is on the under side of a large stele lying on the line of the ancient road just mentioned, where this road ran due northeast, about 2j4 miles east of Babiska, and half a mile southwest of the ruins of an arch over the roadway called by the natives Bab il-Hawa. The stone lies on its face, with its head towards the center of the road, its lower end completely buried, and its upper end projecting so that at the top the face is about two feet above the ground. It was not possible to dig the stone out at the time, so that I was obliged to content myself with digging under the stone a hole in which I could lie, and thus read the inscription upside down.

This inscription begins 28 cm. from the top of the stone: it has nine lines, each about 9 cm. high, and separated

from each other by spaces 3 cm. high. The letters have forms common in the 6th century. Copy of the editor.

I have been unable to make satisfactory sense of this inscription; but I believe that if the stone were dug out, and turned over on its back, the inscription could be read and might furnish some valuable topographical information. Evidently this was a boundary stone. The first two lines are: *Xwpiop* Siaepet T« ©ew or T5 *6eL)x* Oikoj.-*This) place belongs to God,* or *to the divine house,* etc. Lines 6 and 7 contain well-known titles of dignitaries under the later empire, *iravevfTjfiov anb vTrdraiv,* which may be compared with those in No. 305 f.

78. Sermeda. Lintel. On a lintel lying beside the road, at the south of the village. The lintel is ornamented with a door-cap, at each side of which, on the background of the lintel, is an upright eiCeeoCKAIOXPICTOCAYTOYeTOYCHT palm-branch in relief. The inscrip Efs @eos Kal 6 X/aicrros aurou. Erovs fr. tion, on a broad cavetto moulding *One God and his Christ. In (the) year- jpo.* (341-342 A.D.) about the center of the door-cap, is 1.17 m. in length: the letters are 3 to 4 cm. high, and are well cut and clear. Copy of the editor.

Published by Uspensky, *A. M. S.,* p. 108.

79. Sermeda. Stele. On a fragment of a stele lying in the center of a courtyard in the northeastern part of the village: the stone had been dug out recently. The fragment measures 48 cm. in length, 20 in width, and 45 in thickness. The letters are 4 to 42 cm. high. Copy of Dr. Littmann.

The restoration of this inscription is necessarily uncertain. I suppose that the stone has been split lengthwise, so that part of each line 0 c has been lost; but it is impossible to discover with certainty how much e Y T has been lost from each. Probably the text was somewhat as follows: X *J* AN C os, Etuxov *dve'orn'(T)ei,* eov(s) *o(v)'* t N

— *os, (son) of Eutychos,set up (this stone), in the year4.J5 (?).f* (436-437 A.D.) тоут 60уt

Even the date is doubtful, and it is

not even certain that the inscription contains a date at all.

80. Sermeda. Lintel. On a broken 4, TOYCAAtM GMT-UJCAINA lintel in the eastern part of the village, now used as the lintel of the entrance etous af' of a modern house. The stone measures in(the)year53it (482-483 A.d.) io3 x 34 cm-. the break in the center of the inscription 25 cm. The letters are 4 to 7 cm. high. Copy of Dr Littmann. 81. Sermeda. Fragment. On a fragment of some sort of a base, now used as part of the mouth of a cistern, west of the village, beyond the houses. The part of the fragment which bears the inscription is 60 cm. long by 18 high. The letters are 5 cm. high, beautifully carved, deep and 1. 2. regular. Copy of Dr. Littmann. Published by Uspensky, *A. M. S.,* p. 108.

Letters similar to these, particularly the f, occur in No. 64, dated 143 A.d.

M. Uspensky Suggests iejpoi/ vabv... «ctut«' ef *Islcjv* daXw/LiaTtoz/ --_ *tem-ple _ _ _ built at his own expense. 82.* Sermeda. Fragment Of A Lintel. On a fragment now used as the left jamb of a doorway opening on one of the village streets, and facing westward. The stone, which is otherwise perfectly plain, is 76 cm. long, 38 wide, and 47 thick. At the bottom of the stone, as shown in the photograph, are cuttings similar to those found in the bottoms of lintels. In my opinion this was a part of a lintel, on which the inscription was carved from right to left. The letters are 8 to 12 cm. high. Copy of the editor.

Published by Uspensky, *A. M. S.,* p. 108.

Similar words occur on a lintel in Katura, No. 116. See also above, Chapter 1, p. 14. An inscription at Midjleyya, No. 210, is written backwards, as this is. Compare also No. 72. In the same way Semitic inscriptions are sometimes found written from left to right, following the Greek custom. See Part IV, p. 7. 83. Sermeda. A Fragment, built into the wall of a modern house, inside of a courtyard, in the northeastern part of the vil 1 Ti_ i_ 1 r uYri *vireip* uyietas *For* lage. The whole fragment measures 94 by r i »A r 39 cm. The inscription is

in the lower righthand corner, and occupies a space 51 by 22 cm. square. The letters are 8 to 10 cm. high. Copy of Dr. Littmann.

Inscr. 82.

From a photograph of the original stone. *Christ Jesus, cuter! For the health* 84. Sermeda. Stele. A stele now used as the lintel for the entrance to the courtyard of a modern house: the stone is 138 cm. long, Xpurr(i) *'lWov: thkk Jhe* ktters tQ y cm *Christ Jesus/* high. Copy of Dr. Littmann.

85. Sermeda. Fragment. A fragment of a lintel lying on the ground in a ETTjJOYE-VAAB OVnAPAMANN6UUeH(JU "garden" north of the village. The stone is 150 cm. long, the break in the *'I rod eika/ 3(eardrov)l* _ov, „ *aPap(o*-center of the inscription 25 cm. The let *vapiov), aveveoitfrj w ttvkcov?*J. ters are 5 to 6 cm. high. Copy of Dr. *Under the most devout warden, os, this door*-j ittmann *way(?) was restored.*

Published by Uspensky, *A. M. S.,* p. 108.

A *paranwnarios,* the Latin *mansionariiis* or *aedititus,* the German *messner,* was a lesser official who had special charge of a church building. The title evAa/Jeo-Taros was applied to officials of lesser dignity, e.g., to presbyters,2 to deacons,3 or even to the clergy collectively.4 86. 'amud Sermeda. Tomb. In an underground, rock-hewn tomb, three or four minutes' walk from the columns in the direction towards the modern village of Sermeda. Seven steep, narrow steps lead down to a door, 2 by 2 feet square. Within the doorway two more steps lead down to a chamber about 10 feet square, around three sides of which is a kind of a crib, the top of which is 4 feet above the floor and three below the ceiling. This "crib" is divided into two narrow sarcophagi on each side by a narrow partition left in the rock. The inscription is on the front of this "crib," at the left end of the left side, i.e., immediately to the left of the entrance. The lines measured from.91 to 1.08 m. in length, with spaces of from 3 to 5 cm. between them. The letters of the first line are 8 cm. high, the others less, the whole inscription measuring 48 cm. in

height. Copied by Mr. Butler and the editor.

I suppose that this priest had some claim to the use of the other sarcophagi for burying his dead. Such tombs seem to have been used sometimes by large families or groups of people. And doubtless the same sarcophagi were used again and again, when the bodies first interred in them crumbled away. Manlaios, however, secured for himself the exclusive use of this particular sarcophagus, evidently by a special contribution for that purpose. The name MaVXato?, if it is the Greek form of the Latin Manlius, is curiously spelled. The name Aira?, as Dr. Littmann has suggested tome,

'For this reading I am indebted to the 2 Nos. 70 and 73. 4 *C. I. G.* 8619. kindness of Professor Noldeke of Strassburg. 3 *C. T. G.* 8647. may be a *hypokoristikon* of 'aitioxos: perhaps this name may be read in an inscription from Da'el (in the Hauran), published by M. Fossey in *B. C.H.* xxi, p. 48: vA£i£o'? *Kal Za/8Sa5, viol Avra ...?* Kcureuov (i. e., Katrerrou?), crX.

The word itpev?, in view of the early date of this inscription, must be taken in its literal sense: the title, however, occurs in Christian inscriptions. M. ClermontGanneau, in discussing an inscription from the Mount of Olives, says:1 "L'emploi de Upeus, au lieu de *irpeofivTepos,* ne laisse pas d'etonner dans une inscription chretienne." 87. 'amod Sermeda. Bi-columnar Monument. The inscription is on the plinth-blocks, above the pedestal on which the bases of the columns rest, on the southeast side. The face of these blocks measured originally 3.44 by 0.48 m.: probably there were three separate blocks; but the center has been broken out. See Part II, p. 59 f. In the rock on which this monument stands are two tombs, each entered by a narrow stairway, and consisting of a small square chamber surrounded by arcosolia. Close by are other similar tombs.

The first part of the first line of the inscription, twelve letters, is 76 cm. long; of the second line, thirteen letters, 98 cm.; of the third, sixteen letters, 121 cm.

; and of the fourth, eleven lettersj 71 cm.: the last part of the fourth line, ten letters, is 60 cm. long. The fourth line measured originally 2.78 m. in length: hence the break in the cen 1. KYJrelCAAelA 2. rN-NAAe£ANAPO ZT 3. A-VCVNnANTOCOIKO AIACWKPA 4. TOYTOVANTIO 1PIANAIKOVS

Kwpi(o)ts *Wetjdyhpcp Kal Bepviic* (ia) *y* (£)(?) 'AXef*dvhpoy* ZTA—V *o-vviravTo; O'kov* (?) . 8ta ScoKparov row 'AtTiofou, *erovs* — p'. HavSi/cou c'.
For Masters Alexandros and Bernikianos (?) son of Alexandros, of all their /iouse(?) , in the) year 18-, Xandikos 6th. (April, 132-141 A.D.) Published by Waddington, No. 2687.

For this use of Ku/hos, see above under No. 67: for these names, compare No. 64.

88. 'amud Sermeda. Tomb. In another rock-hewn tomb, about fifty feet west of the bi-columnar monument. In this tomb there were three arcosolia, each containing four sarcophagi with their ends towards the center of the tomb-chamber. The inscription is on the end of the sarcophagus at the left side of the arcosolium opposite 1 *Recueil*, v, p. 167. So also " *apxiipevs, evique,* dans l'inscription de la mosaique de Qabr Hirom pres de Tyr, 1. 3." ter of this line measures 1.47 m., a space sufficient for about twenty-one letters. About thirteen letters have been lost from the center of the third line, and about nineteen from the second. There is no evidence on the monument itself as to the original length of the first line. Copy of the editor. the entrance. The letters are similar to those of No. 86, but are badly weathered. Copy of the editor.

The name *Gennadios* 1. rE N N _ I □ *Tevv* a *tou* (*This is the grave) of Gen-* and its abbreviated forms 2. BAP AD BapSov. *naios, son) of Bardos. Gennadi, Gemma', Gennai* or *Genni,* are found, not infrequently, as Syriac names.1 Bd/8o?, on the other hand, suggests rather the Safai'tic and Arabic *Burd,* Compare, however, BdpSa?, in *C. I. G.* 8692 and 8756, *Kairpo/SapaSe* in No. 75, and *Bapa8dvr);* in No. 153.
89. Dana. Tomb. Over an open arcosolium in the rock near the foot of the mon-

ument described below under No. 92. I believe that this is the inscription which is now concealed by a modern house: if so, I do not believe that there is any connection between the monument and the inscription. See Part II, p. 73 f.; de Vogie *S. C* , p. 117 and pi. 93.
The inscription has been published by Franz in *C. I. G.* No. 4457, after copies by Richter, Pococke, Berggren and Steinbiichel; by Texier and Pullan, in *Architecture Byzantine,* p. 194; by Waddington, No. 2688. The following is Waddington's reading: TOYCBOT _ "etod? /sot', *Ltvo% Avcrrpov y',* 'HXioSwpa cc *MdpOwv* MHNOCAYCT PO *irroirja-av p.v7jp.T); yapiv'* o-*fupwre.* Kc *(rot* To. *SiirXa.* HAIOAWPA nOIHCANAITTAA,. n,. „......
In the) year 372, month Dystros 3rd, Heliodora and Mar KMAP0UUN MNHMHCXAPIN *thon made this) for sake of memory: it is consecrated. And* AJIGPUUT *lee P) twce so mucn-*(March, 324 A.D.)
V. 1.: in the first part of the fourth line Richter gives KEMAieiWNen; Pocock KEMAieilNEn; Steinbiichel KKAY NC TT; Berggren K6MAIEX1NE n; Texier and Pullan KMAEI NE; Callier MAICHN.3
In the second part of the first line Richter gives Yr K6COITA; Berggren
Yr KEZOITA; Texier and Pullan (YD KECOITA.
Both *Heliodora* and *Marthon* appear to be feminine names. Professor Noldeke has communicated to me that Mordtmann explained the latter name to him in a letter, a long time ago, as MiimD = *Their Lady* or *Mistress.* Or *-on* may be merely the diminutive termination added to *Martha,* Aramaic for *domina, mistress.*
Franz and Waddington both considered *afaepan-e* to be for *dtepwrat.* It is singular, however, that in all three cases, Nos. 49, 89 and 112, in which I found this word in Syrian inscriptions, it is spelled with a final c, although two of these inscriptions I be 1 But compare *Alp.* Mu«8dvios '*Afjptfia awo* Sttoociov rewtou 3 " C'est-a-dire MAI0X1N ": M. Salomon Reinach, who opaiv 'A *nafieoiv, C. J. L.* v, 8728, and see the notes on No. 48 publishes copies, made

by Callier in 1830-1834, in *R. E. G.* above. in (1890), p. 82, No. 64.
2 See *BopSot* in Wad. 1990 and 2265. lieve to be as old as the second century. Possibly then the form should be regarded as 2nd plu. subj. In any case the word was employed, like a good many other words or phrases in sepulchral inscriptions, as a warning against violation of the tomb, or the use of the tomb or site for any other purpose.
The words *Koi a-ol To.* Sittxo seem odd in this connection. Doubtless they were placed here because of a desire to avoid the envy of others. The phrase occurs frequently on house lintels: compare Nos. 10, 114, 235 and 262.
90. Dana, Lintel. On a large lintel, now the lintel of the entrance to a modern courtyard, on one of the main streets. It is evident from the account given by MM. Texier and Pullan, that this lintel belonged originally to the church described by them in *Architecture Byzantine,* p. 193 f., pi. Lix. The church is not mentioned by M. de Vogiie, however, and was not seen by the members of the American expedition: doubtless it has been destroyed since 1840, when it was found by MM. Texier and Pullan. See Part II, p. 140 f. The inscription was published by Waddington, who describes it as "Sur un linteau de porte, en face de l'eglise." *C. I. G.* 9154, however, to which Waddington refers, is not the same inscription, but one which is at Serdjibleh and is published under No. 95 below. Copy of the editor.
Texier and Pullan, *Archit. Byz.,* p. 194. Wad. 2689. Uspensky, *A. M. S.,* p. 105.
EICeEOCKAIOXPICTOCAY-
TOYKAITOAriONnNEYMABOHGH
ETOYCBAWrOPTTIESKZINAIK'Z +

I
K
O
C

Efs Hcos *Kal* 6 Xptoros *avrov* /cat To "*Ayiov Hvevfia-fiotjdr)* T5 (*oi)kq* O-ouc?). *etou5 /8X£', (ir)(vo;) Fopmeov /c£', ivoiK.* One God and his Christ and the Holy Spirit: help thy house (?). *In the) year jj2, (the) 2jth of (the) month Gorpieos, indiction 7.* (September, 483 A.D.).

line, after erovs, Bnuumhn, and at the end INAK/Z.

My copy shows that there may have been one or two letters in the perpendicular line at the right, above I, K, o, C.

The phrase Otko? *KvpCov* or *Oikos Tov @eou* is of course common in the Psalms. The word Otko? itself is used, in the writings of the Church Fathers, in the sense of *church,* but is generally qualified in some way,as e.g., rows *e &Krqpiovs Oikow;,* Euseb., *deVttaCoust.,*in, cap. 45; *Upbv Oikov iKKr)ria7* ibid., cap. 43; *oifcous eKKr)riov,* Euseb., *Eccl. Hist.,* IX, cap. 9 s.f.; *To. Kara rmv ayuov Oikwv TrpooTdyp.aTa,* Greg. Naz., *Orntio* iv, cap. 86. Perhaps then we might read: *6 Oikos* or *o7fco?,* or simply Tkos eK/ cXo-ia?, or *tov ayiov* etc..

V.I.: after BOH0H Waddington gives u, and below this, in a perpendicular line, the letters T, Uj, K, A, l. M. Uspensky gives, in the perpendicular line, T, III, B,o, C.

Texier and Pullan give, in the first line, BOH9EI, and nothing further on the right; in the second

This inscription is particularly important, as Waddington has noted, because it proves that in this region and at this period the local year began with the first of September, in conformity with the years of the indiction series, instead of with the first of October, as was usual where the era of Antioch was employed. For the 532nd year of the era of Antioch began in the Autumn of 483 A.d. and ended in the Autumn of 484. But the 7th year of the indiction series began in September, 483, and ended with August, 484. Consequently September of the 7th indiction must have been the first and not the last month of the year 532 of the era of Antioch, i.e., of the year 483-484 A.d. See the commentary on Waddington, No. 2689, and also on No. 273 below.

The natives said that this inscription had been copied, about seven years before, by a European, who told them to preserve it carefully, for it stated that if any of the people of that country were bitten by serpents they should not die. Some St. Patrick visited the country of

these people long ago, and there are no serpents there of any account now. But still the people regard this stone with unusual interest, although I am not sure whether they really believe that it has a magic power or not.

91. Dana, Fragments Of A Lintel (?). Two fragments, built into a wall along one of the main streets, near a street corner. The two stones were near together, frag, A on end, frag, B upside down. The fragments undoubtedly belong together and form one inscription, probably that of a house-lintel. The first line is broken by three symbolic disks; but the lower line was continuous, and seems to be complete except at the beginning. Copy of the editor.

Published by M. S. Reinach, after a copy made by Callier, in *J?. E. G.* Ill, p. 82, No. 65. M. Chapot, in *B. C. H.* XXVI, p. 175, Nos. 16 and 17.

Fragment A. Fragment B. On the meaning and purpose AV(d)POVTTA ()NTOCK()9POCOVK f this inscription see above, XVCI6T6AIO 0HMAOUJ!NirfH?DTOV_ haPter P '9 f-The form

K0/ds is doubtless for *iyQpos* / but possibly e'xpos was actually written, for the stone is now placed *Where the cross is present, (the) enemy shall not prevail,* high above the ground and is *Finished in (the) month Loos, indiction 12, of the sgSt/i year.* ,, r-,.

'badly weathered: K(mo-Jvuo-t is (August, 550 A.D.) J for *KdTiorxvcrei* 92. DANA, Monument. On the south side of the base of a monument, consisting of four Ionic columns, upon a base about 8 feet high, supporting a canopy. Part II, p. 73 f., de Vogue, pi. 93. Close to the monument, but at an odd angle to it, as at 'Amud Sermeda, are several tombs in the rock. The first of these is a simple open arcosolium hewn where the rock presents a perpendicular face about 8 feet high, as if there had once been a quarry here. There are other quarries near by. Over the arcosolium are two long palm branches, and between them a star. I am inclined to believe that this is the tomb to which the monument belongs. Next to this tomb, towards the right, is a still simpler arcosolium in the rock. Beyond this again is a modern

house, which appears to have been built but a few years ago. The natives said that behind this house was the entrance to another tomb, with an inscription which, however, could not be seen now, doubtless because the face of the rock formed the rear wall of the house and was plastered over. We did not enter the house, feeling that to do so would make trouble with the natives, who were not well disposed, and especially with the lady of the house, who was very ill-disposed, at that time, and believing also that this inscription could be no other than that published by Waddington, No. 89 above.

The letters of this inscription are large and now very faint, so that only a few, near the end of the inscription, could be read at all. They occupy perhaps a fourth or a fifth of the whole space: there is space for one or two more letters on the right of these. The letters are about 8 cm. high. Copy of the editor.

Li r--r 1 r-A A "O *8eiva* eVoi-*Such an one built this monu*

I V A A T)rev erots aXcr'). *ment in the) year 231 (?). (182 A.D.?)*

This date is of course most uncertain. I have placed r in the hundreds' place chiefly because, in Mr. Butler's opinion, this monument is not later than the third century. The letters also are of the same type as those of the bicolumnar monument at 'Amud Sermeda, dated about 132 A.d. Perhaps, however, we should read the date of the present inscription aM_T', 331 = 282 A.D. 93. Serdjibleh. House. On the architrave of the second story of a colonnade before a building facing south, in the southern part of the town. Of the colonnade five piers in each story remain. The rear wall of the building itself, which seems to have been a private house, is built of unusually large and handsomely dressed stones. See Part II, p. 171 f. The architrave has at the top a plain band, with a cavetto below, 1. 6TOYC O I t MHNOCAOOY S KNONNOC 2. enoiHce

¥Brou5 *dif, firjvbs Aoov ;k NtWos iirovrjcre. In (the) year jip, Loos 26th: Nonnos made (i.e., built this house?).* (August, 471 A.D.) and below that again three plain fasciae. The first line of the inscription is on the first of these, and measures 257 cm. in length: the letters are 6 to 7 cm. in height. The second line is at the right end of the next lower fascia, and measures 31x6 cm. In the lowest fascia, under the o of eVotijo-e, is a cross, measuring 8 by 7 cm. Both the letters and some of the individual words are well spaced from one another. Copy of the editor.

The name No'ios is found in various forms in Syria. Compare *C. I. G.* 9182. See also the next inscription.
94. Serdjibleh. House. On the architrave of the second story of a colonnade similar to the preceding, and almost in a YTneTAN-6AteTOYC NIOAIANONNOY,..,.
„ ' , line with it, but about a hundred paces fur *OW* «"ov-()'. 8« ther east. The profile of the architrave is
Noi"/ov' the same as that of No. 93: the inscription *In year 5i9* (?), *indiction p* (?), js Qn the lowest fascia Qf the mouldings.
through Nonnos. (470-47 A.D.) gee Jj p , f Copy Qf
Evidently Nonnos was the architect of these two buildings.
95. Serdjibleh. Lintel. On a lintel supported on its two jambs, standing alone in a cultivated field, directly opposite the west door of the church, and twenty-three paces distant from it. The inscription is on the fascia next to the lowest in the mouldings of the lintel, and measures 166x4 cm.: I could find no traces of letters in the fascia below. Copy of the editor.

Published by Berggren, */tin. Europ. et Or.,* II, p. 167. *C. I. G.* 9154.
IC9OCKOXPICTOCAYTOYtYC-
TAeiOYNOYMHPAPU

E19 0o? Kc 6 X/aioro? *avrov.* + *Eii/oradiov, vovfirjpapiov.* (There is) one God and His Christ. + Of Eustathios, numerarius (i.e., *treasurer*).

The character X, at the end of this inscription, indicates that it was carved probably in the sixth century. The doorway appears to have been that of the office or the dwelling of a numerarius, a public, perhaps an imperial, treasurer. "Numerarii erant ii, qui publicum nummum aerario inferebant, hoc est, qui pecuniam Regiam, ex tributis, et portoriis,

et vectigalibus partam in aeraria inferebant": A. du Cange, *Gloss. Lat.* Probably then the building to which this lintel belonged was a treasury. Possibly this Eustathios may be the same as the historian mentioned by Evagrius, 1, 19-m, 37, who was born in Epiphanea (Hama) about 500 A.d. 96. Serdjibleh. Lintel. On a lintel lying face up on a pile of ruins, just north of the tower. The inscription is on the fascia at the top of the door-cap. This fascia measures 127 by Sl/2 cm. The letters are 6 cm. high, and most of them 6 cm. broad, with spaces of 4 cm. between them. Copy of the editor.

Possibly there was a cross between o and *foj)d5v.* Possibly also there may be traces IceeeocoBOH9UUNTTACI letters in the fascia next to the lowest, i.e., the v, third from the top; but of this I could not be sure.

Ets ®eo? o *(3or)0»v-naat,.*

At the left of the door-cap, on the flat face of the *(There is) one God, who helpeth all. sXoxvz,* is an A, about 30 cm. high: on the right, in the corresponding place, an w, 38 cm. broad and 24 cm. high.
97. "tokat ou Indjir-keui." Epitaph. Described by Waddington as follows: "Sur une pierre brisee et employee dans une cloture, sur la bord de la route d'Alep." Waddington, No. 2690.

Waddington thought it prob-APT — Brw«..., os *'Aprejuriov* .., able that this inscription gives gTAY *ireXsvrrjo-ev* raiaos cV 'EyiaX.acrip(?), the ancient name of the village. jHCCNrA " y/tfo/os. "This village," he says, "which IANOC is called Tokat by the Arabs Nrl" *In (the) year. .. , on (the) .. of (the) month*
A 111/-1 A r-r 11 *Artemtstos, died Gaianos in Egialosta Ci),a?ed* and Indiir-KeuT or *Village-AmclA* TH-*vears 'S J* ,.. T6NOM *?ears of-figs* by the 1 urks, is situated on the main road from Aleppo to Antioch and Alexandretta, about five hours' march from Aleppo." I have never visited this place myself. The name *Tokat* may very well be ancient, for among the church dignitaries of Northern Syria in the sixth century, mentioned by Wright, *Catalogue,* p. 707, there is one from "Ipn: *TKD,* which

may be rendered *Tokad.* 98. Derit 'azzeh. Sculptured Panel. On a panel of some sort, with figures in high relief, built into the wall of a modern house. Only the left side of the panel is visible: the rest has been broken off, or is now concealed by the stairway which abuts the wall which contains the panel. See Part II, p. 273.

The first line of the inscription is on the upper band, above the figures. The letters of this line are clear, deep and straight. The second line is on the lower band, below the figures: its letters are smaller and less distinct than those of 1. NIKHCAHNH r J fi, 4-1 11 j
„ the upper line, and some of them are entirely covered by mud 2. AiCTTOIHC6N *rr J J* and plaster. Copy, made by the editor, of part of the text only.

Published by Pococke, *Inscr. Antiq.,* 1, p. 3, No. 11. *C. I. G.* 4454. Uspensky, *A. M. S.,* p. 103 and pi. 43.

Pococke's reading is given as follows:
From M. Uspensky's publication 1. NEIKH IEAHNH EPX1Z HA.OI KAINEI-ft g Qf second 2. AllTTIIENTTOAAOIZEYK. ... .g ACnoTHCNnOAAOICY, then space for about nine letters, followed by CnoTUNXAi.

The first line obviously gives a list of the gods whose figures are sculptured below their names: Nike *(Victory),* Selene *the Moon),* Eros *(Love),* Helios *the Sun),* etc. Concerning the second line I must agree with Franz, who says: "Quid ibi dictum sit, exputari nequit."

Admission to the courtyard, where this relief was found, was secured with some difficulty, as the people of the village were unusually unfriendly and suspicious, and because, as it was baking day in this particular family, the house was full of women. It was my intention to return at a more favorable time, and to make a more thorough examination of this relief and its inscription; but our journey to the Djebel Shekh Berekat made this impossible. The natives told me that this house had been built within the last ten or fifteen years, and that, within the memory of some of their number, the relief had been part of a large ruin, which had now disappeared:

the whole relief was then visible.

99. Derit 'azzeh. Fragment. Found lying in a street near the center of the village. The letters are very rude and uncertain. Copy of the editor.

Published by Uspensky, *A. M. S.*, p. 103.

OY AA0 n tne sccond line M. Uspensky read 0 instead of , in the fourth A I x e after tne v: otherwise his copy does not differ essentially from that given B here. He does not attempt to restore the text, nor have I been able to B p V discover any meaning in this inscription.

ioo-io8a. Djebel Shekh Berekat. Temenos Of Zeus Madbachos And Selamanes, 80 To 120 A.u. The Djebel Shekh Berekat, which closes the Plain of Dana on the north, is far the most conspicuous mountain peak in Northern Central Syria. Upon its summit are to be found, besides a modern Mohammedan weli, the ruins of a large sacred precinct, which is shown by the inscriptions upon its walls to have been built at the end of the first and the beginning of the second century after Christ. Doubtless this was the site of a cult much older than these walls.

This mountain was visited at the beginning of the eighteenth century by Johannes Heyman, at that time a pastor attached to the Dutch Consulate at Smyrna, and later Professor of Oriental Languages in Leyden: this traveller was accompanied on his journey by the Dutch Minister, Johannes Aegidius van Egmond van der Nyenburg.1 Heyman seems to have copied only one of these inscriptions, namely No. 104; but about the same time G. Cuper received from a correspondent in Aleppo, probably not Heyman, a better copy of this same inscription and two others, probably Nos. 100 and 102.2 However, the copies of the other two inscriptions do not seem to have been published by him, unless perhaps in his *Dissertations stir Diverses Matieres de Religion et de P.Jiilologie* (La Haye, 1714, 11, p. 47), which I have not yet been able to

'Egmond and Heyman: *Reizen door een gedrclte van Europa, klcin Asictt, Syrien,* etc., 11, p. 401. See Cuper: *Lcttres de*

Critique, pp. 194, 362, 451.

2See Cuper, 1. c, pp. 348, 353, 457,467 f., 573.

see: Muratori, in his *Novum thesaurum veterum iuscriptionum,* 1, p. 64, and iv, p. mcmlxxviii, gives from Cuper only No. 104. Three of these inscriptions were copied two or three decades later by Richard Pococke, and published in his *Inscriptiones Antiquae,* 1752, 1, p. 2 f., Nos. 6 to 9,1 from which they were republished in the *C. I. G.,* in, Nos. 4449-4451. In our own times this mountain has been visited by M. Max van Berchem (1895), M. Rene Dussaud (1895), M. l'abbe Chabot (1897), M. Th. Uspensky (1900) and M. Victor Chapot, whose report on this locality, including two new inscriptions, was published in the *Bulletin de Correspondance HelUnique* for 1902: its inscriptions have been the subject of a learned article by M. Clermont-Ganneau in his *Etudes d' Archeologie Orientate,* Vol. 11, and were also published by me in *Hermes,* Vol. XXXVII.

The summit of the mountain is approached most easily from Derit 'Azzeh, a modern village situated near the foot of the slope on the eastern side: from here the ride to the ancient precinct takes about an hour and a half. The first part of this ride is over very rough and rocky country, but the latter part over the steep but smoother pastureland of the almost conical peak. The road winds about the mountain and reaches the summit on the northwestern side, near the grave of the Mohammedan saint who is said to have given his name to the place. This grave is a small square building with the usual whitewashed dome. Adjoining it on the western side is a newer and still smaller apartment. The lower part of this tomb consists of very good masonry, whereas the Modern buildings at the north wall of the temenos.

upper courses are composed of From a photograph, smaller stones of irregular size, more poorly laid and obviously belonging to a later period. A few yards to the east of the tomb stands a second building of one story and with a flat roof, narrower than the tomb but

nearly twice as long. The greater part is more roughly built than the tomb, and in much the same manner as the smaller chamber of the tomb building and the upper courses of the tomb itself. Apparently the outer wall of the ancient temenos forms the lower part of the northern wall of the tomb and of the south wall of the second building.2

This ancient temenos occupies the summit of the mountain. It is, as the accompanying plan shows, a four-square precinct, oriented correctly to within two or three degrees. In order to obtain an even surface the summit of the mountain was leveled

'See also Pococke's *Description of the East and Some* scriptions or other objects of archaeological interest might be *Other Countries,* 1745, Vol. 11, p. 170. found here: on my second visit, in 1905, I entered these 2 In my article in Hermes, I suggested that possibly inbuildings, but found nothing.

off, and the surface so obtained further enlarged by building up retaining walls, which, r: continued above the level inside, formed the en I closing walls of the precinct. The walls consist r"—=i of large and handsome blocks, laid two courses deep. The blocks which I measured varied in length from one to one and a half meters, and most of them were fifty-five centimeters high.' Most, if not all, of the inscriptions were carved on the outer surface of the temenos wall. They contained the names of the builders and, at least in some cases, the dimensions of those sections of the wall built by these various persons, the cost, the name of the contractor or builder, and the date. They show that these walls were erected at the end of the first and the beginning » of the second century after Christ, by various in

Plan of the temenos, showing the location of..'.

the inscriptions. dividuals, at their own cost, in fulfillment of vows.

In my opinion there can be no doubt about the era of these inscriptions. Muratori, following Cuper's example, assigned them to the Seleucid era; but even then Joseph de Bernard La Bastie, in his *Diatriba de diis quibusdam ig-*

notis, published by Muratori himself in Tome i. of his *Thesaurus,* p. 64 f., had shown that Cuper was wrong, and had proposed either an unknown era of Beroea (Haleb), or the era of Antioch, beginning with the year 49 B.c. For the cost of that section of the wall mentioned in the inscription discussed by Cuper and Muratori is given in denarii, and that could hardly have been the case before the Roman conquest, which took place eighty years after the date adopted by Cuper. Franz, in the third volume of the *C. I. G.* (No. 4449 ff.), proposed for these inscriptions the "epocha Syromacedonica" (ab a. u. c. 585, i.e., 69 B. C.). But, in the first place, it is certainly false, as Prof. Kubitschek has said, to treat the socalled Pompeian era as a provincial era because its introduction in certain cities coincides with the establishment of the province.2 In the second place, as far as can be determined with certainty, all the inscriptions, with the exception of two, in all the region in which the Djebel Shekh Berekat lies, are dated according to the era of Antioch. In three of these the era is determined beyond all question by the indiction number, which is given together with the number of the year, and these three inscriptions are from towns in the immediate neighborhood of the mountain.3 Moreover, the two exceptions mentioned4 seem to belong to the second century before Christ, and therefore do not affect the question at issue. I have no hesitation, 1 See below, p. 107. 3 Der Sim'an: 479 A.d. (Wad. 2692), Dana: 483 A.D. 2In Pauly-Wissowa: *Jieal-EncyclopadU,,.6g.* (Wad. 2689), and Refadi: 510 A.d. (Wad. 2696).

Wad. 27 3 a and 2719.

therefore, in dating the inscriptions of the Djebel Shekh Berekat according to the era of Antioch.1

The sides of the temenos, according to Mr. Garrett's measurements, have the following dimensions: the north side is 67.556 meters long, the east side 67.775 m- the south side 68.406 m., the west side 68.39 m-But since tne sides of the square, as Mr. Garrett tells me, were not measured out with a tape, but with a theodolite and stadia rod, and since at

least on two corners it was impossible to set up the rod exactly at the outermost angle, these dimensions may be incorrect to the extent of two or three feet. The builders of the temenos naturally reckoned its dimensions in cubits, and we should expect that the sides of such a precinct would exhibit some multiple of the local unit. What this unit was may be seen from the dimensions of the several blocks. The thickness I measured on one block only, namely that which bears inscription No. 101: this I found to be 40 cm. But since the edges of the stone were somewhat broken, the thickness may perhaps have been somewhat greater originally. I measured the height of eight blocks, of which four were exactly 55 cm., two 54 cm., and two more 53 cm. high. The irregularity of these dimensions may perhaps be explained by the fact that the edges of some of these blocks also were somewhat broken, for only when the stone was found in what is now the uppermost course, was its height less than 55 cm.2 Accordingly it appears that we have to do here with the socalled Phoenician cubit, which belonged also to the Macedonian system, and that the blocks were one cubit = 41.25 cm. thick, and one and one third cubits, or two feet, high, the foot being 27.5 cm. in length.3 If, then, we assume that this unit of measure is to be found in the dimensions of the temenos, furthermore that each side was in reality 67.65 m. long, and finally subtract from this figure four times 41.25 cm. for the thickness of the walls at each end, we find that the length of each side of the precinct, inside the walls, was exactly 160 cubits. Now 160 cubits, i.e., 240 feet, equal two actus, according to the Greco-Roman system; consequently, the area of the precinct, according to the Greco-Roman system of land measure, was exactly one heredium = two iugera: the actual size, however, of this area depended upon the length of the local cubit of 41.25, or the local foot of 27.5 cm., and not upon the Greco-Roman foot, which was 29.6 cm. in length. 4

In the center of the precinct are still broken drums of columns and rectan-

gular blocks. It is, however, impossible without excavation to determine the character of 1 See also M. Clermont-Ganneau, 1. c, p. 47, and M. Cha-*Handbuch, 2"* Aufl. 1, S. 871 and 859. Hultsch, *Metrologie, 2,c* pot, *B. C. H.,* xxvi, p. 178. Bearb., S. 582 ff. 2 On my later visit I measured a large number of stones 4 Mr. Flinders Petrie, in an article on "The Tomb-Cutters' and found much greater irregularity than I had expected, Cubits at Jerusalem," in the *Quarterly Statements of the Pales*with respect both to height and thickness: at the same time, *tine Exploration Fund,* 1892, p 28 ff., gives the following I believe that the normal course was intended to be approxi-values, in inches, of various cubits: Phoenicia, 22.6; Carmately 55 cm. high and somewhat more than 40 cm. thick. thage, 22.3; Sardinia, 22.1; Haurdn, 22. 2; Egypt, from 20.5 3 Nissen, *Griech. u. Rom. Metrologie,* in Iwan Muller's to 20.7; the old Jewish cubit, probably 25.2; the Roman foot, 11.6, or 11.7 in the provinces. the building which stood here. Farther towards the east there seems to have stood an altar, and north of the center again is a pile of ruins covered with earth, in which a few fragments of columns are visible. This last-mentioned heap consists doubtless of the remains of the stoa, or colonnade, which Pococke believed to have been here.1

The walls of the temenos are now at no point more than two courses above the present level of the interior of the precinct, except at and near the weli, where the ruins are somewhat higher. Without the walls, at their foot and farther down the hill, lie piles of fallen blocks: some of these are parts of an architrave. Still farther from the walls, at a distance of perhaps ten or fifteen meters on the north, east and south sides, are low and dilapidated stone fences, built from the ruins of the ancient walls, and evidently constructed to enclose the sheep which still, as the natives told us, graze on the mountain. Four of the inscriptions are still in situ in the wall itself, the rest lying either in the piles at the foot of the wall, or in or near the stone fences. Their position is indicated on the plan, except in the case of those discovered by M. Chapot, which he shows to have been found at some little distance below the walls, on the east side of the hill.

100. In the southern wall, a few feet west of the southeast corner (No. 6 on the plan). The upper part of the inscription, lines i through 8, is carved upon a stone 1.53 by 0.53 m.: the lower part, lines 9 through 12, is upon three stones measuring 1.26, 0.56, and 1.11 m. in length respectively, and 55cm. in height: the letters are *5/2* to 6 cm. high, and the lines of the lower part about 2. 20 m. long.

Copied by Cuper's unknown correspondent, by Pococke, and M. van Berchem; also by Dr. Littmann, from whose drawing the following facsimile was made. Pococke, */user. Antiq.*, p. 2, Nos. 7 and 8; *C. I. G.* 4449; Clermont-Ganneau, *Etudes*, II, p. 35 ff., No. iv; Chapot, *B. C. H.*, Vol. XXVI (1902), p. 177 f.; M. Uspensky, *Archaeological Monuments of Syria*, 1902, p. 98 ff. =" *Izviestiya " of the Russian Archaeological Institute at Constantinople*, Vol. VII.

V.I., line 2: ANTIOXOY, Pococke; after 8e in the same line, PIIIKIOAEIY-, Pococke; BEUDV H, van Berchem. Line 3, before *airov,* OPY, Pococke; YY, van Berchem; after *i-mKakovfievT* in the same line, PHAX, Pococke; BNA?, van Berchem. Line 5, after *olKoSofirjoavres,* EPO, Pococke; l-KD, van Berchem. Line 9, at the beginning, TTI — Z--vPOYI, Pococke; EZYYDYI, van Berchem; "La premiere lettre 1 *Description of the East, u,* p. 170.

Southeast corner of the temenos. Prom a photograph.

With the evident restorations, the text of this inscription is as follows: 1. Ail *MaS/3d)((i* /cai ScXa/udVei, *7raT/3uoi deois, evj(i)v* 2 *'avti6)(ov, Ko.6' vloOecrCav* Se 0o£i Xov 3 w *avrov,* Kai (0£iXa, 17 *iirtKaXovpivrj* —jrjcu 4 ov, T) yvvr) *avrov, Kal* Sgktcis 17 *pTjnqp,* ai 0eo 5 JftKrei?, 01 uioi *avrdv, oLKoSoprjcravTe;* ejxri 6. cray *eK* Twc Zsiw ef T5 *dpKTLKw Tov Trepifiokov pepei* 7. *8pa)(pwv) _. OlKoS6pr)o-av Kal iv* Tw *peo-r)/p/3pLva Tov av* 8. *Tov ire/*

3iy8oXou *pepei, pijKov; pev d-rrb dvaroXrjs iirl* Suctip 9. fl"??'x a s £ wous 8e Tr»7x«s i#' _, *Spa)((pwv)* JpC-' *dpf)ore* 10. pas 8e rds Oikoso/a la 9 Sid NeiKxTopos rot) Me 11. *Viokov oiicohopov, 8pa(pi!v),arrf* ?'_ "Erous eXp', 'A7reX 12. Xaiou if?'

It is immediately apparent, as M. Clermont-Ganneau has pointed out, that in this inscription we have to do not only with the same family, but with the same members of this family, and with the same builder, as in the inscription which follows: the latter therefore may be used to restore still further the lost portions of the inscription under discussion. It is evident also that the present inscription is the later of the two, for in it mention is made of the work described in the other.

In the second line of the present inscription the name of the father of the principal person is evidently Antiochos, his adopted father, Theophilos. Restoring the lost portions of these names, we lack at the beginning of the line, supposing this to have been equal to the first in length, some eight letters, which must have formed the name of the principal person.[2] Now the number of letters in each line, as shown bylines i, 6, and 8, varies from forty to forty-four. The second line, as we have restored it thus far, contains but thirty-eight. It is quite possible, therefore, that several letters 1 I am not sure, however, that any letter stood between possibly there may have been some connection between him

X and Y. and the family here described, although the date of the Ser - A Socrates, son of Antiochos, is mentioned in the in-meda monument is at least forty-five years later than that of scription on the bi-columnar monument at Sermeda, a-short the present insc rip-tion. The name Antiochos, however, is distance from this mountain (Inscr. 87 = Vaddington, 2687): very common in Syria.

followed the name 8eoi'Xou; but this is by no means necessary. On the other hand, nine letters are lacking at the beginning of the third line. The second line of the following inscription con-

tains the words *Tov dSeXov avrov,* from which these nine letters may be supplied. Curiously enough, I found in 1905, at Kalota, not far from this mountain, a Christian inscription combining the names of Antiochos and Theophilos:

"Erovs *ekv. Zoij. 'TyCa.* Xpiore *f$orjdr)oov 'avtioxp Kc* @eo£i'X(u) (386—387 A.D.). Possibly the word a/ia should be supplied at the end of the second line, so as to read a/ia *Tov d8efov avrov.1* But in such cases the name of the brother is commonly given, as in Waddington, 2221, and also in the following inscription, where the *v* before Tov a8eX£oG is evidently the ending of the brother's name. For a/ia and a name, however, there is not sufficient space, unless this line projected considerably beyond the others. I believe, therefore, that the second line ended with *&eof(ov,* and that this Theophilos was the brother of the man whom he adopted.[2] In that case this person was perhaps an illegitimate son of Antiochos, or at least only a half-brother of Theophilos.[3] Theophilos seems to have been also father-in-law to his adopted son, inasmuch as the latter's wife was named Theophila. If so, the name @eo£i'Xov should be restored at the beginning of the fourth line, so that for Theophila's Syrian name there remains space for three letters in this and four in the preceding line: this name, therefore, consisted of about seven letters, of which the second, third, and fourth were probably HAI.[4] M. Clermont-Ganneau has further recognized that the name of one of the children, which occupied the end of the fourth and the beginning of the fifth line, must be ®e6fio; also, and his restoration of 0d£io ical 2 too-eis fills exactly the lacuna of nine letters at the beginning of line 5. Theophilos the younger was very naturally named for his adoptive grandfather, Soseis for the grandmother: probably then Soseis the younger was a girl, and *ol viol avrav* must be interpreted as *their children,* not *their sons.5*

The rest of the inscription, through line 8, is fairly certain, except for the number of the drachmae expended for the section of wall built by this family on the north side of the precinct and stated at the beginning of line 7. What this amount was may be obtained in the following way. The total cost of both sections of wall is given in line n as *hpaxiv)* txt?', i.e., 1338 drachmae, + a figure which is most uncertain, but which appears to be c', i.e., *l/e* drachma = 1 obol, + another sign, now altogether illegible, but which stood doubtless for some still smaller amount. These last two signs seem to be the same as those given after the units of the sum of drachmae paid for the southern section of wall in line 9. The sum of the drachmae *l'Afui* with the genitive occurs in No. 102, 1. 3: a/xa *Tsv* 3 See the commentary on No. 164.

viav avriLv. See Wad. 2221: rvv 2iov *Kal 'kwlov a&elwv.* 4 Since the A is uncertain, and before H only one letter 2 In adopting this view I have followed the advice of is lacking, Dr. Kampffmeyer has suggested a compound Professor Robert: M. Clermont-Ganneau, however, be-beginning with /3-7X-.

lieves such a relationship improbable. (See *Eludes* (TArch. 5 M. Clermont-Ganneau has kindly communicated to me *Orient.,* 11, p. 52, note 2.) in a letter that vlos not infrequently has this wider meaning in Syrian inscriptions. in this line seems to be expressed in three figures, which in 1905 I read YAA, and of which the last is certain. The sum of the drachmae for the northern section is given in the extant fragment of No. 101 below, where I read XA, these figures, however, being uncertain. From line 7 of the present inscription it appears that this sum was expressed in two figures only, and, if the units of the total cost are eight, while the units of the cost of the southern section are four, it follows that the second of these figures must be A instead of A. Upon examining the squeeze of No. 101, I find that A may in fact be read, and that therefore 8pax(/x5z) xS' might be restored in line 7 of No. 100 and in line 7 of No. 101. The cost of the two sections of wall, therefore, and the total sum would be as follows:

Cost of the northern section, *8pax(pw)* x' = 604 drachmae

Cost of the southern section, *hpaxip-w)* 8' +?' +? = 734 drachmae + 1 obol +?

Total cost of both sections, *Spaxipw)* .citat/ + c' + ? = 1338 drachmae + 1 obol +?

On the other hand it is possible that in No. 101 YA, i.e., 704 drachmae, should be read: in that case, apparently, we should restore *Spaxip-w)* «/8' in line 7, and Spax*(p&p)* x8' in line 9, of the present inscription.

Placed together the letters restored at the beginning of lines 1 to 8 are as follows: 1. A11 MaS/3ax& Ka 5' os Ka'' 2 2. Jiti 6. crow e#f T£v 3. ToS dScXcto 7-8paX. X8' (or V»8')-Of) 4. ©eooV'X 8. tov *nepi/So*

Now a fragment found by M. Victor Chapot,1 and published by him in the *B. C. H.* for 1902, p. 178, contains the following: 1. AIIMAABA 5. cjHAOIKAIZ 2. AIOTENHZ 6. ZANEKTWf 3. TOYAAEA(J 7. APAXYA 4. BOYZ9EOtl/ 8. TOYTTEPI2

There can be no doubt that this fragment belongs to the inscription under discussion, and justifies the restorations proposed: it further supplies the name of the principal person, Aioyevr/s, the end of Theophila's second name,3 and shows that the cost of the northern section of wall was 704 and not 604 drachmae.

In line 9 the dimensions of the section in the south wall are given. In my article in *Hermes*, p. 104 f., I concluded from the copies then known to me that the length 1,1 *En deliors de l'enceinte, plus bas ct plus loin que* 2 Doubtless the forms of these letters are conditioned /;,'(=io8a in this collection). *Pierre compleU a gauche, Ires* somewhat by the type at M. Chapot's disposal, although *bienpolie, gravee en beaux caracleres. Les lettres out mimes* the rectangular □ appears on p. 186.

dimensions qu'ailleurs. " The same fragment was copied, 3This name, then, was _HAIBDYZ, which recalls a and has been published, by M. Uspensky, in his "Ar-chaeo-name *EfuSapow,* in *C. I. G.* 9787: "Y,vda Kirai 'E/niSaou?, *logical Monuments of Syria,"* p. 99. *yapyri)* Kao-

owoC *ToKfiapiov, Kiofiip* 'ASavw. of this section was W'xH5 *V, 7 cubits,* and the height 19 cubits and something more. During my second visit, in 1905, I satisfied myself that these readings are correct. But there remains some uncertainty as to the value of the sign after 7n?ei? *id'*. Professor Robert was of the opinion that this sign stood for the fraction *y2* but I now believe that this may be here a more general symbol for any fraction. In either case, however, if this southern section cost 634 + *ye* + ? drachmae,1 it is impossible to obtain any reasonable cost of building per cubit or foot, either of surface area or of cubic measure. On the other hand, if the cost of this section was 734 + *Ye* + ? drachmae, and if we assume that the unknown sign after /e has the value of r drachma = *l/$* obol, and that the sign after *Tt/jx id'* has the value of 2/3 cubit =1 foot, then the cost of the wall per square cubit of surface is 734 rg-(7 x *X92A)SXA* drachmae, or 5 drachmae and 2 obols. This rate suits very well the figures given for the northern section built by this same family (No. 101), and also for the section next to that described in the present inscription (i.e., the section of No. 102). For if, in No. 101, the section was 12 cubits high and cost 704 drachmae at 5 drachmae per square cubit of surface, the length of the section was exactly 11 cubits, as is natural compared with the other sections. On the east side of the southeast corner the hill falls away less steeply than on the south, and the wall at this point was therefore somewhat less in height than 19 + cubits: supposing it to have been i8 5/g cubits, then in No. 102 we have for the cost *&y%* x 20 x 5 = 1986 drachmae, or in round numbers 1986 drachmae, as stated in the inscription. Furthermore, supposing that a drachma represents approximately the cost per day of ordinary unskilled labor, and reducing the unit of measure to cubic feet (the wall being 2 cubits thick), we have f x f x 3 feet=4z cubic feet costing 5/3 man-days, 27 cubic feet= 1 cubic yard costing 21 man-days, a price which compares fairly with the cost of such masonry in modern times.2

But if the north section built by Dio- genes and his family cost 704 drach- mae, and the south section 734 r, the to- tal cost of both sections is 1438,, and not 1338,' as stated in line 11. Then either a mistake has been made, and 8pax(put) txt/', etc. should be Spaxii- iw),a.v-q etc., or else Neikator, the builder, in view of the fact that Dio- genes' family was contracting for two sections of wall, may have thrown off, as we 1 I.e., the cost of the northern sec- tion, given in Chapot's fragment, line 7, subtracted from the total cost of both sections given in line 11 of the main in- scription.

2In Trautwine, *Engineer's Pocket-Book,* 18th edition, 1002, p. 601 f., the cost of ashlar facing masonry is estimated at $25.14 per cubic yard: "If the stones be *perfectly* well dressed on all sides, in- cluding the back (as was the case in the temenos wall, which was laid without mortar), the cost per cubic yard would be increased about $10." This estimate is based on granite or gneiss, and on wages of laborers at $2 per day of eight hours, masons at $3.50. On the other hand this estimate assumes the use of blasting in the quarries. It also includes an item of 40 cents for mortar, but no transportation other than "hauling, say 1 mile; loading and unloading." In Rankin's *Civil Engineering,* 1872, p. 390, the cost of dressing hard limestone and marble is estimated as about equal to that of dressing granite. An engineer, now actively engaged in construction on a large scale in the neighborhood of Princeton, told me recently that he would not consider it safe to reckon the cost of such building as this temenos at Jess than $30 (i.e., 15 man-days) per cubic yard. My estimate of a drachma per day as the cost of ordinary labor in this work is perhaps too low, and 21 /$ man-days per cubic yard consequently too high. On the other hand wages are much higher in the United States at pre- sent than ever before.

If we proceed here, in the same way as with the foregoing inscription, to restore the lost portion of this inscription from the extant portions of the other, we meet at the outset a very serious difficulty.

For in line 2 only w *Tov* a8eX»oC *ai* is preserved, and, assuming that this line had the same length as line 1, only space for about nineteen letters is available, whereas thirty-seven letters are needed to complete the beginning of this line after the model of line 2 in No. 100. But the same difficulty prevents any other attempt at restoration, for in this space there must have been not only the name of the principal person, but also the name of the brother and some conjunc- tion: if, for example, we supply *aa ®e- ofCovt* there remain but nine letters for the name of the principal person and his father, which could hardly have been omitted. But this difficulty disappears if we assume that the lost portions of lines 2 to 4 extended farther to the left than line i.1 This assumption cannot be made, however, for the succeeding lines, inasmuch as it is evident that no large number of letters can have been lost between the word which ended line 4, *olkoSo/xTj'o-cwres,* and the first re- maining words in line 5, *i K T£v* Zsiw *Kt.* We must assume, therefore, that both the first line with the dedication, and also the last lines with the dimen- sions, cost, and the name of the builder, were indented, while the lines contain- ing the names of the dedicators occu- pied a broader space. Analogies in both these respects are found among the in- scriptions of this same temenos: in No. 106 the dedication, in No. 100 the lines containing the dimensions are indented in this way. If this is true, line 2 must have projected beyond the beginning of the first line by seventeen letters, viz. AioyeVs *'avtloxov K,* and, as in No. 100, must have extended to the block on the left of that now remaining.

The proof of the correctness of this supposition will be found in the restora- tion of the following lines. If we sup- pose that line 2 ended at the same point as the previous line, eight letters are lacking at the end of this line, of which the first three are obviously *jov;* at the beginning of line 3, if this began at the same point as line 1, twenty letters are lacking, of which the last two must be 17 y. To this number must be added the seventeen letters by which line 2 pro-

jects beyond line 1. Thus a total num- ber of forty-five letters seem to have been lost. Inscription No. 100 supplies for this lacuna *tov, Kal 0eo£i'Xa,* 17 eVi/caXou/ieVr? _HAIBDYZ, ®eo/ i'Xou, 17 *y,* or forty-four letters, so that this method of restoration suits very well.

Line3 contains an unmistakable vari- ation from the corresponding passage in No. 100: here, after 17 *yw-q avrov,* follows *Kal /far,* instead of *Kal* Swo- ei? 17 *n-qrqp* as in the other case. The restoration proposed by M. Clermont- Ganneau, *Kal Kara SiadijKrjvt* is most plausible, and, in my opinion, undoubt- edly correct. If so, we have herein an- other proof that lines 2 to 4 occupied a larger space than line 1: for certainly the children did not contribute their share of the expenses by a testament. Conse- quently, before the names 0ediXo? *Kal* Swo-ei 5, which M. Clermont-Ganneau has properly restored in the middle of line 4, and which comprise sixteen of the twenty letters to be supplied 11 owe this suggestion also to Professor Robert. between the beginning of the extant por- tion of this line and the point corre- sponding with the beginning of line 1, there must have been at least two words, the last of which must have been Kcu, the other or others denoting the testator. That this testator was no other than Scoo-eis the mother is not only suggest- ed by the previous inscription, but is in itself most probable. Now *Kara* StaKf, strictly speaking, fills the end of line 3 and leaves one letter over. We may safely conclude, therefore, that the tes- tator's name stood at the beginning of line 4. Assuming that this line was equal in length to lines 2 and 3, we have here a lacuna of thirty-seven letters. Swo-eis *7) fiyjrrfp, /cat 6edc/iXos Kcu* Swo-ei s, however, comprise but thirty-one let- ters. We must, therefore, restore 2ucm? *-q psqrqp avrov* Ktx., corresponding with ©eoci'Xa 17 *ywfj avrov,* and thus obtain a total of thirty-six letters for this lacuna. Various reasons may then be as- signed for the omission of the phrase */card hiad-qicqv* from the later inscrip- tion, No. 100: perhaps these words were thought unnecessary in the second inscription, or perhaps they were omitted merely by the carelessness of the stone-cutter.

In the remaining lines of this inscription the only item which is really uncertain is the length of this section of wall. The height, however, is 12 cubits, the cost apparently 704 drachmae. From No. 100 I judge that the probable rate of cost was 5 drachmae per square cubit of surface: if so, the length of the section was 704 12 x 5 = 11 cubits, which would have been expressed as mfoeis «»'. The division of the lines, however, seems here irregular; for there can hardly have been anything between *£k Twv IhLoiv avaXwfi* draw, in line 5, and *_iv rw apKTiKai Tjou irepifiokov p.pei*, in line 6.

Moreover, the word *acno-av*, which obviously belongs in line 5, does not fill the space of ten letters which, if line 4 ended with 01 koso/xt?-, would be required between *o-avres* and *£k*, in order that this line should correspond in length with lines 7 and 8. Probably, then, lines 5 to 8 were not only shorter at the beginning than the preceding lines, but also shorter at the end. Assuming this to be the case, I propose the following reconstruction of the whole inscription, fully conscious, however, that, where only so small a fragment has been preserved, a complete restoration is necessarily uncertain and hazardous.

1. Ail MaS/Sdw Kcu SeXcutdJpei, *irarpwois* #eois, *evtjv* 2. Atoyo'rjs 'Avnoyov, Ko.6' vlodeaiav 8e ®eofLov, Tov dSekfov avrov, Kcu h 3. ofia, r) ir-riKaXovp-ivq _HAIBDYZ, ®eofLov, r/ yvvr) avrov, /ecu Kard 8iadrjK7)v 4. Scocreis, 17 p.rTi)p avrov, Kcu ed-c£iXos Kcu Swcrei?, ol viol avrcov, 01 ko 5. 8o/LiijcrcuTs *itcricrav* Ck T(sjv ihuav ava.ojj.a 6. T(OV iv TCp dpKTLKW T OV TTtpifiokoV piptl p-lj J. Kous p. ev meis ia', w/»ovs 8 e 7reis t/S', hpapwv) xf/S' (?), 8. 8id NeiKaro/aos rov Mjcvlctkov, olKobofiov. To Zeus Madbachos and to Selamanes, gods of their fathers, (in fulfillment of) a vow. Diogenes, (son) of Antiochos, but by adoption (son) of Theophilos, his (own) brother, and Theophila, who is called , (daughter) of Theophilos, his wife, and

by legacy Soseis, his mother, and Theophilos and Soseis their children, built and erected at their own expense in the northern part of the circuit, in length 11 (?) cubits, and in height 12 cubits, for J04. (?) drachmae, by Neikator (son) of Meniskos, builder. 102. (No. 5 on the plan.) On two adjacent stones in situ, in the east wall of the temenos, at the southeast corner. The first is a corner-stone, and measures 1.71 by 0.54 m. : the second has about the same dimensions: the letters are 4 to 5 cm. high, and are regular and well formed. The fourth line is 2.70 m. long.

Copied by Cuper's correspondent (?), Pococke, M. van Berchem, Dr. Littmann and the editor Pococke, No. 9. C. I. G. 4450. Cl.-G., No. III. Chapot, p. 177.

Inscr. 102. From two copies. Scale 1: 20.

V.I., line 2: ZYMAXOITilN AEIOKAE, Pococke; EYMAXDCTiuNAimKAEIC, van Berchem; ZYMAXOZ, Chapot. Line 4: KATIEГOIPANHTXlNPAN, Pococke; KAIME INBPINHI NHAN, van Berchem; Mezibpinhnkwnian, Littmann; MEZ-INBPINHNHNKUNIAN, Prentice; "kox pevivfipivriv yoviav seems fairly sure," Prentice, 1905. Line 5: APAX'A/MisniK, Prentice, 1905; "Au lieu d'olKoh6nr)a-av, wKo86iM7aravt" Chapot.

1. Ail Ma.8/8ax& xal ZeXa/xaei, 7raT-pa5ois, evxqv 2. Taio? OvaXepios noovXxos Kcli Zw/Li(/u.)aos, T£v A(c)iokx(o)vs, 3. apa Ts)v vSiv avTov, oiKoSofitjcravTes iv T(o avarokiKco 4. p.4pi Tov 7repi/3dXov Kcu ieor)('!)v(3pivriu y)(oviav eV Tov Islwv eKTiaav 5. 8pa)(i(t)v),afrTTQ-OiKo86p. T(rav Tracts pijKOvs p.ev K, w/»ous 8e 6. 77-t? 8iX

With regard to the strange genitive *Twv Aeio/Xeos* (or A(e)ioKx(o)0s), M. Clermont-Ganneau remarks: "Nous rencontrons bien quelquefois dans l'dpigraphie grecque syrienne des constructions analogues, par example: 'PoOos npo«XiWos, Twv MovaLxeiBdvov,1 ou bien: novn-Xios Ktx.,&ixiv7toi vids, TQv BeiWs.8 Mais il s'agit, dans ces cas, de l'appartenance a une famille ou a une tribu; tandis qu'ici on ne peut guere voir dans Aciokxcos autre chose

que le patronymique qui, autrement, ne serait pas exprime, chose peu vraisemblable." The simplest explanation, however, is perhaps that the eye of the stone-cutter was caught by the words rav vuv in the next line of his copy, and that ol Aciokxous was intended: in any case, G. Ualerios Proklos and G. Ualerios Summachos are evidently the sons, or descendants, of Diokles. For the unusual form of the third and fourth letters in /xeo-T/SpiV, I can suggest no probable explanation. I for Z can hardly have been intended. Nor is it easy to read I as 1, which in these inscriptions has regularly the form I. Possibly it is an H turned over on its side. At least for 17 is not found elsewhere in these inscriptions, though often used for «. In any case the word intended is *p.eor)p.fipivTjv*, not *pwqufipivai*, as proposed by M. Clermont-Ganneau, who wished to connect this adjective with pcpei.

1 Wad. 2348. 2 Wad. 2339.

The family of Diokles then, like the family of Diogenes mentioned in the two preceding inscriptions, caused to be built a portion of the temenos wall. For their section they paid the sum of 1986 drachmae:1 the length of their section is given as 20 cubits, m?xeis *fujicovs fiev K*, then follow the words w//ovs Se *mjxeLy* then an empty space sufficient for three figures, and finally the letters AIA. It is evidently impossible to interpret these last three letters as figures. On the contrary, it seems as if the height of the wall should have occupied the empty space after 7njx«?. These figures for some reason were omitted when the inscription was carved, and never added later. The letters AIA are evidently for the word 8i£, and doubtless here, as in Nos. 100 and 101, the name of the builder should follow: 8ia toc 8elvo; Tov Seivos Oiko86ov. But with the help of the price per square cubit of surface derived from the preceding inscriptions, it is possible at least to suggest what the height of the wall at this point may have been; for a section of this wall 20 cubits long, and 18T$ cubits high, at 5 drachmae per square cubit of surface, would cost 1986 drachmae. If this was actually the cost of the section, the fraction of a drachma has been omitted from the sum given in the inscription. The height of wall derived in this way is certainly an irregular figure, but the height of the wall depended upon the irregular surface upon which the wall was built. On the south side of the southeast corner, as we have seen, the wall appears to have been 193 cubits high; on the east side of the corner, the hill seems to fall away less abruptly, and it is not unnatural, therefore, that the wall at this point was not quite so high. I would, therefore, translate this inscription as follows: *To Zeus Madbachos and to Selamanes, gods of their fathers, in fulfillment of) a vow: Gaios Ualerios Proklos and Symmachos, sons of Deiokles, together with their children, built and erected in the eastern part of the circuit and the south(-east) corner, at their own expense, for Iq86 drachmae: they built in length 20 cubits, and in height 18% (?) cubits,* by 103 (No. 8 on the plan). On a broken stone in situ in the south wall, 5 paces west of No. 100: the stone is 1.40 m. long and 53 cm. high. The letters are regular except for the I, which has two forms here as in No. 102. Copied by editor. Possibly this may be the inscription published by M. Chapot, *B. C. H.* xxvi, p. 179, No. 23 H b.

A C AKANEI El 1. Au Ma8flaYa Kou 2 e aucu-a.. ei

Inscr. 103. From a copy. Scale 1:20. *To Zeus Madbachos and to Se/amanes at his own expense, in length 3 cubits, in height.. (the) year* 757, *Audyneos* 2nd. (January, 109 A.D.) , *(son) of Menandros, built and erected* !Not 1886 drachmae, as in my article in *Hermes*, p. 107. In line i, after *ttXadvu*, perhaps we may restore 7rar/ouois, *evxqv*, as in No. 102, line 1. If the south wall had the same height here as five paces farther eastward (No. 100), the figures lBz_ = 193 (or 192) may be placed after x615 at the end of line 3. A section of wall, 193 by 5 cubits, at the same rate as the sections already discussed, i.e., 5/3 drachmae per square cubit of surface, would cost 524+ drachmae: Spax-*4xh"* then may have stood at the beginning of line 4, and, after this, 8ia with the name of

the builder.

104 (No. 9 on the plan). On a stone in situ in the south wall, thirty-one paces west of No. 103. The face of the stone, according to my measurements, was 1. 05 m. long and 41 cm. high. The letters are 5 to 6 cm. high, and perfectly legible. Copy of the editor.

Published by Egmond and Heyman, *Itin.*, II, p. 401. Cuper, *Diss, sur diverses matures de Religion et de Philologie*, 1714, II, p. 47. Pococke, *Inscr. Antiq.*, I, p. 2, No. 6. Muratori; *Thesaurus*, I, p. 64, and IV, p. mcmlxxviii, 7. *C. I. G.* 4451. Clermont-Ganneau, I.e., No. viii. Chabot, in *Journal Asiatique*, 1900, p. 275 f. (see also the drawing which faces p. 300). Chapot in *B. C. H.*, 1902, p. 179.

In the next course below the block which bears that part of the inscription shown in the accompanying drawing are two other inscribed blocks, now almost concealed by debris and weeds. I did not see these other blocks on my first *WfyA$B Ai* X WK AI EE A$ *f0k* Be □ Ii:tta'tpu0i r *k* PAf E A DAtf A P □ N Ef KD E Y/NTTATPW AN E KT Wt 1-AifeNEKTTCEAHl' inscr. 104. Fromacopy. Scale 1:20. visit, but after my return found etdych?pa that they had been copied by others. In 1905 I found these _K myself, and copied the letters here reproduced in type.

The whole inscription then is as follows: YAYNAIDY

If the height of this part of the wall was the same as that of the sections farther east (Nos. 100 and 103), i.e. 19 cubits, and if the rate of cost was the same, then the /ength of this section must have been 1500--19 x 5 = approximately 14 cubits.1 It is worth noticing that the block which bears the first five lines of this inscription is only 0.41 m. high, or, if the upper edge was somew hat broken, 0.4125 m.= i cubit. All the courses do not seem to have had the same height.2 1 143 x 19 x 5 = 1503 drachmae, or 1500 drachmae was 15 cubits long, and that the builder reduced his bill in round numbers: it may be, however, that this section from 15733 to the present figure. See No. 100, p. nz 2 See above, p. 107, note 1.

105 (No. 10 on the plan). This stone is complete, and measures 0.72 m. in length1 by 0.74 m. in height: it was found among the blocks fallen from the south wall, ANAPDNi areas Av8pove6-cov about five yards south of No. 104. 1 he letters are 7 cm. high: they differ from MNTTATPl)*A Krateas,(son)of Andro* those Of the Other inscriptions both in Inscr- F-m a copy. *neikos (in fulfillment of 1* Scale 1:20. *his) father s vow.* their size and in their more ornate appearance. This is probably the inscription which was found but not copied by M. van Berchem, and of which M. Clermont-Ganneau speaks under F'. Copy of the editor. 106 (No. 2 on the plan). I was unable to find this inscription. It was discovered by M. van Berchem near No. 101, and published from his copy and squeeze, and from a squeeze made by M. Dussaud, by M. Clermont-Ganneau, who describes it as follows:2 "'Deux lignes tres effacees. Caracteres moins soignes et de plus basse epoque que ceux des fragments suivants' (M. van B.). Copie et estampage imparfaits. " — "Le bloc forme le jambage gauche de la, porte d'entr£e de l'enclos en pierres seches precedant le wely. II mesure actuellement environ om90 de long sur ora30 a om35 de haut. L'inscription, qui devait se composer seulement de deux longues lignes separees par deux traits, semble etre complete a gauche. La premiere ligne, contenant la dedicace proprement dite, devait etre en vedette avec un blanc d'egale etendue a gauche et a droite." — "La copie et l'estampage combines permettent de lire:

Ail Ma??a'i(ai ai SeXa/xaVei, #eoi? iraT/xwois.... erovs *Tjip* ' Aio(u) 8' *f Ct*"

M. Clermont-Ganneau is of the opinion that this stone formed a part of a lintel, and was originally some 2 meters long. I believe, however, that this inscription, like most if not all of the others, belonged to the wall itself. If so, 2 meters is too long for a single block, and even this length hardly provides room for the proposed reading. Doubtless the inscription was continued on the next stone adjoining on the right; as in the case of Nos. 100, 101 and 102. If the author of the *Etudes* is right in restoring the name of the month, Auv, the date is October, 119 A.d.; but the same editor, who characterizes both the copy and the squeezes as "imparfaits," adds: "l'estampage invite plutot a la lecture materielle AioSoYov." It is possible that, as in the case of the following inscription, the month was lacking, and that the date was placed at the beginning of the inscription, after the dedication. Only it would be more natural to read a nominative, Aio8oto9 6 *Tov* 8ew/os *olKoSofirjo-as 4k T5v ihCwv eKTLaev* Kt., and to suppose that 1 My notes, however, imply some doubt as to the correctness of this measure.

2 *Etudes*, p. 38. the inscription was continued further, in other lines. In any case this inscription shows that as late as the year 119-120 A. D. the wall on the north or west side of the temenos was still in construction. 107 (No. 3 on the plan). On a block which has fallen from about the middle of the east wall, and now lies, with the inscribed side up, on the pile at the foot of the wall. The left end has been broken off. Copy of the editor. Published, from a copy of M. van Berchem, by M. Clermont-Ganneau, p. 44 f.

The P before the names of the gods can hardly be anything but the ending of the date, which consequently stood at the beginning of the inscription. In this respect the present inscription is unique in this series; but other inscriptions of Syria afford examples in plenty.' Moreover, there seems to be a somewhat similar arrangement in No. 106, where the date apparently stands after the names of the gods, but before the name of the dedicator. Finally, a date suits perfectly the space to be filled at the beginning of the first line. For there should be about eight letters here, as is shown by line 2, where ! XeXa/u, may be restored with certainty: Ctous with figures for the units and tens includes seven letters. It is possible also to calculate what this date must be approximately. M. Clermont-Ganneau considers, for palaeographical reasons, that the present inscription is later than No. 102, which belongs to the south end of this east

wall.2 But the two inscriptions of Krateas son of Androneikos (Nos. 104 and 105) show that little dependence is to be placed on palaeographical differences in the dating of these inscriptions. On the contrary, I believe that the wall was begun at the entrance to the temenos, in the center of the east side. The south wall was built in the direction from east to west, *anb ava.Torj; iwl ovo-if,* a statement which is confirmed by the dates of the inscriptions in situ in this wall, No. 100 (86 A.D.), No. 103 (109 A.d.). and No. 104 (120 A.d).3 Naturally the southeast corner must have been finished first. No. 102 refers to this corner, and is therefore earlier than 86. A.d. If the center of the east wall was built before the corners, the present inscription is older than

'Wad. 2557-25576, 2560-25613, 2562 a, 2562 b, etc. paleographiques, par le Gaius Valerius Proclus de l'inscription 3" Elle doit se rapporter, malgre son laconisme, a la suite C." *fijitdes*, 11, p. 45.
de la construction du mur orientale, commencee bon nombre:' See the plan, p. 106. d'annees auparavant, ainsi que le montrent les differences

Nos. 100 and 102. Its date cannot be earlier than erou? *axp'=62-62* A.d., the earliest date consisting of three figures. Consequently the date of the present inscription must fall between 61 and 86 A.d.

In the lacuna at the beginning of line 3 the praenomen МарТМ? would suit exactly. The name Ai/u'xXios, with double lambda, appears in an inscription from Katura, a town on the western slope of this mountain.1 This inscription is found in an unusually large and handsome tomb, before whose entrance stand two tall columns supporting an architrave, like that built by Socrates, son of Antiochos, at Sermeda:2 its date is 195 A.d. Evidently these were wealthy and distinguished people, whose tomb was in Katura, and, although this tomb is more than a hundred years later than the inscription of the temenos, there may have been some family connection between the persons concerned with the one and with the other. In line 4 the

last syllable,-/us, of some Semitic name is preserved: for this M. Clermont-Ganneau proposes the name 'AatX.a/xts, which is known from other Syrian inscriptions.3 Before this there must have been the word *Kol* For, although in the letters OIZ the I is placed so close to the following letter that the two appear almost as a ligature, any other reading than *olz* is hardly possible: if 6 is read some other letter than Z must follow; but the name *Zrjva* seems certain. Evidently we have here to do with two brothers, as in No. 102, and *kcu* AaiXa fills the space of seven or eight letters perfectly. The name of the father is *Zrjvas.* The name of the grandfather, of which the letters Z17 remain, might be, as M. Clermont-Ganneau remarks, either za or *Zrtvavo%.i* But the letters *TLv£rivwv* in line 5 certainly belong to the name of a tribe,6 and, consequently, at the beginning of this line *fvrjs* must be restored, so that only space for three letters remains. Consequently only *Zrjva* is possible, and only the first letter of the tribal name is lacking. At the beginning of line 6 the word *irarpwav* (eight letters) may be restored, after the analogy of No. 104, line 4, and No. 105, line 2. With these restorations the whole inscription is as follows: 1. Erovs *p"* Ail MaSySaw v .-., a „ ', *In (the) year r..: To Zeus Madbachos and* 2. #cai SeA.aJ *fiavei,* t/eois *irarpwots,*

From the fact that the verb *iiroa-av* is used, instead of *oUoSofi-qo-av* or *iKno-av* as in the other inscriptions, it need not be supposed that reference is made to any other sort of building than a section of the temenos wall.

108 (No. 4 on the plan). On a stone on the ground in a rude fence, about 50 feet east of the southeast corner of the temenos: the inscribed face of the stone is towards the west. The block measures 88 by 52 cm. I omitted to note in how far the stone was complete: it is my recollection, however, that it was intact on both ends, but that at the bottom it was broken, so that no part of the fourth line remained except at a point near the middle. Copy of the editor. ANAVAAPX KAI(C Ail MaSySaxM Kch *Ze-To Zeus Madbachos and to*

AAMAlV£H//A, *XafidveL,* *Zr)va;*
Ar)fjiOKpd-Selamanes, Zcnas (son) of
AHMOfCP/ TO YC TV9 OJHSl?TM-
Demokrates, built

Inscr. 108. Scale i: 20.

108 a. One other inscription, belonging
to this precinct, was found and published by M. Chapot1 and M. Uspensky.
2 M. Chapot's description of it is as follows:

"Pierre enlevee du mur d'enceinte et
transporté dans la prairie en contre-
bas, a 50 m. de F (=No. 107). Elle est
bris6e en tous sens, tres fruste, impossible a estamper, tres difficile a lire. Les
lettres ont 4 a s cm. de hauteur, OMNO
TOY9 „ *Tov 7r£p* 1 Bo AO Y TOIXv?
comme dans les autres textes de mcme
provenance.

NAIAOCTO6 "Formules differentes de
celles des autres inscriptions. 'Em TTIK-
TICACKAIA Ktio-o.? lecture douteuse."
TOICKAITW6TTAY A/r TT,,. £... Al, „ _ r.
.

M. uspensky read, in the first line, Ajo/
aou *Tov ©eL,* »n the second, *nepifi6ov*
Tovtov, in the third, if8. 18' erous, in the
fifth, EOirKAP... At.

The first nine of these inscriptions are
divided among the various sides of the
temenos as follows: south wall, 100,
103 and 104, all three of which are in
situ, and 105; east wall, 102 (in situ),
107 and 108; north wall, 101 and 106.
No. 106, however, may belong to the
west wall, which otherwise is not represented. The following are directly dated: 100, family of Diogenes, 86 A.d.;
103, son of Menandros, 109 A.d.; 104,
Krateas, son of Androneikos, 120 A.d.
; 106, Diodotos (?), 120 A.d.; 107, sons
of Zenas son of Zenas, after 61 A.d.
Indirectly dated are: 101, family of Diogenes, before 86 A.d.; 105, Krateas, son
of Androneikos, about 120 A.d. There
remain No. 102, sons of Diokles, and
No. 108, Zenas, son of Demokrates.
From a comparison of Nos. 100 and 101
it appears that about the year 86 A.d.
building was in progress on the north
and south walls at the same time: from
a comparison of Nos. 104 and 106 the
same *1B. C. If.,* 1902, p. 178, No. 21 F'.
2" *Arch. Mon. of Syria,"* p. 100.
conclusion may be drawn with respect

to the year 120 A.d., even if No. 106
belongs to the northern end of the west
wall. Further, it is evident from the dated inscriptions of the south wall, Nos.
100, 103 and 104, that, as has been said
above (p. 120), this wall was built in the
direction from east to west. When No.
100 was carved, therefore, the southeast corner must have been completed
already: No. 102 reports the building
of this corner by the sons of Diokles,
and must be earlier than 86 A.d. For
the same reason No. 108, Zenas, son of
Demokrates, must be earlier than 86 A.
d.: if this Zenasisthe grandfather of the
builders mentioned in No. 107, dated
between 62 and 86 A.d., No. 108 may
be considerably older than the earlier of
these dates. In this way the following
chronological table is obtained:

East wall: No. 108, Zenas, son of
Demokrates: before No. 107.
"" "107, Sons of Zenas son of Zenas: between 61 and 86 A.d.
"" "102, Sons of Diokles: before 86 A.
d.
North" "101, Family of Diogenes: before 86 A.d.
South" "100, " " " 86 A.d.
"" "103, Son of Menandros: 109 A.d.
"" Nos. 104 and 105, Krateas, son of
Androneikos: 120 A.d.
North or west wall: No. 106, Diodotos
(?), 120 A.d.

Now No. 104 is in situ in the south
wall about forty yards west of the southeast corner. Forty yards is less than two-
thirds of the entire side. For the building
of two-thirds of the south wall, therefore, the years from 86 to 120 A.d., or
thirty-four years, were required. Supposing that the remaining third required
a length of time in proportion to the rest,
fifty-one years were required to build
the whole of the south side of the
temenos. The north wall seems to have
been built during the same time. But the
east wall was built before the north and
south walls were begun. Supposing that
this was built in half the time, the work
being concentrated here, some twenty-
five years were required for the east side
of the temenos. The west wall was built
last of all. Supposing the time required
for this to have been approximately the

same as that for the east wall, about
a hundred years were required to complete the whole temenos, that is from
about 50 to about 150 A.d. Moreover,
the extant inscriptions of the south wall,
Nos. 100, 103 and 104, include between
them approximately 27 cubits, that is,
about one-sixth of this wall: these 27
cubits, together with the 11 cubits built
by some of the same persons, constitute
about one-seventeenth of the whole circuit: from the number of persons mentioned in these inscriptions, then, some
estimate may be formed of the total
number engaged in the construction of
this sacred precinct.

The name of the Djebel Shekh
Berekat, in ancient times, was *Kopvij;*
Summit. This follows from a passage
in Theodoretus,1 to which Dr. Littmann
called my *xiX66w 'laropia,* Cap. iv,
Migne, p. 1340 C.

attention: ""*Opos £otiv vrqKov, npbs io)*
pev r»)s 'aktioou, *BepoCas* Se *irpb; io-*
rrepav Zia.Ktip.evov, Tu)v wa-
paKeLpevcDV 6puv vvepKCipevov, Kara
rtfv aKpordnqv Kopv(j)r)v /ccovoeiSe?
pipovpevov o)(rjpa, atrb Tov vjjov rr/v
irpoo-qyopiav 8e$dpevov Kopvr/v yap
avrb ol TrepLoiKoi vpoo-ayopeveLv
el(odacriv. Toutou *irdXai /car' avrrfv*
Tj)v aKpavvylav Tepevos rjv Saipovwv
inrb Ttov ytiTOvevovrwv Xiav Tipdyp-
ivov." The large conical mountain between Antioch and Beroea (Haleb) can
be no other than the Djebel Shekh
Berekat, and, if there could be any
doubt, the identification is made still
more certain by the fact that Theodoretus, a few lines farther on, mentions
a *Kwpi)* Teleda, at the foot of mount
Kopvfrjt the name of which is still preserved in the modern name for a ruin,
Tell 'Adeh, at the foot of the Djebel
Shekh Berekat. The identification of
this mountain with the ancient Kefr
Nabti, once proposed by M. Clermont-
Ganneau,1 is rendered impossible by
the discovery, made by Mr. Garrett, of
the ruins and modern village still called
Kefr Nabu by the inhabitants. The place
was visited by M. Chapot, who has published in the *B. C. H.,* xxvi (1902), p.
180 ff., Greek inscriptions from here,
one of which proves that here also there

was a sanctuary of certain pagan gods. It was also visited by the Princeton Archaeological Expedition in 1905. It belongs to the same group of mountains as Kal'at Sim'an, and is altogether distinct from the Djebel Shekh Berekat. Nor is it, in my opinion, possible to identify *KopvfT)* with the site of the temple at Burdj Bakirha for the reasons given above, p. 70, note 1.

On the other hand, it is very interesting to establish the fact that, as M. ClermontGanneau remarks, the memory of one of the chief gods of the Assyrian pantheon is preserved in the local tradition and in the name of one of the towns in this region, while another Assyrian god, I think without doubt, is identical with one of those worshipped on this mountain. As to the form of the names of these latter gods there can be no doubt whatever: they were called Zeus Madbachos and Selamanes. The older copies of these inscriptions vary from one another only because the inscribed blocks were insufficiently cleaned from the lichen which fills the letters and covers the whole surface. The two squeezes which I had made of No. 101, after the stone had been thoroughly and carefully cleaned, show the letters clearly and unmistakably. But the identification of these gods may still seem questionable.

The second god, *Selamanes,* has been identified by M. Clermont-Ganneau2 and G. Hoffman3 with the Assyrian *Shalmanu* and the Phoenician *Shalman* (D?t£f).4 The same name occurs not infrequently as a man's name, for example in the wellknown inscription from Damascus:5 *%eap.dvov; Tov apxipayeCpov.* The names *taapdvr);, l£twies,* 11, p. 52 ff. 5 Published by Masterman, in *P. E. F.,* 1896, p. 224 f. , 2 *Etildes,* 11, p. 48. and by Germer-Durand in *Revue Biblique,* ix, pp. 91 and 3 *Zeitschrift fur Assyriologie,* xi, p. 246. 307. Also Clermont-Ganneau, *litudes,* 11, p. 149 f.; Lidz 4 See the inscription found at Saida, now in the Louvre, barski, *Ephemeris fur Semitische Epigraphik,* I, p. 221. See and published by Renan in *Revue d'Assyria!.,* 1891,11,p. 75s.; *Journal Asiatique,* 7"

Serie, xix, p. 11 f.; Dussaud et Macler, *Comptes Rendits,* 1890, p. 122; also by Clermont-Ganneau, *Voyage Arch, au Safi,* p. 156.

Comptes Reiidus, 1894, p. 128. SaXai/xas or SaXa/iavo? appear in Waddington, Nos. 2147, 2122, 2262 and 2337, all these from the Djebel Haurän. Several saints of this name are mentioned in the Church Fathers, as, for example, Selamanes of Kapersana, on the west bank of the Euphrates,1 and Selamanes of Bethelea near Gaza.2 The name *Ychw* occurs also in Nabataean and Palmyrene inscriptions.3

As for the other god, Zeus MaSßaxos, Dr. Littmann suggested to me at the first reading that his name might be associated with the Syriac *madbah, altar.* The same explanation had already been proposed by M. Clermont-Ganneau,4 who conjectured a Greek equivalent Zeus Bw/nds, and this very equivalent was found in the following Spring (1900), on the lintel of the gateway in the temenos-wall surrounding the beautiful temple of the Antonine period at Burdj Bäkirhä, a place in plain view from the Djebel Shekh Berekät, and about three hours distant towards the south, across the plain of Sermedä: this temenos gateway is dedicated Au Bw eyaXw eVrj/cow.5 Dr. Littmann has kindly furnished me with the following discussion of this name: "Da die Form MaS/Jaxos nunmehr durch Copien und Abklatsche gesichert ist,8 fallen die Bedenken G. Hoffmann's *Zeitschrift f. Assyriol,* xi, p. 246) hinweg. Da ferner in dem nahe gelegenen Burdj Bäkirhä ein Zeus Bw/aos verehrt wurde, so kann auch über die Bedeutung des Namens kein Zweifel bestehen: es ist das syrische Wort *madhbah,* Altar (in dieser Form, stat. absol., haben wir es wohl wegen der Endung-os anzunehmen). In der Volkssprache lautete der Name also, aller Wahrscheinlichkeit nach, *Ba'al-Afadbah, GottAltar.* Allerdings folgt sonst in den meisten Fällen auf *Ba'al* ein Genetiv, was auch hier das natürlichste wäre; die Formen in den griechischen Inschriften jedoch zwingen zu der Annahme, dass der zweite Name als eine Art Apposition (oder Per-

mutativ) gefasst ist, wie etwa in dem bDD, *Malakbel, König-Gott,* der palmyrenischen Inschriften. Es sei hier an W. Robertson Smith: *Lectures on the Religion of the Semites,* p. 188, erinnert, wo es heisst: 'the sacred stone is altar and idol in one.'7 G. Hoffmann stellt MaSßaxos mit dem i02"U ('Aboda zara, 11 b) zusammen, der wahrscheinlich in *Ba'albeck* angesetzt werden muss, und glaubt *Madbak* sei kaum etwas anderes als *Ba'albekk,* bezw. *MaHbekk* (nach heutiger Aussprache). Ich will die Gleichung flDID = l"OD"Ü nicht durchaus ablehnen: letzteres könnte aus ersterem entstanden sein. Dagegen ist *Madbah = Ba'albakk,* m. E., unmöglich."

Finally," it is an interesting fact that immediately before the temple of Burdj Bäkirhä, a few yards towards the east, where one looks off upon a broad view of the plain, was found a place, partly hewn in the living rock, which I took to be the base of an ancient altar. There was therefore here, as on the Djebel Shekh Berekät, the site of an ancient cult, where the Semitic inhabitants of this region were wont to worship the

'Theodoretus, *Pi66.* 'lon-opta, Cap. xix, Migne, p. 1428 C. 6 See also Clermont-Ganneau, *Htudes,* 11, p. 48 f. 2Sozomen, *Hist. Eccl.,* vi. 32, and vni, 15. 7 Compare also the passage quoted by Smith, I.e., from 3 Lidzbarski, *Handbuch der Nordsem. Epigraphik,* p. 377. Porphvrios, *De Abstinentia,* etc., 11, 56: ovfiaOrvol Sc Ts 4 See above, p. 69, note 4. 'Apaßtas Kar Ctos Zkcuttov iOvov 7ral8a, ov virb ßu/j.ov iOairrov, 5 Inscription No. 48. L xpivrcu isioavy.

god, the *ba'al,* of a "high-place." In both localities were built, in Roman times, temenos-walls, just as described in Nehemiah, chapter iii, a passage to which M. Clermont-Ganneau has referred and which offers a striking analogy. In one place, perhaps in both, a temple was built, yet without giving to the god concerned a proper name. The only strange thing about it all is that on the Djebel Shekh Berekat the local god was obliged at last to share his honors with a naturalized Assyrian. 109. Djebel Shekh Berekat. Fragment, built into a stone

fence, about twentyfive yards northwest of the weli: the face is towards the southwest. This stone was overlooked by me on my first visit, but was found and copied by me in 1905. The total length is 46 cm., the height 34. It is broken at both ends. The inscription is about 20 cm. long, the letters 11 cm. high: at the right 5E0 I t end remain about three-quarters of a disk containing across, 28 cm. Boc0i t Kupie in diameter. Probably this was the lintel of a small door or window. *Help t Lord/*
The inscription was first published by M. Clermont-Ganneau, *Etudes,* II (1897), p. 46, No. vii, from a copy made by M. van Berchem. It was also published by the present editor in *Hermes,* xxxvn (1902), p. 97, note 1, and by M. Chapot in *B. C. H,* XXVI, p. 179 G.

See No. i above, and its commentary.
no. Sitt Ir-rom, near Katura. Bicolumnar Monument, 152 A.d. On an architrave supported by two tall shafts of rectangular section, set above the entrance to a rock-hewn tomb, a couple of minutes' walk southeast of the chapel and cluster of buildings called " Sitt ir-Rum" *The Lady of Rum,* i.e. *of the Greeks),* and perhaps fifteen minutes north of Katura. The monument stands facing northward, on the south side of a small wadi. The two shafts are monoliths, about 16 feet high, 71 cm. broad at the face, and 68 cm. apart. About 9 feet up on the face of each is a socket as if for a tablet or a bust, about 24 feet high, and a foot or foot and a half broad. The whole architrave is about 1.80 m. in length. The first line is on the second band of moulding above the projecting cornice: the other three lines are on the lowest three bands below the cornice. The letters are large, and were originally most handsomely carved, but are now somewhat weathered.
The tomb itself is almost directly below the monument: the entrance is some-yards towards the north,
Monument bearing Inscr. no.
but the dromos, cut down into the sloping hillside, leads towards the south. Within the tomb is a large chamber, having in each side two arcosolia: the first, third and sixth of these, beginning

at the right of the entrance, contain each three sarcophagi, side by side and with their ends towards the center of the chamber. The other arcosolia contain each two sarcophagi.
The inscription was copied by Waddington, and in the following year by M. de Vogue. Inasmuch as these gentlemen evidently did not have the use of a ladder, their copies are not as complete as they would have been otherwise, and for this reason I have not repeated here their variant readings. The following text is from a copy made by the editor in 1905.
Published by Waddington, No. 2698. See also de Vogue, 5. C, pi. 94.
1. TOYCACYTTPB6PTAIOY 2. ICIAO-TOCTTTOA6MAIOYY-ONeAYTUUTTOI-HCeNTATTANTA 3. KAIMAPKIAKOAPA-TOYTHrYNAlKIAYTOYKICTAIAN 4. MAK-PATPITHIAIATHCrAilLUNYAAIAOCnPUJ-TAKICONH
In the fourth line, after TTP, may be O instead of uu: after IC, T instead of I. Around the corner to the right are marks which may be letters, continuing the inscription: these are-jAJN.
"*Erous acr', 'Tnepeperaiov e'. EitriSoro?, YlroXeftaiov vlov, iavrw inoirjcrev rd Travra, Kal MapKLq KoSpdrov, T77 yvvaiKi avrov-jceureTcu 8e iv fiaKpa TpiTrj iSia rrj; iy 8e£i(ov I/kxaisos Trparr(r);) ticriovri. In the) year 201, Hypcrbcretaios jth. Eisidotos, son of Ptolemaios, made all for himself and for Markia, daughter) of Kodratos, his wife: and he shall lie in his own sarcophagus, the third in the first arcosolium on the right as one enters.* (October, 152 A.D.)
The last two words are uncertain; but the meaning of the whole document is perfectly clear in view of the arrangement of the sarcophagi in the tomb, described above. The form *vlov,* in the second line, is doubtless merely a mistake, for vids-Mapa, in the sense of a coffin or sarcophagus, is met with elsewhere; for example, in an inscription on a sarcophagus standing alone in the open country, near Burdakli *'ApCo-ruiv SeXcwou Ty)v fiOLKpav crvv Tw Ttco/m an KaTacrKevdcras aii)c'jPucra 0eois KaT)(8ovioi; erou? /Sicr', p.rjvb;*

Uavip.ov 6k (July, 164 A.d.). In general, compare the present inscription with No. 157 ff.
in. Katura. Tomb. In the vestibule of a rock-hewn tomb, on the south side of the wadi which runs east and west through the ancient town. The tomb in question is the furthest west of those in the wadi: other tombs, farther to the east and nearer the town, contain Inscriptions Nos. 113 and 115. The vestibule is almost cubical, measuring about 7 feet each way: the front is open. The doorway of the tomb itself is very small, and was closed both by a door and also by a large stone of the millstone pattern which was-rolled across it from a sort of slot at the right. Within the tomb 1 Princeton Archaeological Expedition, 1905. See also *B. C. H.,* xxiv, p. 289 f. are three arcosolia, each containing a single sarcophagus. Above the vestibule, carved in relief on the living rock, there is a figure reclining upon a couch, and above the figure an eagle with wings outspread: these sculptures are executed in a sort of niche hewn in the rock. The floor of the tomb is about ten feet above the level of the road through the wadi, and before it the rock has been scarped away, leaving a little platform in front of the vestibule. On the perpendicular face of the rock below this platform there is a rude copy of the figure upon the couch.1
The inscription is incised upon the face of the rock above the doorway of the tomb. There are traces of a dove-tail plate, incised as if to frame the inscription; but the latter has been carved without much reference to the plate. The whole inscription is 1.40 by 0.59 m.: the letters of the first line are *6/2,* of the other lines 3 to 4 cm. high: the letters of the last two words, *Kox rv,* are a little larger than those adjacent to them, and spaced off from the rest slightly. Squeeze.
Published in *C. I. G.* 4452; Wad. 2699; *C. I. L.,* Ill, No. 191 and p. 973; Cagnat: / *G.R.,* III, No. 1007. The following text is from the squeeze made by the Princeton expedition in 1905.
Tomb of Inscr. in, showing the squeeze upon the inscription.
1. T FLAVIVSIVLIANVSVETERANVS 2.

LEGVIIIAVGDEDICAVITMONV-
MENTVMSVVMIN 3. SEMPITERNVMDIIS-
MANIBVSSVISETFLTITIAEVXORISSVAE 4.
INFERISQVEETHEREDIBVSSVISPOSTER-
ISQVEEORVMVT 5. NELICERETVL-
LIEORVMABALIENAREVLLOMODOID-
MONV 6. MENTVM 7. T 4AAOYIOCIOYA-
IANOCOYTPANOCAErEWNOCH 8. CBAC-
THCA(J)lPUJCeNMNHMIONAYTOYAI-
HNKC 9. ee0ICKATAX90NI0ICKA-
IAAIM0CIAYT0YTKAI 10. THCrYNAIKO-
CAYTOYKAHPONONOMOICAY-
TOYKAITOICrrO 11. NO!CAYTUUNOTTU-
JCMHANIIONHATTAAAOTPIUJCAIKATOY
12. AeNATPOTTONTOAYTOMNHMeiON
KACY

T. Flavius Iulianus, veteranus
Leg(ionis) VIII Aug(ustae), dedicavit
monumentum suum in sempiternum Diis Manibus suis et Fl. Titiae, uxoris
suae, inferisque, et heredibus suis pos-
terisque eorurfi, ut ne liceret ulli eorum
abalienare ullo modo id monumentum.
1 See Part II, p. 272 f.
T. 4Xaovi.'o? 'louXiai/os overpavbs
eyeavo; r 2e/3ao-r»7S afaepaxrev
pvr)ptiov avrov 8irveKe; deols
Kara(6ovLoi; Kal Sat/iocri avrov re Kal
rfjs yvvaiKO; avrov, Kr)pov(ovs)6p.oi;
avrov Kal Tois iyyovois avrwv, 07TWS
pr/Sevl itjbv rj anaWorpicoaaL Kar
ovSeVa rporrov ro avrb pvrjpelov. Kal
ou. Titus Flavins Julian us, veteran of
the) 8th legion, (ealled) Augusta, has
dedicated his monument forever to his
manes and (those) of Flavia Titia, his
wife, and to those in the 'world belozv,
to his heirs also and to the descendants
of these, so that none oj them may dis-
pose of this monument in any way. Thou
also farewell)!

The Eighth Legion "Augusta," or at
least a detachment of it, was stationed
in Syria at various times, perhaps even
as early as the reign of Augustus. At
first these troops seem to have been stationed at Beirut: later, under the emperor Philip (244-249 A.D.), soldiers of
this legion were stationed at Ba'albek.
1 Other and similar tombs in the immediate neighborhood2 are dated 152, 195
and 240 A.d. Probably the present inscription belongs to the end of the second, or to the first half of the third, century.

112. Katura. Tomb, 195 A.d. On the living rock, above the doorway of a rock-
hewn tomb in the hillside, facing eastward. Over the dromos leading to the
tomb is built a barrel vault, the front of
which supports two tall columns of Roman Doric order, surmounted by an architrave. See Part II, p. 61; de Vogue, S.
C, pi. 94.
The inscription is in unusually large and
handsome letters, and is very well preserved. The last three lines, however,
are of smaller letters than the others.
Copy of the editor.
C. I. G., Ill, No. 4453 and p. 1172. Wad.
2700. /. G. R., Ill, 1008.
The title for)db; KopviKovhaplw
marLKov signifies what in Latin would
be adiutor officii) comiculariorum
legati) consularis Syriae). 113. Katura.
Tomb. In a dove-tail plate, hewn on the
living rock, above the entrance to a
rock-hewn tomb, in the south side of the
deep wadi which is immediately north
of the village, near the east end of the
wadi. Close by, but farther westward,
are the other tombs and inscriptions described under Nos. 111 and 115. Before
the entrance to this tomb is a vestibule
formed by two free standing columns
and two engaged 1 Eckhel, Doctrina
Num. Vet., ill, pp. 335 f. and 356 f.
2 Nos. 110, 112 and 113. See also No.
128 ff.
columns supporting three arches, all
hewn from the living rock: before the
vestibule is a broad dromos like a forecourt. On the front wall of the tomb, opposite the columns, are pilasters, and on
each side of these, on the tomb-wall, is
a large wreath, with a knot at the bottom, in relief. On each pilaster is what
appears to be a bucranium. Within the
tomb is a chamber, about twelve feet
square, with three arcosolia: those on
the sides contain each three sarcophagi,
two endwise and the third across the
arcosolium at the back: the arcosolium
opposite the entrance contains one large
sarcophagus.
The inscribed plate measures 8s by
27 cm. inside.
Nhmoy Erow T"': UtV The first line
of the inscriPtion fills the length of the
6PUJTA ou' E/,c"(a) Ka plate: the other

three lines extend only one-half of
KATAX9 K 'the length, leaving a space
of about 40 cm. blank.
In (the) year 288, in (the month) Pa-
The letters are well carved, and perfectly distinct. nemos. Ask (the) spirits-of-
the-lower-Copy of the editor. world (?).
(July, 240 A.D.) Published by
Waddington, No. 2701. 114. Katora.
House-lintel. On a lintel upon its jambs,
which have perhaps been rebuilt, among
the ruins in the valley east of the modern village, near the entrance to the wadi of the tombs.1 The whole lintel measures 2.35 by 0.74 m. In the center is
a wreath, within which is inscribed the
word Z6YC. On either side of the wreath
is a palm-branch, upright but with the
top pointing 1 r u 1 r,u u u OCAA6rE
CtIA KAICOITAAITTAA outward. On
each side of these branches is a crescent, with the horns up: in that on the
left is written Xa; Zef 'T-'Oo-a XcreYJs,
j,,,, .1..1 1, T3 1-it. ftke, Kal crol To.
SwrXa. XAPA: in that on the right YriA.
Below is the main r part of the inscription, 2.35m. long, in letters 82 to n4 cm.
high. The wreath, palm-branches and
crescents are in relief: the letters are incised. Copy of Dr. Littmann.
Published by Waddington, No. 2702.
On these words see above, No. 10,
and Chapter 1, p. 25.
115. Katura. Sculptures On Living
Rock. On the south wall of the same wadi as N05. 111 and 113, and situated
between the two, are figures sculptured
in relief, most of them in rude niches:
some of these are in groups, some are
single figures. Below some of them are
inscriptions. These, in order from east to
west, are as follows. Copies of the editor.
Published by Waddington, No. 2703,
from copies made by himself and M. de
Vogue. Also by M. Chabot, in Journal
Asiatiquc, 9= scrie, XVI (1900), p. 273
ff.
A.=Wad. 2703 d. On the base of four
figures in relief, within a niche. The two
figures at the right seem to be women,
to judge by the curls at the sides of the
neck: 1Nos. in, 113 and 115.
the figure at the extreme right, however,
has draperies which cover the feet,

while the other has not. The other two figures seem to be men. The inscription is in two parts, divided by a perpendicular line: the first part measures 50 by 11 cm., and the letters are *2x/2* to 3 cm. high: the second part

I Suppose *i-rroa-r)* to be for Cvoitjo-c, eVoiKa for TYNAIKEI *iiroLTjaa* or *TrenouqKa,* or perhaps for an aorist. erroiKa formed after the analogy of *edqica.* AXovXcuos eVdcrq t5 *iraTpel* /ecu 177 *yvvaiKti Ahdaios* is perhaps a "birthday name," Nhca Arouta T$ *TMrpi Koi rrj ywaKei fiov,* from 'Alul = *September. Evorjuy.*

B.= Wad. 2703 c; Chabot, 1. C, p. 273 f. *Alulaios made this) Jor his father and his*

On the base of two figures, one a man and *ifather's) wife ... . /, Nikandr, made this for my father, Eudlmos,* one a woman, within a niche. 1 he male *and his wife.* figure, on the right as one faces the rock, is in much larger size than the other: on his left arm he is holding something, apparently a child. The woman's head is veiled. The second line of the inscription is 69 cm. long, and all three lines together 24 cm. high.

Waddington's reading is AYCAAapapaiocaay CTXAIP: de Vogue read aaoaaiocaay: Chabot read Paaioc AAYne XAIP6 on the right, and, combining his own copy with that of Waddington, proposes to read on the left AYCAAA (or AYCAA6) AAYne.1 Of the form AYCAAA M. Chabot writes: "Le nom Avo-aXa serait le corresponAyta.»-» r--, dant tres exact du nom sdmitique nbNE'lN.

Avycue, *akwre, XlaiPe* lAA Paaiocaay „ „ On s'attendrait neanmoins a le voir ecrit avec YTTfX TTfXAIPe Paatos, *aKvve, XalP* deux *K* Je ne serais point surpris qu'il fallut le reconnaitre dans un fragment d'inscription grecque tres fruste, copie a Palmyre par M. Mordtmann *Neue Beitrage,* p. 23) ou on lit, d'apres ce dernier: AICAAAAT, e'est-adire probablement: *Ava-aWa T(ov)."* On the other hand M. Clermont-Ganneau, *Recneil,* 11, p. 16, finds Avcm, as genitive of a name Auo-a?, in an inscription from Djerash: *"Ava-a,* ce serait le genitif de *Avo-a?,* forme congnere du nom nabateo-grec, *Avo-os* = Iti'lN."

Compare also Wad. 2064, where Clermont-Ganneau proposes to read Maoeos *Aovaa,* instead of Aoucra8ov.a In the present inscription, however, I believe that the reading Avycue is certain, and would therefore translate as follows: *Aagaios, care-free, farewell! Raaios, care-free, farewell/*

Concerning the second name M. Chabot says: "Le nom propre Paeuos se trouve dans une inscription bilingue de Palmyre (Vogue *P.* No. 16) ou il repond au palmyrenien "'JH. Ce meme nom "'JH, dans une autre inscription (Vogue, *P.* No. 22), est traduit en grec par 'HXidSw/jos." Both names have the masculine form. Possibly one is the name of the man who is represented in this relief, and the other the name of 1 M. Chabot's own reading, however, was AYfA j _-AA -TT6XAIP. 2 *Recueil,* 11, p. 16, n. 2. the child which the man seems to be holding on his arm. The wife's name, then, is not given, perhaps because she had this monument made during her lifetime, in memory of her dead, her husband and her infant son. c =Wad. 2703 b; Chabot, 1. c, p. 274. Below a niche in which is a single male figure. The whole inscription measures 69 by 16 cm., the letters being 6 to 7 cm. high.

The name *BaratJies* appears in the Palmyrene inBAPA6HCA *Bapadrj, dkmre,* scriptions in the form *Bar 'Athe.* M. Chabot quotes a AvnXAlP6 *xaWc-*Palmyrene-Latin inscription found at South Shields, *Barathes, care-free, farewell I* England, and published by Wright in *Transact. Soc. Bibl. Arch.,* vi, p. 438, in which the name has in Palmyrene the form nnjTQ, in Latin the form *Barates.*

D=Wad. 2703 a; Chabot, 1. c, p. 274 f. Below a niche „,' '... BAPAAAC BapXaew: *Barlaas.* in which is a single male figure. The inscription measures 45 by 8 cm. This is a Syriac name, *Barldhd.* M. Chabot cites Assemani, *Bibl. or.,* 1, 401, 406; in, 213.

E. Below a niche containing a group of three figures, with a single figure on each side. The figures are about half life-size. The inscription is at the ritrht of the center. The first line is 64, the

second 80 cm. long: the AAA6IOC,,.., AAYnXAIP letters 7 to 9 cm. nigh.

The first word may be read TAA6IOC or PAAloc, all three forms having Semitic equivalents:, "HJ and "HJH. Consequently I am unable to determine which name was written here: AXSeios (or TaSetos, or 'PeaSeios), *dkvire,* x"P-' Haldeios (or *Gadeios,* or *Readeios), care-free, fare-ivell!*

Probably *Gadeios* is correct, judging by the following inscription.

F. Below the same niche as E, at the left of the center. The first line is 62 cm. long, the fourth 39: the total height of the inscription is 17 cm. The letters are about 3 cm. high, and badly weathered.

The reading of this inscrip OC M H NOC AUJOYA etous ht(s), *u.r)vb Agjov.* .,, -.-..',,.1.1aA'a.v ',-/ « « tion is most uncertain, and this CEANONDC TAAAIOY a, *2edvovo;(*!) ra8(e)iov(?)

□□--'-HrYNH' M«P«, («) *V m* ,S Partlcularly unfortunate, be BAPCIMCH-CA *BaprinrWa.* cause otherwise it would furnish a definite date for these most *In (the) year 270(7), on (the) 1st of (the) month Loos, Seanon(l),* interesting sculptures. In the *(son) of Gadeios (*?), *made this, (and?) his wife Barsimscsa.* (Aueust,,,. T v *'J w v'* second line I am not at all sure 122 A.D.?) that there is any letter between C and A. Probably *Barsimsesa* is a feminine name formed from the Syriac *Bar-Shimshd= Son-of-the-Snn.* Names compounded of *Z'12V* are common in Hebrew (cf. *TW12W= Samson),* in Palmyrene (cf. jttfDEn = Aio-a/xo-os = *Lisamos),* and in Arabic. Compare also *Sam/sigeramos* (Wad. 2564 and 2567).

116. Katura. House (?). On a lintel now lying in a hopeless pile of ruins east of the mouth of the wadi of tombs. Probably it belonged to a private house. The left end has been broken off. The present block is 1.42 m. long; but the length was originally about 0.50 m. greater. The first line, however, which is on the top band of a sort of door-cap, is complete, and probably also the second and third lines. The letters are *6x/2* cm. high. Copy of the editor.

Published by Waddington, No. 2704. 0YXPHCTBOHei 8(£o)5 X,. EfSef6S ICG

OCHONOC /χοvos. ektmtv QaXacrts. 0(ra 6KTIC6N9AAACIC Xeyis, *4&e,* Kc crol ra 8i7rXa. COITAAITTATOVCETTTI-CAeeX "Erovs «rr'. *Eire0e, X(pirr)l Christ of God, help (its)!* (*There is) one God only!* *Thalasis built this). What thou sayest, friend, to thee also (may that be in) double (measure)!* *In (the) year J8j. Enter, O Christ!* (336-7 A.D.) Part of the last line I have restored from Waddington. Waddington, however, gives the date ᴛᴛᴛ=33i-2 A.d. The three letters ᴇᴛᴛᴛ have been so placed that the upper horizontal stroke in each forms one continuous line.

On the contents of this inscription see Chapter i, p. 14. Compare also Nos. 10, 89, 114, etc.

117. Katura. House. On a lintel, without mouldings, standing on its jambs upon the hill north of the wadi and west of the village. Upon the lintel stands the frame of a corresponding doorway in the second story: TOYCAKtM2AN0IKOY uijjing itself has fallen. Below the inscription is a

"etou? 8k£', *L(f)voi) UavdiKov.* disk. Copy by Dr. Littmann.
Published by Waddington, No. 2705 a.
In (the) year 524., in (the) month ..... e. r r .

,,,,,..., '' I he following note is found on Dr. Littmann s copy *Xanthikos.* (April, 476 A.D.) f *CJ* of this inscription: "It is not certain whether there were any figures after *"EavOacov,* but perhaps ᴀᴀ could be read." **117 a. Katura. Same House.** On another lintel, without mouldings, in the same house as the foregoing. This doorway, like the other, has above it a second doorframe. Below the inscription is a disk. Copy by Dr. Littmann. TOYCd "OMHZANeiKOYd K

Published by Waddington, No. 2705 b. *Erovs 8k£', fJ.r)(vo;) Uavdixov Sk.*

The form of A in this inscription is noteworthy: *In (the)year 524, in (the) month Xan 4* is diamond-shaped, the perpendicular stroke coin-*thikos the)* (April *4?6 A D)* ciding with the diagonal.

Three other inscriptions were found in Katura by the Princeton Expedition in 1905. One of these, on a house-lintel

close to Nos. 117 and 117 a, is dated October, 391 A.d. Another, on a house-lintel in the valley directly east of the mouth of the wadi, is dated in the year 466-7 A.d. The third was found near the tower, in the wall of the Mohammedan structure which the natives call the "djami'," and which probably was a mosque once: this inscription I have not been able to decipher yet.

118. Refadeh. House. On a lintel in situ, in a small house in the northwestern corner of the town, facing southward. The stone is large and without mouldings; the inscription incised in large letters. Copy of the editor.

Published by Waddington, No. 2695. ɪX9YC + APXHTOYNEUKTICTOY 'io-oSs) X(pioro5), @(eoS) T(tos), *tonip).* Xp(ioros) *dpXi* ETOYCZTTYPI-IANAIKOYA *Tov vewKTiorov.* "etous £,irv, p(r)vb) BavSiKov a. Jcsus) Christ), the) S(oti) of God), our) Savior)! *Christ) the beginning of the new-created 7 In the) year 4.87, on the) 1st of the) month Xandikos.* (April, 439 A. D.)
On the letters ɪX9YC, see p. 23 f. The following sentence is to be compared with Colossians i, 18: os *io-riv apxv nponoroKos* eVc *Twv veKptov,* and Revelations iii, 14: raSe

Xeyei 6 'Apijv, 6 pdprv 6 moros Ko.1 dt)div6;, rj dprj TV' KTurea»s Tov QeoC. The word *vecoKTLOTov,* or *Vt)o)ktlotov* (Waddington) is obviously for *veoKTLorov;* it doubtless refers specifically to one admitted into the church. See the very interesting article by Dolger, " Die Firmung in den Denkmalern des Christlichen Altertums," in the *Romische Quartalschrift,* Vol. xix (1905), p. iff.

119. Refadeh. House. "Sur le parapet de la galerie exteYieure d'une maison antique. Bien conserve." Waddington, 2696. See de Vogu6, *S. C,* pi. 110. Also Part ɪɪ, p. 252. *%vp.eaPT);. + Kv(pie) evk6yt)oov rr)i elaohov Kou Tt/v eijoSov r)p.5v, aprjv. 'EsirXrjpoOr)* oroa *iv pfavi) Acjov is' (?)» ipoucruttvos) rpiᴛᴛjs, Tov r)vf erous-'Arjpa/irjs Symeones. + Lord bless our coming in and our going out. Amen. This) stoa was completed on the) 16th ?) of the) month*

Loos, indiction third, in the 558th year. Aerames. (August, 510 A.D.)
Dr. Littmann has suggested to me that probably Ahpamhc should be read ABPAMHC, A/U/sa/ATjs and kindred forms of the name *Abraham* being very common in Syria.

M. Waddington, in his commentary on this inscription, remarks: "Su/iewis et 'Ar)pdp-r); sont les proprietaires de la maison. On remarquera combien lc nom propre *tvpeavr);* est frequent dans cc district." The word *orod* here doubtless means a bazaar, in which the goods for sale were exposed in the lower story of a portico before the building itself, very much as in the modern bazaars in Syria. See No. 59 and Part ɪV, Syriac 14 and 15.

On the content of this inscription see Chapter 1, pp. 14 and 22.
120. Refadeh. House.. On the lintel over a w indow, facing' w est, in the second story of a house in the northeastern part of the town. The window is divided in two by a small pier, the face of which is ornamented with an engaged column and capital. On either side of the inscription is a disk. The let-+ iHtrjNAZLuPEur: + 'I(oOs) 6 Na&upew?, 6 ters are 334 to 5 cm. high, and rjEKMAPIACTENNE CK MaPl'a? *yewed(e)i;,* 6 *v(ib);* are still distinct: the first part eiCDYCTnYETYENGA *Tov 8(co)S, ada Karol-pi* of the last line has been lost. Katdikimiectukae fan. o8e _ __. 'E „ . T. T... ETEA'T»»24TOVC+ T«x(&#») *Tov bows.* +
Copy by Dr. Littmann. v" r

Published by Waddington, No. 2697.

Waddington, however, read the last line as follows: mt/j/os *'Xirek(aiov) t, ef£' erou?.* +

See Chapter I, p. 23. Compare also the inscription from Herakeh, quoted on p. 19.

Five other Greek inscriptions were found at Refadeh by the Princeton Expedition in 1905, one of which, a fragment, gives the date 73-74 A.D., another, on a tomb, the date 341-2 A.D., and a third, on a house, the date 427 A.d. : this last inscription mentions an architect (tcxvtj?) Maris (Mapis). One of the undated inscriptions is as follows:

IX9YC 'it; Vou? *XprjaT* t + os, BeoC
Ttjos, *2,(orqp. + Jesus of Nazareth, (he)
that was born of Mary, the Son of God,
dwells here! Let not . This was finished
in the 565th year.* + (December (?), 516
A.D.) line as that of the sacred road
which led up the hill, on the opposite
side of the wadi, to the church and
monastery of St. Simeon Stylites. In the
center of the lintel is a disk inclosed in
a square, measuring 51 cm. each way:
the first two lines of the inscription are
above this square, the other lines are at
the right side of it. The second line is
1.47 m. long, the third 0.39. The letters
are rudely carved, and are 5 to 7 cm.
high. Copy of the editor.

Published by Waddington, No. 2691.
De Vogue, *S. C,* pi. 114, and text, p.
128.

In the fifth line de Vogue also read
PIMHC. Waddington's text, however,
beginning with the second line, is as follows: *Ucurfi if' rov erovs.* X(pior)c *fior-
jOt. Xifitwvqs*

Tou/xiwas *t* eVoM7rev. T
On the letters XMr see Chapter i, p.
23. For the spelling of the name Su/
xews compare Nos. 119 and 123. *Mvo-
dy* is often used in this way: compare
Wad., 1886 a, 2270, 2277 and 2278,
2464, and *B. C. H.,* 1902, p. 182.

See also Waddington's very interesting commentary on this inscription, and
M. Uspensky, *A. M. S.,* p. 94. Evidently
the building which bears the inscription
was an inn to accommodate the
strangers whom the fame of the sanctity
of St. Simeon brought to this place. But
from the size of the building it would
seem as if food rather than lodgings
were provided here. See also the following inscription.

122. Der Sim'an. Inn. On a lintel in situ,
on the north side of the same street as
No. 121, but farther up the hill towards
the west. The building to which it belonged has been destroyed; but it is evident that this building, like the other,
was of no great size. The lintel, however, measures 2.64 by 0.93 m. The inscription occupies a space 79 by 18 cm.
Above it is a disk, 48 cm. in diameter,
containing the letters A and U) upside
down. The letters of the inscription are

distinctly legible. Copy of the editor.
Published by Waddington, No. 2692.

It seems to me, however, more natural to read the third line: 'Tyi'a Tois
Kv/jiois auroS Kcp8o9. The inscription
then may be translated: *This inn was
built in the) month Hyperberetaios, on
the) 15th day), indiction j, in
the527thyear. Health to its masters is)
gain!* (October, 479 A.d.)

I think that *Tou* Kv/k'ois does not refer to the emperor or to the members of
the imperial family, but to the gentlemen who were expected to patronize the
inn.

In the second line of this inscription
the iota has on each side a dot, so that
it has the form T. These dots are found
with iota in other Syrian inscriptions, e.
g. in No. 319. Compare also Waddington, No. 2619 and its commentary.

123. Der Sim'an. "Sur un autre linteau;
devant la porte il y a plusieurs auges."
Waddington, No. 2693. Below the first
line are three disks, one between and
one on each side of the last two groups
of letters. tEKTECHNKYPOC MNOJ
M. Waddington has rendered this as follows: CYMEW + *EKTeor)v Kvpos* Sv/
xewtr? oik080*fios*-NHC MOC

The first word, *£kttt)v,* is evidently
for *hcrurtv.* Waddington believed *Kvpos*
to be for *Kvpios;* but we should expect
here rather a proper name, and KCpos
occurs as a proper name e.g. in Nos.
57 and 288. I would therefore translate
thus: *+ Kyros had this built :Symeones
was the) builder.* 124. Der Sim'an.
Church. In the extreme northeastern
corner of the town, not far west of the
first arch over the sacred road, on the
lintel of a doorway in the south wall of a
small church. The inscription is incised
on a dove-tail plate in relief, in the center of the uppermost band of moulding.

The plate measures 33 by *i9y2* cm.
The let-+tujoikujcoy x(pun)s t TS ters
are *y2* cm. high. Copy of the editor.
TTPTTI-MAC *oucV a-ov* irpcVi dyia

Published by Waddington, No. 2694.
Renan: *Mission en* MAK Plt *afia,* Kupie
t *Phenicie,* p. 611. See Clermont-Ganneau, *Recueil,* IV, p. 85 ff., and V, p.
290. *Christ conquers,* t *Holiness bc-
cometh thine*

In the dove-tail on the left are the letters XC, *house, O Lord!* t and in that on
the right RT.

The words in the body of the plate are
found in Psalm xcii, 5. See Chapter 1, p.
16.

Three other inscriptions were found
in Der Sim'an by the Princeton Expedition in 1905: one of these, probably a
house lintel, contains the date 334-335
A.d. There is also an inscription in the
mosaic pavement of a small church near
the southwestern corner of the town,
discovered by Sig. Edoardo Martinori
in 1880, during an expedition described
by him in the *Annuario 1888-Q1 delta
Sezione di Roma del Club Alpino Ital-
iano.* CHAPTER III INSCRIPTIONS OF THE
DJEBEL RiHA 125. KAL'AT Il-mudik.
Statue-base. Block built into the mud
wall of a modern house, a little above
and to the left of the doorway. It is 51
cm. high and 47 broad. The letters are
3 cm. high. Copy by the editor, and a
squeeze.

Published by Sachati, *Reise,* p. 73.
Uspensky, *A. M. S.,* p. 58. /. *G. R.,* Ill,
1532.

AvTOKparopa Ncpovav *Tpaiavbv* Kau-
rapa, #eo0 Nepoua *viov,* SejSaordV,
VeppaviKOV, Aolklkov, Kkrjpo y op.01
'Amriov "HpKov a.yi6v)Ka.v. *(This
statue of) the emperor Nerva Trajan
Caesar, son of (the) divine Nerva, Augustus, Germanicus, Dacictis, (the)
heirs of Appius fiercus (?) set up.*

In the third line M. Uspensky gives, after Wo-apa, 9luuTATOYNPOY; but between 66 and P there is room for three
letters only, as may be seen from the
AYTOKfRTOPA
NPOYATPMIKJOi
ioNceBKCTOMret MANLKQNAAK&r
KAHfO'MOMOI
nnioyHPKay

Inscr. 125. Cast from a squeeze: the
letters colored by the editor.
photograph of the cast, and the hole in
the stone at this place is so deep that no
traces of the missing letters remain. In
the last line M.Uspensky read 'A7ri'ot.
-'*AmrUm,* however, is certain. At the
end M. Uspensky reads'Hp/couXtfW,
omitting the verb, and this is altogether
plausible: in fact there is room for not

more than four letters after HPKOY, so that if *avedrKav or avea-rqerav* was really written it must have been abbreviated or continued on the right side of this block, or on a block below this one. Since Trajan is called

Dacicus but not Parthicus, the date of this inscription falls between 102 and 116 A.D.

138

126. KAL'AT Il-mudik. Stele. In a pile of stones in the middle of a yard in the modern village, near the house of Shekh Ahmed Agha. The block is 63 cm. high and 56 wide. It is broken at top and bottom. The letters are 3 to 4 cm. high. Copy of the editor.

The emperor whose name is mentioned here may be Antoninus Pius, Marcus Aurelius or Commodus. In line 9 f. I have assumed that this town was called *'AvTOiveivovirokis;* but I have found no other evidence that the city of Apamea ever received this name. There was, however, a city, apparently in Mesopotamia not far from Edessa, which was called at one time Antoninopolis, and later Maximianopolis, and Constantia or Constantina.

On the other hand *'Avravetvov,* in the present inscription, is perhaps to be construed with *aTTapxop.4vov.* Moreover there may be a letter between TTaAU)C and ATTAPXOMN. Inscriptions of somewhat similar content may be seen in /. *G. R.,* ill, Nos. 1274 (= Wad. 2306), 1353 and 1364. An inscription found by M. Uspensky in Kal'at il-Mudik, and published by him *A. M. S.,* p. 60), possibly contains a part of the present document. His reading is as follows: HMUJN TO

OAONAHMOCIANKA

I TT OCHKOATAM6

ACTHC6 YHNOY 6KACTONKION Y0YCK

OTIKOYCYNCA OYKAIT

HCrOPCUCTOI A 127. KAL'AT iL-MupfK. Pillar. On a fragment of a large pillar, lying upon the ground about half an hour east-southeast of the ruins of Kal'at il-Mudik, close to the road which leads to the modern village, and on the south side of this road. The space occupied by this inscription is 50 cm. broad and 43 cm. high: the letters are 6 to 7

cm. high. Copy of the editor.

IN CISARMA

DIVICOM

TERDIVI

NKPOS 1. IMP (erator) 2. Caesar, divi Marci An-

3-tonini Pii Germani-

4. ci Sarmatici filius, 5. divi Commodi fra- 6. ter, divi Antonini Pii 7. nepos, divi Hadriani 8. pronepos, divi Traiani 9. Parthici, divi Ner 10. vae, abnepos, Lucius 11. Septimius Severus *The emperor, Caesar, son of the divine Marcus Antoninus Pius Germanicus Sarmaticus, brother of the divine Commodus, grandson of the divine Antoninus Pius, great-grandson of the divine Hadrian, descendant of the divine Trajan and the divine Nerva, Lucius Septimius Severus*

I have restored the text of this part of the original inscription from *C. I. L.,* in, 211 = Waddington, 1838, which seems to have been exactly similar. Its date falls, obviously, within the reign of Septimius Severus, 193-211 A.u. At the end possibly *vias et milliaria renovavit* might be supplied, after the model of *C. I. L., in,* 205, etc.

128. KAL'AT iL-MupiK. Stele. Built into the outside face of the wall of the Saracenic castle on the acropolis of the ancient city, within which the modern village is built. The inscription is on the western side of the castle, in the south side of the first tower from the southwest corner. It is about 12 feet from the ground. The stone is 1.43 m. long and 53 cm. wide. Above the inscription, in the center, there is an oblong plate sunk in the face of the stele, perhaps a foot long and half as broad, rounded at the top, which doubtless contained a figure in relief now battered off. On either side of this plate are the letters DM. The letters of the main inscription are 4 to 5 cm. high.

Published by Waddington, No. 2643. *C. I. L., Ill,* 187 (see also p. 972). Perdrizet and Fossey, in *B. C. H.,* XXI (1897), p. 74 f.

According to MM. Perdrizet and Fossey, "Les lectures ZENOSTRATO, NONAPRIN, MLITAVIT sont certaines. Detail plus important, le n de la legion est bien 1 et non 11, comme l'avait lu

Waddington et comme l'avait admis Mommsen": these readings, however, were obtained "a la lorgnette." I examined the inscription from the top of a ladder, and my copy is as follows: *To the Divine Manes. To Septimius Zeno, of Stratonicea, soldier of the 2nd Parthian Legion, (which is fiamed) Severiana, the Devoted, the Faithful, the Fortunate, the Eternal, second centurion of the second line in the ninth cohort, who lived 34. years (and) served 22 years, Flavius Maximus, heir of three-fourths of the estate, and Muciatius, legatee, in gratitude erected (this monument).*

The abbreviation *Strato.* occurs again in No. 131. Consequently the reading *Strato(nis filio),* which Waddington thought possible, must be rejected. I have not hesitated to adopt the reading *Strato(nicea)* which Waddington himself preferred. Stratonicea was a town on the east coast of the ancient Chalcidice, which in the Roman time formed part of Macedonia. The Second Parthian Legion was founded by Septimius Severus (193-211 A.d.). But the name *Severiana* seems to have been received, not under this emperor, but under Severus Alexander (222-235): before Alexander the legion appears to have been called *Antoniniana,* and later, under Gordianus (238244), *Gordiana The* titles *Pia* and *Fidelis,* moreover, were conferred2 by Elagabalus (218-222), *Felix* apparently under Severus Alexander.' I have not discovered when the title *Aeterna* was acquired, but I believe that it is clear that this inscription is to be dated in the first half of the third century after Christ.

In M. Cagnat's exhaustive article on the Roman legions4 it is stated that at least a part of the Second Parthian was brought to Syria by Caracalla (211-217): that when this legion declared for Elagabalus it was stationed at Apamea.5 And I believe that this is approximately the date of the other six military inscriptions found by this expedition at this place. For of the persons whose names can be read in these inscriptions, four are named *Aurelius:* of these, two are of the Second Parthian Legion, and one of the Ala Britannica. If these men, as their names indicate, were born in the reign of Marcus Aurelius (161-180), and were between thirty-one and seventyfour years of age when these inscriptions were written, then the inscriptions belong to the reign of Caracalla, Elagabalus or Severus Alexander. Two others, both of this same legion, are named *Septimius*. But these men may have assumed this name, as other soldiers assumed similar names, when they received the Roman citizenship," perhaps at the end of the Parthian wars of Septimius Severus. The only other nomen which can be read with certainty in these inscriptions is that of *Flavius* Maximus.

I have adopted Waddington's rendering of the letters D D, as *(ex) d(d)d(rante)*, although this explanation seems to me most doubtful: the usual interpretation, *d(edit), d(edicavit)*, which is accepted by MM. Perdrizet and Fossey, seems to me to be impossible in this instance.

In editing this and the following Latin inscriptions I have had much assistance from Professor J. C. Egbert, of Columbia University.

1Henzen, in *Annali deW Institute*, 1858, p. 27 ff. But 4 In Daremberg et Saglio, *Dictionnaire des Antiquites*, see also Borghesi: *Diploma di Decio*, p. 31 ff. = CEuvres Com-s.v. Legion. *plctes*, iv, p. 294 ff. 5 Cassius Dio, Lxxviii, 34. 2 Bouch6-Leclercq: *Inst. Rom.*, p. 308. 6 See Wolters, in *Mitth. d. deutch. Arch. Inst., Ath. Apt.*, 3Henzen, I.e. xxvm (1903), p. 296. 129. KAL'AT Il-mudik. Stele. On a fragment of a stele or pedestal ofastatue, in the ruins of the ancient city (Apamea) about 30 yards south of the north gate, where there are the remains of a wall running southward from the western end of the gate. This wall seems to be part of a sort of dipylon built probably in medieval times, of ancient materials, some of which were stelae taken from some ancient necropolis, which probably lay north of the ancient city wall.

The present block is 65 cm. long and 60 wide. It is broken at the bottom, and the sides are much battered. The inscription is in a panel, sunk in the face of the

stone, 38 cm. wide, and about 38 cm. long from the top to the break at the bottom. About this panel is a border ornamented with an egg and dart moulding. On the right side of the stele there appears to be a rude bucranium. The letters of the inscription are 5 to 6 cm. high. Copy of the editor.

Published by Sachau, *Reise*, p. 74. *C. I. L.*, Ill, 6700.

Professor Hiibner, in his note on this inscription (Sachau, I.e.), says: "Poetovio, Pettau in Steiermark on the Drau (cf. *C. I. L.*, in, p. 510) was, from the time of Trajan, a colony, and consequently had the name Ulpia, which is here placed instead of the name of the tribe, before the cognomen, as was customary among the soldiers."1

With regard to the date, see the commentary on No. 128 above. Mommsen, on the other hand, considered the letters to be of the second century.

130. KAL'AT iL-MuptK. Stele. On a broken stele found face down in the same wall as No. 129, a few feet farther south. It was turned over on its back in order that a copy and squeeze might be made of it, but was finally left upon its side, to protect it as much as possible from the weather.

The stele, in its present condition, is 98 cm. long, 60 wide and 53 thick. The upper half of the face is occupied by the figure of a Roman centurion in relief. The figure is shown in front view. The girdle draws the tunic up slightly above the knees, and makes somethingof a fold above it. The cloak is clasped above the right shoulder, and the front is thrown back over the left shoulder, leaving the right arm wholly bare, and showing the left forearm. The right hand rests upon the hip, while the left rests over the heart, as if the thumb had been caught in the sword-belt which hangs from the right shoulder, passing across the breast to the left side. I could not determine 1 Compare, however, the titles in an inscription of 149 A.D., from Pannonia Sup., published by Bormann in *Arch.-Rpigra/h. Mitth. aus Orsterr.-Ung.*, 1893, p. 224 f.: I Aelia (militaria) sag(ittariorum) et I Ulpia Pannon(iorum), etc.

whether there is anything held in the left hand or not. The scabbard hangs at the left side, reaching nearly to the knee. On either side of the figure are the letters D M: D(is) M(anibus).

The stele is broken through the middle of the eighth line, the rest being lost. The present inscription occupies a space 50 cm. high. The first line has been mutilated, evidently with intention, so that only the last nine letters can be read with any degree of certainty. Copy of the editor, squeeze, and photographs.

D(is) M(anibus). Se-ti—o vs-pori, dupliciario le g(ionis) n Part(hicae), Severianae, P(iae), F(idelis), F(elicis), Aet(ernae), (centurioni) (cohorte) vi pr(incipi) pr(iori), qui militavit annis xxi dies xxx, vixit annis Xli, hoinini incomparabili, Septiiriius Andra, imm(unis) bucinator, et Aurelius Mucianus, im(munis) bucinator, heredes, bene merenti posuerunt.

To the Divine Manes. To , an officer on double pay in the 2nd Parthian Legion, Severiana, the Devoted, the Faithful, the Fortunate, the Eternal, first centurion of the second line in the 6th cohort, who served 21 years and jo days, (and) lived 41 years, an incomparable man, Septimius Andra, a privileged soldier and trumpeter, and Aurelius Mucianus, a privileged soldier and trumpeter, (his) heirs, (in gratitude erected this monument).

The date of this inscription is probably not far from that of Severus Alexander (222-238 A.d.). See the.commentary to No. 128 above. Concerning the dupliciarii, Varro says:1 "Duplicarii dicti quibus ob virtu tern duplicia cibaria ut darentur institutum." 131. Kal'at Ilmudik. Stele. Found in a wall similar to that mentioned under No. 129, running south from the east end of the north gateway: it lies about opposite to No. 132. The wall is double, and the present stone was found, half buried, on the east side of the wall with its face in. In the dampness of the earth where it lay the face of the stone had become so soft that it was impossible to clean it thoroughly without damaging the letters, or to make a squeeze. A drawing of the stele is shown in the accompanying cut. See also Part II, p. 286. The stone seems to be broken at the bottom. From the top of the stone to the top of the inscribed panel is 47 cm. The height of the space occupied by the inscription is 78 cm. From the bottom of the inscription to the bottom of the stone is 14 cm. The whole stele is 69 cm. wide, the inscribed panel 53 cm. Some of the letters are very well carved, others very 1 *De Lingua Latino,* v, go. Cagnat: /. *G. R.,* Ill, No. 1022. badly: the letters had been painted in red. At the end of the letters of the first line is a blank space sufficient for four or five letters. Copy of the editor and photograph.

D(iis) M(anibus). Aurelius Maximianus (S)trato(nicea?), prae(fectus) alae Britannic(a)e, s(t)ip(endiorum) vm, vixit annis xxv, tacianus, eques alae s(uper)s(criptae), heres et c(o)nt(u)bernal(is), b(ene) m(erenti) faciendum curavit in acceptis(s)imo.

To the Divine Manes. Aurelius Maximianus, of Stratonicea ?), prefect of the Ala Britannica, of 8 campaigns, lived 25 years, tacianus, eques of the said ala, (his) heir and tent-mate, for (his) well-deserving (friend) cared for the making (of this monument) in most welcome service.

Inscr. 131. From drawings and a photograph.

The fifth line is so uncertain that I have not ventured to include it in the text. Possibly it may be read as follows: m(enses) v, (di)es 1. Se(p)(ulchrum) Sep(timius) Lutacianus:' *5 months, 1 day. This sepulchre Septimius Littacianus,* etc. The last phrase also is most obscure, and the translation, given above, is offered with much hesitation.

The Ala Britannica2 was doubtless a squadron of cavalry, normally five-hundred strong,3 stationed here together with the Second Parthian Legion and perhaps other troops. See the commentary on No. 128 above. The date probably falls within the second quarter of the third century.

132. Kal«at iL-MupiK. Stele. On a fragment similar to that of No. 129, and found in the same wall, a few feet farther south. The stone is broken at the left side and at the bottom, and much of the surface of the remaining portion is so damaged that only a few of the letters are legible. I think, however, that only one letter is lacking from the beginning of the first line, and the inscription is evidently complete at the right. Copy of the editor.

See the commentary on No. 128 above. The second name is perhaps *Magno.* 133. Kal«at Il-mudik. Stele. Fragment of a stele lying upon the ground a few feet east of No. 132, evidently having been part of the same wall. The whole

'Or Lutatianus.

2 An Ala Britannica is mentioned in a military diploma of 149 A.d. from Pannonia Sup., published in *Arch. Mitth. aus Oesterr.-Ung.,* 1893, p. 229 ff. :t See Mommsen, in *Hermes,* xxiv (1889), p. 256. fragment is 73 cm. long and 61 wide. Above the inscription is a moulding, 222 cm. in height. The stone is broken at the left and at the bottom, possibly also at the right. The letters were originally good; but are now badly weathered and almost illegible. Copy of the editor.

I am indebted to Professor Egbert for the following text of this in-A IV LP I VERIEQVI scription:

S I N C AVC

M. Ulpi Sejveri, equi(tis) sing(ularis) Aug(usti), tur(mae) Victoris, heres. TVRVINTC *The heir of M(arcus) Ulpius Severus, trooper of the emperor's mounted) guard, of the* R I S HERES *turma of Victor?)* .

The end of the fourth line should perhaps be read *viatoris.* Small bodies of mounted guards, *turmae,* were sometimes known by the name of their commanders, as, for example, in the Egyptian papyri, *lirneix; Tvpp.r);* 'ATrokkivaptov: *trooper of the turma of Apollinarius* Compare also *'ettoulov Mudov,2 'HpaKXe&ov pepfc,3* etc.

134. Kal'at Il-mudik. Stele. Fragment of a stele found in the same wall as No. 131, and similarly placed, about opposite to No.. 129. The fragment is 47 cm. high and 86 cm. wide. On either side is a series of mouldings, framing the inscribed panel, which is 54 cm. wide. The stone is broken irregularly at the bottom, but seemed to be smoothly dressed at the top. The letters are *6/2 to jy2* cm. high. Four letters of the fifth line were broken off while the monument was uncovered, the stone being very soft. I replaced these letters in their original position; but later on, finding that a native was carrying them off, I took charge of them. They are now in the library of Princeton University, where they may be had if the monument is ever brought to a safe place. Copy of the editor.

F . mil(iti) leg(ionis) *To,a soldier of the 2nd*

V, 11 Part(hicae), Severianae, P(iae), *Parthian Legion, Severiana, the De* F(idelis), F(elicis), Aet(ernae), 7 *voted, the Faithful, the Fortunate, the* ORE'BMVC lv Vj (=centurioni) (cohorte) 11 pr(incipi) *Eternal, first centurion of the second issS1* pr(iori), oriundo Pannunia Superi-*line in the 2" cohort, of Upper Pan*

Inscr. 134. From a drawing. ore domu CroWonia) SavTarial *nonia, whose home was at Colonia* Senile 1 20 qui vixit annis--etc. *Savaria, who lived* .

Savaria or Sabaria, now "Stein-am-Anger," was made a Roman colony by the emperor Claudius, and in consequence was called Colonia Claudia Savaria. Here Septimius Severus was declared emperor. See also the commentary on No. 128 above.

1 *Aegypt. Urkunden aus d. kiinigl. Museen zu Berlin,* 4Aurelius Victor: *Epitome,* cap. xix: "Hoc tempore NiGriech. Urkunden, I, No. 142, 1. 11 ff. ger Pescennius apud Antiochiam, in Pannoniae Sabaria 2 Inscr. 48 above. Septimius Severus, creantur Augusti." 8 *Griech. Urkunden,* No. 95, line ,*etpassim.* 135. KAL'AT iL-MupiK. Columndrum. On a drum of a column in the open field near the southeast corner of the ruins. The circumference of the column is 2.01 m., the height of this drum 1.25. The lines vary from 92 to 20 cm. in length, and all nine lines together occupy a space 83 cm. high. The Latin letters are 5 to 9 cm. high, the Greek letters 32 to cm. Copied by Dr. Littmann.

136. KAL'AT IL-MupiK. On a round

block of stone, found by Professor Sachau in the center of the modern village.

Published by Sachau: *Reise*, p. 73 f.

If, as I believe, Dr. Neubauer is right in considering that these dates are reckoned according to the Seleucid era, the two parts of this inscription are dated October 133 and November 148 A.d. respectively.1 For *ftvpapov, ov Mdpov* might be read: *Mapdoov* is possibly for *Mapdwv*, a name which occurs in No. 89.

137. KAL'AT IL-MupiK. Fragment. On a fragment found by Professor Sachau "in der Nahe des Stadtthores." Doubtless the north gate of the ancient city is meant.'"'

Published by Sachau, *Rcise*, p. 80.

"etou? 17011' *Ylavffp.ov. In the) year 4.78, (in the month) Panemos.* (July, 167 A.D.) 138. KAL'AT IL-MupiK. Fragment. On a fragment in the stone fence of a yard, near the center of the modern village. It is 64 cm. long and 52 high. The first line is 24 cm. below the top of the stone. The letters of the first line are 5 to 6 cm. high, the others 3 to 4/2 cm. The stone is broken at the right. Copy of the editor.

Dr. Neubauer renders these dates 135 and 150 A.d.

-See Sachau, I.e., p. 76.

Inscr. 135. From a drawing.

Scale 1: 20.

In the year 4.4.5, in the month Hyperbereteios, Thy mam, care-free, farewell! In the year 460, on the nth of (the month) Deios, Marthoon, carefree, farewell!

Dr. Littmann has proposed to me the reading xuSeiW for *KvByjvai*. If this is correct, the inscription may be translated as follows: *May good cheer crown these things. In the year 547, month* YBYMIAKYAEINA? *Hyperbereteos..* YTEPBE?

Then possibly, as Dr. Littmann suggests, this was T □ Y the inscription over the door of some wine-shop. Other-rn1 ,a,, n 1 *1 hjJvVvpia Kvo)eua _iJ Tavra.* wise I should read the text: *KvXeta raira,* (nw) *rdav.* (erous) *Cfif',* '*TirepftepeTeov,* and translate: *By the good will of Kyleinas this was built, in*

the year) 547, month) Hyperbereteos. (October, 235 A.D.) 139. KAL'AT Ilmudik. Stele. On a stone in the east wall of the ancient city. Its height is 1.16 m. , its width 55 cm. The inscription occupies the whole width. The letters are 3 to 3)4 cm. high, and the space occupied by the twelve lines is 70 cm. high. Below the inscription are carved two large leaves. The following text is from a copy made by Dr. Littmann.

Published by Sachau, *Reise,* p. 78.

140. KAL'AT Il-mudik. Stele. On a tombstone found by Professor Sachau in tbe east wall of the ancient city, a little north of No. 139, and published by him in his *Reise,* p. 79 f. The description of this monument and the reconstruction of its inscription, given by its finder, is as follows:

"Die Inschriftist in schonen, grossen und regelmassigen Schriftziigen gehalten und gehört etwa dem i. Jahrhundert nach Chr. an. Sie ist auf allen Seiten beschädigt, doch fehlt vorn nur ein geringes Stück in der Breite von 1-2 Buchstaben, rechts ziemlieh genau die Hälfte; oben und unten fehlt, wie der Inhalt zeigt, abgesehen von der Verstümmelung der Zeilen, nichts. Die Inschrift war in Distichen abgefasst in der Weise, dass Hexameter und Pentameter je eine Zeile bildeten und so dass der Pentameter immer etwas eingerückt war. Es war wohl die Grabenschrift einer jungen Frau, die bei der Geburt eines Kindes starb, das ihr unmittelbar folgte. Der ihr die Grabschrift setzte, ist der Gatte. Die folgende Ergänzung ist nur ein Versuch, der zeigen soll, in welchem Zusammenhang die erhaltenen Reste gedacht werden können:

H *KK.ryro Ko rj p.kv ird pdevos, rjv Se Kai dyvrf* '*iovXi'a iv Tclvtj)* Buy8pias eari Tar.

H *£eiV»7 Tov aeivov* e *cxko/xcvt/ viov vlov Kardavev, &» dp.fo Tvjxßov eovriv ha.* A, *Tl ir6ov evcrovcra Tov alvbv ip.' ov cruvairffyei* Tola *(fioTTopy(ü 8' affßov (Lyr) 7r/* 3oXiVes, otkov c'pTj/AOKTas, es 8' dXXo 8a7roi fienovcra (?).

4eu, avXoi' *dvrjTois fiolp* CTreicXwae

fjLopov. Zeile i und 7 sind die Buchstabenreste sehr unsicher. In Z. 2 dürfen die Reste ®TB kaum eine andere Möglichkeit der Ergänzung offen lassen. *%vßpLd%=%vßpLd;* ist auch sonst nachweisbar als Adj. fem. zu *dvp. ßpi;.* Julia war demnach eine Römerin, weshalb sie in Z. 3 als bezeichnet wird. Dem jungen Kinde war, wohl nach dem Vater, der Name Ecu/o? gegeben; mit diesen beiden Worten wird in Z. 3 gespielt. Julia zog als eine f«« den kleinen Heifo? nach sich, als eine Fremde den kleinen mit in die Fremde, für die ihn sein Name bestimmte; in einem anderen Zusammenhange wären Z. 3-4 (o? *ap.f)ü) Tvp.ßov exvo-iv iva,* was dem ursprünglichen doch nahe kommen dürfte) schwer zu erklären."

It seems to me, however, that *geZvov* is as little a proper name as the mother was a stranger, coming perhaps from distant Rome, and her son was a stranger too, coming from that still more distant land whence babies come, and together they two had passed as strangers into that stranger land beyond the tomb. So I would translate as follows: *She that was called a maiden fair, she so divinely pure, Julia, from the Tiber, lies within this tomb. Herself a stranger she has drawn away the stranger tad, her) new-born son, in death, so that they both a single tomb possess. Ah, why, when about to face the dreadful voyage, hast thou not taken me with thee, but hast left to me), tenderly-loving, such a wealth of woe, bereaving (my) house, removing to another land f Alas, a miserable lot hath fate to mortals meted out!* 141. Kal'at Ilmudik. Sarcophagus. On the side of the cover of a sarcophagus, lying half buried about five minutes' walk north of the north gate of the ancient city. The cover has the usual four acroteria. Copy of the editor.

The word *Humerus* was used, especially under the later empire, for a special *troop* or *corps,* either of infantry or of cavalry, composed of soldiers who + ENeAAEKITAIAITEPIOC + *Ev0dBe k1t(u* »Arrtr,., n ,. TPIBOYNOCNOYMEPOY 0 ,, . , did not possess Roman citizenship,

AAKUUN *rpipowos vovpepov Ao.kwi.* and whose organization differed + *Here lies Asterios, tribune of (the) numerus of the) Dacians.* from that of the regulars of the imperial army.. The numbers of such a troop varied from 300 to 900: its commander was called commonly by the irregular title of *praepositiis,* rarely *praefectus,* or, as in this instance, *tribimus.1* The cross, at the beginning of the present inscription, appears to be original, and seems to me, therefore, to indicate that this inscription falls in the time after Constantine.

142. Kal'at Il-mudik. Fragment. On a fragment found by Professor Sachau "in der Nahe des Stadtthores" (cf. No. 137). Pub AAONKOYTYONHBOYAH..,,. c. o u u r 11 lished by Sachau, *Reise,* p. 80, where the following: NAPXIACTHCBO..
_.,,.
account is given: "Dass.... nicht mehr als zwei nicht ganz sicher lesbare Zeilen iibrig geblieben sind, ist um so mehr zu bedauern, als es eine Inschrift politischen Inhalts gewesen zu sein scheint." "InZ. 1 sind nur ganz unsichere Buchstabenreste erhalten. Vollkommen sicher ist die Lesung der 2. Zeile: 143. KAL'AT iL-MupiK. A Plain Block. In the center of one face of a block, 65 cm. long and 45 high. The letters are well carved. Copy of the editor. x X(/ 3iore) (£(vafoi/)C?). *O Christ,save (us)!* 144. Kefr Ambil. Tomb. In a rock-hewn tomb in the northern slope of the hill, a short distance southeast of the village. The tomb consists of a small chamber with an arcosolium in each of the three sides, each arcosolium containing two sarcophagi with their ends towards the center of the chamber. At each side of each arcosolium is a bust, rudely carved on the living rock, and now badly preserved. At the back of the arcosolium opposite the entrance is a figure, standing, and with the right arm held across the breast. Inscription A is over the arcosolium on the east, B is opposite the entrance, c is on the west. Copied by Dr. Littmann and the editor. 1 Th. Mommsen, in *J/er//ifs,xix,* p. 219 ff. The name A/3/3i/3a9 is interesting because it shows that at this time and in this region the double consonant was

still pronounced. In the next inscription the form 'A/Si'/Ja? appears. See Part IV, p. 52 f. Compare also *C. I. L.,* v, 8728. The original of this name is doubtless the Syriac *Habbiba.* The name Max"»' is doubtless from the Aramaic *Malkhu.* 145. Kefr Ambil. Tomb. In a similar tomb, farther towards the west. The letters are rudely painted in black. The inscription A is over the arcosolium on the left, the cross in the center of the inscription being at the top of the arch. Inscription B is opposite the entrance, and ends before the crown of the arch is reached. Inscription c is over the arcosolium on the right, and ends about at the top of the arch. The letters of B are 24 to 3/2 cm. high: those of c, 6 to 7 cm. Copy of the editor.

The letters of these inscriptions are faint, and the reading very uncertain, especially of B. Possibly this contains the name of the emperor and a date: or possibly A and B should be read together: *Abramos, physician of the emperor.* "The title 0eos," says Waddington, in his commentary to No. 2585, "given to an emperor during his lifetime, is by no means unusual in the Orient. At Rome they awaited the emperor's death before decreeing to him the title *divus* but Asiatic peoples were long since accustomed to show more reverence to their sovereigns." But if this is the name of the emperor Severus Alexander (222-235 A.d.), the cross in A would seem to prevent combining A and B. Abramos apparently was a Hebrew Christian physician. In No. 349 another man with a Hebrew Christian name, Ioannes, is called *'larpbv* 2e/3(ao-ToO): *Physician of Augustus* (i.e. the emperor?). Later on, Jewish and Christian physicians were in great repute in the East, and perhaps this was so as early as the period of these inscriptions.

The name *Kaiamos 'vi* not infrequent in Syria. Compare Wad. 2103, 2253a, 2413, 2436. The original of the name seems to be *Kaiyam.1* Apparently Kaiamos and Habibas shared one sepulchre together.

146. Kefr Ambil. Stele. "Sur une stele tres-fruste." Waddington, 2662.

Waddington's reading of this inscrip-

tion is as follows: etovs 7tu'?... TDYCBTT, ,,,, ME ATTN A aU7re Eucre/Set, I.e., *In (the) year 4.89 (?) 0 sorrow-free, farewell/* AAYTTE *Be reverent* (respect this tomb)! (177-178 A.D.?) XAI P E The name of the person buried beneath this stele is evidently contained in the second line of the inscription. Perhaps we may read *Mikiraa.* The imperative cuo-e/to. is doubtless used like *afaepwre* (see Nos. 49, 89 and 112) and similar expressions, to warn against profanation of the tomb or removal of the stele.

147. Kefr Ambil. Tomb. In a tomb hewn in the rock, a short distance west of

No. 145: the tomb is of the same type as No. 34. The inscription is on the north side of the shaft, above the arcosolium. The letters are badly weathered. Copy of the editor.

I have thought that

With vapa one might un-XAPAErgiC-NX-ANH-AQYT7   Xapa-Ero(v)?-(), nunxF   uucllll8"lU11 CEAEYKrJCZrjBQJNDCTTATHP, *7Q* derstand i/fur «mu; but HMIUNEIAECENTD-KDIMH, ,/Wv s,, perhaps *xapa* is only a Thpinmneiandihthptujn 'T"." r r nEaluN   Z61"" (Pa)T7?(l')(-) TM" 7r£6a'1'mistake lor xatPe-See *tyikTarq* 17001? XPa in an *Joy! In (the) year6j-(?), Panemos —, Seleukos (son) of Zobon, our , r A, father, completed this sepulchre, a visible memorial of his children.* (July, inscription from Asty-*J ' 1 r' J* w' ,, c 340-348 A.D.?) palaea, /. G. xn, fasc, 3,

No. 236. The noun xaP however, occurs in No. 114. With *Zobdn* the ancient Aramaic names pi and may be compared.

148. Kefr Ambil. Lintel. On the lintel of a richly ornamented doorway. The space occupied by the upper line is 1. 61J/2 m. long, that of the lower line 1. 48 m. The letters are 4 cm. high. Copy of the editor.

Published by Waddington, No. 2662 a.

__O0OCTujNAINOMa.N()IAA?IKAlAHCI t 'O ©cos *Twv* Sivo/acw £iXa£i ai *ikeijart   Tov*   tTON6ICLjAONHHu. NKAlTON6Ju.AN + *Tw Ko Tov gaSov.* t +

The God of Hosts shall preserve and shall have mercy upon our coming in and our going out. +

On o for A in Sivop.eW see Waddington's notes on No. 2662 a and No. 1916. Compare also in this publication Nos. 25 and 26. As for the contents of the inscription see Chapter i, pp. 14, 22 and 25.

1 See Part IV, Safa'itic No. 39. 149. Kefr Ambil. Fragment. On a small irregular fragment of fine, white limestone, without mouldings, built into the wall of a house above the entrance, and too high up to reach. Seen from the courtyard of the house the letters appeared to be somewhat over 2 inches high: the letters themselves are very good. Copied by Mr. Butler. 150. MA'ARRIT Betar. Tomb, 250 A.d. Six fragments of the architrave of a ruined aedicula, about fifteen minutes' walk southeast of Hass. The monument has been so completely destroyed that scarcely one stone remains on another; but the ground plan is still clear, and in the fragments the important features of the building are preserved. The building was square, measuring 3.30 m. at its base on each side. It was roofed by two slabs of stone, flat on the under side and cut to a gable form above. One of these is still intact, and measures 3.30 m. in length: the inscribed fasciae of the architrave therefore, which must have been 10 or 15 cm. shorter at each end, must have had a length of from 3.00 to 3.10 m. See Part II, p. 74 f.

Fragment 1 is a corner-stone, and obviously the beginning of the inscription. Its place was doubtless at the southeast corner of the building. Fragment 3 was broken through the upper line of the inscription; but the two pieces were found and fitted together. Fragment 5 is also a corner block, and doubtless had its place at the northeast corner of the building. If fragments 1, 2, 3, 4 and 5 are placed together, and if an allowance of about 30 cm. is made for three letters in the lower line between fragment i and fragment 2, the inscription which these fragments form will measure 3.01 m. in length. I believe that this was the inscription of the east side, i.e. the front.

Fragment 5 shows that the inscription was continued on the adjacent side, i.e. the north side, of the structure. If then the right end of fragment 5 is placed together with fragment 6 and the block numbered 7 in the drawing, a total length of 2.61 m. will be given, or.40 m. less than the corresponding part of the architrave on the east side. This difference of.40 m. would allow room for about four letters between fragment 5 and fragment 6.

The letters are about 8 cm. high and were painted red. Copied by Mr. Huxley and the editor.

vetous a£f" Ba.povfjifiov Tov kiovvaLov, (TTpa,Tr)(y)ov kwjii 179, Zttl iyevo/juqv. Mtji/os Ha.vijfi.ov 8k'. EuSe. *In the) year 561: under Barummas (son) of Dionysios, strategos ofthis) village, I was (made)?. On (the) 24th of (the) month Panemos. Sleep!* (July, 250 A.D.)

The reading of this inscription which I have given here is not entirely satisfactory. The date however is certain. Barummas would be a name natural enough in this region: its Semitic form would be *Bar Ummd*, ID. But neither the construction nor

Inscr. 150: north side. From drawings. Scale approximately 1:20.

the case of the name is clear. Furthermore the position of em seems strange, as also euSe at the end of the inscription. As for the latter, one is tempted to read the last letter of fragment 3 as I, instead of Y, and to supply between fragments 3 and 4 TAIEN9A, i.e. Kcirai *iv66. Be.* But these letters would increase the length of fragments 1-5 beyond the limits of the east side of the monument.

The lower line seems to have been an afterthought. But it appears less unnatural when it is remembered that the month in this case is placed immediately under the year. That even a could have a *orparr/yds* is attested by Waddington, 2399.

151. MA'ARRIT Betar. The Same. On three other blocks found among the ruins of the aedicula described under No. 150. The first of these was on the west side. The stone has a smooth face: the letters are at the bottom, near the right

end. The letter T is 17 cm. high. The second block was found on the south side near the southwest corner. It is a corner block of a base moulding, having the corner at the right of the letters. The letters are at the left end of the stone: the P is 18 cm. high, the w 14 cm. The third block is a small fragment, 20 cm. long by 14 cm. high, which seems to contain the single letter H, 14 cm. in height. Copied by Mr. Huxley and the editor. 1. 2. 3. Apparently these letters were not in the same tier, TW pw H for No. 2 is on a moulded block, while No. 1, at least, was not. It may be assumed that they belonged to this building, for there were no other ruins near from which they might have come: probably they belonged to the west wall of the aedicula. But whether they were part of an inscription, or whether as letters they had some significance of their own, is uncertain. Possibly they are to be combined as follows, in T$ rpu(t,): *to the hero,* or d£ie/a»rai Tw Vp0')-sacred to the departed herd). 152. HAss. Oil Factory, 372 A.D. On the face of a pier, in a large building, now partly underground, just outside of the southwest corner of the modern village. The interior of this building is divided longitudinally by two rows of three square piers, on which rest arches supporting an upper floor or roof of stone slabs. If there was an upper story, as I think, it has now disappeared. See Part II, p. 270. The inscription is on the second pier from the entrance on the left, facing the central aisle: it is above the cap of the pier, at the springEfs 0os ixovos mS f tne arch. Though completely sheltered and "En-ovs Snx', Ai'ov dry, the letters are almost illegible, because of the *6", rvveTeerdr) To* poor quality of the stone on which they were cut. *(There is) one God alone. In the) year 68j, Dios pth, this oil factory zuas completed.* (November, 372 A.D.)

The whole inscription occupies a space 60 cm. long and 65 cm. high. The letters are rude and vary from 6 to 11 cm. in height. Copy of the editor.

On the words Efs Beos /aovos, see Chapter 1, p. 18 f. The form *iXtor-pifSzov* is for e'Xcuor*pifieiov.* 153.

HASS. Lintel (?) Of A TOMB, 376 A.d. On a block of stone, about ten minutes' walk southwest of the village, beside a path which leads to the ruined church called by the natives Kasr il-Benat (see Part II, p. 219 ff.), and not far from the church itself. The stone lies on the south side of the path, half buried, and the inscription is on the south side of the stone. The block had no mouldings nor ornament of any kind. It is 2.24 m. long, 0.74 wide, and 0.41 thick. The lines are irregular in length, the first being 1.19 m. long, the second 1.89, the third 1.39. The letters are *Sy2* to 6 cm. high. Copy of the editor.

In the third line I believe that the a has been omitted by mistake and the *To* placed on the wrong side of the *v:* or perhaps *Ovvct4vt(o.v) Top p-v-qplov* should be read. The explanation of the letters K6Y, *nal vloi*, is certainly not entirely satisfactory: I know of no other example of« for ot. The reading itself is uncertain, and there may be another letter before the first in this line.

The name *Baraddncs* is probably the Syriac *bordond: mule*, or perhaps from *Barad* (or *Bord*) with the diminutive termination *-on!* Animal names are common among the Semites, and the mule is not without honor in the East. The name *Zeoras* is the Syriac *Ze'ord: small.* See Part IV, p. 55.

154. Hass. Tomb, 378 A.d. On the living rock, above the arched vestibule of a rock-hewn tomb facing south, in the old quarries, a short distance northwest of the village. See Part II, p. 104 f. The inscription is incised on a dove-tail plate, which is in low relief. The plate is 85 cm. long by 37 cm. high. The letters are irregular both in size and shape: those of the first line are about 6, those of the last line 3 cm. in height. The whole inscription is very carelessly carved; but, with a very few exceptions, the letters are all perfectly legible. The letters were once painted red. Copy of the editor. Published by Waddington, No. 2660.

"etovs *Ottx*', 'ApTefiio-tov e", iirl o-rrov8rj; Inscr. 154.
'Aypimra rov Mapivov /ecu Ad/xfa rr?; Seyva, ywe/cos avrov, iTtXuodr). *In (the) year 689, Artemisios 5th, at the*

direction of Agrippa, the (son) of Marinos, and Domna, the (daughter) of Segnas, his wife, (this tomb) was finished. (May, 378 A.D.)

If my reading of the fourth and fifth lines is correct, the author of this inscription seems to have formed the genitive of the feminine name *Aopva* after the analogy of the genitives of the masculine names AypiWas and %eyva. But perhaps *A6p.v(r));'* should be restored. JSee No. 88 and its commentary. 155. Hass. The Samp: Tomb. Over the doorway, within the vestibule, where the rock is carved to represent a door-cap. This doorway had no door, but was closed by a stone like a cart-wheel, which was rolled across it.

The length of the space occupied by the inscription measures 1.05 m.: the inscription itself is O.78 m. long, the letters 4 to 4 Cm. high. Inscr-'55-Cast from a squeeze.

The letters are well formed and clear. Copy of the editor, squeeze and cast.

The letters X M r appear not infrequently in these ElceEOCXHrMONOC Syrian inscriptions. They have been interpreted by *Eh* eco's X M r /xoVos, i. e. *Eh* de Rossi1 de Vogue,2 and others, to mean Xpun-o's, r, r ,*K* MixaX, *Tapiqk.* Such an interpretation makes these *vrjdeis), fiovos.* .

letters most inappropriate here, unless we consider *(There is) one God, Ch(rist) biorn),* ,,,,, .. that they had become mere conventional symbols, (f/) *M(ary), alone. / J* the original meaning of which had almost faded out. Waddington's explanation, given in his commentary to No. 2145, seems to me to be the correct one, and has therefore been adopted in these inscriptions. The phrase is given in full in No. 120 above = Wad. 2697. See also Chapter 1, p. 23. 156. Hass. Lintel. A lintel found upside-down in a field north of the village. Above the inscription is a moulding like the classic egg-and-dart without the darts, and above this, in a sort of frieze, a disk containing Christian symbols. The stone is 1.83 m. long. The inscription is 1.68 m. long and 4 cm. high: the letters are very well formed, sharp and regular. Copy of the editor, squeeze and

cast. t AOlATTATPIYIUUAriUJTTNeYMATI + CWCONKYPI6TONAAAONCOY t Adfa *War pi*, TiaS, 'Ayi'to *UvevpaTt.* + *xSxrov*, f *Glory to Father, Son and) Holy Spirit'*. + *Save, Kwpie, Tov XaoV crov. Lord, thy people/*
See Chapter 1, p. 10.
157-170. Hass. Tomb Of Eusebios And Antoninos.3 The so-called "Tomb of Diogenes" at Hass has attained considerable notoriety through the account given of it by M. de Vogue in *La Syrie Centrale*, p. 103 f., pis. 70 and 71. Various histories of architecture since that time have referred to it, and have reproduced M. de Vogue's drawings. Several of its inscriptions have been published, by Waddington, No. 2661 a, b, c, d, e, and f, after copies made by himself and M. de Vogue, by Burton and Drake in *Unexplored Syria*, 11, p. 214 ff. and p. 380, and again by M. Clermont-Ganneau in a recent article in his *Recueil d'Archeologie Orientate*, iv (1900), pp. 122-130. 1 *Bulletino di Archeologia Cristiana*, 1870, p. 25 ff. 3 The following account is reprinted here from the *Prince -T.a Syrie Centrale*, p. 90 ff., and p. 108 f. *ton University Bulletin*, Vol. xiv, 1903, pp. 74-88.
The architectural features of this building are discussed by Mr. Butler in Part II, p. 160 ff. It was originally a small structure, of two stories, situated a few minutes' walk southwest of the modern village. Near by, on the side towards the village, are the ruins of several other built tombs, and north of these lie the quarries in the sides of which are the entrances to a number of rock-hewn sepulchres. This was then the necropolis of the ancient town. Beyond, a walk of about five minutes farther to the southwest are the Tomb of Eusebios and Antoninos, from the southwest.
ruins of the convent church, called by the natives " Kasr il-Benat." The ground slopes quite steeply towards the north, where there is a broad wadi, and consequently the tomb, which was built near the top of this slope where the rock was scarped, as M. de Vogue's drawing shows, was so constructed that its upper story could be entered directly from the higher ground on the south, while the

story below was entered from the lower level on the east.

The lower story is partly excavated in the solid rock, and partly built. The entrance, on the east side, is now completely blocked up by earth and debris, so that only a glimpse of a part of the lintel and of the top of the door itself can be had, and that only through a hole where the earth has washed in through the partly open doorway. The walls arc complete, except that above and to the left of the doorway a single block has been removed about ten feet

East elevation, restored.,, n.. above the floor, leaving an opening through which I entered, as doubtless those who made the hole entered before me. Within is a high chamber, containing in its walls five arcosolia, two on each side and one across the rear end. These arcosolia are cut in the solid rock. In the center of each side, covering the space between the two arcosolia and resting on the set-off at the base of the sarcophagi, is a pier of masonry, the top of whose cap is about 7 feet above the top of the sarcophagi. On these caps rests an arch of thirteen voussoirs, which supports the center of the floor above. In the keystone is a hole which once contained an iron plug, doubtless for the chain from which a lamp or a chandelier was suspended. The caps of the piers are level with the first course of stone above the solid rock. The inside measurements of one sarcophagus, the second on the left, I found to be 181 cm. in length, 72 in width and 82 in depth. Evidently then the owners of this tomb

Plan of the lower story. were not yery tal At the wegt end of me sarcophagUS the bottom has been left somewhat higher, and this higher portion has been rounded off to form a sort of pillow for the dead. Its front wall is 32 cm. thick, and at the back and ends is a ledge 11 cm. deep to support the cover.

The floor of the chamber is filled up to the top of the sarcophagi, and in some places higher still, with earth and stones, most of which are comparatively small and seem to be the broken pieces of large blocks. As the roof and walls are intact, these stones can only be the

fragments of the sarcophagus covers, which were doubtless broken by those who rifled these tombs and who were unable to move the covers entire. One large piece, which was still in a sarcophagus, was of the common prismatic shape. The earth in the chamber must have been blown in or washed in through the doorway. For this doorway an opening was made in the face of the solid rock 220 cm. wide. In this, on each side, was set an upright block of limestone about 50 cm. wide, and into these blocks again was sunk the door-frame, which is of black basalt. The width of the doorway is 119, and its height about 133 cm.: I could not reach the sill because of the mass of debris there. The doors are of black basalt also, and opened inwards. M. de Vogue, who seems to have seen the whole doorway, gives a detailed drawing of it in plate 71. The rest of the tomb, except the plates which formed the balustrade of the colonnade, and doubtless the door-frame, of the second story, was r i-1 1 1.,1 Cross-section through C-d. of limestone, which is now gray and coated with gray and white lichen, but which was white when first cut, so that the contrast between the white building and its black trim must have been very striking.

No inscriptions of the inside of this chamber were visible from without; but on digging away a little earth from the face of one of the sarcophagi I found letters there. I then had the debris cleared away from the face of each sarcophagus in turn, and found inscriptions which are evidently the counterparts of those on the broken sarcophagi of the floor above. The inscriptions in the lower chamber are in almost perfect condition. But when each had been read, it was found necessary to replace the debris which had covered it, in order to be able to reach the next. These inscriptions, according to my own copies, are as follows: 157. On the first sarcophagus on the right—(a), in the lower story. The inscription is in a dove-tail plate, outlined on the face of the sarcophagus: the plate measures 136 x cm.

TA ANUUICTONNAONKAIIUU

NANTU)NINOYAIOΓNOY CUUCAY
TWCT Akatuukae5iuunttiapk
TONTAAYOANTWNINOYAIOΓNOYC

Ta avo) eis Tov vaov cc heiwv 'Avra-vivov Aioye-The part above on the right as one enters the temple vow wcravTus To. Korea 4k Scijicav eVl dpKTOv, To, belongs to Antoninos, son 0/Diogenes: in the same way 8vo, vtoivlvov Aioy(c)i/ous. tne Part below on the right towards the north, the two places), belongs to Antoninos, son of Diogenes. 158. On the second sarcophagus on the right—(b), in the lower story. The plate measures 119 x 39, the letters 5 to 6 cm. in height.

TAANWICTONNAONKAe5IW
ANTWNINOYAIOΓeNOYCUJCAY
TWCTAKATWKAIIUJNniAPK
TONTAAYOANTWNINOYAIOΓN OYC

To. dvo) et? Tov vaov eV heijix(v) 'avto-jvcvov Alo-The part above on the right as one enters the temple yevovs-wo-avr-ws To. Kara ex Setjiwv «r! dpKTOv, belongs to Antoninos, son of Diogenes: in the same To. Suo, 'avtovivov Aioyei/ovs. way the part below on the right towards the north, the two places), belongs to Antoninos, son of Diogenes. 159. On the first sarcophagus on the left—(c), in the lower story. The plate measures 136 x 37 cm.

Kaltaaaxontaanwycbiw
62apict6pwthcicoaoyo
Moiuuctakatwtoyaytoy
6ycbioymchmbpinon

Kcu To. a)(6vra aval EucreyStw i£ dpiorepSv) rrj; Also the part above which fell to the lot of Eusebios lo-68ov 6p.oim To. Kara Tov avrov Rbo-efiiov, p.zot)p.-(« on the left of the entrance: likewise the part befipivov. lw belongs to the same Eusebios, the) south side).

Perhaps we should read here: The part above which fell to the lot of Eusebius is) 011 the left of the entrance, as well as the part below belonging to the same Eusebius, i.e. the) south side). 161. On the sarcophagus at the west end of the lower story—(e), opposite the door. The plate measures 128x39, tne rst ne 94 tn second line 120 cm. in length: the letters are 6 cm. high.

KAITOMCONTTI
BATTONTATTITHNeY
PANTTIKOINAYCBI

OYKAIANTWNIN OY

Also the middle (place), looking towards the door, belongs in common to Eusebios and Autoninos.

The upper story, referred to in these inscriptions as the "naos," evidently had the form of a little peripteral temple facing the south. The walls of the cella were superposed above the front part of the arcosolia below on the north, west and south sides: the east side had no arcosolium below, and hence the east wall of the cella above must have rested on the east wall of the lower chamber. The east wall of the lower chamber then must have been provided with a portico which supported the east side of the peristyle above, while this peristyle on the other three sides rested upon a kind of podium built upon the rear portion of the arcosolia of the lower chamber and upon the solid rock which lay behind these. The inside of the cella then had nearly the same dimensions as the lower chamber inside of the arcosolia: it contained three stone sarcophagi,

South elevation, restored, and cross-section through A-b.

Plan of the upper story.

one at each side and one at the back. Nothing is left of this upper portion of the building, above the podium, except the northwest angle of the cella wall, and the remains of the three sarcophagi, very badly mutilated. These, however, still bear parts of the original inscriptions, two of which at least may be restored in their entirety from those below. 162. On the sarcophagus on the right—(f), in the upper story. In a dovetail plate like those below, but broken at the right. The first line measures 56, the second 78, the third 85 cm. in length: the letters are 42 to 6 cm. high.

Published by Waddington, No. 2661 d. Burton and Drake, No. 18. M. Clermont-Ganneau, 1. c, p. 125.

TAANW6ICTC

WNANTWNlNo Ii

Wcaytwctakatuu6

WN6TTIAPKTONTAA

WNINOYAIOrENOYC

Td *ava)* eis To *y vaov Ik* 8ef t *wv 'Amwvivov The part above on the right as one enters the temple*

At oyeVovs wo-aurws ra *Kara* e/c 8efi&y eVt *belongs to Antoninos, son of Diogenes: in the same way apKTOv, To.* S wo, 'ait *wvivov* AtoyeVovs-*the part below on the right towards the north, the two places), belongs to Antoninos, son of Diogenes.*

M. Clermont-Ganneau, in his most acute discussion and reconstruction of this inscription, was at a great disadvantage because of the lack of the inscriptions in the lower story, and of fuller information than was furnished by M. Waddington and M. de Vogu6. Consequently the learned author of the *Recueil d' Arche'ologie Orientate* assumed, tentatively, as he himself states, that both stories of this mausoleum were entered from the south. This, however, is not the case: the upper story was entered from this side; but the lower story was entered from the east, as described above.

163. On the sarcophagus on the left—(g), in the upper story. Length of the inscription, 51 cm.; height of letters, 6 cm.

Published by Waddington, No. 2661 f. Burton and Drake, No. 16. Clermont-Ganneau, I.e., p. 130.

1 vctJloYMtw,

Kai *Tol Xaoura dvoi* Evo-/8i'a *ii; dpLcrrepwu Also the part above which fell to the lot of Eusebios* r% 10-00W 6/X01W9 ra xartu row avrou E *vaefiiov, is) on the left of the entrance: likewise the part below (ierr)iil3pLv6v. belongs to the same Eusebios, the) south side).* 164. On the sarcophagus at the north end of the upper story—h), opposite the entrance. The plate measures 79 cm. at the top, and 88 across the fourth line. The first line of the inscription is 59 cm. long, the second 77, the third 82, and the fourth 61: the letters are 5 to 6 cm. high.

Published by Waddington, No. 2661 e. Burton and Drake, No. 17. Clermont-Ganneau, I.e., p. 128 ff.

Waddington gives K instead of N at the beginning of the second line, and renders the inscription as follows: Atoyc Vr/s O /cos *Evaefiiov Kai 'AvTaviPOvd. &efov iirl Koiva.* M. Clermont-Ganneau, on the other hand, would read: AioyeVrjs, 6 e/cSi/cos (or 6 crwSi/co?), Eio-epiov Kui *'avTwlvov* dScA.os, eVi

Kolvo.. It is significant, however, that this sarcophagus occupies the most conspicuous position in all the tomb, as though Diogenes AIOrNHCO Atoyei O Were P6TM11 f diSnity Eu" NOCYCBlOYK?oCEio-'ou*Kolv*-sebios and Antoninos. And yet the latter TWNINOYAAAt *rtavivov a§ef* were the real proprietors of the mausoleum, TTIKOINA« *ivld.* as js evident especially from the following inscription, No. 165. This Diogenes may be the same as the Diogenes who is mentioned as the father of Antoninos. But it is a curious fact that while the father of Antoninos is mentioned in all the inscriptions which concern Antoninos in particular, Nos. 157, 158, 162 and 170, the father of Eusebios is not mentioned anywhere. It seems to me then quite possible that the Diogenes of this inscription, whether he was the father of Antoninos or not, stood in some other relation to Eusebios, and that Eusebios and Antoninos were not brothers in the ordinary sense, but perhaps "brothers in Christ," or, as Dr. Littmann suggests, foster brothers: in the latter case Eusebios may also have been a natural son of Diogenes. See the discussion of the term *brothers'*in Part IV, p. 37 f. I would therefore suggest reading Kl instead of K or N at the beginning of line 2, and adding an I at the end of line 1. The whole inscription would then be as follows:

AioycvTjs, Oi(ki)o? *TLvaefitov* Kcu ai *Twvivov,* aSeXfwi', C7ri *Kolvol. Diogenes, kinsman of Eusebios and Antoninos, brothers, in common.*

That is: *Diogenes (is buried here), a kinsman of brothers Eusebios and Antoninos, (to whom this sepulchre belongs) in common.* 165. A stone, which is now the right jamb of the village mosque, was evidently the lintel of the doorway in the upper story of this tomb. It is heavily ornamented, and measures 194 cm. in length, by 56 in height. It contains an inscription in letters 5 cm. high. My copy of this inscription marks a break in the stone, immediately after the last letter. I have no record whether this break was through the entire stone; but I should judge from my copy that it was so. In that case the lintel has lost its right end. The inscription, however, seems to be complete. The text which follows is from copies made by both Dr. Littmann and the editor. The letters are badly weathered.

YMHAIKWNA APTIWNYCBIOYKAI ANTWNINOY V.I., YMHAIKWNA4. Ap Kt. (Dr. Littmann); in my own copy I noted that the third letter may be X, instead of M.

Eu(y) (8)ikcw a£' a.)_fiapTiC)v Eucre/ 8tov KaX 'avtwvivov. *Resting-place of Eusebios and Antoninos, justified from their sins.*

I am indebted to Dr. Littmann for the suggestion that AIK6UJN should be read (8)iKeW, i.e. SiKauov. The use of this adjective with *airb* seems a little strange. But SiWoi (sc. cto-i) is used, evidently in the sense of the passive of Si/cguow, in Romans ii, 13: *ov yap oi aKpoaral vop,ov Si'kcuoi napa Tw % ea, dxX' oi notr/Tal vop,ov hiKaioiOr-fo'ovraL.* Compare also 8i7ccuo9 in Galatians iii, 11:6 Sikguo? *i nto-Tews It-fo-erai,* with 8iKaia0evTe? in Romans v, 1: SiKGucofleVres *ovv Ck 7ri'oT6a»? eiprjvrjv exa)H-v-*The verb is used with *avb* in this sense in

Romans vi, 7: *0 yap awodavuiv SeStKatWcu dirb rrjs d/tAaprux?.* The adjective Suceos = *"lejtiste"* is found in a Christian epitaph, probably of late date, published by M. ClermontGanneau, *Recueil,* v, p. 167.

This reading, if correct, gives the true name of this interesting building, and shows that this was not the "Tomb of Diogenes," but the Tomb of Eusebios and Antoninos.

The cornice of the lower story of the mausoleum, which formed the podium of the naos, was ornamented with a cy-matium whose profile is given in Mr. Butler's drawing, Part II, p. 163, Fig. 69a. On the south side this cornice must have been very near the ground level, and it was broken by the steps which led to the entrance of the upper story. On the east side this cornice was doubtless borne by the ends of the slabs which roofed the portico of the lower entrance. The western section of the cornice, with an inscription carved on the upper inward curve of the cyma, remains almost

intact in its original place. See Part II, pp. 160 and 162.

166. On the cornice of the podium, on the west side. The inscription is about 8 meters long. It began about 1.18 m. from the northwest corner of the building. The corner block has been lost from the north end, and one block or more from the south end of this cornice; but the inscription is evidently complete. The letters are 9 to 11 cm. high, and regular, well-formed and clear.

Published by Waddington, No. 2661 b. Burton and Drake, No. 15. Clermont-Ganneau, I.e., p. 123.

eniCKYOYTHNrHNKAIM6eYCACAYTHN-ACTACYNePIMMATAAYTH-COTieCAAYeH 'Emo-Ko/iou *rfjv yrjv Kal e/u.e#was avrrqv eacre rd ovvQplp. p.ara aurs on eoaXev#n. Thou hast visited the earth and watered it: heal thou the breaches thereof; for it is shaken.* 'Knio-Ka(tov *is for eVeo-K«/»ct), iaae for lacrai, ouvdpip.paTa for ouvrpLp.p. ara.* Waddington says that he was unable to find these passages in the Holy Scriptures. As M. Chabot discovered, however, in the case of the first, and M. Clermont-Ganneau in the case of the second, they are quotations from Psalms lxiv, 1 o, and lix, 4. Swete, in his edition of 1891, has adopted *io-aXevdrjo-av* in the text of the latter passage: see his critical commentary. Doubtless these psalms were familiar to all Christians through their use in connection with the church service. The Codex Parisinus 476, of the so-called "Liturgy of St. James," contains in the concluding prayer a sentence which was perhaps based on the second passage, and suggests that possibly these words may have formed part of the burial service, or of some early form of worship: *Avros Kal w, beo-Trora, lao-ai rd 0-vvTplp.p. ara Totv tcaphioiv r)p.£v, Kox /Jvcrai r)p.ai anb Ttjs fo/3epas Kal avivido-TOv Kal £/3iktt??* 17/u.epas Tss *Kpiaem, Kt.* 1 Compare, however, Isaiah xxx, 26, and Jeremiah iii, 22. On this and the following inscriptions, Nos. 167-170, see Chapter 1, pp. 9, 20 and 12 f. 167. The inscription on the cornice of the north side of the podium seems to have been still intact when it was copied by

Waddington and M. de Vogue. Only a small portion of its western end now remains. The letters are like those of No. 166: the last of them is about 1.25 m. from the northwest corner of the building.

Published by Waddington, No. 2661 a. Burton and Drake, No. 15.

The eleven letters which were still to be seen in March, 1900, are CKAIlTItAN. M. Waddington's reading is as follows: *E.voyT)fjLevo; 6 ipop-evo iv ovopan Kvpiov. @eos Ku/atos, Kal iirifyavtv rj-plv. Blessed (is) he that cometh in (the) name of (the) Lord. God is (the) Lord, and hath shown us light.* 'Eirtyavev *is for inefavev.* The words of this inscription are taken ultimately, as M. Waddington noted, from Psalms cxvii, 26 and 27. But in view of the facts presented on p. 9, above, it seems to me that this inscription is not only liturgical in the more general sense, in which M. Clermont-Ganneau uses this word to distinguish the inscriptions of the cornice from those of the sarcophagi, but was a part of the liturgy actually in use in this community. As has been said, the same may be true of No. 166 also. And it is not impossible that the clue to the following fragments is to be found in the literary tradition of the early forms of worship.

Besides the cornice inscriptions, two inscribed fragments were found by both M. Waddington and myself in the immediate vicinity of the tomb, and apparently belonging to it. The profile of these fragments is that given by Mr. Butler in Fig. 6 b, and they were, in his opinion, parts of the architrave of the portico on the east side of the lower story. They seem to contain portions of two distinct sentences; but as the two sides of the lower-story cornice contained each two short sentences joined together in one inscription, there is no reason for believing that these fragments do not belong together also. They are as follows: 168. On a broken block in a stone fence immediately south of the mausoleum.

The moulding is broken at the top. The total length of the AYNAM—4IAA--CONH letter-space is 184 cm., the height of the letters 7 to 8 cm.

Published by Waddington, No. 2661 c.

Waddington gives:--AYNAMIA t»ACA-CONH.

169. On a block in a stone fence immediately northeast of the northeast corner of the mausoleum. The total letter-space is no cm. in length: the KAH-PONOWIANC. „ *S.t.. r.* height of the letters is 8 to 9 cm. Three other pieces of the same moulding, but without letters, lie near by.

Published by Waddington, No. 2661 c. Burton and Drake, No. 19.

1 Swainson, *Greek Liturgies*, p. 331.

Sentences SUCH as *aaaov Tov Xaov crov, Kal evXoyqaov Trjv KX-qpovopLav crov,*1 or *evXoyqaov Tov a6v aov, Kou hiavXaov Tt)v KXrjpovofj.iav aov* are common enough in the traditional liturgies: the former occurs for example in the "Liturgy of St. Basil,"2 and the latter in the "Liturgy of St. James."3 In fact the short prayer, in which the former is contained, occurs both near the beginning and again near the end of the "Liturgy of St. Basil," and suggests a possible combination of the fragments under discussion. The whole prayer is as follows: Kvpios 6 ©eos *r/pwv, awaov Tov Xaov aov, Kal evXoyqaov Ttjv KX-qpovoplav aov To irX-qpcapa Trjs eKKXiqaias aov iv elp-qvrj oi.afvXa£ov, dyLaaov* row? *dya77wra? Tt/v evn peireiav Tov Olkov aov. av avrovs dvTiootjaaov Tt) de'iKfj aov Svvdpei, Kal pr) eyKaTaXLirr)s* 17/u.as, 6 ©eds, Tov? *eXirilovTai tVi al* Possibly the two fragments might be united in some such way as this:

Kupios *dvTLOoaaov-qpd; Trj deiKr aov ovvdpei* xat *(ev)X(oy)* tj *aov (T)rfv KX-qpovoplav aov Glorify 7ts in return, 0 Lord, by thy divine power, and bless thine inheritance.*

The total number of letters here is sixty-six, or two more than in the inscription on the west cornice and five more than in that of the north side. But the letters in these fragments are somewhat smaller than those of the cornice inscriptions. It is interesting to note in this connection that a handsome lintel, which was also found at Hass, and which probably belonged to the church of that place, bears this inscription: Ad£a riaT/31 Kal *Tia Kal 'Ayiq HvevpaTf aoaov, Kvpie, Tov Xaov* 0-ou.4

One more inscription completes the number of those belonging to this mausoleum which have been found as yet.

170. On a slab of black basalt, lying in a field a few yards southwest of the tomb. Mr. Butler tells me that this was one of the plates inserted between the columns of the peristyle, to form a kind of balustrade, such as is found in the upper stories of the porticos which form the fronts of most of the houses in this region. The length of the slab is 91, the width 69, and the thickness 19 cm. The two ends of the slab are notched, leaving a projection of about 5 cm. at the back. These projections are rough dressed at their outer edges, and were evidently intended to be inserted in the columns. All the other surfaces of the slab are smoothly dressed, and were doubtless highly polished.. A plain panel, 73)4 by 52)4 cm., is sunk in the face of the stone. The inscription, in twelve lines, runs across this panel and its border as well, and fills the whole face of the slab. The letters are from 4 to 5 cm. high, and are poorly arid lnscn '»0-Cast from a sueeze irregularly carved, doubtless in consequence of the extreme hardness of the material: 1 Psalm xxvii, 9. 3 Swainson, p. 322. 2 Swainson, p. 76. 4 No. 156. they are now much worn, but still legible. Two squeezes of this inscription were made, and are at present in the library of Princeton University. It was my intention, when I had finished with the original stone, to turn it face down, in order to preserve it better: I cannot now recall whether I did so or not; but in either case the stone can be found easily, for it lies only about 10 yards from the original building. *Thou who gavest life to the human race, and didst enjoin death on account of transgression, and in thine own loving-kindness and tender mercies didst promise the resurrection, and gavest a pledge* (i. e. the Holy Spirit), *Christ, visit with thy salvation thy servant Antonitios, son of Diogenes, and Dometia, his wife, and the others who lie at rest here, that they may see the good of thy chosen.*

In spite of its lofty tone, this inscription abounds in mistakes. Most of these are orthographical however, as the following list will show: yeVi for *yivei.*: K4 for *Kox*, five times OUt of six: *ivTikapevos* for *eVriXd/Aei*09: iSois for Z3toi9: *iTTa.vyikdp.tvo'i* for *inayyeikdpevos; dpa/3a)vo-a* for *dppa./3(avicra.;*; *inicrKeie* for *cVur/co/icu*: Avrmvivov for *'avtojvlvov*. Aioyevov for Aioyevov?: *IBiv* for *IBelv; iykerwv* for *iKkeKTwv*.

The phrase *iv e'Xe'ei Ko.1 oitcrippoh* is found in Psalm cii, 4; but it also occurs frequently in the liturgies. Lines 7 and 11-12 are quoted from Psalm cv, 4 and 5: *eVio-K«/»ai ij/xas iv* Tw *crayrqpup crov, Tov Iseiv iv Tjj xP7lrrTVTl Tv ixci£Tj)v crov*. But the whole inscription is distinctly liturgical in character, and may have been taken entire, except of course for the proper names, from the actual church service. A comparison of the successive phrases with passages contained in the "Liturgy of St. Basil" will be found above, p. 13, and also in my article in the *Transactions of the American Philological Association*, 1902, p. 96 f.

It will be noticed that this inscription refers primarily to Antoninos and his wife. Undoubtedly it was placed in the south side of the peristyle, between the first two columns at the right of the entrance to the naos, where it could be read easily by those ascending the steps. This would bring the inscription about opposite the end of the sarcophagus in the upper story which belonged to Antoninos. Perhaps there was another inscription in the corresponding position, on the left of the entrance and opposite the end of Eusebios' sarcophagus, which referred in the same way to Eusebios and his wife.

In conclusion then it is evident that Eusebios and Antoninos, two Christian "brothers," built this mausoleum for themselves and their families in partnership. Each reserved for himself three out of the eight sarcophagi, Antoninos those on the right of the entrances, one in the upper story and two in the lower, and Eusebios those on the left of the entrances. The two remaining sarcophagi, one in each story opposite the entrance, were owned in common; but the owners agreed to grant the one in the upper story to a kinsman of theirs named Diogenes. The sarcophagi, though not very long, were wide and deep, and doubtless were used, as such graves are used in many parts of Europe still, to receive other bodies after the first had crumbled away. Thus three or four sarcophagi would amply provide for a man and his wife, together with their immediate descendants. And thus this "Resting-place of Eusebios and Antoninos" may serve as a typical example of the family tombs of the more wealthy inhabitants of this region, about the fifth century of our era.

170 a. HAss. Fragment. Published by Burton and Drake, *Unexplored Syria*, 11, p. 380, No. 14, and Drawings, p. 2: "On Moslem tombstone at Shaykh Sawadan." EKGEMEAIwN... «c 0e/eXiW ...... *from the) foundations...* 171. Khirbit Faris. Tomb. In a dove-tail plate on a stone, otherwise perfectly plain, lying among other blocks at the west side of a shaft-tomb, in the southwest corner of the main part of the town. The tomb is covered by a lid with six acroteria. The stone now faces eastward: it is 1.34 m. long, 0.83 wide and 0.56 thick. The letters of the first three lines are well made and 6 cm. high, while those of the last two lines are carelessly made and scarcely more than 3 cm. high. Copy of the editor.

In the fourth line d8i£e and *Kvvijo-e* seem to have been intended for dSi/oJo-ai and *Kivijo-ai; elva* gives another example of « for i. In the fifth line perhaps we should read Xup/iava or *vmliava. A* close parallel to the fervent desire expressed here is furnished in a Greek inscription from Nablus, published in the *Statements of the Palestine Exploration Fund,* 1902, p. 240 f., and there translated as follows: *"The single (i.e. separate,private) tomb of the Blessed Doxasia, daughter of Dora and Megale, whose lives have closed. And / adjure the God of these bones, and the mystery of death, and the hour of judgment, that no one here tear either relic or bone out of me."* 172. Kefr Ruma. Tomb, 349 A.

d. On the front of a rock-hewn tomb, with a vestibule before it, north of the village and facing southeast. The letters were originally painted with red; but now the whole inscription is coated with a black substance, as hard as shellac, which fills up many letters, and makes the reading of the inscription difficult and uncertain. The same black coating covers a part of the wall, and the ceiling of the vestibule: it is probably due in part to the smoke of many fires, built by those who used the tomb as a dwelling. The inscription is in a dove-tail plate, the body of which measures 0.52 by 0. 49 m. Copy of the editor.

The use of the word *rpk.iov* for tomb was not unnatural for these people, for they were accustomed to the use of -*qprn* in the sense of the *"dear departed":* cf. No. 151.

If o-a£eo-0e (for o-w£eo-0ai?) is in the middle voice, rather than the passive, it is quite possible to understand the verb in the sense of *keep in mind, remember,* as in Plato's *Republic,* 455 B: 178' a *epaOe o-oitfliTo.* The last sentence might then be translated: *kindly remember this, I pray.* At the same time one would expect to find here a request that the tomb may remain undisturbed. If so, then the words must mean something like this: *be obedient to me to preserve this tomb ofours.* In either easel believe that the last two words are intended for *einjuooL* and *poL* The word after *Av&vrlov* must be either his father's name, or some title. One naturally thinks of 4tXtir7rou.

The monogram, outside of the dovetail plate, is perhaps by some other, later hand, and certainly has no apparent connection with the text of the inscription within the plate. Possibly there may have been other similar letters, which with these made up aXvjTre, xaipe: *sorrmc-free, farewell,* written after Auxentios' death.

173. Kefr Ruma. Columnar Monument. On the stump of a broken column, standing on a pedestal, north of the modern village. See Part II, p. 63. Burton and

Drake, *Unexplored Syria,* 11, p. 213. The pedestal, which is about 8 feet high,

rests upon the living rock, in which a plain sarcophagus is hewn on the south side of the monument. All about are similar sarcophagi, and in the hill nearer the village there are other tombs, so that this was evidently the necropolis of the ancient town.

Only six drums of the column now remain: the inscription is on the uppermost of these, about 18 feet from the ground, on the south side, facing the town. The stone has crumbled badly, so that the central part of the inscription, including the date, is lost beyond recovery. The inscription was incised in a plate, sunk in the face of the column, 442 cm. in height and about 97 cm. in length. The last letter of both the first and the second lines is outside of the plate. The letters occupy a space of about 5 cm. each in breadth. The break in the first line is about 56 cm. long, in the second 50, in the fourth 6 cm.: in the fifth line the space between rYNAI-KI and E, and the space after E, seem to have been blank. When I saw this monument again, in 1905, the inscribed drum had fallen, and had been broken in two pieces and still further damaged. Copy of the editor.

I have not been able to decipher this inscription satisfactorily. In 1900 I read, in the first part of line 2, NOYMHN; in the first part of line 1-ETOYC AAC,,,,, ... Tr.

TTPOMAAO; in the second half of line El. If it may 2-NOYMh AAO y '.7 3-TTPOMA OINA be supposed that the text was written in two columns, 4-KAIANT-GTH-WNETTOI the following recon 5. rYNAIKI E struction is possible: "Erous Xas, *Novfirjv Xdov, In the) year,for Numenios, son of Promachos, and Antia, his pofid(x)ov,* «r! K *oiva wif£m Ko)* 'Avruf, Tt) *Wv eVoi'ei. las, son) of laos, conjointly (i.e. by way of sharing in) ywaiicL what he made.*

This reading is, of course, most uncertain. On *eVi nowd,* see No. 164.

In 1905 I found on a block, which seemed to have been a part of the pedestal of this same column, the following letters: CEPATT. These letters are 5 to *6/2* cm. high. The stone is broken at both ends; but before the letters is a blank space, 42cm. long, showing that this was the beginning of an inscription. 174. Kefr Roma. On a plain block 4 meters in length, half buried in the ground, east of the monument. The first line of the 6YC6 B I C Ewre/Jis, *Bdpyov.* ....,,, _ . *rr* inscription is 0.40 m. long, and begins 0.80 m. from B APrOY r & b the left end of the stone: the second line is 0.39 m. *Euscbis* (i.e. Eusebios), *(son) of Bargos.* , 1, 1 1. 0 v 'x *'J 6* long-The letters are 4 to 4J4 cm. high, except the

B of the second word, which is 7 cm. high. Copy of Dr. Littmann.

On the name *Bargos* see Nos. 3 and 336 a.

174 a. Kefr Ruma. Fragment. Published by Burton and Drake, wM MAriC *Unexplored Syria,* 11, p. 380, No. 13, and Drawings, p. 2: "On broken sarcophagus." 175. Kefr Ruma. Graffiti on the south wall of an ancient building, probably a church, but later made into a mosque by breaking through the south wall and adding a mihrab. The letters are on the east side of the niche. The first are mere scratches, which I think were intended for Greek letters, but of which I could make nothing whatsoever. Further towards the east, upside down, are the letters CE.

176. Khirbit Hass. Grave Stele, 187 A. d. "Sur une stele employee dans une cloture." Waddington, 2655. I did not find this stele myself; but Waddington says-TYCH9YAY etovs Ij9u,aa8u that the following inscription in his publi_mhahca "c"ou ' At8r?s cation, No. 2656, is close by. The latter was _japoy-aa *Spov, £X(We,* found, among other stelae, in the ruins of walls XAIP XatP which form a kind of enclosure On the sOUth *In the)year 498, Audynaios 20th, Diomedes* and west sides of the church. See the next *(son) f Dexandros, sorrow-free, farewell!* inscription. '(January, 187 A.D.) 177. Khirbit Hass. Stele. On a stele in the ruins of walls, perhaps of cloisters, on the south and west sides of the church. See Part II, pp. 82 and 93 f. These ruined walls contained other stelae, two of which at least were inscribed (Nos. 176 and 178). Probably there are other inscriptions here also, and I regret that we did not have suffi-

cient time or a sufficient force then to examine this place thoroughly. For evidently these buildings, which belong to the Christian period and are now in ruins themselves, were built from the ruins of a pre-Christian settlement: some of these remains of the earlier time were the gravestones of a pagan cemetery. MHNOCAY he stee s Drken immediately below the sixth line AYNAIOY Mtjj/os AuSuvaiou Gf the inscription, which therefore may be incomplete. TTCMTT-TH Trein-fl, *Xpurrap*-ye remaining portion measures 1.33 m. in length by A ?cimkbw S *Aavpov* ave 0.59 in width. At the top of the face is a moulded border,

AciANArO Y o"rnT(v ANCTHC6N 7/ cm-deep. Below this, the surface is cut in the form *On the) fifth oj'the) month Andy*-of a panel, having a plain border in relief on each side, *naios, Aristarchos son) of Dexandros y2* cm wide. The upper half of this panel is occupied *set up this stele).* an eagie presenting a front view, with wings half raised. Below this is the inscription, occupying a space 0. 42 m. high. The letters, which are about 5 cm. high, are fairly well made, but irregular and not deep. Copy of the editor.

Published by Waddington, No. 2656.

The date of this monument is probably about the same as that of the preceding one, i.e. about 187 A.d. 178. Khirbit Hass. Grave Stele. On a stele, broken at the top, found near No. 177, at the foot of the wall on the side towards the church. The length of the stone is 1.60 m., the width 0.59, the thickness 0.40: the width of the space occupied by the inscription is 0.43 m. Copy of the editor.

avo xov Tv i»ioC *avrov-aXiwc Xa'Pe (in memory?) of his son: sorrow-free, farewell /* 179. Khirbit Hass. Tomb. On the two ends of the cover over a tomb like that of No. 34. The tomb is in a corner formed by two buildings, about 50 feet west of No. 177. See Part II, p. 277 f. The cover has six acroteria, of which the one at the center of the east side contains a bust, the one on the west side a kind of "disk" (Part II, p. 32 f.). The bust is very rude: its drapery, where it crosses the breast, is so stiff that the folds

look almost like the ribs of a skeleton. The face has been battered off. Inscription A is on the north end of the cover. The first line is 0.64 m. long, the second 0.53. The letters, 3 to 7 cm. high, are very rude. Inscription B is on the south end of the cover: the letters have the same forms as those of the other end. Copy of the editor.

A. ETOYCHOXOVPANIC A. "*etous rjox', Ovpdvi? EvKevrpCov,* VKNTPIOY

B. BACIAYcBoNBore B-acriXevs, *Bovoye(yeov,* eVo«jre rOVTTolHC-MAOoVIB ftvos) *Aoov ifi.*

In (the) year 678, Uranis (son) of Eukentrios, king (?), from Manbdg (?), made (this

sarcophagus), (on the) 12th of (the) month Loos. (August, 367 A.D.)

In B, the letters BoNBorereov all seemed to me certain, excepting the third, which might be V or Al. With regard to these letters I am indebted to Dr. Littmann for the following note: "I believe that *Bovfioyeyeov* stands for *Bovfioyeov,* the y« having been repeated by mistake in the second line. Booyios is only another way of spelling Ma/ioy-aZo1 The Syriac form for *Membidp* is *Mabbog* or *Manbdg.* In *Bovfioy*-we have for the first time the prototype of the modern variant *Bumbudj.*" The word here seems to agree with the name of Uranis' father, as if the father alone came from Manbog. But I have not discovered what the title /3ao-iXev? can signify in such a case as this. I suppose it is possible that both Bao-iXetk and *Bovfioyeos* are proper names, 1 See Wad. 2554 f. 3 Many of the natives call the city *Bumbudj* instead of 2 The modern name for the city, which is about 50 miles *Membidj:* the Greek name was *Hierapolis.* northeast of Haleb.

Inscr. 178. From a drawing. Scale 1:10.

the former like the names *King, Kaiser, Le Roy,* etc.; the latter like *Bremer, Berliner,* etc. See Clermont-Ganneau, *Recueil,* v, p. 86 ff.; Dittenberger, *Orientis Graecce Inscrr. Selectae,* No. 426. Two examples of BcunXevs as a proper name are cited by Pape: with Boioyeos we may compare Aftaios, Boiwrios, etc. In this latter case Basileus, son of Bon-

bogeos. was the man who made the tomb, Uranis the man who lay in it. 180. Khirbit Hass. Lintel, 566 A.d. "Sur un linteau de porte qui n'est pas a sa place originaire." Waddington, 2658. t TOY-CZOWI«1APTMC fErous £oo/, fi-qvbi) Aprf/xeo-lou + *In (the) year 877, in (the) month Artemesios (May, 566 A. D.)* 181. Khirbit Hass. Tomb, 430 A.d. Over the entrance to a rock-hewn tomb, northeast of the town, and facing southeast. The tomb is approached by a passage with eight steps. Before the door is an arched vestibule 1.95 m. wide, with engaged columns at each side. The doorway is 0.69 m. wide, and from it two more steps lead down to the floor of the tomb itself. This consists of a single chamber with four arcosolia, one in each side and two in the wall opposite the entrance. See de Vogue, *S. C*, pi. 82, No. 1. The space occupied by the inscription is 1.30 m. long by 0.16 m. high. In the center is a disk, which breaks both lines. The letters were originally painted. They are from 3)4 to 4 cm. high. Copy by Dr. Littmann.
Published by Waddington, No. 2657.
ETEAIU9HTOWNHM ONETOYC AM 'EreXiw To *fivlov* erovs ap/»', /xt/(j/os) N/IANAIKOYK£f INAI TIONOCI rtf *BavBucov K, Iv8lktl5po; iy'. This tomb was finished in (the) year month Xandikos 20th, indiction Ij.* (April, 430 A.D.)
I have restored the 1 in *vuov* from Waddington.
182. Khirbit Hass. House. Lintel of a two-story house, of simple quadrated masonry, facing south in the southern part of the town. The ground floor of this house consists of two large square rooms: the present inscription is over the entrance to the room on the east. The lintel is ornamented with the usual raised plate, surmounted by a door-cap. On either side of the plate is a disk containing the chrisma. The first word of the inscription is carved on the raised plate: it measures 21 by 6 cm. The other word is below the plate, and measures 29 by 3*l/2* cm. The plate itself is 36 cm. long. The letters are well formed and clear. Copy of the editor.
Published by Waddington, No. 2659 a.

Uspensky, *A. M. S.*, p. 61 f.
IX9YC IXOTS *(ixdvs: aJish), '.t.* 'ictocs) AAHAOYIA e(eoG) T(Ios), *t(amjp).* 'axtjxouio. *J(esus) Ch(rist), (the) S(on) (of) G(od),(our) S(avior). Aleluia!*
See Chapter 1, pp. 15 and 24.
183. Khirbit Hass. Same House. On the lintel of the other doorway in the ground floor of the same house, opening into the room on the west. The lintel is similar to the other: the inscription is at the bottom, below the plate, and measures 26 cm. by 3 to 4 cm. Copy of the editor.
Published by Waddington, No. 2659 b.
AAHAOVIA *'Ar)ovia. Aleluia!* 184. Khirbit Hass. House. Lintel on the east side of a house, of simple quadrated masonry, in the northeastern part of the town. This seemed to have been a side door to the house. The space occupied by the inscription is 1.10 m. long and 0.19 m. high. The tallest letters are 14 cm. high. Copy of the editor. 185. Khirbit Hass. Same House. Lintel of a door on the north side of the same house as the foregoing: evidently this was the main entrance. The space occupied by the inscription is 1.41 m. long and 0.18 high. The letters are 12 to 13 cm. high. Copy of the editor. 186. Khirbit Hass. House. On the lintel of a doorway in the second story of a house in the southeastern part of the town, facing south. The letters are $yA cm. high. Copied by Mr. Butler and Mr. Garrett.
Inscr. 186. From a copy and a photograph. Scale 1: 20.
See Chapter 1, p. 25, and Chapter 11, pp. 39 and 64 f. Compare also Nos. 89, 114, 116, 235 and 262.
187. Il-barah. Press. Carved on the outside of the north wall of a building, about the center of the town. See Part 11, p. 270, and M. de Vogu6, *La Syrie Centrale*, p. 84 f., and pi. 35. The building was about 12 meters long and 8 wide on the outside, and the span of the arches which supported the roof was 20 feet. It was evidently a factory for wine or oil. Above the inscription three blocks of stone, flat on the under side but with sloping
Inscription 187.
tops, project horizontally from the wall,

forming a shed-roof over the inscription and over an opening cut through the wall below the inscription, through which the fruit was poured into the factory. The top of this chute is now barely visible, and the shed-stones are less than a meter and a half above the ground; but I think there is no doubt that the original ground level here was much lower: the floor of the factory is two or three meters lower than the ground outside. The inside of this opening is 97 cm. wide and 30 cm. high, and below it the wall has been cut out somewhat, as if for a bin into which the fruit fell.
The western wall of the building is destroyed and most of the roof has fallen in, so that the interior is filled with large blocks of stone and debris. But the east wall has been preserved, and one arch, supporting the first row of roof-slabs. At this end of the building some of the old apparatus remains, and doubtless if the rest of the interior could be cleared out this factory would be found as complete as the bakeries at Pompeii. In the northeast corner is a circular stone, about 4 feet in diameter. The top is hewn into the form of a flat-bottomed basin about Press at ii-Barah. 6 inches deep, with a socket in the center, the top of which is flush with the top of the basin's rim. I took it to be the under stone of a machine for crushing olives, like some that are in use among the modern natives. In such a machine there is first a circular stone laid upon its side, like a lower millstone, with a socket in its center and a rim around its edge. In the socket stands a revolvable post, into which is set, horizontally, a beam, the inner end of which serves as the axle of a second stone like a grindstone or a cart-wheel. By means of the beam the grindstone is made to roll around upon the millstone, crushing the olives placed in its track.
In the southeast corner of the factory, in the east wall, is a very large socket for the lever of a press, 47 cm. wide and 1.04 m. deep, the jaws projecting a foot or more from the wall. I could not find how high this socket is, because of the debris on the floor. In the jaws are holes at two different heights, evident-

ly for the pins which held the lever. These holes, which are 20 cm. in diameter, pierce the left jaw, but are not carried entirely through the right one, so that it must have been difficult for anyone, who was not left-handed, to adjust these heavy pins. In front of this lever-socket are two stones, placed side by side: I could not see that they had been fastened together in any way: but they are doubtless mortised into the stone floor. They are cut so as to form between them a cylindrical vessel, 27 cm. in diameter. On the side towards the lever-socket this cylinder has an opening, 20 cm. wide, extending down 22 cm. from the top. In the opposite side there is an opening, 9 cm. wide on the inside, and 17 cm. wide at the front. The back of the cylinder is 84 cm. from the front of the jaws of the lever-socket. I have seen a similar apparatus used by modern natives: it consisted of a tube, made of a tree-stem, about a foot in diameter, and hollowed out until it was like a section of 1 o-inch pipe, set upright under a long lever. The top was open, and through the tube, for most of its length, there was a slit, about 3 inches wide, through which the lever was passed. The olives were crushed, made into a mash and packed in little, round, shallow baskets, which were then piled in the hollow tree-stem and pressed by the lever.

I have no doubt that all the apparatus which I have described here was used for making olive oil. But the stone cylinder seems absurdly small, when compared with the size of the lever-socket. And the inscription on the outside of the building indicates that this was a factory for wine rather than for oil. M. Waddington, in his very interesting commentary on this inscription, says that the grapes of ilBarah are still famous in northern Syria, and that he himself found them most delicious. Waddington believed that these were the uvae Apamenae, which were brought to Rome at great expense under the emperor Elagabalus. The present expedition unfortunately visited this region at the beginning of April, when the vines were being pruned and the joints smeared with some tarry substance; when the first shoots were starting from the old stocks and the first furry leaves were unfolding; when there was nothing whatever to suggest grapes, much less wine, save the remarkable thirst engendered by the climate. But undoubtedly this was a great wine country, and would be still, if wine were not forbidden to the Mohammedan natives by their religious law. Probably then this was originally a wine-press, in which a huge lever pressed upon a vat now concealed by the debris. A lever which fitted this socket must have been a tree-stem more than a foot in diameter.

But the Mohammedans occupied il-Barah in comparatively early times, as is known from the Arabic literature, from the local traditions and from the many ancient graffiti found among the ruins. And it seems as if the ban of Islam must have fallen on the old wine-press too: then, in a later age, this factory appears to have been used for crushing olives and for making oil, on a comparatively humble scale.

Published in the *Bibliotheca Sacra*, 1848, p. 92. Waddington, No. 2644. M. de Vogiie, *S. C,* pi. 35. *C. I. L.,* in, 188 and p. 972.

NECTAREOSSUCCOSBACCHEIAMUNER-ACERNIS

QUAEBITISGENUITAPRICOSOLEREFECTA

Nectareos succos, Baccheia munera, cernis, *Here draughts of nectar, Bacchus' gifts, you see,*

Quae bitis genuit aprico sole refecta. *which his vine bore by the warm sun revived,*

Bitis is for *vitis.* 188. Il-barah. House, 412 A.d. Graffito inside of a very plain house, facing the east, at the edge of the deep wadi which is on the 6TOY-CAKYMHNOCA-OYAKK eagt Qf the and fer frQm the southeast

"Erou? 8w/»', fir)vb; Aiov *Uk ia.* corner of the ruins. The inscription is in the main room, on the north side, on the soffit of the central arch near its springing. It is 79 cm. long, and the letters 3 to 8 cm. high. Copy of the editor. *In (the) year J24., month Dios 21st.* (November, 412 A.D.) 189. Il-barah. Tomb, 417 A.d. Above the entrance to a rock-hewn tomb in the wadi between the modern village and the ancient town, about three minutes' walk west of the former. Above the inscription are three disks, the central one of which contains a +, and the letters A w. The tomb contains three arcosolia, two of which have two sarcophagi each.

The inscription is scratched on the face of the rock, rudely, but deeply enough to be perfectly legible still. The letters vary from 4 to 7 cm. in height, and are not in a straight line: the distance, in a straight line, from the first to the last letter is 1.25 m. Copy of the editor.

Published in *C. I. G.* 9152. Waddington, No. 2645. M. de Vogue", *S. C,* pi. 80.

TOYCHKYZANAlKOYSMAAXOCrOYPA.

belifVe ±e dafc iS' aS in similar inscriptions on tombs, the date when ErovS, SoriucoS MaxxoS *ToUpa.* Makhos had the tomb made PerhapS) hQW *In (the) year 728, Xandikos 6th: Malchos* ever, as the editor of the "Corpus" believed, it is *(son) of Guras.* (April, 417 A.D.) the date of Malcnos' death.

On the name *Malchos* = the Semitic *Malk* or *Malik,* see the discussion by Renan, in *Journal Asiatique,* 7, xix (1882), p. 11. The form *Vovpa* is doubtless a genitive from Toupas. Cf. "*AvSpa* or *'Avhpea* in No. 29. A genitive rWpov, however, occurs in No. 257. There is a Palmyrene name NIIJ, transliterated into Latin in the form *Gums,* in the bilingual inscription (Palm.-Latin) found in Keransebes, Hungary.1 190. Il-barah. Tomb, 416 A.d. Over the doorway of a rock-hewn tomb, southwest of the ruins. A wadi formed the southern boundary of the ancient town, and on the slopes of the wadi and in the southwestern corner of the town itself were a number of the handsomest tombs. Some, close to the houses, were of masonry. One of these, with a high pyramidal roof, is still almost intact. See Part II, p. 243 f. Another, which has lost most of its pyramid, still constitutes one of the most beautiful buildings of this region. See Part II, p. 244 f. Other tombs, among which is the tomb of the present inscription, are hewn in the rock on the south side of the wadi. See also the next inscription.

This tomb has a sort of vestibule, with two arches springing from a central pier, all hewn from the living rock. Within the tomb are five arcosolia. Above the doorway 1 *C. I. L.,* 111, 7999.
is a sort of frieze of upright acanthus leaves, in the center of which is an ornamental disk containing a cross and the A and w. This ornamentation had been badly damaged shortly before I saw it. It seemed as if some of the natives of this neighborhood resented our reading words which were Greek to them. Many of the natives certainly believed that these writings contained the clue to hidden treasures which they thought we were trying to find for ourselves. And most of the natives, as we found from actual experience, were far too ignorant to distinguish between writing and mere ornament.

The first line measured originally 1. 11 m. in length; but from twenty to twentyfour letters, occupying a space of 0.84 m., have been lost from the center. The second line was 0.89 m. long, and seven letters have been lost: these however can be restored with certainty. The letters were well cut, and were painted red. They are 4 to 5 cm. high. Copy of the editor.

P." OIIAITOY SI ouatTOV.

MHNIA _ TOYCZKYINAI *Mrpi* (A)*vcr-rpov,* Ijtous £fa/»', *ivB.* (S)i'. *In* (the) *month Dystros, in* (the) *year* 7.27, *indiction* 14. (March, 416 A.D.)
Over the N in INA there are two dots, which I think were intended to indicate that the following letter is to be read twice, or else that IN stands here as the abbreviation for Ivsiktiwi/09, instead of the usual INA. In any case the year 727 of the Seleucid era falls in the fourteenth year of the indiction series.

191. Il-barah. Tomb. On a column of the portico of a rock-hewn tomb, on the south side of the wadi, near the foregoing inscription. Probably there were quarries here, from which part of the town was built. At any rate, an open space has been cut out of the rocky hillside, 25 feet square, leaving at the back

a wall some 8 feet high, in which is the entrance to the tomb. In this open space several olive and fig trees are now growing.

The portico of the tomb consists of two attached pilasters and two free columns, all executed in the living rock, and with the living rock above them. Within is a square chamber with six arcosolia. The inscription is on the right side of the column on the left as one enters, and towards the back of the column. On the same column, below and to the left of the inscription, is an unusually well-cut cross, with broad arms. The whole center of this cross was battered out in ancient times, evidently in a determined, though clumsy, effort to obliterate a Christian symbol: possibly there tVCBI tEure/8ios. t*Eusebios.* was a figure on the cross. There are other rude letters and crosses on the front of the tomb. The tomb is briefly described by Burton and Drake, *Unexplored Syria,* n, p. 212. The inscription measures 18 cm. in length, including the cross, and the letters are 3 cm. high. Copy of the editor.

192. Il-barah. House. On a handsome lintel near the southeast corner of the town. The lintel is in place, but has been cracked through along the line of the inner face of the right jamb, so that the right end of the main part of the lintel has dropped down nearly a foot, and rests against the side of the jamb. Before the doorway is an arch, under which a square door-frame has been set. This second doorway obviously dates from a comparatively late period, but seems to have

Lintel which bears I user. 102. 1 u-ik. ru 1 v been built of older material.

The house behind the door has been destroyed completely; but such a doorway, with an arched vestibule, was commonly the entrance to a dwelling house of the handsomer sort, or to a villa. The broken lintel is similar to that of the great pyramidal tomb (Part II, p. 244 .), but on a smaller scale.

The total length of the inscription, in its original position, was 2.02 m. The letters are 4 cm. high. They are very well formed, clear and deep, and were

painted red. Copy of the editor.

Published by Waddington, No. 2646. Uspensky, *A. M. S.,* p. 68.
t   iTiPclJYAAIHTHNICDAD-NCDYKAITHNEinADNAnDT-DYNYNKAIEliJCTuJNAIuJNliJNAMHN   +
Kv/3(to?) *j)vdt;r) rrjv IcroSov aov KaX Ttjv itjoBov dirb Tov Vvv* /ecu ews Twv *aldjvwv. 'Afiijv.* + (*The) Lord shall preserve thy coming in and thy) going out from this time forth) and for evermore. A men.*

The form *fvd$T)* is for (*frvXdgei, ZooSov* for *elo-oSov.* These words, with some slight variations, are found in Psalm exx, 8. See Chapter 1, pp. 14, 20, 22 and 25: also the three following inscriptions. In 1905 I found a fifth inscription in il-Barah, beside the present road through the northern part of the town, containing essentially the same text; K(upio)? *(fvdrj rrjv lto86v oov Kal Tr/v ioSov crov dnb Tov Vvv Kox* eo 193. Il-barah. House. On an elaborate lintel, now in two pieces, lying in a heap of ruins before what appeared to be an ordinary house, near the southeast corner of the town, about fifty yards east of No. 192. The two lintels are almost precisely alike, but differ somewhat in their dimensions and in the forms of the letters.

The inscription seems to be complete, for the last letter is at the extreme end of the inscribed fascia, and I could find no letters on any other part of the stone. The Syrian stone-cutters seem often to have spared themselves the trouble of calculating accurately how much space each letter should occupy, or even of drawing these letters with a crayon before carving them. The total length of this inscribed fascia, on the two fragments together, is 2.03 m. The letters are 4 cm. high. They are well formed, deep and clear. Copy of the editor.

KYttiYAAIHTHNICDADNCDYKAITHNEI-DADNAnnTnYNYNKAIluCITuJNAIiiJ
Ku(pios) *(fvXdr) TTjv loo86v oov Kox rrjv ioSov Oltto Tov Vvv* /cai(e)fe)? *Twv aicavcov). The) Lord shall preserve thy coming in and thy) going out from this time forth) and for evermore.*

See the preceding inscription, and Chapter r, p. 14.

194. Il-barah. House. Lintel of a plainer

house, in the southeastern part of the town. The inscription is on a splay-faced moulding, which forms one of the upper members of a door-cap. At each end of the inscription, and near its center, is a disk, 12 cm. in diameter. The distance between the first two of these is 57, between the second two 74 cm. Below is a row of dentils, and below these a plate in relief, having at each end, and near its center, a disk about 30 cm. in diameter. The smooth surface of this plate may have contained paintings of some sort.

The letters average 7 cm. in height. Some of them are good, while others are very irregular and grotesque. In four places letters have been combined in a ligature. Copy of the editor.

Kupio? /vafi *Ttjv elooh6v oov (kol) Tt)v t£oBov crov.*

Door-cap bearing Inscr. 194.

(The) Lord shall preserve thy coming in and thy going out.

This reading is, of course, very uncertain. See also the preceding inscriptions. Phrases such as *Kvpic* etc., *Porjdei. T£ Sovxco O-ov,* are very common in the Syrian inscriptions. See Chapter 1, p. 22.

196. Il-barah. House. On the lintel of a doorway within an arched vestibule, on the north side of a narrow street running east and west, in the southwestern part of the town, a short distance southeast of the southernmost pyramidal tomb. The entrance appears to have been that of a handsome residence, although the building itself has been completely destroyed. The lintel has a large ovolo door-cap like that of No. 192, uncarved but smoothly dressed: probably it was painted with a rinceau design. Before the door is an unusually large vestibule, faced with a broad arch ornamented by simple heavy mouldings, and roofed by long slabs of stone. The base of this arch, on the right side, bears inscription No. 197.

The present inscription is scratched, not carved. It measures 1.33 m. in length. The letters, *3l/2* cm. high, are fairly clear but somewhat rudely formed. Copy of the editor.

AluSAENYYICTDICGEluKAI-

ETTirHCEIPHNHENAePlunDI EYADKIA t

Atafa *iv* M//icttois ®ew, /ecu eVt *yijs eipyjvrj, iv Glory to God in the highest, and on earth peace, a(v)dpamoii evhoKia. + good will among men.* t

These words are found in Luke ii, 14. It is of interest to know whether the form euSoKia was actually written here, or cuSoKias. On my second visit to il-Barah, in 1905, I examined this inscription again most carefully, with the purpose of determining this point. It is barely possible that there was a C under the left arm of the cross, which is rather high in proportion to the letters, so that such a C would be almost in its proper place. I do not believe, however, that these marks were really intended for a C. Moreover I found in 1905 another inscription in the northern part of the town, containing precisely the same text: in this inscription, which is well carved, *eiBoKia* is certain. Compare Nos. 197 a and 213. See also Chapter 1, p. 9f.

197. Il-barah. Same House. On the front wall of the vestibule of the same house as No. 196, on the right of the entrance, near the spring of the arch. The inscription, like the foregoing, is not regularly carved, but merely scratched. The first line measures *Ko* by 2V2 cm., the second 37 1. _-wTOVBETOVnOI-HENviCTONNVKA, _ r , by K cm. Copy of the editor. 2. KYPICBOhbI *30 VJ*

I have been unable to decipher the first of these lines. Possibly Tog *derov* Itoio-guto?.-of *the adopted sou, who made this),1* or, at the end, *iv Tovtw vUa.* But neither of these readings is plausible, in view of the two copies made of this graffito in 1900 and 1905. The second line is the familiar Kupic *fiorjOi.: Lord, help I* 197a. Il-barah. House. On the lintel of a doorway between two windows in the second story of a large house a short distance east of No. 187. This house faced 1 See Romans viii, 15: *id/3tTt nvtv/M. vloStaias, iv S Kpaofuv* "A/J/8o 6 *irar-qp.* southward on a court, from which a doorway led to a street on the east side. The doorway of the lintel is in the north, i.e. the rear, wall of the house, and must have opened on some sort of balcony.

Published by Waddington, No. 2647. Uspensky, *A. M. S.,* p. 68.

+ Adf*a iv w/uaroi?, Kal iirl yfj elprjvr),* + *Glory to God in the highest, and on earth peace*

At the end of the inscription, after *elpvvy,* Waddington read NIAIEN. I read NKNDI t or NKAICDI. M. Uspensky gives simply «Vl *yfjs Iptjvrjv.* Possibly the original was *y Kal croL; and may) this (de) to thee also.* This inscription could undoubtedly be read with the aid of a long ladder: I did not find it in 1900, and on my second visit to il-Barah, in 1905, I unfortunately did not bring a ladder with me.

On the content of the inscription see the commentary to No. 196.

198. Il-barah. House. "Sur deux linteaux de ported'une grande maison antique." Waddington, No. 2648. M. de Vogue, 5. C, pi. 46.

A. "eswkcis *poi v(fpocrvvrjv* tis *Tr/v KapsCav pov f 'atto Kapnov Oltov Kox olvov Kox iWeov iveir7jo-0T)pev iv IprjvT). Thou hast put gladness in my heart. -J-From the) harvest of corn and wine and oil were we filled in peace.*

These words are found in Psalm iv, 7 ff. See also Chapter 1, p. 16.

B. Ad£a IlaTpl *Kal Tlw Kal 'Ayia HvevpaTi. Glory to Father and to Son and to Holy Spirit.*

See Chapter i, p. 10.

The first of these two inscriptions I found in 1905, a short distance north of No. 187 and a short distance west of No. 201. I was able to verify Waddington's reading and restorations. The first line is on a fillet, and is in letters 2 cm. high: the second line is on the main plate, in letters 42 cm. high.

199. Near Il-barah. Lintel. Two fragments of a plain lintel in a stone fence, on the north side of the road to Belyun, about half a mile north of il-Barah, where the road turns towards the west. In the center of the lintel was a handsome disk containing a large cross: the lintel was broken through the middle of this disk, a part of which remains on each fragment. The disk was 35 or 40 cm. in diameter, and the whole lintel originally about *2l/2* m. long by 0.45 m. high. The letters are well cut and clear,

and 6 to 8 cm. in height. Copy of the editor.

Published by Waddington, No. 2649. Uspensky, *A. M. S.*, p. 68.

t Kypidctlunayna () MEuNMEeEMluNEC-TI

+ Kvpios *Totv Svvdpecav ptd kpoiv* eori.
+ *The Lord of Hosts is with us.*

M. Waddington read the last word Coto. These words are taken originally from Psalm xlv, 8 and 12. The phrase Kv/ne *Tuv Swdpecov,* however, occurs not infrequently in the liturgies, for example in Swainson, pp. 282, 306, 89, etc. See also Chapter 1, p. 16.

200. Il-barah. House(?). "Sur un linteau de porte." Waddington, No. 2650. K(v/oio)s TTOLfiv(i) fie + Kal ovSeV *poi vaTeprjcr(et).*

The) Lord is my shepherd, + arid nothing shall I want.

These words are taken from Psalm xxii, 1. But see also Chapter 1, p. 10.

201. Il-barah. House. "Sur un linteau de porte." Waddington, No. 2651. This doorway is within a vestibule, and evidently belonged originally to a dwelling house; it stands a short distance north of No. 187: the rest of the building has disappeared.

Xpior6s *del Vlks,.* + IltoTi9, Cxttis, *ayamj.* + *'Eytpei dirb yr; Ittw)(ov Kox airo Koirpiai aw)ol irhnTa. Christ ever conquers.* + *Faith, hope, love.* + *He raiseth (the) beggar from (the) earth and lifteth up (the) needy from (the) dunghill.*

The words of the second line are found in Psalm cxii, 7. See Chapter 1, p. 17. Compare also *C. I. G.* 8912.

202. Il-barah. House (?). "Sur un linteau de porte." Waddington, No. 2652. + *Yevoiro, Kvpie,* To eXcds *rov if* 17/j.as, + *Kaddnep rfK.iTicrap.tv* eVt re.

+ *Let thy mercy, O Lord, be upon us,* + *according as we hoped in thee.*

These words are quoted from Psalm xxxii, 22. See Chapter 1, p. 15 f.

203. Il-barah. On a lintel, facing the north, in the north center of the town. The building to which this lintel belonged is completely destroyed, and the doorframe itself is buried to within 3 feet of its top in a pile of large stones and debris. Immediately opposite,

across a narrow street, is a large arched vestibule before another square doorframe. About 10 feet farther towards the west along the street is a third doorframe, and about 10 feet farther in the same direction is the southwest corner of the building in whose north side is the lintel containing inscription No. 204.

The present inscription measures 2. 09 m. from the beginning to the end of the letters, including a space of 6 cm. in the center, which is occupied by a cross 44 cm. broad. There is also a cross at each end of the inscription. The letters , O and C are from 4 to 5 cm. high: the others 6 to 7 cm.: they are regular, well cut and clear. Copy of the editor.

Published by Uspensky, *A. M. S.*, p. 68.

t MrAAHHAYNAMICTHCAriACTPIAAOC t OKOMICTTPICKOCNTOYTuJNIKA t t *Meydkr) r)* Swafii? Tijs dyias T/naSos. + 'O + *Great is the power of the holy Trinity.* + *The*

Ko/ais HpicTKOs iv Tovtw viKa. t *comes* (counselor) *Priskos conquers in this.* +

The title Ko/as *comes)* was, in some cases, an honorary one, and held for life. See the commentary to VVaddington 1906 a. It was also given to counselors of the emperor, who from the time of Diocletian formed a kind of ministry: these were salaried officers. Moreover the higher members of the bureau *officium)* of the governor of a province were called Kotcs. Possibly, and if so then probably in this case, the head-man of a town may have received this title, inasmuch as he held office nominally as deputy of the governor and was nominally a member of the governor's officium, though resident in his own town.

204. Il-barah. Baptistery(p). On the lintel of one of two doorways, close together and facing northward in the north center of the town, a few yards northwest of No. 203. These doorways are buried to within about 2 feet of the top. On the west side of the inscribed doorway there appears to have been a window. Through the doorway one entered a room or passage, about 15 feet square, the rear wall of which abutted the street

on which No. 203 is situated. There seems to have been a doorway in this rear wall also, opening on the street.

That part of the lintel on which the inscription was carved measured originally 2.13 m. in length, of which 13 cm. have been broken from the left end, 46 from the right end. Parts of twenty-three or twenty-four letters remain upon the stone, and these measure about 1.53,5/2 m. in length. The letters are 4 to 5 cm. high. There would be room, if the lintel were intact, for five or six letters before *Ttlotls,* and from eleven to thirteen after *fiaTmo-fia,* supposing that the inscription completely filled this band of the moulding. Copy of the editor.

--CTLAniCTICENBATTTILMAHnPI X 7T10T15 *iv* a7JTlO"/i,a(Tt) 7T0O .

faith in baptism

The words of Ephesians iv, 5: Eis Kvpios, *ftia 7rurris, ev fidimcrixa,* suggest /'a 7rtoTt9, *Iv* /3a7rTio-,a as a possible reading for this inscription. But I could not reconcile this reading with what remains of the beginning of the inscription upon the stone.

205. Il-barah. Fragment. "Dans les ruines du palais,1 au milieu du grand clos; fragment en grandes lettres." Waddington, No. 2653.

Undoubtedly this is a fragment of the trisagion, prob OCICXYPOC ably in the monophysite form. If so, the whole inscrip NMA r 3 r tion may be restored as follows:

"Ayios 6 Beos, ayios 'Io-u/ad?, ayios 'AddvaTos, 0Tavpt«0eis 8t' f))fLa._;, iXerjcrov 17/01615.

Holy God, holy Mighty One, holy Immortal One, crucified for us, have mercy upon us! 1 I understand this to be the Saracenic castle north of the main part of the town: I did not find the inscription.

The second line may have been spaced out, perhaps with a cross at each end and a cross in the center, so as to be nearly equal in length to the line above. It is however uncertain whether the inscription contained the monophysite addition, i.e. the phrase (o) *o-ravpwdeU hi as.* See inscription No. 6 above, and also Chapter i, p. 8 f.

206. Il-barah. On a large block of stone

near an arch, which seems to have been the central arch of a small, plain house, in the east center of the town. The block is 1.44 m. long,.66 high and.57 thick: except for the inscription, it is perfectly plain. The inscription is in the upper left-hand corner of the stone, ZOHYrlA beginning 5 cm. from the left end and 13 from the top. It is 91 cm. long, *Zorj. 'TyCa.* and the letters vary from *8l/2* to 13 cm. in height. Copy of the editor. *Life! Health! Zor)* is for *t,o)Tj*, and *vyia* = *vyeta* for *vyUta*. Compare Nos. 114 and 338 f. 207. Midjleyya. Sarcophagus, 463 A.d. On the north side of a sarcophagus at the southeast corner of the town, just beyond the houses. The first line is immediately below the top: it *4, Inscr. 207. From a drawing. Scale 1: 20.* measures 2.06 m. in length. The second line is in a series of shallow mouldings which frame the panel, in the center of which is an eight-arm cross in a circle. The third and fourth lines are at the top of the panel, immediately below the mouldings. The letters are 4 to 6 cm. high. They are irregular in size and shape, and in several cases the same letter has two or even three different forms. The inscription is badly weathered. Copy of the editor. ('O) *kcltoikuv C(v) fiorfdia. Tov 'tilcttov i)eicr6v pe /cara (t)o peya crov eXeos. Ets@e6so 0or)dov Tov ypdiavTo;) Kal Tov dvayvo _crKovTo;).* etovs *8oi//', prjvl HeptTtov ft, iKaTecrrdOi To pvrfp(iov).* 'iSi. a'. *Thou that dwellest in the help of the Most High, have mercy upon ttie according to thy great mercy! There is) one God that helpeth him that wrote and him that reads. In the) year 774, in the) month of Peritios the) 2nd, this monument was set in place, indiction 1.* (February, 463 A.D.)
The first line is taken in part from Psalm 1, 1: 'EXeo-oV *pe,* 6 @ed?, (card To //. eya eXed? o-ou, zeal *Kara To 77X0? Tov oiKTipp.ov crov i£deifov To av6p-qp.dp.ov,* and in part also from Psalm XC, I I 'O *Ko.tolku)v ip fSorOtla Tov 'TxfricrTov, iv crKewji Tov Beou Tov oipavov avkicrdrjcreTcu.*

This quotation from Psalm 1, i is found also in No. 267 below = Waddington 2672: see also Chapter 1,

p. 16. Phrases such as that contained in the second line are frequent: see, for example, No. 25. The genitive with the participle *fior)0av* is not altogether unnatural where Semitic influence was strong; but perhaps o *fio-qdo-;* should be read. Compare, however, No. 58. The double augment in *eKa.recn6.di* for *KaTecrrddrj* is worthy of notice.
208. Midjleyya. Sarcophagus. On the east side of a handsome sarcophagus, standing in the open just beyond the last houses in the northern part of the town, north of the church. The upper righthand corner had been broken off and the sarcophagus otherwise damaged shortly before our arrival, and I was not able to find the broken pieces: the sarcophagus was doubtless intact when it was seen by MM. Waddington and de Vogue. In the center of the inscribed side is a cross in relief, 35 l/2 cm. high and 31 cm. broad. The letters are 9 cm. high. They are somewhat irregular in shape and badly aligned, but unusually well cut, so that most of them are still deep and clear. See Part II, p. 250. Copied by the editor. The letters which are now missing I have restored to the text from M. Waddington's copy.
Published by Waddington, No. 2654. M. de Vogue, *S. C,* pi. 87.
TONYYICTON690YKATA
YOYTTPOCAeY CTTT
KAKAIMACTI £OYK I
(OCKHNCOMATICO Y
Top *"tilcttov edov KaTcufyvyrjv crov ov trpocreXevcreTe np6;)* are Ka/ca, *Kal /Aa0-Ti£ Ovk evyii ev Tw oKrjvap.aTt crov. Thou hast made the Most High thy refuge; there shall 110 evil befall thee, and a scourge shall not come nigh thy dtvelling.*
Inscription 208.
These words are taken from Psalm xc, 9 and 10: "On *o-v, Kvpie, rj cXirw p.ov, Tov "tio-tov edov KaTaf)vyrjv crov. Ob irpooeevcreT(u irpos ere Kaicd, Kcli p.dcrTL Ovk eyyiei Tw crKr)idp,a. Ti crov.* See
Chapter 1, p. 16.
209. Midjleyya. Factory. On the rock wall of an underground chamber in the north center of the town, a short distance southwest of the basilical church.

1 This chamber is large and almost circular, although the north side is but slightly curved: its walls are rough and uneven, except where a place has been made smooth for the inscription: it is doubtless a natural cave, which has been enlarged somewhat, and fitted up as a factory for wine or oil. See de Vogue,.S". *C,* pi. 34, which presents a somewhat different view.
One enters from the east, through a passage 6 feet broad, cut down into the rock. At one side of the doorway is a cistern. Inside of the cave, a few feet from the entrance, there is a large opening in the roof, now covered with slabs of stone. This 1 Part II, p. 96.
Alui a
Inscr. 209. From copies. Scale 1: 20. may have been intended merely to admit light and air; but perhaps the fruit was poured in here from the ground above, just as in presses at il-Barah and Ruweha the fruit was poured into a regular chute in the side of the building.1 There seems to have been another entrance at the southwest corner; but, if so, it has been blocked up. Possibly this was the original entrance, for, if I remember correctly, the cave is situated in a small hill, which rises like a knob in the midst of the city, and the ground level on the western side is nearly as low as the floor of the cave itself. In the northwest corner were sockets in the rock, as if for the lever and beams of a press.
The inscription is *KvPi)e* X(/Hor)e *pmjdi 'loviai6v* carved on the east wall, #ca! *ArjfitjTpLou* on *irekea-av.* north of the entrance, *Lord Christ, help Iulianos and Deme-above* an irregular *trios, because they completed!* niche, at the bottom of which is a kind of trough or basin, hewn in the rock. I thought at first that this trough might be a tomb, but decided afterwards that it was not. The edge of the trough is 4J/2 feet above the floor, and a couple of steps lead up to it. A dove-tail plate is inscribed about the inscription, and above the plate is a cross with *h* and w. Inscription, plate and cross are all formed by incised lines painted with vermilion. The letters are somewhat rude in form, but are all beautifully clear because completely

protected from the weather: they are 4 to 5 cm. high. At the end of the plate a little cross in a circle is painted in red on the rough wall, and between the cross and the plate is the letter C, painted as if to try the brush. Copied by Dr. Littmann and the editor.

I do not know exactly what was completed. Possibly it was this factory. Possibly the words mean that some vowwas paid, or that these persons finished their course, i.e. their life. But I am inclined to think that they mean that Iulianos and Demetrios completed their course of instruction, were confirmed and admitted into the full membership of the Church.
2IO. MIDJLEYYA. GRAFFITO, on a blank wall, on a street north of the hexagonal church mentioned in Part II, p. 237 f. The inscrip oking east.
Street in Midjleyya, on which is Inscr. 210: tion is about i J/2 m. above the original level of the street: including the cross it is !See No. 187.
55 cm. long, and the letters are about 8 cm. high. There are other crosses and scratches, some of which may be letters, on the same wall. + Nucae: *Let the cross) conquer/*
What is interesting about this graffito is that it was obviously written from right to left, as the native Aramaic was written. See Nos. 72 and 82, and the commentary on each: also
'*J* Inscription 210.
Part IV, p. 7.
211. Midjleyya. House. On the lintel of a doorway opening upon a portico, in the west center of the town, facing south. The three letters together measure 39 cm. in length; but the distance between the first and second letters is 16 cm., or about twice the space between the second and third. Probably whoever carved the inscription intended to space the three letters at equal distances apart, but through some carelessness failed to put the third in its proper place. There are marks on the stone immediately before the M which resemble a C; I do not believe however that these marks are really the remains of a letter. The letters are 4 to 5 cm. high, and have the same forms as those of the following inscription. Copied by Dr. Littmann.

X M r X(/toTo?) (6 «e) M(apias) y(ei/Tj0e«): *Christ) born) of) Mary).*

See Chapter 1, p. 23, and Inscription No. 155.
212. Midjleyya. House. Lintel of a house in the western part of the town, facing south. The lintel is ornamented with the usual door-cap, the lower part of which is a raised plate. This plate measures 1.50 by o. 18 m., and bears the inscription. In the center of this plate is a cross inscribed in a circle, and on either side of the plate is an ornamental disk.1 The three letters occupy the left half of the plate, and are spaced at equal intervals: the right half of the plate, from the cross to the right end, appears to have been blank. The letters are 5 to 6 cm. high. Copy of Dr. Littmann.

X M r X(pioTo?) (6 «c) M(a/3tas) y(tPvr)0efc): *Chrisf) born) of) Mary).*

See the preceding inscription.
213. Wadi Marthun. House. Lintel of the entrance to the courtyard of a handsome, two-story house, facing northeast. The right half of the inscription has AU5ANYYICTOICeU KAI, NAN9P, and I. Acifa *iv* Ui/hotois Hea, + /ecu *iv* dvdp _wtto Is euSo/aa.
Glory to God in the highest, and among men good will!
!See Part II, p. 32 f.
been broken off; but two fragments of the broken part were found on the ground, one of which gives the tops of the letters NAN9P, the other the upper part of an I. The letters are about 4 cm. high. Copy of Dr. Littmann. See No. 196. 214. 'allaruz. Lintel, 572 (?) A.d. North of the town, a broken lintel, now used as a jamb in the entrance to the courtyard of a modern house. The lintel has the common form of a door-cap. The inscription is at the bottom, below the mouldings: it measures 0.88 m. in length, and ends 9 cm. from the end of the stone. Probably about a third of the original inscription has been lost from the beginning.
On the upper concave portion of the cymatium of the door-cap, near its right end, are two letters, B2: at the right of the mouldings, over the M of the inscription, is a N, and somewhat higher up, above the SAN, are the letters EBB.

I do not believe that these letters have anything to do with the inscription, and I doubt whether they have any significance at all: perhaps they were carved by the stone-cutter to give his hand practice before he carved the inscription, or perhaps they were cut here by some one else, in mere idleness. The letters of the inscription seem to have been fairly well made, and Dr. Littmann tells me that all but two seemed to him perfectly clear. They are 3 to 5 cm. high. Copy of Dr. Littmann.

I am altogether uncertain as to what this inCtdybyettjcxkenihamzan b _, r „, scnption means. 1 he following interpretation, however, may be acceptable in part: s *Tov ®(eo)v,* eros *k, iv* (t)# 8' *(rjfiepq) fi(r)pb;) SavOiKov.)* of God, in (the)year 620, on the 4th (day) of (the) month *Xanthikos.*

At least this date is not likely to be correct. For it appears that inscriptions of this region were dated according to the Seleucid era, the year 620 of which is the year 308-309 A.d. This date seems to me too early for an inscription which I believe to be Christian. Furthermore, it is the custom in these inscriptions to arrange the letters which form the date in their alphabetical order, rather than in the order of their numerical values. Perhaps therefore KY, i.e. 408 A.d., or MY, i.e. 428 A.d., should be read. On the other hand, this inscription, like No. 215, may be dated according to some other era, perhaps that of Antioch, the era in use throughout the region immediately north of this (see Chapter 11): if so, the date is April, 572 A.d.

At the beginning of the inscription perhaps DAOrn might be supplied, i.e. 'O Aoyo? *Tov* 0(eo)u.-*The Word of God,* or 'O X/jioto? *Tov* ©(eo).1 *The Christ of God.* Compare the inscription from Herakeh, quoted in Chapter 1, p. 19.
1 Compare No. 40. 215. Baboda. Tomb, 474 (?) A.d. In a rock-hewn tomb, in the northeastern part of the town. Before the tomb are arches supported on columns. The walls are ornamented with trees, birds and fishes in relief.

The first inscription is at the left of the entrance, in a dove-tail plate, the body of which is 24 cm. long by 12 cm.

wide: the letters are 3 cm. high. Below the plate is a fish. The other inscription is at the right of the entrance, in a similar plate measuring 25 by 17 cm. There is a fish below this plate also. Copy of Dr. Littmann.

A. B.

+ wXMr TOYCB
IXGYC KtMHY
NDY + UJ X(/3io-to?) (6 ix) M(apias) y(evin)dei). Erovs /8k£', fir)(vb;) (A)v8u veov. 'l(ricrovs) X(ptcrrds), 0(eou) T(ids), (amjp). f UJ Christ) b(orn) (of) M(ary). J(esus) . In (the) year 522, in (the) month Audyneos. Ch(rist), (the) S(on) (of) G(od), (our) S(avior).

I do not know what the significance of the u in the first inscription can be, unless it is that n, being common in Christian symbols of every sort as part of the An, came to be regarded as a symbol of the Christ by itself, the original meaning of the letters An having been entirely lost. On the very common symbols XMr and IXGYC see Nos. 155 and 182.

The date of this inscription, if reckoned according to the Seleucid era, would be 211 A.d. This date I believe to be impossible, in view of the general character of the whole inscription. If then the figures were copied correctly by Dr. Littmann, I believe that this inscription must be dated according to some other era, perhaps that of Antioch: if so the date is January, 474 A.d. See the preceding inscription: also Nos. 263 and 264.

216. B'uda. Sarcophagus. On the west side of a sarcophagus, among the last houses on the east side of the town, somewhat north of wrENANOMATYX-PYCTOY the center: the cover of the sarcophagus overhangs the X(ptoros) (6 Ck) M(aptas) y(ev-inscription. The sarcophagus is similar to that shown loci's). 'E«/ dvofiarv Xpvirrov. m part 11; p. 251. Below the center of the inscription Ch(rist) o(om) (of) M(ary)! In (the) is an unusually handsome +, 40 cm. high, and 35 cm. name of Christ! broad. The inscription itself is 1.44 m. long, the letters 8 cm. high. Copied by Dr. Littmann and the editor.

There are traces of one or possibly two letters before the first letter in my copy; but I feel sure that there were no other letters on the stone, either at the beginning or at the end, although the first letter of my copy begins 58 cm. from the left end of the sarcophagus, and the last ends 47 cm. from the right end. Moreover, the first letter of my copy may be H instead of M, and in the second letter, r, are marks which may represent a small □. It is possible therefore that we should read t 'Hy6 (for cyw) iv avofiaro xpva-rov, or rjyov, or something else.

The word avofiarv is of course for ovoaTi, Xpva-Tov for X/aio-ToO: on the confusion of a and o compare Nos. 148 and 295.

217. Serdjilla. Hath, 473 A.d. The following inscription was once in the center of the mosaic floor of the main hall of a bath.

The bath has been described by M. de Vogue in La Syrie Ccntrale, p. 94 (. , and pis. 55-57, the bath and the mosaic by Mr. Butler in the Revue Archeologique, Tome XXXIX (1901), p. 62 ff. , and in Part II of these publications, pp. 165 and 288 ff.: also by M. Uspensky, A. M. S., pp. 63-67.

The mosaic was discovered by Mr. Butler in the spring of 1900, at a depth of about 18 inches below the surface. A large part of the mosaic was uncovered at that time, drawings and photographs were made, and the floor covered again with the soil which had lain upon it. On our return to Serdjilla in 1905, we found that all the soil from the entire room had been removed, and that the mosaic was almost wholly destroyed. I looked for some piece of the inscription, and found what seemed to be a part of one letter, but nothing more. The natives told us that a party consisting of two Russian gentlemen and a lady had visited the place shortly after our departure, and, being informed of the mosaic, had had the soil removed, in order to make new drawings and photographs.

The inscription was in black and white mosaic, in a circular field enclosed by a border in various colors. The diameter of the circle occupied by the inscription was 1.27 m.: the letters were 5 to 6 cm. in height. The following account is reprinted here from the Reime Archeologique, Tome xxxix (1901), p. 68 ff.

The text is evidently metrical. But it is not altogether clear what metrical form the author chose. The first two lines are in the form of an enhoplius, consisting of a choriambus and an ionicus a minore.1 inscr. 217. From a drawing and Next follows a pure iambic dimeter, and then what photographs. appears to be an ionic dimeter consisting of a mo lossus and an ionicus a minore. A second enhoplius, ending as before in an ionicus a minore, completes what may perhaps have been intended for a metrical period, which would then be as follows: —:, ww—: ww

But such a mixture of ionic and iambic measures is unnatural. Furthermore, one would expect that an epigram of this character, belonging as this does to the fifth century of our era, would be in hexameters. Professor Blass and Professor Earle convinced me that this is actually the case, and that the metrical irregularities are due 1 'iovkmvos: See below.

to the ignorance of the versifex, or his lack of skill. And on the whole, when we read it so, the verses sound better, and the metrical periods correspond in the main with the sense. Besides this, most of the metrical mistakes may be explained without great difficulty. The name 'IoiAiads (verses 1 and 3) is scanned-www, instead of w — w — w, in other epigrams, e.g. in the distich quoted by Zosimus, 11, 34: 'ioiakwos perd Tiypiv aydppoov evdaSe Kcitou.1 This scansion is doubtless due to the position of the accent. So also d-n-aa-a in verse 1, as Professor Blass suggested, counted as a dactyl because of its accent. In the same way the accent may excuse the false quantity of tvv in the second verse. In the first verse again the author seems simply to have overlooked the fact that the final syllable oferevgcv is long by position, although the last syllable of ZxL in the same verse is made short before diraa-a.-The fourth verse presents greater difficulties. Perhaps it was meant to be cretic. But u was so often written K4 at this time, that it may easily have been considered short. As for Kvsos (instead of a)8os), which seems to serve as a spondee here, this poet, like most of his contemporaries, was very uncertain of the quantity of the o-sounds, as is shown by the *ivhiKTiovos* of line 11. The word *vppiv* as a trochee is common enough in Homer, at least in the manuscript readings if not in the original text. 3 In eVi *iriov* the author seems to have fallen between eVl *irkelov* and *4mireov*, of which only the latter really suited his purpose. Lastly, ATPOI is doubtless intended for *dipoi*.

The reconstruction of the last verse is necessarily somewhat uncertain. In consequence of a hole which was broken in the mosaic, the ends of lines 13, 14 and 15 were lost. Had the circle in which the epigram is enclosed been preserved intact, there would have been space for six letters at the end of lines 13 and 14, for five letters at the end of line 15. But as some of the lines do not fill entirely the space within the circle, it is impossible to fix exactly the number of the letters lost from the mutilated lines. Furthermore there is some doubt as to the letter which follows nPATTIAEC. While working at the mosaic itself, I read an E; but after studying the epigram more carefully than was possible at that time, I am convinced that this letter was probably C. The difference between C and E, in this mosaic, lies in the color of a single mosaic-stone. And the dark red crust with which the whole pavement is coated so obscures the original colors, that in many places it is impossible to distinguish with certainty even between the black and white, unless the stones are thoroughly scraped. But as this particular stone was at the very edge of the hole and liable to be broken off, I was unwilling to scrape it as much as the others, and hence could easily have mistaken its color. Believing that this was the case, Professor Blass 1 See *C. I. G.* 3806 (Kaibel, *Epigrammata Graeca*, 355), 3E.g. *Iliad*, xiii, 95; *Odyssey*, xi, 336.

found at Flaviopolis in Bithynia. 4 An I with two clots occurs elsewhere. See Wad., No. 2619 2 See the very interesting article by Mr. F. D. Allen in the and commentary. It appears also in the date on the lintel *Papers of ihe American School of Classical Studies at Athens*, of the ancient city gate at Khanasir, of which a facsimile 1885-1886, p. 110 f. is given under No. 319 below. suggested to me *ir0.rjuri npanic)eo-o-iv 86£av kwv (rvvepi.dov*, while Professor Earle, proposing of course only what he thought the author of these verses might have written, recommended ts e'o-0Xi-jis 7r/Gnri8eoyi *Kal* So£av x.av awe-jC6ov. It seems to me unlikely that even the author of this epigram repeated so without point a word like eVflXds from the preceding verse. But however that may be, I believe the letters AHK to be certain, and in fact they can be seen distinctly in several of our photographs.1 The K is in all respects the same as the other examples of this letter in the epigram, while on the other hand 2 in this epigram always has the form C, never c. Moreover, the I in this mosaic is always straight, whereas the character which follows AHK has the form . This is clear from the photographs, and not only is the form of the character itself distinct, but also the white stones, which are about it, are seen to be laid irregularly, as they would be only where the space about some curved character was to be filled in. This character appears four times in this inscription, twice in the form /, lines 3 and 4, and twice in the form , lines 13 and 14. In lines 3 and 13 it is evidently an apostrophe, i.e. 8'and *T68* In line 4 it seems to mark the end of a word. Such signs were often used in the later inscriptions, especially in the East, to mark the end of a word written in full,2 or after an abbreviation,3 or even as a sign for xaL The character after Ad/m/i seems to belong to the first class of these signs, and to mean here that the 1 belongs to this word:5 the character after AHK apparently belongs to the second class mentioned, and marks an abbreviation. The *K* then stands for *aL*, and was doubtless the more easily understood because the sign alone was sometimes used for the conjunction. If this is the case, I would suggest for the verse /8ovXf/ . npairtSeo-

criv 8dfai e-v awipt dov. With 8d£cw avvipiQov may be compared a Christian epigram from Corcyra, dating from about the end of the fourth century (C. /. G., No. 8608; Kaibel, No. 1060): *Tt'uttiv ko)v fiao-'ikiav ifiSv p.evewv crvvipiQov.* Compare also ApollinariuS, Psalm XXXvii, 42: *Kol fie 8007? crvvepiOov enecr/3oij)o-iv efi-aXov.*

The whole epigram then, if the length of its lines were not conditioned by the circular field in which it is contained, would appear as follows:

'IovXiavos p.ev erevijev, X,Ptv XL d-iracra Kwp.T),

Aofj-vr/L aw aXdw, *Kal aanerov amacev okfiov*

irdrp-qv Kvoatvwv dXXd f66vov eKTos ekavvoi

Sofa *Kal* Kusos vp.jxiv iirl nXlov alev atpoi.

'etcxkwt/ To Xovrpoi' *firjvl Tlavep. ov, Tov* 8771/1' eroi/9, *IvSiKTlOVOS La'*.

®aXXao-iov eo0Xos iral? 'louXiao? Tos' erevf ev,

y8ouXjj (al) 7T/3a7ri8co-criv 80 far *eaiv crave pi dov.*

1 There remains of course the possibility that the work-4 Wad., Nos. 1997 and 2068 d. There is another use of man who laid the mosaic misread the written copy which such a sign, namely, to mark the end of a metrical verse, where he had of the epigram. an epigram is written continuously, as in Wad., Nos. 2145, 2 As in Wad., Nos. 1951, 1954, 2035, 2399 2643 and 2473, 2474 and 2475. But this can hardly be so here. 2661 e. 5 Why the 1 is written in the line is a mystery, unless the 3 Wad., Nos. 1997, 2110, 2327 and 2328. author intended -fit) Ao/ait;i to be a ditrochaeus after all.

Julianos had this made—and the town is grateful—together with Domna his spouse, and he has conferred great happiness, glorifying his country. Well, may your good repute drive out envy and ever increase your glory! The bath was finished in the month Panemos, of the year 784., indict ion 11. Thallasios' noble son Julianos had this made, a man of reputation to match his qualities of mind and heart. (July, 473 A.D.)

Julianos was the donor of the pavement, possibly of the whole bath, and not the artist. The verb Tevx«" is commonly used in this sense in the inscriptions of the East. Compare for example Waddington, No. 2381: M/ua *fie....* *'Povfivo; he p.'* erev£e.... SaSo? Neo77om7s *olKoSo/x-qa-ev* curves. Plainly Rufinos was the owner here, Sados the architect or contractor for the monument.1 Furthermore, in these Syrian inscriptions it is customary for a man, who dedicates a tomb or monument or statue, to join with his own name that of his wife, and sometimes the names of other members of his family. Compare Waddington, No. 2225: 4X. Mafi/xos... To *pvTjpa 4k Twv ihLa(v) AKo86p7)re(v)* o-w 8o/t8exfl *ywaiKi1* Hence the last verse does not refer to the artist's skill, as e.g. in *Odyssey* vii, 92: ous "Haio-ros *erevijev ISvCyo-L rrpaTriSea-a-i,* but is merely a general compliment like that in an epigram in the *Anthologia Planudea,* No. 281, which happens to refer tO a bath also: *Kcu yap 'AkeijavSpos* Ni/caeW *lepevs, ao(fCr)s ipucvSeos dcrijp, revtje piv Oiklol; XpijfJ-acri. Kcu Sandvais,* or in Waddington, No. 2349: ®*copevTelvo;,* apioros *djrrjp Kal VTreipo)(os* aXXow *Oikov iSeCparo* roVse *per'* cwcXefys *crofvq; rat* (i.e. Tc'j.

Professor Blass suggested that the latter part of the second verse may refer to an endowment of the bath. But *danerov amaaev okfiov* is a conventional and almost stereotyped phrase. Compare with it Hesiod, *Erga,* 379: *p£a-8e #eev irXtovto-ai tropoi* Zev? *do-ntrov okfiov,* or *Theogonia,* 974: *rbv* 8' *dfvabv iffrjKe, Ttoxw re ol omaaev okfiov.* Such a phrase is not likely to have here so special a significance.

Julianos and Domna are not uncommon names in Syria. There was a Julianos who was an imperial legate in 236 A.d.,4 and another, who seems to have held the same position, about 149 A.d.5 One was a bishop at Bosra in the year 512 A.d.8 But more important, in connection with the Serdjilla epigram, is the T. Flavius Julianus, who built a tomb for himself and his family at Katu-

ra, a town on the next mountain, about 60 miles from Serdjilla. This tomb, cut out of the living rock, is ornamented with figures in high relief, and bears a bilingual inscription in Latin and Greek. 7 On a lintel of a house in the ruins of Katura there is a Greek inscription containing the name *Thalasis.* The inscription is Christian, and one of the earliest Christian inscriptions found in Syria: it is dated 331 A.d.8 Perhaps the Julianos, son of Thallasios, of the Serdjilla bath, belonged to the same family as T. Flavius Julianus and

Thalasis,1 and came originally from Katura. At Kokanaya, not far from Katura, a certain Domnos, an architect, built a house in the year 431 A.d.2 Possibly there may have been some relationship between Domnos of Kokanaya and Domna, the wife of Julianus.

The date is evidently reckoned from the Seleucid era, the usual reckoning in this region.3 The 784th year of the Seleucid era corresponds to the year 472-473 A.d., and was the eleventh year in the indiction series. The date is therefore July, 473 A.d.

From the literary point of view this epigram has little to commend it. The best of it, both metrically and in literary flavor, consists in reminiscences, principally from the epic poets. Not only the phrase *do-nerov wnao-ev oXfiov,* but also the expression eVro? e'Xavvoi in verse 3, are part of a poetaster's stock in trade. Compare for example *Odyssey,* xiv, 11: *o-Tavpovs* 8' *Cktos eXao-o-e.* The *naTprjv KvSaCvojv* in the same verse savors of Pindar, e.g. *Nem.* ix, 12, or *Pyth.* i, 31; but still more of Homer, e.g. *Iliad* x, 69: *7rdVras KvSaww /X7j8e /ieyaXt£eo 0uua.* The latter part of this verse also calls to mind Bacchylides v, 188 f.: *(j06vov dfujoTepaioL xepTM dirwadp-evov;* but it is highly improbable that this versifier knew anything of either Pindar or Bacchylides. Finally, the last two verses seem to have been tacked on as an afterthought, perhaps only to fill up space, for they add nothing but the father's name.

In conclusion it may be noticed that the Serdjilla epigram lacks all the poetic imagery natural and common to bath

epigrams, such as are to be found in the Greek Anthology. There is no allusion here to the charm, the x/315-of the bath, or to the charm which the bath bestows, or to the Nymphs and Graces, Aphrodite and Eros, who were so naturally associated with baths and bathing, and who were often spoken of in these bath epigrams as bestowing upon the bath, or the bathers there, something of their own charming loveliness/ This difference may be seen clearly if we compare with this epigram one discovered recently in Pontus, near Amasia, Strabo's birthplace:5

Nuaeai (10071777-015 *ivl Swpacri vcueTdovrai*
dOop-evai Toirdpotdev erev)(ov dyXabv vScjp-
r)X@eT0 8' *H£aioTos-vvv* 8' anracre
'Id/Sios aureus
yepovcov 0% dpioros *iif vtvktol; 6aXdp. oicnv*
Xuoi7rdvot5 *Nvp,faicrL Kabv* credos, *otypa. Kox aural n p.* 77 Tats *pitfixriv dya.kk6p.evai Xapirecrcnv.*

xThe difference in the spelling of these names is of little may be dated according to the era of Antioch. But in the consequence, for there are few inscriptions in Syria without case of this bath epigram, although it is the only dated insome mistake in orthography, and perhaps the name in the scription found at Serdjilla, the indiction number fixes the Serdjilla epigram would have been spelled *Thalasios,* if a date with certainty.

dactyl had not been required at the beginning of the verse. 4 See the articles by Dr. Rubensohn in the *Berl. Philol.* 2 No. 37 = Wad. 2683. *Wochenschrift,* i8c)i,Sp. 161-4; 1894, Sp. 986 f.; 1895, 3 See Nos. 180 f., 188 ff., 207 and 225 f. There are, how-Sp. 380 ff. ever, a few inscriptions from the region to which Serdjilla be-5 Published first by M. Hubert in the *Revue Archeol.,* longs, including No. 273 = Wad. No. 2667, and some others xxiv, 1894, p. 308 ff. Also by Dr. Rubensohn in the *Berl.* discovered by this expedition, Nos. 214 f. and 263 f., which *Philol. Wochenschrift,* 1895, Sp. 380 ff.

Such verses, shorn of all their pagan

imagery, would be the counterpart of the Serdjilla inscription. There is nothing Christian about the latter, nor indeed in the whole mosaic; but the avoidance of anything which, however appropriate, might be associated in any way with paganism, is noticeable both in the epigram and in the rest of the pavement, and may be accounted for by the fact that this was of course a Christian community. And this conclusion is further borne out by the three crosses which I found, after long scraping away the lichen which had completely obliterated them, on the lintel of the doorway which leads from the outside into the room marked D in M. de Vogue's plan of the bath. These crosses, although on an otherwise plain surface, were so well and so elaborately carved, that I believe them to have been carved there when the bath was built.

218. Serdjilla. Arch. On blocks now forming an arch in a ruined wall, immediately south of the ancient church. There seem to have been several small apartments here, on the south side of the church1 court, perhaps lodgings for the clergy. In later times the Mohammedans made a mosque out of the southernmost of these apartments, breaking through the south wall of the original building, and constructing the mihrab, or niche, by attaching to the outside of the wall a rude half-dome, which has now fallen down. The opening in the wall was framed by an arch, for which the voussoirs were sought among the ruins of the earlier time. Perhaps they belonged to the apse of the church itself, for they are very large, and their curve is too wide for the narrow arch in which they stand at present. In order to form the narrower arch the blocks had to be refitted, and this was done in very clumsy fashion. In particular the upper mouldings of the third block from the left pier do not match those of the second at all. The upper left-hand corner of this third block is several inches lower than it should be, and it is clear that when it was placed in its new position, the lower left-hand corner must have projected down several inches below the curve of the arch. This lower corner was then

cut away, and the lowest fascia recut so as to match roughly with that o the block on either side. But the next fascia above, which on other blocks carries the inscription, lost by this process about half its breadth at its left end. A few lines, which are perhaps traces of letters, are still to be seen at the left end of this block, where the upper line of the inscription might have run. The fourth block has no certain trace of any letter. The fifth has traces of a few letters at the right end, where the upper line would come. But these letters are not quite in line with those of the sixth block, because the lower end of the fifth also slipped down a couple of inches when the present arch was set up, and its under side was cut away to make the curve of the arch uniform. The fifth and sixth blocks however may have belonged together originally.

All the blocks are badly weathered and incrusted with lichen, so that very few of the letters can be made out with certainty, and I have been unable to make any satis xSee Part II, p. 95. factory sense out of the inscription as a whole, or even to determine the order in which the blocks should be read. I copied the following letters, many of which are most uncertain: c. On the third: D. On the sixth: YOWWOYK E AJn YKAlToC

CnNAYTolC

B and D may be read together, as follows: a/xa *MaCfJiov d8ekfov*, /cat *nacnv* e cuXd*yrj&ov* auro(u)s.

On *apa* with the genitive see No. 102. 219. Serdjilla. House. On the soffit of an arch, in a house about the center of the town. The house, the front of which is shown in Part II, p. 258, was a characteristic one for this region. It consisted of two parts, exactly alike and separated by a party wall, each consisting of two similar rooms one above the other. Each lower room had a door and two windows in the front, while each upper room had a door and a single window, the doors opening on a portico. The lower rooms measured 19 feet by 21, and each was spanned by a single arch, which supported the floor above. Before the house was a paved court, and

what I took to be a cistern.
The inscription is on the soffit of a voussoir of the arch of one of the rooms in the lower story, on the right as one enters. It is not carved, but painted in red on the stone, which was once-- ANOYHAXMT..

X P I c T o C N i K A whlte-but which is now yellow with age. At 'EavowjX, X(picn-os) (6 Ik) M(o-*Emmanuel, Christ) born) of)* archeg there_ pi'as) y(ewTJ0«s). Xpioro? *viica. Mary) Christ conquers!* fore, in such houses, were not covered with stucco.1 Above the inscription is painted a cross inscribed in a circle: as usual, the Greek P grows out of the head of the cross, and in the lower quadrants of the disk are the A and U). The inscription is 0.72 m. long, the letters 5 to 8 cm. high. Copy of the editor.

Compare Wad. 2068; also Nos. 318 and 155. See Chapter 1, pp. 21 f. and 23. I have no doubt that the presence of such inscriptions in houses is due chiefly to the superstition of these people, and that their object was primarily to guard against evil spirits and to avert ill luck. But at the same time words like these, painted in so !See Part II, p. 293 f. prominent a place in a private room, cannot have been without a strong influence upon the family who lived here: successive generations of children must have wondered and asked what these words meant. 220. Serdjilla. Lintel. On a lintel near the center of the town, facing northeast. The lintel is a large one, measuring 2.54 m. in length: it has a door-cap consisting of simple mouldings above a broad plate in low relief, containing the inscription. Before the doorway was a simple colonnade of five rectangular piers, one story high, and with a sloping roof. Within is a small room, 7 feet by 10, at the back of which is another, but much smaller, doorway, opening on what seemed to be a court beside the church. This then was the vestibule of a side entrance to this court. The front of the inscribed lintel is in line with the fronts

Of Other buildings On each Side. The Passageway, showing the lintel which bears Inscr. 220, and 1,, *r* .1 «. 1 the doorway at the back opening into the courtyard of the church rudely cut, but perfectly clear: they are about 10 cm. high. There are no other traces of letters. Copy of the editor.

These letters have, as numerical signs, the value 8051, which is the sum of the numerical values of the letters which make up the following sentence:

Kupios *fvd£r) TrjV eicroSov crov Kal Tt)v efoSoV crov airo vvv Kal eo? al(ovav. 'Afiijv. The Lord shall keep thy coming in and thy going out from now even for evermore. Amen.*

See Chapter i, p. 25.

Traces of another inscription were found in 1905 on the lintel of a house in the extreme eastern end of the town; but I was unable to read a single word, and very few letters, with certainty: the writing has been almost completely obliterated.

Inscr. 220. From a drawing. Scale i: 20.

221. Delloza. House. On the lintel over the entrance to the courtyard of a -t EieEwCYnEPHMDNTICwKAeHMDNXMr t + Ei @co)s *vTTtp rjfjLov, ns d Kad' rj/ iov; t If God (be) for us who (is) he that is against X(pior6?) M(a/3iV?) y(evvrj0e). t tis? Ch(rist) (is) b(orn) of M(ary).* t house: the doorway of the courtyard faces eastward; but the house itself faces the south. The inscription is on the highest band of the plain, right-lined mouldings: the band is 1.90 m. long and 8 cm. wide. The letters are 4 to 5 cm. high. Copied by Dr. Littmann.

These words are from Romans viii, 31. See also Chapter 1, p. 17. On XMr see p. 23 and No. 155.

222. Delloza. House. On the lintel of the entrance to the courtyard of a house in the western part of the town, facing 'eastward. The lintel is 2.15 m. long and 60 cm. high. The band occupied inscr. 222. From a drawing. Scale 1:20. by the letters is 1.88 m. long and *jy2* tEi 0eo? *vnep ip.av,* rt's 6 *Kol0' Vwv* Sdfo, avrw cm. high: the letters themselves, *y2 wavTore.* to *y2* cm high, are handsomely formed t // *God (be) for you, who (is) he (that is) against you:* and wejj cm Q , Dr Littmann *glory (be) to*

him alway!
Published by Waddington, No. 2666 b.

Possibly uyxwi/, pronounced *himon,* may have been intended for *;*see the preceding inscription.

223. Delloza. Same House. On the lintel of a doorway of the house, the entrance to the courtyard of which bears the foregoing inscription. The house faces southward. It has three doorways, the central one of which bears the present inscription. Before the house was a two-story colonnade. The inscription is upon the highest band of the plain, right-lined mouldings of the lintel. The whole lintel measures 2.22 by 0.57 m.: the inscribed band is 1.91 m. long and *6/2* cm. high. The letters are 4 to 5 cm. high. At each end of the inscription, on the return of the inscribed fascia and below the line of the inscription, is a so-called "Maltese" cross, with broad arms. Copy by Dr. Littmann.
Published by Waddington, No. 2666 a. De Vogue, 5". C, pi. 39.

t   KYPBOHGITu/OIKLJTOYTKAlTOY-CYKOYCINeNAYTujAMHN +
+ *Kvpie, fiorjdj* T& *Oikco Tovtw,* Kou Tovs *Vkovctiv iv* avrw. *'Afjirjv.* +
+ *Lord, help this house, and those that dwell in it. Amen.* +
Evidently *Vkovo-w* is for *Oikovo-iv.* probably TOIC was intended, before *Vkovo-iv,* instead of TOYC.

In 1905 Dr. Littmann found a third lintel belonging to this same house, and containing almost the Same words as No. 222: Ei Oeo? *vnkp vp.5v,* n's 6 /ca#' *vp.ov Sofa avrov iravrore Kal Vvv.* This lintel seemed to have been part of the doorway in the south wall of the courtyard: it now lies, broken in two, in a fence adjoining the southwest angle of the court.

224. Dell6za. House. On the lintel of a house facing westward, a short dis tance south of No. 221. The whole lintel measures 2.00 m. in length '"t X T?fYi « space 1.34 by 0.22 m. The letters are 5 to 9 cm. high. Copy of Dr. Littmann.

Compare No. 221, No. 219, etc.; and see above, p. 23.

225. Der Sambil. Tomb, 399 A.D. "Sur un tombeau creuse dans lc roc; audessus de l'inscription on voit le monogramme

du Christ, accoste des lettres A Q." Waddington, No. 2663. De Vogue, S. C, p. 109. XMH "Errow? *uji, firj(vbs)* Agjov 8k', *ireXeo-drj To ipyov.* + 'HXiaSou. *Ch(rist) b(orn) of M(ary). In (the) year yio, on the 24th of (the) month Loos, the work was finished. (It belongs to) Hcliadcs.* (August, 399 A.D.)
Heliades, as Waddington says, was evidently the proprietor of the tomb. On the letters XMr see p. 23.

226. Der Sambil. Tomb, 408-409 A.d. On a rock-hewn tomb north of the town. Above the entrance are traces of painting and a disk. The lintel also is ornamented with disks and other ornamentation. The space occupied by the inscription measures 1.07 m. by 6 cm.: the letters are 3 to 4 cm. high. Copy by Dr. Littmann.

Published by Waddington, No. 2664.

The genitive, *Aifiavtov,* at the end of such a sentence seems strange. Possibly, as Dr. Littmann has suggested to me, the Al is a rendering of the Syriac preposition *le, to* or *for,* etc. In that case the name may be *Bavtov,* and may be treated here as indeclinable. The name *tafieivos Baviov* occurs in an inscription found at Namara, Wad. 2268. But see the foregoing inscription (No. 225), where the same sort of a genitive is found without the possibility of there being a preposition involved, viz. 'HXtaSou.

227. Der Sambil. Tomb. Over the doorway of a rock-hewn tomb with an arched vestibule, in the northwestern part of the town. In the center of the lintel is a disk, containing the +, with A and Uj. On either side is a simple-f: under the left one of these crosses are the letters OBIOC, 22 cm. in length; under the other the letters MAT6QC, 30 cm. in length. Below these letters is a band, about one meter long and 4j/2 cm. broad, the whole of which seems to have been inscribed. But in the first half only the letter o remains, 31 cm. from the left end and 23 cm. from the beginning of the letters in the right half. These letters are INITAC: they are 16 cm. long and 2 to 3 cm. high. Below this inscribed band is a row of disks, and below these a band, similar to the first, in

which the letters A Y or AOY were read. These last are under the letters 16 of the upper band. The inscription was copied by Dr. Littmann. In 1905 I saw the inscription myself, and noted that the letters INI and, below, AOY seemed to me certain.

'O £i'os /ictreos. o IN I ereX«r(0)77.
Life (is) vain was finished.

Probably this inscription was similar to the foregoing, and the date was probably about the same. This date was probably contained in the first part of this upper band, and the letters INI may stand for *Iv(8lktlo)vos) l; in indiction 75.* Inscription No. 229 is on the arch of the vestibule of this same tomb.

228. Der Sambil. Tomb. On a band of the mouldings, on the face of the arched vestibule of a rock-hewn tomb. This band of the mouldings is 7 cm. wide, and the span of the arch 2.35 m. The letters are 5 *x/2* cm. high. Copy by Dr. Littmann.

Published by Waddington, No. 2665 a.

ITDYKYPIOYHrHKAITnnAHPUJ-
MAAYTHCKAITT--TECDIKATDIKYNTE-
CENAYTH *txMri Tov Kvpiov r) yrj Kox To TrkTjpcjfta avri; Kcu irdvTe; ol Ka. ToiK(o)vire; iv airy. + X(/hot6s) M(a The earth is the Lord's, and the fullness of it and they that dwell in it. + Ch(rist) b(orn) of M(ary).*

These words are from Psalm xxiii, i: they are quoted also in No. 229 and, for example, in *C. I. G.* 8937. See Chapter 1, p. 16. On the letters XMr see p. 23.

228 a. Waddington reports another inscription on the doorway within the vestibule of this tomb, which Dr. Littmann did not copy. Waddington's reading is as follows (Wad. 2665 b): etou? aXi/»', (1705) *TlayT)iLOV Ln (the) year Jji,in (the) month Panemos* (July, 420 A.D.?)

In 1905 I examined the doorway of this tomb, but found no inscription there. But on the right wall of the vestibule is the inscription given under No. 237 below.

Rock-hewn tomb containing Inscr. 22S.

229. Der Sambil. Tomb. On the mouldings of the face of the arched vestibule of the same tomb as No. 227. In the

middle of the inscription is a disk containing a-f with A and u. The last five or six letters are in a horizontal line beginning with the end of the inscribed band of the mouldings. This band is 7, the letters 3 to *l/2* cm. high. Copy of Dr. Littmann. TLJKYPI0J6CTINOIOYPANOI t HrHKAITOTTAHPWMAAYTHC-TAYAOCpAYN

Tw Kvpiio iarlv ol ovpavoi, + To the Lord belong the heavens, f) yfj Kai To irTjpcop.a avrs t the earth and the fullness of TAYAOCDAYN-*H*

On a brief visit to Der Sambil in 1905, I copied anew the last few letters of this inscription. I read, after *avrr,* ErPAYAoC©AYN, the first three letters being written together in a ligature. I Jhink the © in the last word may be for 9, and so would read *iypayjja 09 i(d)aiev +: I wrote who buried. +*

On the contents of this inscription see No. 228, and Chapter 1, p. 16.

230. Der Sambil. Tomb. On a rock-hewn tomb with an arched vestibule, facing southward. Within are columns. The inscription is on the topmost band of the mouldings of the arch. The letters are 4 to 5 cm. high. Copied by Mr. Butler.

Doubtless life is like a wheel in that the part which is now on the top will soon be down below. But perhaps the potter's wheel was also thought of, on which man is as the clay. On the other hand I am not entirely sure that we should not read here *T/adxo?: a race-course.* Ecclesiastes i, 2: see Chapter 1, p. 17.

231. Der Sambil. The Same Tomb. On the lintel of the rectangular doorway, within the vestibule, of the same tomb as the foregoing inscription. The band of the

The latter part of the inscription is of course a quotation from mouldings which is occupied by the inscription is I. ii m. long: the letters are 4 to 4 cm. high. Copy of Mr. Butler, + Tpets, *rpew.* Ai-tos *irov;* Alto? toScu. +

+ *Thou runnest, I run.— Unto where? Unto here.* +

Tpex is for Tpcxeis, attu? doubtless for »8ai for 5Se: for the expression «us S8c see Genesis xxii, 5; II Kings xx, 16; III

Kings xviii, 45; IV Kings viii, 9.

It seems strange to find a reference to the grave so cynical, and yet framed by the symbol of the cross. But we may compare an inscription from Shekh Miskin, the two fragments of which were published by MM. Macrides and Mordtmann in *Z. P. V.,* 1884, p. 123, and by Professor G. A. Smith in *Edinburgh Crit. Review* for 1892, p. 55 f. : these two fragments were combined by M. Clermont-Ganneau and published by him in *P. E. E.,* 1902, p. 25, with the following translation: *'Asiamos* (Aslamos?), *the son of Anthos, made this sepulchre by his own labor and that of his children, and he says: 1 Hail, passer-by! As thou art, I was; and as I am, thou shall be! for life and riches all end in) this house of the tomb!"* Compare also the words *p-era ndma* ra£os: *After all the) tomb,* found by M. Loeytvedon the lintel of a tomb at "Irbid," and published by M. Clermont-Ganneau in his *Recueil,* 1, p. 17.

232. Der Sambil. Tomb. On the lintel of the doorway of a rock-hewn tomb with a vestibule, facing southward, in the center of the town. In the center of the mouldings is a disk containing a cross and certain other symbols which I do not understand. The inscription is on the highest band of the mouldings, above the disk, 1.50 m. in length: the top of the disk crosses this band, causing a break in the inscription 21 cm. long. The letters are 24 to 3 cm. high. Copied by Mr. Butler. t ENiuNOMATiT-TATPCCKYDY KAriOYTTNlAMHN t + *'Ev wvopari Ylarpbs K(oi) 'tov Kcu) 'Ayiov + In name of Father and of Son and of Holy Uv(evp,aTo;). 'Aprjv. + Spirit. Amen-+*

In each case the K, which stands for *Kai,* has a bar closing the lower angle: the figure after TTN I take to be a sign of abbreviation rather than I or 2. From the forms of the letters I judge that this inscription is not older than the last quarter of the fifth century.

233. Der Sambil. On the lower part of the door-cap of a lintel. The letters of

E(i) a Ke(e)os *virep ipav,* Ti? *a Ko.0' lp.wv;* X(/3kttos) M(a/otas) *y(vv7)9ei;). If God (be) for us, who (is) lie (that is)*

against

Inscr. 233. From a photograph and copy. Scale i: 20.
the lower line are 1.20 m. long, the five letters above the end of this line are 34 cm. long. The letters are 4 to 6y2 cm. high. Copied by Mr. Butler.
Dr. Littmann suggests that the first word here, EN, may not be merely a mistake of writing, and intended for the Greek «£, but may be in reality the Syriac word *en* which means *if.* It is strange to find in the same inscription both e and t standing for *v*-On the content of the inscription see Chapter 1, p. 17: also p. 23.
234. Der Sambil. House. On the door-cap of a lintel of a doorway in the second story of a house in the eastern part of the town. Before the house was a twostory colonnade of piers. The space occupied by the inscription is 1.18 m. long and 14 cm. wide, the letters are 5 to 6 cm. high. Copied by Dr. Littmann.
XMrXYTONIKOCJ)EVrECATANA
X(/oicrr6s)   M(a/n'as)   y(evur)0ei;).
X(picrro)G To *Ch(rist) (is) b(orn) of M(ary). Christ's (is) the vicVikos. tevye tarav*a. *lory. Flee, Satan/*
On XMr see p. 23: for the rest see p. 19. This is one of the inscriptions which show most clearly that such symbols and words were intended as charms to avert evil spirits from the entrance of the house.
235. Der Sambil. On a lintel over the entrance to the courtyard of a house, facing northward, near the foregoing inscription. The lintel is 1.82 m. long and 62 cm. high: both ends have been broken off. The inscription is at the top of the lintel, in letters 3 to 5 cm. high: there was originally room for about nine letters after the TA. Copied by Dr. Littmann.   OCIOCNIKAOMOieEAICI-
AEKAICOITAA- otrios *Viks..* 0 *fiol* #eXi?, £iXe, /ecu *holy conquers. What thou wishest me, trot To.* 8 i7rXa. *friend, may that be to thee also, twofold.*
Before oo-ios I think iras might be supplied (compare Psalm xxxi, 6): *everyone that is),* and before this, probably *iv Tovra; in this (sign).*
On o *fiol* c'Xcis Ktx. see No. 10, etc. Also see Chapter 1, pp. 14 and 25.

236. Der Sambil. House. On the lintel of a house in the western part of the town, facing southward. The inscription is on a part of a door-cap measuring 1. 24 by 0.25 m.: above the inscription are several disks. The t XPICTEBDEBt.,. 0,,,t length, from cross to cross, is 78 cm., and the letters are 0/2 + Xpiore *BoeOL.* ... _.-, _ T. to gem. high. Copied by Dr. Littmann. t *O Christ, help (us) & V J ..*
See Chapter 1, p. 22. Compare also the inscription from Der Sambil published by M. Uspensky, *A. M. S.,* p. 69, which is similar, if not actually the same.
237. Der Sambil. Tomb. of which bears Inscription 228.
    Within the vestibule of the rock-hewn tomb, the arch
The present inscription is painted on the wall at the
right as one faces the tomb. The inscription is 48 cm. long, and the letters 6 to 7 cm. high. Below it are painted two Christian symbols, consisting of the + with A and u below the horizontal arm. Copied by Mr. Butler.
    De Vogue, *S. C.,p.* 151. See also p. 109.
TOYTONIKA Tooto *vUa: This conquers,* i.e. the sign of the cross painted below. See Chapter 1, p. 21. 238. Der Sambil. House. On the lintel of a small house in the western part of the town. The letters are in XQYC 'I(i7o-oi)s) x(pioTds), 0(coC) relief. The portion of the lintel T(Ids), %(a/rrjp). on which the letters are carved is *J(esus) Christ, the) So,i) of G(od), our) S(avior).* 1.80 m. long and io cm. high: the inscription itself is 48 cm. long, the letters 8 cm. high. Copied by Dr. Littmann. See No. 182.
239. Der Sambil. Sarcophagus. On the inside of a sarcophagus hewn in the rock, south of the town and near the church. One side of the sarcophagus stands free of the rock, and is carved with 9T!T 6tovci a figure of a boxer. Part II, p. 277 f. OCYI OGIOYCY
The inscription is rudely scratched on the inner face of the Uun Oyano west side of the sarcophagus near the north end. The space Xaa Acoa-o occupied by the letters is 48 cm. long and 23 high: the letters themselves are 3 to 5 cm. high. Copied by Dr. Littmann and the

editor.
    I have been unable to decipher this inscription. Dr. Littmann has suggested to me as perhaps possible the following: Ev0a8e *KelraL* Tovcnco?, vio? *'ovavjfwvov, anb Kuix.* AaoS i/ceias.
240. Frikya. Lintel, 324 A.d. On a handsome lintel over a doorway in a wall, about the center of the modern village: it faces westward. The right end of the lintel has been broken off, and the left end is imbedded in the wall, so that it was impossible to measure the length of the stone accurately: the width of the present doorway, however, is 1.27 m. I understand this to have been a modern doorway for which this ancient lintel was used. The lintel, then, is not in situ. It is about 92 cm. high and 50 cm. thick. The inscribed portion of the lintel is badly weathered and broken, so that most of the letters are quite illegible. The lengths of the mutilated spaces and the remaining letters are as follows: a space of about 91 cm.+ I DTD = 142 cm. + 136 cm. + MIDYSAY = 20 cm. + about 23 cm. Copy of the editor. IDTD N (t)oc Cxx'c?) erous. , *in the 636thyear.* (324 A.D.) 241-247. Frikya. The Tomb Of Abkdrapsas, 324 A.d. This notable tomb is situated in the hillside south of the town. It has been described by Mr. Butler in Part II of these publications, p. 278 ff., and by the present editor in the *Princeton University Bulletin,* xv (1904), pp. 224-240. Two of its inscriptions were copied by Pococke about 1740, and published by him in his *Inscriptiones Antiquae* (1752), 1, p. 64 f.: the first of these and part of the second were republished by Franz in *C. I. G.* 4463 and 4464: the other part of the second inscription was published by LeBas-Waddington, No. 1834, and also by Kirchhoff, who united both parts of the second inscription in *C. I. G.* 9899. The text of the inscriptions in the present publication is based on copies made by the editor.
The approach to the tomb proper consists of a dromos, 3 meters wide and a little over 3 meters long, hewn in the living rock and covered by a barrel vault of fine masonry. The dromos is now partially choked with soil and stones;

but I think it was originally open at its north end. At the opposite end is a broad arcosolium hewn in the face of the rock, within which is a large sarcophagus-lid, of the usual prismatic shape and with acroteria at the corners, covering the top of a shaft sunk perpendicularly into the rock, like that of Eusebios' tomb at Kokanaya (No. 34). Hewn in the south side of this shaft is a second arcosolium, within which is the grave. The shaft is 2. 08 m. long and 87 cm. wide. The grave is of the same size as the shaft, and is about a meter deep: its top is a meter and a quarter below the top of the shaft. 241. The top of the upper arcosolium is perhaps a meter below the level of the ground outside, and in the middle about 2 meters below the inner surface of the vault. The gap at the end of the vault, above the ground level, is now filled chiefly by one large block, on the inner face of which is a dove-tail plate. Most of Inscription 241 is carved on this plate: the last word, however, in the eighth line is at the right of, the ninth line is below, the plate. The body of the plate is 1.12 m. long and 54 cm. wide. The letters in the plate are 4 or 5 cm. high. The ninth line is 1.37 m. long and its letters 5 to 6 cm. high. All these letters are well carved and regular, and were painted red: the reading is certain.

End of the dromos leading to the tomb of Abedrapsas, showing Inscriptions 241 and 242.

Published in the *C. I. G.*, No. 4463.

1. eTOYCSAXMHNOCAPT6MICI 6. MWC-TONBIONMETAAA 2. OY-AKeTeAGCeNTOMNHMI 7. BONT6CK-AITAC6YXAC 3. ONAB6APAYACAIONY-CIOY 8. AnGAWKANTOICTTATPUJOIC 06OIC 4. KAIAMA9BABeATHCeYTTOAe 9. 0APCIYYXHOYAICA9ANATOC 5. MOYrAMeTHAYTOYeYGY

"Erov? *S-x't H-Vvo,; 'Aprep.ioiov aK, irieo-ev rb p.vT)plov* kySeSpcu/ias *Aiovvcriov* Kai 'Ap,ad3a/3ia *rfjs Ein-roXip.ov, yaperrj avrov, evdvp,a; Tov fi-iov p.eTaa/36vres,* Kai rds evicts *dniBwKav* Tois *7raTpe5ois* deols-©d-pcri *VXV'* u8is *addvaTos.* In the) year *6j6,* on the) 21st of (the) month Artcmisios, Abedrapsas, sou) of Dionysios, and Amathbabea, daughter) of the

daughter) of Eupolemos, his wife, finished the tomb, having shared life cheerfully, and they paid their vows to their ancestral gods. Be of good cheer, my) soul: no one is immortal! (May, 324 A.D.)

I have translated the fourth line literally, although I am inclined to believe thatrrjs is a mistake for 17, and due to the influence of the genitive following. If so, Amathbabea was the daughter, not the granddaughter, of Eupolemos. Otherwise, the explanation of this unusual wording may be that Eupolemos was a more distinguished person than Amathbabea's own father.1

Both names, *Abedrapsas* and *Amathbabea,* are of Syrian origin. The former is doubtless compounded of *labd=servant,* and some god's name, perhaps *Rapsha* for *Raskpd,* r, identified with the Greek Apollo. The latter is doubtless from *Amath=handmaid,* and the name *Bdbai,* which occurs as the name of a person, but is here probably the name of a goddess. The same name occurs in No. 263 in the form *Mathbabea.*

An interesting parallel to this inscription is furnished by another, from Apameia Kibotos in Phrygia, published in *C. I. G.* 3962: *'AirfyLa eyw Kelp.ai MeveKel p.iya TwSe avv dvSpu Kai yap £gw9 6pou Tovto yepas dxopev. Kai iirop.ev Svo TKva, viov hi ye Aprepi-hwpov, os X-PLV cvo"e/8«7s revfi' rvp.f$ov $6ip.ivoio-iv, Xcup ere 8' 01 V apiovres, Kol euas2 Oiaff inep avrov.*

I, Apphia, lie here, united with this my husband Menekles: for, living together, this the reward we have. And we leave two children, and Artemidoros, a youth who for sake of piety has built this) tomb for the dead. Hail, ye passers by, and offer ye prayers for him.

The last sentence of the present inscription, *Qdpo-i xjjvxv Kt.,* occurs frequently in epitaphs of Syria, e.g. Wad. 1829,1897, 2459, etc-! F-r893, P-178; R. A/., xxxiv, p. 196. In one case the words eV Tw /8uj» Tout»: *in this life,* are added *(R. R. G.,* vn, p. 296). It seems to be primarily a pagan formula, but not exclusively so: see Wad.

1 Or possibly rijs *Em-oefiov* means daughter) of the slave of Eupolemos. -See Ramsay in *K. E. G.,* 11, p. 32. 2459. Sometimes the phrase o£ *deol ada.va.T01* is used in inscriptions otherwise similar in character, as, for example, 0a/o-ei, Ac dim, o *I Oeol dddvaroi.* Er«w t/3.1

I think there can be no doubt that the date of this inscription is reckoned according to the Seleucid era: if so, it is one of the latest pagan inscriptions in this region.

242. Above the upper arcosolium, and immediately below the preceding inscription is another and still longer document. The first eighteen or nineteen letters of the first five lines are carved on a block of stone, 72 cm. long and 24 cm. wide, inserted in the rock evidently because of a defect there. The inscription on this block was published by Franz, after Pococke, *C. I. G.* 4464: in *C. I. G.* 9899 it was combined with the rest of the inscription by Kirchhoff, who however places it at the right of the other. The rest of the inscription is on the living rock, at the right of the inserted block. Around the edges of the block the rock is somewhat crumbled, so that between the two parts of the inscription there is a space sufficient for three or four letters in each line. The seventh and eighth lines of the second part begin farther to the left than the others by three and four letters respectively, so that the first letter of the seventh and the first two letters of the eighth line are below the corner of the inserted block; but there is no trace of letters at the left of these. This fact indicates that the block was inserted before the inscription was first carved, and was not inserted to repair the inscription at some later time. The letters are not so large or so well shaped as those of No. 241, but have the same forms. They are also painted red. Published by Pococke, *Inscrr. Antiq.* I, p. 65. *C. I. G.* 4464 and 9899. Waddington, No. 1834.

1. TAYTAeYXAPICTUUNAeiT ABGAPAY-ACeMOYeH AIKIAC 2. ONTOCOTTATP-WOCMOYee OCAPK6CIAAOYAHAUUC-MOI4) NO 3. MeNoceNTTOAAoicMeeYe preTHceNuuceTWNrAPKenAPeAO 4.

eHNeiCMAGHCINTeXNH   CKAIAI
AOAITOYXPONOYTTAPeAA 5. AABON-
THNAYTHNT6XNHN   KAI6TIAIATHCAY-
TOYTTPONOI AC 6. enPIAMHNAYTWXW-
PIONMHAeNOCrNONTOC   7.   KAI-
HAeYeePUUCAAYTONMHKATABeNI-
NAYTONSIO   8.   THNnOAINKeeTU-
UAIKeOCHMHNK6AIKeUJCOAHrHeH

Taura *evapio-rov X4yi) 'Afie8pdfia;-
'Epov if' These tilings Abedrapsas says
in gratitude: "When rjkiKias Ovtos, 6
Trarpwds pov 0eb 'ApKecnXdov, I was
of age,my ancestral god, the god) of
Arkesilaos,*

St7'Xw9 *poi jiv6pevo;, iv Ttoxxois
pe evepyerrfaev appearing visibly unto
me, showed kindness to me in c2s ircov
yap ce' irapSoO-qv «s pdBaiv re'Xi/r,s,
Kox many (waJ's) for when M TMnty-
five years of age), svw / r / n _a » _v
J. I was given over to learn a trade,
I both acquired this oiaoiy-
ovpovovTTapKaKayfiov   rqv
avrr)VTe)(yr)v, Y same trade in a short
time, and furthertnore on my own ini-
tiative I bought myself a place, no one
knowing it, and I freed myself from going myself to the city: I both was righteous and itas rightly led."* 1From "Fik"
near Djerash, published by M. Germer-
Durand in *Rev.Bibl.* 1899, p. 25. See also an inscription published by Dr. Schu-
macher in *Z. P. V.* ix, p. 322. 2 The red
pigment, still in the cross strokes of the
A, shows that A A was carved here, and
not M as Pococke thought. The form
MyO is, Of cOUrse, for Xeyei, *fev6ievo;*
for £au;d/tei'OS, *KaTafieviv* for *KOLTaf-
taiveiv, Kc* for Kcu, Si/ceo? and Siew?
for SiVaios and Si/caiws.

In my article on this inscription in
the *Princeton University Bulletin,* I expressed the opinion that the name 'Ap/
ceo-iXaou was in apposition with the
pronoun /xou, and that the speaker was
this *Arkesilaos,* quite another person
from Abedrapsas. Now, however, I believe that this is not the case, but that
Abedrapsas is the speaker throughout. I
am indebted to Professor Dittcnberger
for the suggestion that probably
Abedrapsas' ancestral god had no name
of his own, but was called simply "The
god of Arkesilaos." The existence of
such nameless gods has been discussed,

first by Professor Noeldeke, in *C. I. S.,*
n, No. 176; then by M. Clermont-Ganneau, in *Ms Recueil cf Archiologie Orientate,* v, p. 154 ff. The latter, speaking
of this matter on p. 160 f., says: "Nous
rencontrons souvent en Syrie des ded-
icaces faites a des dieux innomds,
lesquels sont seulement designes par le
nom de leur adorateur au genitif: 'au
dieu *d'un tef;* et le nom de cet adorateur
n'est pas celui de l'auteur de la dedicace, mais d'un autre personnage, probablement, au moins dans certains cas,
celui d'un de ses ancetres dont il a herite
le culte familial. C'est ainsi que nous
voyons divers personnages adresser
leurs hommages a un Heos Av/aou, a
un £eos *Ovaa-eddov,* a un ©«s *'Apepov,*
etc.'' See also Dittenberger, in *O. G. I.
S.,* No. 637, note 1.

Arkesilaos does not seem to have
been of» the immediate family of
Abedrapsas, for his name does not appear among the family names carved on
the other walls of this tomb. Possibly he
was some remote ancestor, possibly the
patron or even the owner of Abedrapsas, for the fact that the latter's father
is not mentioned here suggests that perhaps he was a slave.

Lastly the pronouns, in the last part
of the fifth line, and in the sixth and
seventh lines, present a certain difficulty. Perhaps the first, *awov,* refers to
Abedrapsas' god, by whose providence
he was guided: perhaps this pronoun
and the others, *avrS* in line 6 and aww
twice in line 7, refer to Abedrapsas' patron. But I now believe that these pronouns all refer to Abedrapsas himself,
and should be read *avrov, avrw, airov*
for *ifiavrov, e/xavrw, ifxavrov.*

It would be interesting to know what
is meant by the words / *was given over
to learn a trade,* and why this person did
not begin to learn his handicraft until he
was twenty-five years of age. This im-
plies some very special circumstances
in his case. I think it can be accounted
for best by the supposition that this craft
of his required some unusual talent,
which was discovered in him comparatively late in life. What craft was there
in those days, for which unusual natural
talent was required, and favor of the

gods, and the assistance of some patron? I think sculpture most of all. Perhaps then the very remarkable sculptures of this tomb, which are described
below, are by the hand of Abedrapsas
himself.

As for the reasons for his *going down
to the city,* probably Abedrapsas, successful though he was, did not intend
outsiders to know the precise nature of
his obligations.

243. Beside figures sculptured on the
right wall of the dromos. These figures
are life-sized, and are executed in high
relief on the living rock. They constitute
a single group. In the center are a man
and woman, reclining upon a couch before which a small table, spread with
viands, is set. The head of the couch is
towards the right, and on this the man
leans his left arm. He is represented in
full face, his right hand resting on the
woman's shoulder. The woman is also
represented in full face and leaning upon her left arm: she is in front of the
man but nearer the foot of the couch, so
that her body does not completely con-
ceal his: her right arm is stretched towards the viands on the table. At the left
of the table and facing the woman stood
the figure of a little girl, perhaps ten
years of age; but her body, which was
sculptured in the round, has been broken off. At the left of the group, behind
the foot of the couch, stands a young
slave-girl, clad in a tunic which is fastened over the left shoulder by a brooch,
but, passing under the right arm, leaves
the right arm and shoulder nude. She is
turned towards the right, so that her face
is shown in profile. Her right hand is
held close to her hip, her left is stretched
out before her: with both hands she is
holding up the draperies which form a
background for the principal figures. By
the head of the couch stands a youthful
male figure, completely draped, represented in full face. In his right hand,
which is raised above the head of the
couch, he holds something which looks
like a serpent; in the other hand something which I took to be a torch, but
which may have been a cornucopia. The
figure is taller by a head than either the
man, who is propped up fairly high on

the couch, or the slave girl, who is standing.

A. C. I P H N H *ElpyvT, &ovr).* A B 6 A P A 'A/SeSpctyas.

A O Y A H *Eire tie, a slave.* Y A C *Abedrapsas.*

The first of these inscriptions, or titles, At the left of the man's head. The first is at the right of the slave-girl's face. part is 28, the second 16 cm. long, both The first word is 27, the second 25 cm. together 14 cm. in height, long, the two together 12 cm. in height.

D.

B-TYXHAFA9H *'AaaOfia/Bea*-Aua0/ 3a/3ea, *Tychc Agathe, i.e. Good Fortune.*

A M A0 BA B A.,

A, 1 A o A A *ttvyarrip.* At the left of the head of the male fig AMA0BAB6A & GYΓATHP *Atnathbabea, (and) A mathure* at the right of the group: the letters *babea (her) daughter.* measure 35 by 6 cm. This name is

At the left of the woman's head. The properly that of a female divinity, who was three words measure in length 46, 43 and thought of sometimes as the personifica34 cm. respectively: together they meas-tion of good luck and sometimes as a kind ure 19 cm. in height. Gr gUardian angel of a nation, a family or even a single individual. The figure, on the other hand, is that of the corresponding male deity, whose name was properly 'Aya06s Aou/wof. Snake and cornucopia are common symbols of this god. 1

These inscriptions add nothing of philological interest to those already given, Nos. 241 and 242: their interest lies only in that they are the titles and explanation of a unique and beautiful work of art. A family is here represented in a group whose composition is both symmetrical and effective. The wife occupies the central and most prominent position: on her left is her husband and on her right her daughter. The slave-girl who stands behind her mistress' feet, and who perhaps represents collectively the servants of the household, is balanced by the figure of the youth who stands by the master's head, and who represents the Good Spirit of the house.

Unfortunately the faces of all have been completely demolished, probably by the Mohammedans, excepting only the lower part of the slave-girl's face. This face shows the thick lips of a negress; but what is left of the nose suggests rather a Semitic type. In spite of their mutilation, however, all the figures, except that of the youth on the extreme right, are sufficiently individualized to indicate that they were really portrait statues. The central figures, which are fully draped, show both a dignity and a tenderness of feeling which is very impressive. The figure of the slave-girl is graceful, tense and full of spirit. If this was the work of Abedrapsas, it is no wonder that he was successful in his calling: the god of his fathers must indeed have been manifest unto him. I think he could have had but few competitors, judging from the other 1Preller-Robert, *Griechische Mythologie,* I, p. 543.

sculptures which remain in this region. And I think the same man must have produced the original sculptures of another tomb in Frikya, described by Mr. Butler on p. 281 f.; but his work here was marred, in a later and I think a Christian time, by one of little talent or even skill. The sculptor of Abedrapsas' tomb was one of the last representatives of the pagan art, which was dying lingeringly in this remote region, when in the world's centers art was already dead.

Above the life-sized group which I have just described, at the top of the wall of living rock which forms the side of the dromos, is a frieze of small figures also in relief, about 30 cm. high. On the left is a seated figure turned three-quarters to the right: the head is supported upon the right hand, while the left rests upon the seat. Next on the right are six draped figures, upright and turned towards the left, as if walking towards the seated figure: the last two of these appear to be carrying between them a large chest. Next on the right are four figures, which apparently face towards the right. The second and third of these appear to be mounted, while the fourth appears to be stepping upon the

lowest step of an altar which, at the extreme right of the frieze, balances the seated figure at the left end. These figures have been so badly mutilated that little can be made of them now. In my article in the *Princeton Bulletin* I suggested that two scenes from the life of Abedrapsas might be represented here, first Abedrapsas and his five sons fulfilling the obligation in the city, secondly the worship at the altar of the "ancestral god." 244. On the left side of the dromos of the same tomb, immediately above a row of ten heads, sculptured in life size on the living rock. The heads have been completely defaced, so that only the general outline and something of the neck of each remains. No attempt was made to carve the shoulders of these figures, but where the shoulders should be the rock has been cut back at an even slant, extending continuously for the whole length of the row, and reaching at the top a depth sufficient to allow the sculptor to execute the heads in high relief below the original surface. Below where this slant begins the rock shows only the rough-dressed surface natural to the wall of such a dromos.

Every other head, beginning with the first, is that of a man: the other heads are those of women. In spite of their mutilation the latter are easily distinguished from the former, not only because the arrangement of the hair makes the outline of the women's heads much broader, but also because of the long curls which hang down, one on each side of each woman's head, in some cases apparently before, in others apparently behind, the ear. See the description of the busts in the medallion described under No. 246. The slanting surface of the rock below the heads is unbroken save for these curls which fall across it.

The inscription is carved on the lowest tier of the vaulted roof, at the bottom of the stones. It consists of five names, each of which begins above a man's head.

The first four letters of the first name are 20 cm. long and 7 high. The last four letters of this name, which have about the same dimensions, are upon a corner of the block which has been cracked off from the rest and which fell down when the debris was cleared away from it. Between the two parts there would be space for about one letter. Between the first and second names was a space of 15 cm. The second name measures 33y2 by 5 cm. Between it and the next is a space of 13 cm. The third name measures 21 by 6 cm., and is followed by a space of 23 cm. The fourth name measures 33 by 5, and is followed by a space of 20 cm. The fifth name reaches almost to the inner corner of the dromos. The last two names were copied by Pococke, and appear in C. I. G. 4464.

T6NN AAIC PWWANOC BIZOC IAN(tIAOC AIONYCIC Few ej ai9, Ptu-jaai'os, Bi£os, n dpfios, Aioiwris.

Genncalis, Romanos, Bizos, Panphilos, Dionysis.

Perhaps the first name should be read rWa(S)is, for TeiWSios. I believe, with Mr. Butler, that these are probably sons of Abedrapsas, and the unnamed women their wives.

On the left spandril of the upper arcosolium (at the south end) of the same tomb, at the right of a medallion, carved below the surface of the rock, and containing in relief a life-sized head and bust of a woman. Her figure is fully draped, and a veil, which hangs apparently from the back of the head, is brought forward over the shoulders. She wears a necklace with a pendant. Her face is turned slightly to the left, and bent slightly forward, with a pensive expression. The nose seems to have been straight at the bridge and clearly cut, the cheek-bones high. The hair stands high over the forehead and is brought down at each side in a wavy mass, well over the upper part of the ear: the arrangement of the hair at the back is hidden by the veil. The figure is badly weathered. The inscription measures 34 by 7 cm.

I think that perhaps Heraklia was an unmarried daughter: if so, the difference between her head-dress and that of the other women is significant.

246. On the right spandril of the same arcosolium, at the left of a similar medallion containing two busts. That on the left is of a man, his head turned three-quarters to the right. His figure is

fully draped, his forehead high, his nose straight at the bridge. The bust at the right is that of a woman. Her head is turned slightly towards the left and slightly upward. Her draperies OYAPMI-AN are open a little at the throat, disclosing a necklace. She *Ovape/xuave* .... .. *O Uaremianos!* wears no veil, but her hair is brought down at each side in a long curl, which falls forward over each shoulder and thus seems to give a frame or setting to her face. Both these busts also are badly weathered. The inscription is 44 cm. long, and the letters are from 3 to 5 cm. high.

The vocative here seems strange in view of the other inscriptions of this tomb. I have been tempted to read *ovaXe* for the Latin *vale I* But I have been unable to account for MIAN as a name. The same objection has prevented my reading here two names, the first being Ovapos: *faros* or *Icarus.* Dr. Littmann has suggested to me that possibly *OvapeWiave* should be read, for *Ovakept,avc; O Ua-lerianos (ISalerianus).* 247. On the right side of the dromos of the same tomb, close to the inner corner, by the medallion with the two busts to which the preceding inscription belongs. The present inscription is on the first course of the vaulted roof of the dromos. It is 7 cm. from the bottom of the stone, and begins 11 cm. from the corner: it is 40 cm. long and 8 cm. high. Pococke combined this name, and two of those published here under No. 244, with his first inscription from this tomb. See C. I. G. 4464.

Bapaxos is of course the Aramaic name *Barakh.* BAPAXOY BapdXOv: *Of Barachos.* R immediate,y oyer the seated figure at the left end of the frieze described under No. 243 above. Possibly it may have some connection with that. It seems more probable, however, that this word should be taken together with that given under No. 246 above, although the letters of the one are twice as large as those of the other, and although there was room for the letters BAPAXOY on the spandril of the arcosolium, under the latter part of OYAPMIAN. Taking both inscriptions together, we should read *oiapepiave Bapdxov; O Uaremianos? son of Barachos.* JOr *OiaptXXmvt:* see

above, under No. 246.

Perhaps this man was not a son of Abedrapsas, but was adopted by him into his own family.
248 FRIKYA. HOUSE EICBEDCMONDC E TDVCEDX Ets @cos "etov? eoX' 364 A. D. On a rudely cut Dcaujdvbk.... OvClk AAw lintel in the northern part *(There is) one God only. In (the) year 675, on (the) 29th of (the) month of the town, facing south-Loos (August 364 A.d.) ward.* The space occupied by the inscription measures 1.36 m. by 20 cm.: the first line of the inscription is 1.32 m. long, and the letters 6 cm. high. Copy of the editor. See Chapter i, pp. 13 f. and 18 f. 249. Frikya. House. On the lintel of a doorway in the lower story of a simple quadrated house in the northern part of the town, facing eastward. The house originally had before it a two-story portico, which has fallen down. At the right of the doorway is a small niche, as often in this region, and beyond that a window. The inscription is 1.74 m. long, the letters 4 cm. high. Copy of the editor. ICBEDCKAIDXPICTDCI/TDAriDNnNEY-MADBDHBlJJNnACIEEIN f

E is Oeos *Kox 6 Xpioro? (kcu) To Ayiov* nVcv/ia, *(There is) one God and the Christ and the Holy 6 fior)&av Traoo-)uv. + Spirit, that giveth aid. -f*

The form *irao-o-uv* is evidently for *iraa-iv:* compare *nao-eiv* in No. 250. See also Chapter 1, p. 13 f.
250. Frikya. Same House. On the lintel of the doorway in the upper story of the same house, immediately above the preceding inscription (No. 249). The present inscription was copied for me by Dr. Littmann, who climbed to the top of the lintel and, lying upon it, read the inscription from above. The lintel itself is 2.16 m. long and 52 cm. high, the top band of the mouldings which bears the inscription is 6l/2 cm. broad, and the letters are 3 to 4 cm. high. In the center of the upper mouldings of the door-cap is a disk with a cross in the center. EICBED-CKDXPICTDCKTDAriDNnNEYMADBD-HBuNnACEIN t

Eis Qeos *K(al) 6 Xpioros /c(cu) To 'Ayiov* Ilvev/xa, *(There is) one God and the Christ and the Holy 6 fio-qOwv TTao-eiv t. Spirit, that giveth aid. +*

See the preceding inscription.

251. Frikya. On a lintel in the courtyard of a modern dwelling, in the center of the village, facing southward. The inscription is 1.64 m. long, the letters 3 to 4 cm. high. At the left end is a space 14 cm. long. Copy of the editor. IAT-POCKAIAYCICKAKO-NIACOYCOXPTCo-eninANTvuNee 'IciT/aos zeal Xucris Kclkwv, 'larovs 6 X/3i(ctt6)s, 6 *A healer and a deliverance from ills (is) Jesus the* c'n l iraivTcav @e(ds). *Christ, the God over all.*

Below, in the lowest band of the mouldings, are the following letters, 3 cm. high and together 17/2 cm. in length: IX9YC

'I(rjtrous) X(pioTos), 0(coC) T(ids), *(tarqp). Jesus) Christ), the) S(on) (of) G(od), (our) S(avior).*

On the first line see Chapter 1, p. 15: on the second see No. 182.

252. Frikya. On a very artistic lintel, close beside that of the preceding inscription. The present inscription is in the center of the fascia next to the lowest in the mouldings. The whole fascia is 1.42 m. long, and 8 cm. broad: the inscription is 17 cm. long and 3 cm. high. Copy of the editor. IX9YC

'I(i7roGs) X(/3i0rd?), 8(eou) T(i6s), *t(arrrjp). J(esus) Ch(rist), (the) S(on) (of) G(od), (our) S(avior).*

See No. 182 and its commentary.

253. Frikya. On a lintel in the northern part of the town, just south of No. 248, and facing eastward. The inscription is 34 cm. in length and 7 cm. in height. Copy of the editor. IX9YC *'(t)a-ovs)* X(p«TTos), e(eoi)) T(ids), *t(anrjp). J(esus) Ch(rist), (the) S(on) (of) G(od), (our) S(avior).*

See No. 182 and its commentary.

254. Shnan. Tomb. In a rock-hewn tomb, east of the town, and facing eastward. The inscription is painted on the rock on the under side of the arch of the arcosolium opposite the entrance: this arcosolium contains two sarcophagi. The eleventh line of the inscription and the + at the beginning of the sixth line are painted in red: all the rest is in black or green.

The first line is 1.24 m. long, the letters *2j/2 to t.y2* cm. high. The B, at the

end of the line, is 10 cm. high: the three following letters, Y H r, are somewhat smaller. Of the other odd lines the longest is 1.49, the shortest 1.00 m. in length. The even lines vary from 70 cm. to 1.00 m. in length: the letters vary from 3 to 7 cm. in height. The eleventh line is 1.30 m. long, and its letters are *6/2* to 9 cm. high. The lines are spaced at irregular intervals from each other, as if no definite plan had been formed: e. g. the second line is 24 cm. above the third, the fourth is 5 cm. above the fifth.

About 12 cm. below the tenth line and perhaps the same distance above the eleventh, is a group of letters of much larger size: these vary from 11 to 19 cm. in height. Two of these letters are evidently I X, which probably stand for '1(170-01)5) X(pio-Tds). In a line with the X, but some little distance to the right, are two letters, 5 or 6 cm. high, which seem to be C. Between them and the X there is room for four, perhaps five, letters of this smaller size. Possibly then we may read xpeior(d)s. At the left of the I, but apparently turned sidewise, are letters which seem to be I or 9 or 9 I or 9 Y. Below the I is a large M upright, or possibly a sigma of the old form (I) turned on its side. Possibly then the painter meant to write IX9YZ. Copy of Dr. Littmann.

The letters,BYMr have numerical values whose sum is 2443. This is also the sum of the numerical values of the letters of the refrain, 'iijo-oG? 6 Xpeiords. The other lines, exclusive of the refrain, begin with the letters A, r, A, E, and z respectively, as M. Petrides has pointed out.1 The refrain therefore, which appears first as the second !S. P&ridfcs in *Echos d'Orient,* May, 1904, p. 185.

line, when written in the cryptogrammic form supplies the missing initial B, and the alphabetic sequence of the first letters of the lines is complete from A through Z. Possibly the letters BYWr have also a second significance, as, for example, *orjdi),*

T(ie) *M(ovo)y(eves)* or B(t), T(ic) (eVc) *M(apLa;) ye.vvT)6d;); Help, Only-begottetl Son, OX Help, Son of God) born of Mary* Compare Wad. 2145, where, at the end of parte, I believe we should

read XMr?9, i.e. X(/3«rros) (6 *Ik)* Ma/ nas y(evin)0zCs). ?#' =99= 1+40 + 8 + 50 = '*Afirfv.*

In the first line, *inrcpivev* is doubtless for *vTT(fi.uvv',* in the fifth, Tracrc is evidently for *Trdcry.* In the seventh line the reading is uncertain. I had thought of "EXc(o)s (Sic) o/e *v ig ovpavwv* eVl *yfj;,* comparing Psalm lxxxiv, I I f.: Eeos /ecu *aXrjOua. crvvyjprr)(rav* /ecu *SiKcuoo-vvr)* eVc Tov ovpavov 8ie/ «A//e. With line 9 compare Luke i, 70 (Acts iii, 21): Ka0tk *iXdkrjcrev* Sid cr-roViaTos *To»v ayiatv air aXsivos ir-poiTiv avrov.* Also Psalm XV, I I (Acts ii, 28)'. 'Eyvw/aio-a?/xot 68ous u%. And Matthew xxii, 16 (Mark xii, 14): Ai8d-cr/cae, oiSa/xei/ on *dr)0r);)* et /ecu *Ttv ohov Tov &eov iv dkrjdeia* 8t8acr»ceis.

On the content and significance of this inscription as a whole, see Chapter 1, p. 12.

255. Shnan. Same Tomb. Painted on the rock at the back of the same arcosolium as the foregoing inscription (No. 254). The span of the arch is 1.94 m., and the top of the soffit 1.00 m. above the j0 CH sarcophagi. In the center of the wall space at the back is a M I uu N large disk. The inscription is painted in black on each side of TOY N I this disk. The letters are 4 to 6 cm. high. Below the letters T 0 K A on the left side is a small disk in red containing a + and the *To arfiribjV togto vlK*letters A and CO. Copy of Dr. Littmann. *This sign conquers!*

See Chapter 1, p. 21.

256. Dana, Fragments, 428 (?) A.d. On six fragments of a block, found lying in a field about a hundred yards west of the tomb of Hyphinos and Olympiane (Inscr. 257). The outlines of the various fragments are irregular. The stone seems to have had a plain face, without mouldings. It was probably a lintel. Fragment A is 42 cm. long and 22 high. Fragment B is 38 to 42 cm. long and 24 cm. high: the letters are 6 cm. high. Fragment c is 26 cm. long at the top, 32 at the bottom, 25 high and 28 thick. Fragment D is 34 cm. long and 24 high: the letters are 4 to 5 cm. high: it fits on the right side of c. Fragment E is 32 cm. long and 22 high: it fits on the right side

of D. 1 See above, Chapter 1, p. 23. I thought, at one time, that as certain. In deference to Professor Kroll, and mindful of the B should be emended to 9, and, in my article in the No. 120 in this collection = Wad. 2697, I have written *Transactions of the Am. Philol. Ass. , 1902, p. 95 f.*, read X(purros) (6 t«) M(optas), or X(/j«jtos) M(o/jios), *ytvrtfidi),* in ®*(tov)* v(los) M(apt'as) *y(arftai).* This reading was criticised interpreting the letters XMI-. In the present instance, howby Professor W. Kroll in the *Berliner Philologische Wochen-*ever, I believe that the B is certain, and that the numerical *schrift,* 1904, Sp. 950, on the ground that " Even then it explanation given above is correct, was not Greek," and 0(eov) «(J6s) ft(ovo)y(evs) was proposed

Fragment F is 29 cm. long and 28 cm. thick: it is 47 cm. high. The upper part contains the ending of two lines of inscription and at the right of these lines across, about 10 cm. high. This part of the stone is 15 cm. high. Below is a blank space, 12 cm. high. Below this again are the endings of three more lines of inscription. Evidently then this is the right end of the block, which bore originally five lines of inscription, two above, doubtless with a cross at each end, and three below. I believe that Fragment A. contains a part of the two upper lines, Fragments B, C, D, and E parts of the three lower lines. Copies of the editor.

The first fragment suggests the words 7reWa0Xos and EuyeVows, the upper part of the last perhaps *eto-eXOel* and roVse. I have not been able to make anything of Frag. 13. The other fragments are as follows: *Kixre/3tov iracrav a-noyhrfv ...*

(a)irb Tov dvaXdj/xaTos rrjs *Kaifirjs ....* AErOY */jL(r)vb);* (A)iov-'(?), Tov *ixxp' erou(?). of Eusebios the) whole enter-prise*
at (the) expense of (the) village
in (the) month Dios (?), of (the) yotli year.
(November, 428 A.D.)
The M of the date, i.e. 40, is doubtful: the Y i.e. 700, is, I think, certain.

257. Dana. Tomh. On the architrave of a canopy, supported on four columns, over the entrance to a rock-hewn tomb. This entrance is now filled up; but there seems to have been a straight shaft, sunk perpendicularly into the living rock. The inscription begins at the southwest corner, and extends across the south and east sides. Seede Vogue, *S. C,* pi. 78. The inscription on the south side is 2.01 m. long, the fascia on which it is carved is *Sy2* cm. wide, and the letters 6 cm. high: the inscription on the east side is 1.90 long, begins 9 cm. from the southeast corner, and ends 23 cm. from the northeast corner. Copy of the editor.

Published by Waddington, No. 2673.

rtINOCrOYPOYKTHCNMNHMOCYNONA-MA

CYNBIOYAYTOYOAYMTTIANHC

Waddington read at the beginning of the inscription KOINOC, and in the middle of this side CTHCN. The first two or three letters are above the capital of the col 1 Compare the end of No. 116.

umn at the southwest corner, and are consequently very difficult to read from the ground. But I examined them first standing on my horse and later from a ladder. I believe that the t is certain: also that there is but one letter before it and this almost certainly Y. *T(fivo; Tovpov eKTT)oev pvrp6ovvon apa ovvfilov avrov 0vpinavrj;. Hyphinos (?), (son) of Guras, built this monument with his wife Olympian?.*

On *apa* with the genitive see No. 101. The father's name was doubtless rW-pas: *XyyGiird* see No. 189.

258. Dana. "Sur un linteau de porte, entre deux crois." Waddington 2674.

X M r X(pio-Tos) M(a/sias) y(evjT?0ei's). *Ch(rist) b(orn) of M(ary).*

See the notes on No. 155, and also p. 23.

259. Dana, Fragment. On a fragment of a lintel, found lying in a field in the northeastern part of the town. The inscription is 82 cm. in length and the letters 5 cm. in height. Copied by Mr. Huxley and the editor.

Published by Waddington, No. 2675.

These words are quoted from Psalm cxxi, 7: see the variant readings of the original text given in Swete's edition of the Septuagint. See also above, Chapter 1, p. 17.

260. Dana, House (?). On the lintel of a doorway, about a hundred yards northeast of No. 261. The inscription was carved upon a plate 1.60 m. long and *22l/2* cm. high, with dove-tail ends. In the center is a disk, 23 cm. in diameter. In the first line, on the left side of the disk, is first a space of 30 cm., then two letters, which seemed to me to be Nl, 5 cm. in length, then a space of 7j/2 cm. , then the letters AYN 12 cm. in length, and lastly a space of 4 cm. to the rim of the disk. The letters of this line on the right of the disk measure 67 cm. in length, and end 8 cm. from the end of the plate. In the second line, the letters at the left of the disk measure 57 cm. in length, at the right of the disk 29 cm.: at the end of this line is a space of 35 cm. which seemed to be blank.

The letters are 4 cm. high. They were not deeply cut, but sharply, and in straight lines. I thought that they showed traces NI--AYN AME9HMUU-NANTH c,.. ,....., AIMTUJH-IUUNOe EO-CEIAKOJB f red but COuld n0t be Certam f this. Copy of the editor.

Published by Waddington, No. 2676, from a copy of M. de Vogue.

M. deVogiie has given a different reading. See Waddington's publication.

Kvoio(s T)o)i' *8vvdpe(ov pe)@' rjp-wv, avnjk(-qTr)TOi(p) j)Pv 6* ®os ElaK-cifi.

The Lord of Hosts is with us, the God of Jacob is our defender.

Compare No. 199, and see also Chapter 1, p. 16.

It is not impossible that *dvrr)klprap* was actually carved: if so the spelling of this word and also of EzaKw/3 are worthy of notice. I believe that the stonecutter, in carving the inscription, skipped over from the ME of *Swdpewv* to the ME of *ped* and thus omitted, unintentionally, four letters of his copy.

261. Dana, House (?). Lintel of a doorway with an arched vestibule before it, in the eastern part of the town and facing westward. The inscribed fascia of the mouldings measures 154 by 19 cm. The first line of the inscription is 1.18,

the second 1.16 m. long; the letters are 5 to 9 cm. high. The letters were incised and painted red. An upper band of the mouldings also bore traces of paint, as if a painted inscription or some ornamental design had been there. Copies by Mr. Garrett and the editor.

Published by Waddington, No. 2677.

M--APIOCANePWTTOCOG
TTI--PIONKOYMHATTW

Mcucapios *dvdparrros 6 i_kiri£(ov iirl Ku-Blessed (is the) mail that hopeth in (the) Lord, and piov, Kc ov pr)* a7r-tuXetTat. *'he shall not perish!*

The last letter of the first line was read by M. de Vogue C; but both Mr. Garrett and I, independently, read 6. If M. de Vogue's copy is correct, however, Waddington's reading must be approved: os eXm'£«. Waddington compares Psalm xxxiii, 9: *Tevo-aa$ /ecu tSere on octto? 6 Kvpios-paicdpios dvr-jp os iXnifci in" avrov.* Compare also verse 23: *Kcu oi pr) TrXrjppeXrjo-ovo-Lv irdvTts oi c7ri£oiTs eV avrov.* The first part of verse 9 occurs in the liturgies apparently as the beginning of a hymn, of which only the first words are given in the manuscripts (e.g. Swainson, p. 316 f., etc.). With the reading of the inscription which I have adopted, compare Psalm lxxxiii, 13: See also Chapter 1, p. 16.

262. Dana. On a lintel lying on the ground just north of the foregoing inscrip AArliAKAlC—-AITT tion' This inscriPtion is on the uppermost A x /,/x x r v vn rx-moulding of a doorcap. The first fifteen .... ,...... .... letters measure 67 by 5 V2 cm. After them wv/rt/ *thou say est, friend, to thee also (be) the double!* 'J u/ is a space, 28 cm. long, from which the letters have been obliterated. The last three letters are 20 cm. in length. Copy of the editor.

Compare Nos. 10, 89, etc.

263. RuwfeHA. Tomb, 384-5 A.D. In the pediment of a temple-tomb, in the southeastern corner of the town, facing northward. See Part II, p. 113 f. Within the main doorway of the temple is a chamber, 13 by 14 feet square. Doubtless it contained three sarcophagi, like the tomb at Hass, Inscr. 157 ff. But these sarcophagi have now disappeared,

and a large part of the floor has fallen in. The temple is built upon a podium which contains a chamber, of the same size as the cella of the temple, and entered from the south, where the ground level is lower. This lower chamber contained three arcosolia, the arches of which are built, but the sarcophagi hewn in the living rock. The fronts of these sarcophagi have been broken away, in order to enlarge the chamber by including these vaulted alcoves. For the whole building, in both stories, has been used for a dwelling and a stable, the inner surface of the walls being plastered with mud and whitewashed.

The space occupied by the inscription, in the north gable, is 99 cm. long and 31 cm. high. The letters vary from 4 to 7 cm. in height: they are all very well cut and regular, except that in several cases an , and in one case a 9, seems to have been left without the cross stroke, so that it is like a C or an O. The inscription, however, does not show clearly to one on the ground below, because the shallow lines of the letters, now covered with lichen, blend with the unusually white stone. Moreover the inscription is in so unusual a place that it is easily overlooked now. Waddington failed to find it from Pococke's description: it was found for me by accident and one of the camp servants. I think that originally the letters must have been painted: if so they would have been conspicuous enough. With a ladder I found the letters still perfectly clear, although in some cases is not distinguished from C: the reading given here I believe to be certain. Copy of the editor.

Published by Pococke, *Inscr. Antiq.,* I, p. 64: also by Franz, *C. I. G.* 4462.

ICOOCMONOCOBOH0_ Efc eeos pfeoc 6 /3o-qd(wv). YTT6PCUJTHPIACKAIMNHM (TWNZONTWNANNeW „ n *Ti)v Lovtwv. Aveveaxrev aacrCCNBACCIMACK-AIMAGBA %* „ BCACTOYCrAY *ri/tas ai Ma0/ia/ja Ctov9 yKv. (There is) one God only, that giveth aid. For the safety and remembrance of the living. Bassimas andMathbabea renewed (this tomb) in the year 4.Jj.* (384-385 A.D.)

The name Bao-o-t/ua? is perhaps for Ba/o-i/xas = Syriac *Bar Sima: Son of Si-*

ma. Compare Ba/30Tj/i.os in No. 310. Professor Noldeke suggests that it is more probably from the Syriac *bassima = lovely. MaBfiafiea* is undoubtedly the same name as *'Apadfiafiea,* discussed in the notes on No. 241. It is noteworthy that pagan names figure here in an inscription which is evidently Christian. If *Bassimas* really meant, originally, *Son of the god) Sima,* and *Mathbabea* means *Servant of the god* or *goddess) Babai,* these names must have lost their significance for these persons, and paganism must not only have died out, but must have been practically forgotten in this region in 384 A.d.1

There are many inscriptions similar to this, although the common phrase is *virkp fj.vrj; Kol avanava-em*-Compare Waddington, Nos. 1920 and 1997, or *C. I. G.* 8624 (= LeBas 980 =*B. C. H.* vii, p. 502 f.), 8857, 8860 and 8867. The last mentioned was found at Bethlehem, and is as follows: *'Tirep pvijpr); Kal dvaira-vo-ecos Kal dofeo-ecds dpapnwv Sv 6 K(u/5io)? yr)v6o-KL To. ovopaTa: For the) memory and repose and remission of sins of those whose names the Lord knoweth.* Dr. H. Gelzer, in *Mittheilungen d. d. Palaestinavereius,* 1895, p. 17 ft, compares the phrase *inep rwr-qpai = "urn des Seelenheils willen"* in the "Kollektengebet": so for example in the "Liturgy of St. Mark,"2 and the "Liturgy of St. James' *'Tircp r»J? dvwdev elpijvr); Kal @eou ikavO paytr-la; Kal cra/TTj/ai'as Twv pv)(av fjixcov, Tov Kvpiov hvqdojp.ev.* Compare also the following, from the same liturgy:4 YETM

Se *Kal virep TtiTnqpLali Kal d/ecrecus dp-apTiSiv Tw ir-pocreveyKavTi dSeXpai -qpcov. Kal vtrep pvTjpiqs To)v oa-'unv TTarepoiv-fficov Kal dSeXowi/, LTT(op.ev Ttolvtzs eKTevcos,* Ktx. In the present inscription I believe that the words *Tup £,6vtov* refer to those living in the world beyond the grave, as in the prayer for the dead in the same liturgy:5 'E/cel avrous *dvdi-ravo-ou iv xPa Cvroav, iv /3acriXei'a ovpavwv, ci? Koxttovs 'Afipadp., Kt.-. There give them repose in the land of the living, in the kingdom of heaven, bringing them) unto the bosom of Abra-*

ham. If so, and if the punctuation which has been adopted in the text is correct, then this inscription illustrates the belief of these Christians in the efficacy of prayer for the estate of the dead, a belief which was fully developed in the Church at least as early as the fourth century.6 For compare the following passage from the lecture of Cyril of Jerusalem to the newly baptized:7 *Etra Kal virep Twv irpoKKoi.prjp4vo)v dyltov traripoiv /ecu iiTLO-KOTTcov, Kal irdmoiv a7rft)5 TOiv iv-qplv irpoKeKocprjpevwv, peyicrTTjv ovqTLV iTLorevovres ecrecrcu Tcu?*

I/wx"s. vntp &v V Sojo-is dvafepeTai; Then also for those who have fallen asleep, holy fathers and bishops, and for all in a word who among us have, fallen asleep before, trusting that greatest benefit will be to the souls for whom this petition is made, etc. Compare also No. 265. At the same time too much stress, perhaps, should not be laid on this phrase in the inscription, *vwip o-omipCas Kox pvtjpr);,* which might easily have been suggested by the stereotyped formula *vwep o-amjpLas Kal vU-qs; pro salute et victoria Au* 1 I am indebted to Dr. Littmann for these observations. 5 " Liturgy of St. James," Swainson, p. 300.

-Swainson, p. 44. 6 See Gelzer, /. c. 3 Swainson, p. 224. 7 Swainson, p. 210. "Liturgy of St. James,"Swainson,p. 312. *gusti),* which occurs frequently in the inscriptions of Syria, for example in Wad. 2035, 2071=392 below, 2545, etc. See also above, p. 14 f.

With regard to the date of this inscription, it seems to me obvious that it cannot be reckoned according to the Seleucid era, for if it were the year would be 122-123 A-D-I believe therefore that the inscriptions of Ruweha, like those of Ktellata and Riha, must have been reckoned according to the era of Antioch, which was in general use in the region immediately north of the Djebel Riha: the three towns mentioned are all situated on the northeastern slope of this mountain. See No. 264, No. 273 and the commentary to Wad. 2667, and Nos. 278 and 282: also Nos. 214 and 215.
264. Ruw£ha. "villa," 396 A.d. In the

entrance to the villa, in which Inscr. 267 was found. See Part II, p. 122. The inscription is on the lintel of the rectangular doorway in the middle of the arched passage through the tower, which forms the center of the west side of the villa and leads into the courtyard. It is on the outer, i.e. the western, face of the lintel, and measures 2.23 m. in length. The letters are 5 to 6 cm. high, are irregular in form, and very badly weathered: the Y of the date, however, and the following MHN are certain. Copy of the editor. eTOVCAMYMHNOSylTANEMOYrAyiS POI--KBKAP
"Erous 8/u,u', /xrji'o? *Uave/xov y, wtyi;%) In the) year 444., on the) third of the) month . Panemos,* (July, 396 A. D.)

The date is not altogether certain: on the era see the notes on No. 263. Twice in the present inscription the sign S is used, apparently for a final sigma.
265. Ruweha. Tomb. On a square, built tomb with a spherical dome, immediately south of the southeast corner of the North Church, facing westward. Part II, p. 247 f. Within the tomb are three arcosolia, each containing a sarcophagus. The whole tomb is exceedingly well built, and almost perfectly preserved. The lower edge of the lintel, however, has been broken away: at the left end a very small portion of the lowest fascia of the mouldings still remains, and shows a trace of what may have been an inscription. If there was an inscription here it is most unfortunate that it has been lost, for it probably contained the date of this most interesting tomb, and would have furnished also an approximate date for the handsome "North Church," on which No. 266 is carved. The tomb is assigned by Mr. Butler to the sixth century.
The present inscription is cut on the outer face of the western wall, at the left of the doorway and on a level with the lintel. The letters are fairly well made, but neither the lines of the inscription nor the strokes which form the letters are straight. Copy of the editor.
Published by Waddington, No. 2670. *C. I. G.* 9151 a.
BIZZOCTTAPAOY   Bi££os   *Hdp&ov*

eVtjSiiTjo-a KaXws, T?X0a /caXws, 6TTHAHMHCAKAAUJC *Kal Kc /caX«£?.* Eufipxu VTrep roC.
HA9AKAAluCKAIKIM
KAALUC6Y2HTAIYTTEP *Bizsos, son) of Pardos: I sojourned well, I journeyed* H MOY *well, and well I lie at rest. Pray for me* (?)!

The inscription is strangely worded and strangely spelled. 'ETrrjSro-a is evidently for eVcS/Aa-a, *ripe for /cel/xai,* 17/xoO for *Ipov.* But it is hard to determine what is meant by eufTcu. Certainly one would expect, with Kirchhoff, *evxo-Oe* or possibly *evgar0e.* Possibly *evgrjTcu* may be the 3rd sing. aor. subj. mid., used instead of an optative, after the analogy of the aor. subj. with *prj:* in that case *iinBrjprfa-a* KaXws *id/ie* caXus must be regarded as words of Bizzos quoted here by the author of the inscription, who then added for himself: "May he pray for me." My friend Dr. S. Angus suggested to me that possibly this may be an aorist middle, used as a passive form, = *May prayer be offered for me.* But I believe that the clue is furnished by an inscription found in the Sakhra at Jerusalem, and published with a commentary by M. Clermont-Ganneau in the *Academy* for Nov. 7th, 1874, and also in *P. E. F.,* 1875, p. 56 f.: *"Evda KardWe evtjeTe vir)ep) avrov diro Ttj? ocias pv7)p.T);,* prj. *AeKep.fi.,* + *lv8. a, erovs ph'. Here lies :ye shall?) pray for him,* etc. Consequently I believe that the evroi of the present inscription was intended for Cvtc or *evtjere,* and that the chief irregularity is the use of the active voice of a deponent verb. A similar request is contained in an inscription of Phrygia, *C. I. G.* 3962, discussed by Professor Ramsay in *R. E. G.,* 11, p. 32. At the end of this inscription Professor Ramsay reads Kal cvxas 0eo"0' *vnP o-vrov' and prayers offer ye for him* Professor Ramsay believes this inscription to be earlier than Constantine.

Concerning prayers for the dead see the notes on No. 263.
266. RuwfiHA. North Church. On the lintel of the west portal of the North Church. Part II, p. 225 ff. De Vogue,.S". *C.,* pis. 68, 69 and 91. The inscription is on the topmost band of the mould-

ings, immediately below a door-cap or-namented with a row of upright leaves. The letters are well formed and well cut: they are about 8 cm. in height, and the whole inscription, which was too high to be measured accurately, is about 1.35 m. long. There is a space of about one letter between the two words. Copy of the editor.

Published by Waddington, No. 2671. *C. I. G.* 9151 b. Uspensky, *A. M. S.,* p. 70. BIZZOC TTAPAOY Bi'££os *Udp8ov. Biz-zos son) of Pardos.*
Waddington says that after these words there are "trois lignes martel6es." Both Dr. Littmann and I searched for these lines with the utmost care and a ladder, but 1 The era and the date are uncertain: perhaps the era is that of Diocletian and the martyrs, the date 388 A.d.-1 am not sure, however, whether the pronoun refers to the dead father or the living son mentioned in the inscription: the text is quoted in full above, p. 206.
found no certain trace of them: I do not believe that they ever existed. But on one of the lower bands of the lintel there are dowel-holes, as if a narrow metal plate, perhaps 3 feet long, had been af-fixed here.

On the names *Bizsos* and *Pardos* see the notes on Nos. 73 and 88. A Bizos, bishop of Seleucia, is mentioned by Photius, *Cod.* 52, as present at a church council held at Side in 383 A.d.; but this is evidently not the person to whom the Ruweha inscriptions refer.

267. Ruweha. "villa." On a lintel in a large villa, similar to that described in Part II, p. 122 f., in the east center of the town. One entered by an arched passage through the tower, which forms the cen-ter of the row of apartments on the west side of the large courtyard. The north side of this courtyard is formed by a row of handsome dwellings, provided with a two-story colonnade. The inscribed lin-tel is over a doorway about the center of these dwellings.

The lintel is ornamented with a door-cap, the upper part of which consists of a row of heavy dentils, a narrow band, and, above that, a heavy cyma recta. In the center is a large disk, in the form of a wreath, which stands out from the overhanging curve of the cyma, and at the bottom breaks through and below the line of the dentils. Below the dentils is a plate in relief, 1.26 m. long and 20 cm. wide, having at each side a disk,, connected with it by an arm, 4 or 5 cm. wide and 3 or 4 cm. long, which pro-jects from the center of each end of the plate, in a line with the center of the disk. The bottom of the plate is 5 cm. from the bottom of the lintel.

Four lines of the inscription are upon this plate, painted in red but not carved. 'The central disk broke into the first line. The other lines were originally un-broken; but the rain, trickling around the disk, has washed away about four letters from the middle of the second, third and fourth lines, leaving this space stained and covered with moss. Below the plate there are traces of a fifth line; but these are now so faint that I was un-able to read a single letter with certain-ty. The letters are 4 to 4 cm. high. Copy of the editor.

Published by Waddington, No. 2672. Uspensky, *A. M. S.,* p. 71.
+ OKA-OIKUJNEN BOH9IATOYYYIC TOYNCKTTHTO YTOYOYPANOY + 0HC-TAI UUKYpeiWANTI TWPMOYE ATAtYrHMOY
Above the inscribed plate there are let-ters painted between and on the dentils. These are now scarcely legible. Perhaps they may once have given the date at which this part of the villa was built; but, if so, I was unable to read it. The letters on the right of the central disk seemed more like the common formula Efs Beos, with a cross at either end.

On the lintel of another doorway in the same row of dwellings, at the left of the doorway just described, traces of letters in red paint are still to be seen at the right of the mouldings. They seemed to have the form shown in the accompa-nying figure. Possibly this may be *efiv erq: 445 years,* or, *err)* being perhaps for erei, *in the year 445,* i.e. 396 A.d. See No. 264.
268. Ruweha. Villa. On a lintel in the entrance to a villa like that of the fore-going inscription, in the central part of the town. The entrance is a broad arch-way through the basement of a tower, and was closed by a door set in a rec-tangular door-frame in the center of the tower: the lintel of this doorway bears the inscription. On either side of the archway are rooms in which a modern family was living in 1900: the rest of the villa has been destroyed. The whole in-scription is 1.66 m. long, and the letters 34 cm. high. The letters were original-ly fairly well formed, but are now bad-ly weathered. The first word is in the form of a ligature, XC: the sign S ap-pears once for a final sigma, as in No. 264. Copy of the editor.

Published in part by M. Uspensky, *A. M. S.,* p. 71.
XPCErENHT NAPMAPECEMACEdJUCE-NATTDTTANTDSKAKDYAMEN t
Xp(«rro)s *iyevr)To* NAPMAPEC-C/ass *icraxrev dtrb iravTos Kclkov. 'Afiev.* + *Christ was born He saved us from all evil. Amen.* +

Perhaps we may read, after *iyevrjro,* ex *Uapdevov.* Compare the first of the Syriac inscriptions discussed in Chapter 1, p. 15.
269. Ruw£ha. Villa (?). Painted on the lintel of a doorway within a large arched vestibule in the southwestern part of the town, a short distance west of the South Church. This was probably the entrance to a villa: it faces towards the south.

The first line of the inscription was painted on the topmost band of the mouldings. The band measures about 2. 23 m. in length, and 8 cm. in height: the letters are 4 to 5 cm. high. These let-ters are almost obliterated; but I thought I could read the following:--O-AC o _TTAN. This may be the date: vEros 8ov?, HH IW *jiov :In the) year 474, in (the) month Panemos* (July, 426 A.d.); but this is altogether uncertain.

Below this band is another broader band containing a plate, sunk in its sur-face about 2 cm. deep, and containing in the center + with A and w. This plate seems to have contained an ornamental design of some sort, or letters. Below this again is a band of carved ornament, and, below this, simple right-lined mouldings. In the highest of these is an-other painted inscription of which I read the following letters:TTT AIT OATA6 T UJC. These measure together 50 cm. in length: the rest of the band is 1.61 m. long. The letters are 3 to 4 cm. high. In the lowest band are the letters NA: these also are painted, and measure 9 cm. in length and 3l/2 cm. in height.

I have been unable to read any part of this inscription except perhaps the date, for most of the paint has been washed off, leaving no visible trace whatever. 270. Ruweha. Villa(?). On the lintel of a doorway within an arched vestibule, in the extreme southwestern corner of the town. It seemed like the entrance to a villa, and if so it opened upon the courtyard at the southeast corner. Through the outside corners of the vestibule were holes to which animals might be tied.

The lintel is ornamented with a door-cap, the upper part of which is formed by a cymatium. The lower part is a plate in relief, 1.54 m. long and 32 cm. broad, with small dove-tail ends. In the center of the plate is a disk, within a square. The disk contains the +, and in the upper quadrants A and w. In the lower quadrants, and in the four corners of the square, are figures which I did not understand. Traces of red still remain on various parts of the lintel, as if the Π6ΤΡΟC ΤΤΑΥΑΟC...,, „ j whole had been originally painted.
Π ΤΤ O J I IIcT/)05, IlavAos.
The inscription consists of two names, 22 and 23 cm.

Peter (and) Paul. long respectively, one on either side of the disk. The letters are incised, but not very deeply nor well: they are 3 to 4 cm. high. Copy of the editor. 271. RuwfiHA. House. On the lintel of what appeared to be a private house, described by Professor Sachau, situated in the west center of the town and facing northward. The lintel is 2.11 m. long, 65 cm. high and 58 cm. thick. The inscription is on two dove-tail plates in relief below a heavily moulded door-cap. Between the two plates is a disk in relief, containing a cross, and, in the upper quadrants, the letters A and U), in the lower, figures which perhaps are merely ornamental and intended only to fill up the vacant space. In the left upper quadrant there is also a curved band attached to the upright arm of the cross, which, if it were on the right side would

complete the monogram +. Per .. .r r ,.,.. teiceeoc tKAioxpicToc haps the real significance of this curved line ,,,,. . 1 11 'Ets ®09 ' *Kal* 0 XpiOTOS had been lost, and possibly it was placed on + (*There is) one God + and the Chrtst.* the left here because there was more room beside the A than beside the w. Similar curved lines may be seen in both left quadrants of disk No. 8 on p. 33 of Part II. The plates are 65 cm. long with the dove-tails, 39 cm. long without, and 24 cm. high. The letters are 8 to 10 cm. high except the last four, which are in the right dove-tail of the second plate, and measure 44 to 6 cm. in height. Published by Sachau: *Rcise in Syrien und Mesopotamien,* 1883, p. 97.

Below the dove-tail plates there is a second inscription, to which Professor Sachau does not refer. It is however so badly weathered that I was unable to decipher it.
6KYI WKYPI6 I.OT7P Y Y--
The only letter of which I feel certain is the P. This is 6 cm. high. All the traces of letters given here measure in length 1.41 m., and about fill the space from the beginning of the body of the first plate to the end of the body of the other. The second word seems to be Ku/ue. 272. Ruweha. Tomb. On the lintel of a rock-hewn tomb, about five minutes south of the town, on the way to Djeradeh. The tomb consists of a dromos, whose sides are crowned by a sort of cornice with simple mouldings. Before the entrance to the tomb is a sort of portico, whose pediment is supported by two free and two engaged columns with capitals, all hewn in the living rock. The doorway of the tomb measures 87 by 63 cm. It is ornamented with mouldings consisting of four plain bands. Above the mouldings over the doorway is a space, 14 cm. high, which perhaps contained painting of some sort, above which is a plain, high door-cap. Within the doorway is a chamber about 8 feet square and 7 feet high, having three arcosolia in its sides, each of which contains two sarcophagi.

The inscription is on the top band of the lintel. The letters begin 7 cm. from the left end of the band: together they

are 21 cm. long: the rest of the band, to ' the right of the letters, is one meter long. The letters are 7 cm. high.

It seemed to me that this was the beginning of an unfinished inscription, and was a part of some proper name. But Dr. Littmann has suggested to me that this is possibly M(a/3ta) 'l(rjrov) MVp): *Mary, mother of Jesus.* 273. Ktellata. Cap Of A Well (?), 449 A.d. "A la fontaine, en une seule ligne." Waddington No. 2667: copy of M. de Vogue. t'Eiri *vrbvivov lklttttov* K(cu) 'i/jov/ hov1 *Herpov* IKENTATTPWTWNA *erous C$v, Iv8(lktlwvo;)* TP'»?T(17S) Perhaps we may read, after *Uerpov,* eyeWo 17 fpcan'a, or something similar: *Under Antoninos Philippos and Ibnrios Petros this well was made ?) in the year 4gy, indiction third.* (September, 449 A.d.)

This inscription is evidently dated according to the era of Antioch: see No. 264 and its commentary. Furthermore it is clear from this inscription, as Waddington has shown, that in this region the year began with the month of October. For the 497th year of the era of Antioch began in the Autumn of 448 A.d. and ended in the Autumn of 449. But the 3rd year of the indiction series began in September, 449 A.d. Consequently, if the 3rd indiction coincided on any day with the 497th year, the former must have begun before the latter ended: this could only be if the month of September was the first month of the 3rd indiction but the last month of the 497th year. This year therefore must have begun in October, 448, and ended in September, 449 A.d. See the notes on Waddington, No. 2667; and also on No. 90 above.

Waddington, in his commentary on this inscription, suggests that the ancient name of Ktellatamay be contained in an inscription found at Rome, *C. I. G.* 9730: *d-n-b Kcj Aar .... opoiv 'Airafiewi/.* As Mordtmann has shown, however, in *Z. M. G.,* Xli, p. 305, this is probably not the case. 274. Tomb, about five minutes northeast of Ktellata. The tomb is hewn in the rock and faces northeast. It has a large and handsome arched vestibule with two plain columns and two pilasters supporting the arch. Above the arch are two small crosses and one large cross in relief. The doorway within the vestibule is ornamented with simple, right-line mouldings, on the bands of which three lines of the inscription are painted in fine, straight strokes of black. But the paint has weathered off so completely that neither M. de Vogue nor I was able to decipher the writing. The band occupied by the first line is 1.28 m. long; but I think it is likely that the inscription began some 12 cm. or more from the left end of the band, and perhaps ended before the end of the band was reached. The next two lines of the inscription are naturally somewhat shorter than the first, because they are on the lower mouldings of the doorway. The letters of the second line are from 2l/2 to 3 cm. high and occupy about that same space in length. The third line is on the broadest moulding: below it, on the plain face of the lintel, are a few letters of much larger size: the whole space on which they are painted is 1.04 m. long; but the letters given below extend only 45 cm. from the left end of the space. The letters are about 7 cm. high. Above the inscription are three disks, the central one of which originally contained a cross, +, which has been battered off. Copy of the editor.

Published by Waddington, No. 2668, from a copy made by M. de Vogue.

1. AINTDNACYADNAYM 7 ENAXAXAN APoNoYKYPION 7 YAH INEAPIP 2. 7— KAIY-r-KYPIAA7C--HAPCY-EN-CATIAI- CI 3. rEIAADYM-P — KAJTANATr 4--A H M! O Y

Waddington read only the words *Top dovXov,* in the first line. I think the names *WegavSpos* and *KvpCkas* may be recognized in the first and second lines.

275. A Rock-hewn Tomb, about five minutes north of Ktellata. The inscription is carved above the doorway of the tomb, within a vestibule. Both vestibule and doorway are perfectly plain. The inscription is roughly cut: it is 29 cm. long, and begins *$l/2* cm. from the left corner of the doorway, the total width of which is 62 cm. The letters are *x/2* cm. high. Copy of the editor. _ A v TT E

X AXv7re x."Pe Sorrow-free, farewell! 276. A Fragment Of A Lintel, on the road from Kefr Inneh to il-Mgharah. The length of the fragment is 89 cm. , the height of the mouldings together 48 cm. The inscribed band is cm. high, and the present inscription 61 cm. long, the letters 5 cm. high. Copy of Dr. Littmann. INYAABBOAYMTTIOY 'Em *To)v £va/3(rrdTa)v) 'OXvp.iTLov #ccu rov Under the most devout Olympios and ,*

Scij/os, *irpeo-ftvTepoiv. presbyters.*

I have assumed that there was a second name after *'OXvpurCov* because the remains of the letters before the title cwXa/8. indicated a plural rather than a singular form: this title, *evkaf3erTa.Tos,* was commonly given to church officers not of the highest rank, and on this account I have supplied *Trpeo-ftwepav.* Seethe notes on No. 85. Presbyters are mentioned elsewhere in pairs, as in No. 29.

277. Tomb in the rock, twenty-five minutes south-southeast of Riha, and facing northward. A passage of five deep steps leads down through the rock to a small doorway, once closed by a stone like a cart-wheel, which could be rolled aside into a slot cut for it at the right of the passage. Passing through the doorway one descends by three more steps into a chamber about 10 feet square and 5 feet high. In the front wall near each corner, and in each side wall near the back of the chamber, there is a rectangular alcove containing a sarcophagus: there is no such alcove in the rear wall. The inscription is roughly scratched on the inner face of the front wall, immediately to the right as one enters: the space which it occupies is 45 cm. wide and 63 cm. high. Copy of the editor.

I have tried to read here *ba-awd* and c/Soa-as, or, after ANNA, '-qrov); AAT O M x(piords). But I am inclined to believe that what the author meant to 0 C write was as follows: ANNAiC, A,

Aarouos *vvcu* (or Awatos) *ravra eiroir)ra.*

TlDCAC r.' *Stone-cutter Hannai* jri; *did this.* BOH CAC

The character C at the end of each of the last three lines may be, like /, mere-

ly a sign to mark the end of a word. *Twra* may have been written for *ravra* or *Tovro.* See Clermont-Ganneau, *Recueil,* in, p. 247, and compare Inscriptions 25 and 26 above.

278-281. Mughr Ramdan. This is the name given by the modern natives to a group of tombs in the hillside about fifteen minutes' walk east of the village of Riha. Before the tombs, cuttings in the rock show that there were once quarries here, and doubtless these quarries were older than the tombs. For often in this country old quarries were used in this way, the perpendicular walls of the quarries affording convenient places for such excavations. There are no buildings, either ancient or modern, near the tombs, and hence the tombs must have belonged to the ancient town whose ruins are almost entirely concealed from view in the modern Riha.

Three of these tombs were inscribed, Nos.278f., 280 and 281. Another tomb, the next towards the east to that which bears inscription 281, is almost buried by the soil which has washed into and about it from the slopes of the hill. This tomb also may have borne an inscription; but I was so uncertain whether there were even traces of letters above the doorway, that it seemed unwise, in the short time at my disposal, to undertake the excavation which a thorough examination would have required. On the wall of the vestibule a bracket for a lamp was executed in the rock. On the next tomb towards the east again there may have been still another inscription, but I think not.

Another tomb, east of that which contains inscription 280, has a large + painted in red on the rough wall of rock at the right of the door, within the vestibule. Perhaps there was some painting over the doorway also.

I believe that these tombs belong to the Christian period, though there is little distinctively Christian about them, except the cross just mentioned and the very small cross in the vine ornament below inscription 280. On the formula Efs ©cos /udTM? see p. 18 f. In general, however, the tombs themselves, with their inscriptions and ornamentation, are such as we might expect to find dating from the end of the fourth century. If so, then inscription 278 must be reckoned according to the era of Antioch, and dated 386 A.d. These tombs are so similar that I believe all must belong to approximately the same date. But if they date from this period, and if the extensive quarries in which they were hewn were, as I believe, no longer in use at the end of the fourth century, the ancient town must have flourished comparatively early.

278. Tomb, 386 A.d. On the front wall of a double tomb, consisting of two large chambers opening on a broad vestibule, hewn in the rock. The vestibule is 8 paces long and about 6 feet deep. At present there are no supports for the roof of this vestibule, so that it appears like a great hood, over the entrance to the tombs: on the under side of this roof, however, there are the remains, either of piers hewn from the rock, or of sculptures such as that on the soffit of the arch of the tomb at Frikya shown in Part II, p. 281. The front of the vestibule was provided with mouldings, or with some other ornamentation, which has crumbled away completely. Within the vestibule are twin doorways in the face of the rock. Their lintels are simple, but the mouldings are well drawn and well carved. The holes for the doorfittings are unusually sharp and well preserved. The doorway on the left seems never to have been inscribed: that on the right however bears inscription 279.

Each doorway admits to a roomy central chamber, each of which contains in its walls three arcosolia. The surface of the walls is rough, but the apartments themselves and the arcosolia are regular in shape and well proportioned. At the beginning of April, when I was there, each of these apartments contained water to a depth of a foot or two. The water in the apartment on the left was coated with a thick scum, light green in color and very beautiful: the water in the apartment on the right was of a sorrel color and seemed alive with many things with gills and tails that crept or swam about in it. While I was at work

on the inscriptions natives came and both drank and drew in pitchers water from both apartments, generally from that on the left, and generally blowing aside the green scum for this purpose. The inscriptions were copied by Dr. Littmann and the editor.

Inscription A begins at the left corner of the vestibule and extends to the middle of A. the space above the left-hand doorway. It is 1.66 m. long l l C e o C M o N O C ancj its letters 17 to 18 cm. high. The letters seem to have been scratched rather than carved; but they are fairly deep and regular. B.

Inscription B is above the lintel of the same doorway, in the right-M N H M H hand half of the space. The first word is 40 cm. long, and its letters BACCOY 6/2 cm.high: the second is4l/2 cm.long, and its letters vary from 12 to6 cm.in height. c Inscription c is on the wall at the right of this doorway. HP5ATOBACCOC The whole inscription occupies a space 1. 12 m. long, and TAlwceN9OCBIC Q,6g high: the letters are 8cm. high. HTYN-HAYTOYMeTA Inscription D is still farther towards the, M UD'U . TWNAYTu,N6T.,. ,. .,..., t N H H N I right, about midway between the two door-Ttan e M o Y AlvuCNCKOYN 1 it-A"noctxnithc wavs-The whole inscription occupies a K6ToYAAY space 0.77 m. long, and 0.56 m. high. The ToYC letters vary from Sy2 to 14 cm. in height.

Eis ©cos ftovo;. yivTjftT) Bacrcrov. "Hparo Bao"cros-CTeXiwcrev ®ocre/ 8is, rj yvvrj aurou, fiera Tojv avratv irekuixrcp Sckovvslvos, revirq. 'Ev firjvl Have/iov K& ', Tov Ov erovs. (There is) one God only. Remembrance of Bassos. Bassos began (the tomb): Theoscbis, his zvife, together with their (children), completed (it): Sekundinos, (the) artisan, completed (i.e. constructed) (it). In (the) month of Panemos (the) 29th, in the 4.34th year. (July, 386 A.u.)

I think, however, that m = remembrance, is probably used here for /iva or /j.ur)fjLelov = a monument or tomb. Note that the feminine form of the name @eoo-e)Sios is here B«xre£is, instead of the more usual ©eoo-eySia or Qeooefieia; but possibly it should be read

©eoo-eySfs for ©wxre/Jifc.

A certain Aurelios Bassos is mentioned in an inscription, found at Concordia (?) and published in C. I. L. v, No. 8725, which contains the ancient name of a town in this neighborhood: Avprjios Batro-o?, Svpos, Io£mt(.otos, KWfLrjs Zaxfrecw (op)ov 'Anapewv. See also Mordtmann in Z. M. G. Xli, p. 304.

On the era of this inscription see the notes on No. 264.

279. On the same tomb as the foregoing. Inscription A is on the mouldings over the doorway on the right. The first line is 96 cm. long, the second 78 cm. The third line is on the lowest fascia of the lintel, except the last letter, which is level with the others, but is carved on the return of the second member of the mouldings: exclusive of the last letter the third line is 60 cm. long. The letters of all the lines are about 5 cm. high. These letters have different forms from those of inscription 278.

A. eeoTeKNoYKAIAPTEBANoY AAEAtUUNTKN AH AM ANoY ATTETEAhCANhPoE I O N

Inscription B is on the wall of rock beside the lintel. The first line is 66 cm. long, the second 94. The letters vary from 5 to 12 cm. in height. The N of TAI(JL)CN was omitted in carving this word, and then inserted above the line between the final 6 and the following C. The letters have the forms of those in inscription 278, but are more carelessly executed.

B. N TAIUUCC KOYNAINOCT6XN T!-i C &ot4kvov Kox 'Aprefidvov, aScXwv TeKva Of Theoteknos and Artebanes(?), brothers: (t/ic) Uapdvov dneTerja-av ripotiov. children of Patnanos finished the) tomb.

'EreXuocrei' ,kovv8ivo;, Ttxyvrq;. Sekundinos, (the) artisan, constructed (it).

The word d8efot, brothers, may perhaps mean brothers in Christ, perhaps monks. See No. 164. Also the discussion of this word in Part IV, p. 37 f. On rjpoelov see No. 151, and also Wad. 2537 e, Dittenberger, O. G. I. S., Nos. 526 and 554.

The names Artebanes and Pamanos are curious: they have a Persian sound.

They do not seem to be Greek and they are not Semitic, as Dr. Littmann tells me. There is an Egyptian-Aramaic name DD, and a Pa-mu-nu in Babylonian. Or is *Pamanos* for Panamos? See Clermont-Ganneau, *Recueil,* 11, pp. 102 and 107.

280. On the face of a double rock-hewn tomb with an arched vestibule, east of that described under No. 278, and facing northward. The tomb is similar to that of Inscription 278. At the right end of this vestibule there appears to have been a stone bench.

The inscription is over the western doorway. At each side of the inscription there seems to be have been originally a palm branch; but, if so, the branch at the left has almost disappeared. The space originally occupied by the letters and branches together was about 1.20 m. in length: the inscription itself is 75 cm. long, and the letters 10 to 12 cm. high. Below the inscription is a border of two vines intertwined: in the central loop of these there is a small cross inscribed in a circle. Above each corner of the doorway is a disk. That on the right contains a six-point star, carved and painted. The disk on the left is similar to No. 1 on p. 33 of Part II. This disk was carved, and was also painted in three alternating colors, one of which was the usual red and another probably yellow. Below this disk there was a large palm branch, painted in red but not carved, on the wall of rock which, though as a whole it does not present an even or regular surface, was evidently smoothed off somewhat to receive this painting. Copied by Dr. Littmann.

EIC9EO.C Efs ®cos. *There is) one God!* See the notes on No. 16, etc.

281. Over the doorway of a rock-hewn tomb within an arched vestibule, a few steps south of the foregoing. The inscription is somewhat rudely scratched on the rock; but the lines which form the letters are broad and deep. The first line of the inscription is 1.50 m. long, the second 0.98.. The letters are 13 cm. high, and were painted red. Copy of the editor. BET1 A' I am inclined to think that the second name is feminine, AD-STINAC *f f* ,. and that *h.ovylva.%* is for

AoyyiVs. See *C. I. G.* 11, 1064. *V3OTKVOV Kdl AoVyiVO.5. 7*

But a masculine name, AovyiVa?, appears in *C. I. G.* 111,5063 *Of Theoteknos and Longina.* and 4716 d24 (in the addenda), and might be thought to be treated here as indeclinable. However, *Aopyivq.* occurs in *C. I. G.* 1964, plainly as a dative feminine. Dr. Littmann suggests that Bcoreos is the Greek form for the Syriac name *Barldhd,* which sometimes appears in Greek as BapWs. See No. 115 above.

282. RiHA. Tomb, 422 (?) A.d. On the face of a broad, fine arch hewn in the rock before a rock-hewn tomb in the hill immediately south of the village, and facing northward. The inscription is carved on the mouldings of the arch. Both lines are broken by a disk in the center, which seems to have contained the-f with A and U) in the lower quadrants, but which is now almost obliterated. The total length of the first line, including spaces between the words and the disk, is 1.83J/2 m. The two parts of the second line measure 1.60 and 1.30 m. respectively. The letters are 5 cm. high. The whole inscription is badly weathered. Copied by Pococke and the editor.

Waddington, 1833. *G. I. G.* 9150.

+ ETDYC DY MHNDC A w □ Y f t
AAEZANAPQCAONETTTDTTDCK-
AIKANKE AAAPIOYEnA PXUNYIDYA-
IAECriDYAI

ArDPTDNIDY Pr?

t "Erous *Ov, firivbs* Awou *y.* f *'Adv8po(v)(1)* + *In (the) year 470, month Loos 3rd.* f *(This is the*

A kif-TT-r-nrrnr-» w ' » / « « *tomb) of Alexatidros and chancellor of* AONEMT-DTTDC *Koli KavKthkapiov tirapwv, Vlov" governors, (and of his) son Lidesgios (?), through Gor AiBeayiov (' !), Sid VopyovLov (i)Pr ohorov.. .. /A.*

'v' ' v / L j *gontos, superintendent (1:). (August, 422 A.D.)*

The reading of this inscription is most uncertain. Perhaps the word before Kcu *KavKeXXapCov* is T07ros, *place ox sepulchre.* I do not know what manner of official a *KCLVKkdpi.o; iirdpxoiv* may have been. As to the era of this inscription see the commentary on No. 164.

283. RiHA. Tomb. On another tomb, west of the foregoing, and facing northward. The doorway has simple rightlined mouldings, in the corners of which traces of a band of red color, 1 cm. wide, are still visible. Within is a chamber with three arcosolia. The arcosolia in the side walls contain each one sarcophagus set parallel with the wall: that opposite the entrance contains two sarcophagi set at right angles to the line of the arch.

The first part of the inscription, A, is over the doorway. The letters of the last two words are both incised and painted red. The second part, B, is at the right side of the doorway, beginning after the O of *Mevdvhpov.* these letters also are painted red. Copy of the editor.

Published in *C. I. G.* No. 4455.

A. o Y B. H O OZ GNO HAAX-
ocw6NANAPOY KMA AXO Y
TXN I
TUU N

OY OZ 0NO MaXxo? *MevdvSpov. Malchos, (son) of Menandros* HO Kc *Mdkov, Ttxyirwv.* and *Malchos, architects (or artisans).*

The first letters are possibly a date, namely *ov* = 470, i.e. 421-422 A.d. CHAPTER IV INSCRIPTIONS OF SELEMIYEH AND KINNESRİN, AND OF THE DJEBEL IL-HASS AND THE DJEBEL SHBET. ALSO INSCRIPTIONS FROM BA'ALBEK, TELL NEBT MINDO, HAMA, MA'ARRIT IN-NU'MAN, KHAN SEBİL, ISRIYEH, PALMYRA, KHAN IL-ABYAD ON THE ROAD FROM PALMYRA TO DAMASCUS, AND DMER.

284. SELEMIYEH. LiNTRL (?), 432 A.D. On a stone, doubtless originally a lintel, now used as the right jamb of the doorway of a modern house, in the northeast corner of the city. The left end is concealed by the sill of the doorway. The face of the stone is divided into parts, of which the first and third are inscribed, the others contain ornamental designs. Copied by Mr. Butler and the editor.

6MNHC A w

N6NTH IX9YC COY 6TOYC6MY t X/wot e *fivyja-#77*TM *W v v "HI* ySatriXctqi *O Christ, remember us in thy kingdom. ' Alpha and) aov.* A XI. 'Io-ovs) X(/

3«rro's), 0(coC) T(tds), *Omega! Jesus! Ch(rist), (the) S(on) of G(pd), (our) tiumjp).* "etovs ep/»'. *S(avior) In the year 745.* (432-433 A.D.)

The missing portions of this inscription are supplied from No. 293. The words evidently reflect Luke xxiii, 42, where some manuscripts have at the beginning *'l(r)o-o)v,* and some *Kvpie.* See Chapter 1, p. 17.

285. Selemiyeh. Fragment, 542 A.d. On a small fragment built into a mod ern wall, about fifty yards southwest of the castle. It is Etdyl: Etou? broken at each side and at the bottom. At the right end is N ID *&vw.* a portion of a disk, amounting to about a quarter of the cir 5 *I"tlear85'* S42 cumference, from which I judge that the stone was originally nearly twice as high, and that it may have contained a third line of letters. Copy of the editor.

The first letter of the date may have been A, which would make the date 539-540 A.d. 236 286. Selemiyeh. Fragmhnt, 489 A.d. On a small block of basalt, in the entrance to the castle, in the curb on the west side. The block is about a foot square. Copy of the editor. 3YAUUTO Tou aw' erous. *In the 801styear.* (489-490 A.D.) 287. Selemiyeh. Lintel, 604 A.d. On a large lintel of basalt, near the center of the town. The opening of the doorway has been closed by stones laid in mud, and against the face of the solid wall thus formed a modern kubbe has been built, so that the lintel can be seen only from the interior of the kubbe. The lintel is apparently in situ. It is 3.47 m. long and 76 cm. high. The lower half of the lintel is framed by a sort of torus moulding, like a twisted rope, which stands out from the surface of the stone and is returned at each end. Below this is a conventionalized grape-vine, executed in low relief in a band, 22 cm. wide, sunk below the surface: below this again is a band of ornament, half as wide as the other but similarly executed, like two pairs of strands, twisted together in such a way as to leave a succession of loops. Above the torus the face of the stone is plain, except for the inscription, which is executed in relief in a single band, sunk below the surface.

The inscription is 3.02 m. long, the letters 9 cm. high. In the center, after the letters GEO, five letters have been erased completely, as if with a chisel. The other letters are well preserved and certain. Copy of the editor.

Published by Hartmann in *Z. P. V.* XXIII, p. io8f.

'EnXrjpoOi To KTLO-fia Tovto e' o vo /la a t *L rrj;* H)eo tokou, eti /at/ih *'lovviov, IvS. rov* «9/ rrous. *This building was completed in the) name of the Mother-of-God, in the) month of June, indiction 7, of the 915th year.* (June, 604 A. D.) 288. Selemiyeh. Colonnette. On the base of a small column of reddish marble, built into the inner wall of the castle, on the left as one enters, at the angle formed by the wall of the entrance and the wall of the courtyard. The base is 42 cm. high, 35*lA* wide and 35 thick: the whole fragment, including the base and the remaining

Inscription 287.

Inscr. 288. Cast from a squeeze. portion of the column itself is 60 cm. high. The letters are rudely carved, and from 3 to 4 cm. high. Copy of the editor, squeeze and cast.

Published by Waddington, No. 2633. Burton and Drake, II, p. 379, No. 10. Oppenlieim and Lucas, in *Byz. Zeitschr.* , xiv, 1905, p. 27.

M. Waddington renders the first partof the inscription as follows: 'H 7rvXi7 /caXj a-wovSfj Ktx. But there is room for but one or at most two letters before the first letter of the present inscription, nor could there have been a line above the present first line upon this base, nor could I find any trace of letters on the stump of the column. We might read *rrj KaXy o-rrovSfj* as Dr. Lucas does: "*Durch den vortrefflichen Eifer.*" But I am inclined to believe that the inscription is complete, and that *xakrj* stands for /caXia or KaXts, a small *chapel or niche.* A column such as this was would seem to me much more like the ornamental column at one side of a small niche, than like a part of the ornamentation of any sort of door or gateway. Dr. Lucas defines Trc/noSevr-rjs as "*Ein vom Bischof mil Inspektion-*

sreisen betrauter Geisllicher." See Waddington, 2011, and Professor Sachau, in *Monatsber. der Berl. Akad.* , 1881, p. 175 fif. An inscription published by Professor Domaszewski in *ArchEpigraph. Mitth. atts Oesterreich,* vn, p. 183, No. 49, similar in many respects to the inscription under discussion, mentions a certain work accomplished under two officers, to each of whom two titles are given, *TTporrow-pea-fivrepos* and *Trepio8evn;,* to one, and Siaxofo? and *oiKov6p.oi* to the other. A presbyter Sergios is mentioned in an inscription, dated 568-569 A.d., which was found at Horns and published in *Musee Beige,* 1901, p. 265, by Pere Lammens, and again in an inscription dated May, 592 A.d., which was found near Horns and published by the same editor in *M. B.,* 1899, p. 300, No. 36.

289. Selemiyeh. On a block of basalt, about 1 m. in length by 30 cm. in width, built into the outside of the wall of the entrance to the castle, on the south side, about 12 feet from the ground. In the center of the stone was a disk. The inscription was in three lines, on each side of the disk. The letters were in relief, and were originally well formed; but they have been hacked off so that the face of the stone is now almost smooth. The letters on the right of the disk are wholly illegible. Copy of the editor.

290. SELEMiYEH. A fragment high up in the outside wall of the tower in which is the entrance, on the south side of the castle. The stone is badly weathered. The left end of stone is occupied by the monogram , at the right of which is a rude dovetail, as if the inscription were in a dove-tail plate. Below the monogram are letters which are perhaps Arabic. The stone is broken at the right end. The line of the break is curved, and suggests that there was perhaps a disk after the letters given below. Copy of the editor, made with the aid of a telescope.

The last letter of the first line might be w: the last letter of the second TT P Lu T o j-ne jjg-ht be M or N: the last letter of the third line might be N, after which 5 V H, &, &' tJ, u there may have been I.

M t Y *J*

Possibly the second and third lines were intended for *Canj* and *pov:* in any case, I believe that a second part of this inscription, at least as long as the present fragment, has been lost.

291. Selemiyeh. A fragment still higher up, and a little to the left of No. 290, in the west side of the same tower. The letters are large and well made, and

B 0 c are well oreserved. The stone lies now upon its right side. Copy of the V A editor, o C

Published by Waddington, No. 2637.

B

Possibly this maybe read 'laKu/?os, 8oCXos, e(ir) oi'rjo-e: *Iakobos, a servant, made this).* 292. Selemiyeh. A fragment in the outside of the south wall of the castle, between the tower in which is the entrance and the southwest corner, close to the ground. The letters are at the right end. Most of the stone is ornamented with a rude design in relief below the surface, like a conventionalized grape-vine, in which appears a chalice. Below this is a simple right-lined border. This seems to be the

V! "r! lower part of a larger block, which was cut down to fit this course in the r E T wall of the castle: the original block was cut through the first of the rePeto......

A A E H mammg lines of the inscription, so that the upper parts of four letters, and perhaps other lines, have been lost. The other letters are fairly clear. But the whole stone is rudely carved, like most of the blocks of this sort in Selemiyeh. Copy of the editor.

Published by Waddington, No. 2636. Oppenheim and Lucas, *Byz. Zeitschr.,* 1905, p. 28, No. 12.

293. Selemiyeh. "Dans le haut d'une tour du fort, du cote de l'ouest; inscription encadr£e." Waddington, No. 2634. Burton and Drake, 11, p. 379, No. 11.

Xpiore *ivurdeu Tjfiwv iv rfj* /SacriX cuj oou.

O Christ, remember us in thy kingdom I Waddington reads nv«rdeu as yLvrjaO-qn. See No. 284.

294. Selemiyeh. On a stone close to the ground, in the front wall of a shop built against the south wall of the castle, east

of the entrance. The letters are rude, but most of them clear. In the center is a diamond-shaped figure, within which is a cross within a circle. I believe that the inscription is complete. Copy of the editor.

The first line of this inscription obviously contains the words K(ypi)(e)t KCBOH0I *ftoj$i: Help, Lord.* In the other two lines I believe that two names IKY P & «««»k) were contained, both in the genitive, signifying perhaps: *this is the house of , son of .* Dr. Littmann, however, has suggested to me that possibly a name 'ikv/3ov/3cjvv should be read, derived from the Aramaic *'ekurbd = scorpion,* in Nabataean and Safaitic 2"lpJ?, in Arabic *lakrab.* A name A/cpa/3os, doubtless from the same root, is found. On the other hand, BlpN = A/coTraos occurs in a Palmyrene-Greek inscription, Waddington, 2571 b.

295. Selemiyeh. On a fragment in the southwest corner of a modern house, a short distance east of the castle, at the top of the stairs to the second story. These stairs are built into the wall of the courtyard, which is a continuation of the south wall of the house. The inscription was partly concealed; but the owner of the house very kindly tore down a part of the obstruction so that I might copy the inscription. The whole stone was 58 cm. long, 19 wide and 14 thick: it was broken at the right. The letters are poor and badly weathered. Copy of the editor. + ArioCA0OC I. vAytos d ©eos, dyio? 'Icru/ads,

ArioCAOON 2. dyios *66v_a.roi,* e'Xojcrov T/ass, vnoxeicME 3 Sl *Holy God, holy Mighty One, holy Immortal One, have mercy upon us, (thou who wast) brought to judgment for our sake.*

This is an unusual form of the trisagion, with the monophysitc addition, the phrase *vTraxOeU Si' tid?* being substituted for the common *o-ravpcjOeU Si* tids. See No. 6 and also Chapter 1, p. 8 f.

The confusion of o-sounds and a-sounds in this inscription is noteworthy, i.e. d for 6, *a66varoi* for *addvaTos,* viroxk for U7rax«. See No. 26 and its commentary, No. 148 and No. 216.

296. Selemiyeh. "Dans le mur d'une ca-

bane; grandes lettres." Waddington, No. 2635. Burton and Drake, 11, p. 379, No. 12. 1. *"ttv* K(upioVS 7rpos Tiuds v, P *The) Lord said unto us: I am t lie God of Abraham,* 2. Ey& ei/ii o Beo? *Apa Isaac (and) Jacob: (he is) our God, not (the God) of* 3. a/xj. 'W, 6««« *(the) dead* 4. IjjflWt', *oil vtKpmv To....*

As M. Waddington has noted, this inscription is an adaptation of Matthew xxii, 31 f.

(Mark xii, 26 f.; Luke XX, 37 f.): fepl 8c T175 daordo-cft?) *rwv vexpwv Ovk aveyvwre* To *p-qdev vp.lv Vtto Tov* Bfov *eyovro;-'Eyw el/ju 6 Heos 'Afipaap, Kal 6 Bco? 'craaK Kal 6 s)ebs 'laKco/ 3-Ovk ZaTiv*

Beos venpuv aXka £,avTtoi. See above, Chapter 1, p. 17.

Waddington supplies *vpa* in the first line, and *vp,Sv* in the fourth, rather than i?/a? and *riixcov.* 297. Selemiyeh. On two fragments of a large basalt lintel, lying in a street about 150 yards northeast of the castle. The smaller fragment, A, is 53 cm. long and 36 wide: the letters are 19, 17 and 16cm. high. The larger fragment, H, is 1.43 m. long and 36 cm. wide: its letters are about 15 cm. high. At the right end of fragment A, and the left end of fragment B, are the halves of the same disk, containing a broadarm cross, and in the lower quadrants the letters A and uu. Copy of the editor.

FRAGMENT A. FRAGMENT B. A?/T HNE-IC0A'I0YKAIE?0A'

+ Kvpios £uXa£(i) *Tj)v* Lcro8(6v) crov Kal i£o8(ov).

+ *The Lord shall preserve thy coming in and thy) going out.*

The first part of this inscription, on the left of the disk, seems to have consisted of fewer letters than the second part. However, the three remaining letters of the first part are somewhat larger than the others.

These words are derived from Psalm cxx, 8: see Chapter r, pp. 14, 22 and 25. 298. Selemiyeh. On the two halves of a block of basalt which has been split lengthwise. The left half is in the curb of a cistern just outside of the city, towards the north, about opposite the middle of the north side. The right half is now the sill of a modern house in the northeast corner of the city. The pieces are 1.13 m. long and 25 cm. thick: each is about 15 cm. wide. The letters are *2l/2* cm. high. Below the inscription is a blank space of 40 cm. Copy by Mr. Butler.

I have restored the name of the martyr from *C. I. G.* 8842, an inscription from Medjdel, a town in Palestine near Joppa: *MapTvpiov) Tov aylov KiqpvKov.* Probably the name *KrjpvKos* is an incorrect form for *KvpiaKo,* and, if so, should be accented on the last syllable, *K-qpvKos.* At the same time, one cannot help wondering whether the name, both in the present inscription and in the inscription from Medjdel, is not really *KypvXov,* for *KvpiWov.* 299. Selemiyeh. On a stone, upside down, in the upper part of the wall of a modern house, at the northeast corner of the city. It was partly concealed by the corner of a cross wall, which the owner of the house very kindly demolished for me.

The stone was of basalt and very much weathered. It was 91 cm. long and 29 wide: the letters, which are together 43 cm. in length, occupied the left half of the stone only.,. _.., Copy of the editor.

I ᴀᴀ C E I *rj*

Perhaps this should be read £(uX)ao- «, for £vafei, and, if so, this is probably a part of the same text as that contained in No. 297, etc.

300. Selemiyeh. On a lintel, now the right jamb of a modern doorway on a street in the northwest corner of the city, at the end of a second street joining the first at right angles. The stone is 1.87 m. long, measured from the ground upwards, and 41 cm. wide. In the center is a disk, containing a Latin cross, and in the lower quadrants the letters A and u: the U) is upside down. On either side of the disk is a plate, each with a single dove-tail end on the side towards the disk. The stone had flaws in its surface, even before the inscription was carved. Now the surface has flaked off in irregular patches.

I was unable to read any of the inscription on the plate at the right of the disk. The present inscription, therefore, is that on the first plate only. Of this at least twelve or thirteen letters have been lost from the beginning of the first line, at least 3 or 4 from the beginning of the second. The letters are *3l/2* to 4 cm. high. Copy of the editor.

Published by Hartmann, in *Z. P. V.,* 1900, p. 109 f. Oppenheim and Lucas, in *Byz. Zeitschr.,* 1905, p. 26 f. No. 10.

The adjective *aX-qddpyqTov* may mean rather *of continual service.* Dr. Lucas proposes *avap.dprrjTov,* "im Sinne von *dixep,Trrov."* My reconstruction is uncertain, and the precise meaning of the text is not clear to me.

301. Selemiyeh. On a lintel now in use, upside down, as the lintel of the entrance to a modern courtyard, on a narrow street in the western part of the city. It has been broken lengthwise about through the middle, so that only the upper half of the original block remains: both ends have also been broken off. In its present condition the stone is 1.40 m. long and about 18 cm. wide. In the center of the original block was a disk consisting of a circle within a square, of somewhat unusual form, as shown in the accompanying drawing. Both letters and ornament are executed in relief on an otherwise plain surface: the letters are about 12 cm. high, and comparatively narrow. Copied by Dr. Littmann and the editor.

I believe that *dvrjXOe* is here like *dveyeipev,* which is constantly used in this sense in late Greek. On the other hand I am not sure that there is any letter at all between e and M. Perhaps after the M we might supply as follows: *fiaprvpiov Tov ayCov of the holy ....*

From a drawing and photograph. Scale 1:20.

this) chapel 302. Sel-emiyeh. On a much battered stone lying in a street south of the castle. The stone measures 1.19 m. in length and 26 cm. in width: it seemed to be broken on all sides. At the left of the inscription is a blank space 21 cm. long. Copy of the editor.

EIC BEOCXPICTH
BO H9E YBOY

303. Near Selemiyeh. Lintel, 379 A.d. On a small lintel found on its face in a brook just east of a mill, about half an hour's walk west of the city. It is 1. 35 m. long, 33 cm. wide and 40 thick. The letters are of good size and form, and perfectly legible. Above the inscription are two circles, and between them a face, rudely carved, and badly weathered. Copy of the editor. 6TOYCAMX-TOYC "etovs a?x'erous. *Year 69i year.* (379-380 A.D.) 304. Near Selemiyeh. Graffito, upside down on a large column in the gristmill mentioned under No. 303, about a half hour's walk west of the ᴍʜᴋᴀʜᴍʜ/ city. Copy of the editor.

Possibly this may be *ɴUa, 7 firjy,* or (ToOro) t *Vlko., fnjv Conquer, in very truth,* or *This cross conquers, in very truth.* I did not note, however, that there was any cross upon the stone.

This graffito is mentioned by Hartmann in *Z. P. V.* xxm, p. no: see also ibid., p. 74; Van Berchem, *Recherches,* 16, n. 1.

305. Kinnesrin. Fortress (?), 550 A.d. On a stone now used as the lintel of the stable below the house of the Shekh, facing eastward. The stone was probably a lintel originally. It is 1.91 m. long and 56cm. high: except for the inscription, the face is plain. The inscription occupies a space 41 2 cm. in height. The letters, which are incised, are about 5 cm. high, and the average space allotted to each letter is about 34 cm. The fifth line, which is the longest, is 1.68 m. in length. The third is 1.64 m. long, the fourth two letters shorter, the first and second probably shorter still. The first letter legible in the first line is 62 cm. from the beginning of the stone, the last 47 cm. from the end. In the second line the first legible letter is 30 cm. from the beginning, the last 34 from the end. In the other four lines there are spaces of 15, 13, 16 and 16 cm. respectively at the beginning, and of 12, 16, 7 and 13 cm. respectively at the end, which seem to have been always blank. The stone is badly weathered, and many of the individual letters are uncertain. Copy of the editor.

Published by Oppenheim and Lucas, in *Bvz. Zeitschr.,* 1905, p. 55 ff., No. 88.
l AIHAYT!KHTTACATT-YPAKe6MA 2. UCKTUNYCBlJN(J)IAOTIMIUJNTOYrAAH-NOTATOY   777777   3.

HMUNACnOTOYtAIOYCTINIANOYTOY-
AIUJNIOYAYrOYCTOYKAIAYTOKP OC 4.
nPONOIA-OrriNOYTOYNAOI-
KAinANYj)HMOYAnoenAPXUJNYnATLJN
5. KAICTPATHAATOYKAIANACTACIOY-
TOYNAOIAnOYnATUNKAIICIAUPOYTOY
6. MrAAOnPAAOYCTPIOYKAIMHX-
ANIKOYNINAATOYBEUTOYC t «
I believe that the word KYPIDY was
written at the end of the second line; but
I was unable to make certain of this. I
have restored the first line in part from
No. 306.
'FiKTicrOr) criiv s(e)w /c al r/ Svrucr)
naca Tt X evpd With God the whole
west side also was built from
Ck 6e.fj.ek uav a?, e#c Twv evcrefiuv
the) foundations , out of the pious mu-
nifi jikoTip.iSv Tov yar)vora.Tov
KvpCov ? r)iJ.wv Scotto-cence f our
most serene lord (and) master Flavius
Jus Tov, X. 'lovmvivov, Tov alwvlov Aiy-
ovo-Tov Kal tinianus the ever august,
and emperor, by provision of AirroK-
pldTopjos, irpovoia Koyyivov, Tov iu8o-
Longinos, the most glorious and all-
praiseworthy ex ft / 1 » v 5 / / v, c /
prefect and ex-consular, and commander (i.e. dux or £oTaTOV)Kaif-
favevpr)povawoenapxtovKaL)vTra.
T(ov x v, ' x,,, 5. magister militum),
and of Anastasios, the most gloriKcll
oTpaTt)KaTov, /cai Auacrracriov, Tov
evoo , v, v t / s/ ,,. ous ex-consular,
and Isidoros, the most magnificent
c(oraTov) airo vnaToiv, /cat Icriowpov,
Tov ueyaXo-...., ...,, ,,.
% t t illustris and engineer, in indiction
14, of the 862nd irp(eireo-Td.Tov)
IWovarpCov Kai p,7)xxvLKov, iv ivO.
ygar (550 AD) 18', Tov fiija erous. + 'i
On irkevpa, in the sense of a side of
a rectangle, see Plato, Sisyphus, 388 E.
Evidently the inscribed stone was a lintel of a doorway in some great wall, for
the whole west side is spoken of as if it
were, of itself, a considerable work, and
the men concerned are men of high titles even for an age when titles bloomed
most exuberantly. And I think that this
wall can have been no other than the
wall of the city of Chalcis itself, or at
least of its acropolis.

On the persons and titles mentioned
in this inscription see the very interest-

ing commentary by Dr. Lucas in B. Z.
, 1905, p. 55 ff. Dr. Lucas thinks that
Longinos' title was iirapxol? Ttj?
troXew;, and quotes numerous references to a city-prefect of this name, who
was most prominent during the reign of
Justinian I, and who is probably identical with the Longinos of the present
inscription: "Prokop berichtet, dass er
(this Longinos) von Justinian vor seiner
hohen stadtischen Wurde in besonderer
Mission nach Emesa gesandt wurde."
"Mehrere Konstitutionen Justinians
sind an ihn addressiert, Nr. 43 Novella?,
ed. Schoell, a. 537), 63 und 64 (a. 538);
auch am Schluss von 79 ist der Long-
inus gloriosissimus praefectus urbis
genannt. Bekannt ist, dass ein Longin
von Justinian an Stelle des Narses zum
Statthalter von Italien ernannt wurde,
und weiterhin bei Bestrafung der
Morder Alboins (t 573) alspraefectus
Ravennae eine Rolle spielte: vermutlich
die gleiche Personlichkeit."

Isidoros is doubtless the distinguished architect of that name who,
with Anthemios of Tralles, Chryses of
Alexandria and others, designed the famous buildings erected under the emperor Justinian I. Dr. Lucas cites Procopius, De Aedificiis, 1, p. 174, 6; p.
177, 18; p. 180, 9; 11, p. 217, 23: also
Strzygowski, Kleinasien, p. 130 f.,and
Byz. Zeitsclir., 1904, p. 565.

On the titles see also Ducange, Glossarium, Hirschfeld's article in the
Sitzungsber. der Berl.Akad., 1901, p.
579 ff., "Die Rangtitel der romischen
Kaiserzeit," and Koch's Dissertation,
"Die Byzantinischen Beamtentitel von
400 bis 700," Jena, 1903. The titles
cfSofdraros = gloriosissiniUS,
iravevjt)fio; = famosissimtis, and
/AeyaXoTT/oeTreoraTos = mag nificen-
tissimus, were given to officials of the
highest rank. See Koch, pp. 58 ff., 94
f. and 45 ff. The title IWovo-rpios =
illitstris, in the sixth century, denoted,
like Patricius, a rank conferred honoris
causa, and independent of any rank or
title, such as magnificentissimus, which
pertained to any particular office held
by the bearer of the title. Hence the titles
magnificentissimus and illitstris might
properly be combined, as in this inscrip-

tion. See Koch, p. 44: also P. Lammens
in Musee Beige, 1899, p. 303 f. For examples of the titles a.TM indpxov xal
virdTwv see Koch p. 67. The word /xavi/
cds would naturally signify engineer
rather than architect: in the next inscription the verb ipyoSorelv is used of this
same Isidoros, and in Procopius, De
Aedificiis, 1, p. 174, he is

Called p.Tyavoiroi6i. 306. Kinnesrin.
The Same Fortress (?). On a stone, now
the right jamb of the doorway of a house
immediately south of the house of the
Shekh. It is evidently the left half of a
lintel. On its face was a dove-tail plate,
having in the center a disk, 21 cm. in
diameter, containing a cross. The stone
was broken through the center of this
disk, so that half of it, half of the plate
and the left dove-tail remain on the extant fragment. This half of the plate is
88 cm. long without the dove-tail, and
46 cm. high. The disk crosses all the
lines except the first and last: consequently, while the first and last lines
of the fragment contain twenty-nine and
thirty-one letters respectively, the others
contain twenty-four to twenty-six letters
only. The letters are /2 to 5 cm. high.
Copy of the editor.

Published by Oppenheim and Lucas,
in Byz. Zeitschr., 1905, p. 57, No. 89.
With God the %vhole west side also was
built from the) foundations , out of the
pious munificence of our most serene
lord and) master Flavins Justiuianus,
the ever august, and emperor, by provision of Longinos, the most glorious and
all-praiseworthy ex-prefect and ex-consular, and commander, and of Anastasios, the ex-consular, Isidoros, the most
magnificent engineer, directing the
work.

Doubtless this was a lintel of another
doorway in the west side of the same
wall as the foregoing: see No. 305.
having built from the) foundations up).
... ... of the holy M, in the month
Panemos, in diction 9. but otherwise
complete. The inscription is executed in
relief, in three bands, oy2 cm. wide and
sunk below the surface. The letters are
"l/2 cm. high: the width of the lines of
which they are composed is about i cm.
, and the height of the relief about 3

cm. At the top, bottom and right end of the three bands is a border *2l/2* cm. wide, between the bands a space of 1 cm. Copy of the editor.

In the upper angle of the second N of the third line is a sign of abbreviation like a small upside down, and through the right-hand stroke of the A is a small cross-stroke. For the meaning of this inscription see No. 309 below.

308. Rbe'ah. On a stone, face down in a corner of a square building of mud, with a dome, like a weli. I cannot discover from my field notes whether the stone lies on the ground inside of the building, or is actually built into the wall, immediately below the dome. The right end of the inscription is concealed in some way by the wall. The three lines of the inscription are in a plate, without any separation between the lines. The visible portion of the inscription measures 38 cm. in length and 18 cm. in height. Copy of the editor.

The second line of this inscription perhaps contains the word *Koip.-q(r)piov, cemetery,* or perhaps *K!w* and *'P./3,* the ancient name of this place. The third line suggests *fvdKwv TS)y of the guards of the* 309. Rb&ah. A fragment found north of the village. It is 36 cm. long, 38 wide and 36 thick. The letters are 6 to 6)4 cm.

high, and are contained in three bands, 10 to lujAN *l'* IftMU,V»7s e 0e &, _.,, _ T. HEAlu 2. ueuui/ u 11 cm. wide. Copied by Dr. Littmann.. „TVyo, r /ax r *J* APTYP 3. *aprvpj.ovl)*

This inscription looks very like the begin *r ,v r u-1 Xt loannes from (the) foundations* ning of the inscription of which No.-307 is *J* v *'J*

& r. 0' *(built this) chapel (?).* the ending. But the descriptions of the fragments do not agree exactly, and I do not know whether the letters of the present fragment are in relief or not. If these fragments do belong together, they were doubtless part of the lintel of the chapel of some saint, and should be read as follows: 1. *'(iiavyq; j /cruras K 6e* 2. *LekLa)y* To *tvKTrjpio v Tov ayiov fi* 3. *dprvpo; ev, p,T)(vb;) Uav(cfiov), lv8. Joannes having built from (the) foundations this chapel of the holy martyr ....*

..., *in the month Panemos, indiction p.* 310. Rbe'ah. Sarcophagus (?). On the end of a trough, now lying beside a well. Perhaps this trough was originally a small sarcophagus: the whole stone is 1.15 m. long, 55 cm. wide and 40 cm. thick. The inscription, on the east end as the stone now lies, is 42 *y2* cm. long and the letters 9 cm. high. Below it is a cross in a circle. Copied by Dr. Littmann and the editor. Dr. Littmann read BAPCIMn. *Bap(T7jp.oy; of Barsemas.* Compare the name Bao-o-ijaas in No. 263. Perhaps, however, we should read in the present inscription Bap *%-qp.ov* or Bap *2ij(iav, Bar Simon,* i.e. *Simonson.* 311. Mektebeh. Lintel, 508 A. d. On a lintel, upside down in a wall built roughly of ancient material upon an ancient pavement in the northern part of the village, nearly opposite the door of a modern dwelling. The lintel forms part of the first course of the wall, resting upon the pavement itself. Upon it is a small, ancient stone door, set upright between two jamb-stones, but without a lintel. The face of the door is ornamented with a ring in relief, below which is a fish, also in relief. Above the ring is a horizontal band, which reaches from the left side almost across the door, and has near the left side a perpendicular band reaching down from it, perhaps to represent the long leaf of a strap hinge, with a rectangular brace, such as might be employed on a wooden door. A photograph of the door, and below it the inscribed lintel, is reproduced on p. 45 of Part IV. The lintel is 2.02 m. long, 37 cm. wide and about 36 cm. thick. In the center is a cross, of the "Maltese" type, inscribed in a circle, and executed in relief below the surface. On the left side of this cross, when the lintel was in place, was a Greek inscription, and on the right an inscription in Syriac. Both inscriptions are incised. The stone has no mouldings or ornament other than that described.

The Greek inscription, including the cross at its beginning, is 68 cm. long. The letters are 6 to 7 cm. high, and t A w x M r K u „;... are well cut and regular in size t A in. X(p«rrfc) (6 *4k)* U(apte) y(aqfc). pbw) form Copy Qf t *Alpha) and) 0(mega).*

Christ) born) of M(ary). In the I believe that the line above *year) 820.* (508-509, A.d.) the ietters KLuis intended to signify that these letters, unlike the others, are to be understood as figures, and therefore as a date.

The Syriac inscription is published by Dr. Littmann in Part IV, p. 45, No. 21. His translation of the Syriac is as follows: t *O God, mighty) above all ?), helper) of Bar Bassos,* t But see Dr. Littmann's commentary.

312. Mektebeh. On a fragment, probably of a lintel or an architrave, found at „ the foot of a pile of stones near No. 311. t AriOCOeE Ayios 6 «eos, ayios Io"xu-, *i,... .,. „ ra,* I he fragment measures 64 cm. in length POCAriOCA *pos,* ayio? A0aj/aTO?. by 32 in width; the back is rough, so that *Holy God, holy Mighty (One), holy Immortal (One) „,.. „ J* 'the thickness varies. The letters are 7 to 9 cm. high, and executed in relief in two bands, about *()/2* cm. broad, sunk so that the face of the letters is flush with the face of the stone. Between the two bands is a space 3 cm. wide. The letters are well-formed and regular. Copy of the editor. This is the beginning of the "trisagion": see No. 6, and Chapter I, p. 8 f. 313. Mektebeh. On a corner block, found half buried near Inscription 312. Two adjacent sides of the block are moulded. At the bottom is a band of ornament, consisting of vines intertwined, above which is a single line of letters in relief, above which again is a group of heavy, overhanging mouldings. The left end of the first side showed a broken surface. The right end of the second side seemed to be the end A. B.

t ATIMAPIA BOE9IAOM6TIC + 'Ayt(a) *Mapia, fioedi* Ao/neri?; f *Holy Mary, help Dometis!* of the original block. The mouldings, however, were not continued upon the third side, on which the block now rests. The block might have been a part of the cap of a pier supporting one side of the apse-arch of a church. The whole stone is 39 cm. high. The first side, A, is 60 cm., the second side, B, 69 cm. long: the letters are 8 to 9 cm. high. Copy of the editor.

The name Ao/xms is for Aoenos or Ao/

aitio?. In the inscription the name seems to be treated as if indeclinable, and perhaps therefore it should be accented as if it were a Syriac form, Ao/xen's. In the same way the form ayi may be due to the influence of the Syriac feminine adjective, *hagitha,* the form *hagia* in Syriac being masculine.

314. Mektebeh. Panel. On a stone like a panel of a balustrade or parapet, found upright about the center of the ruins, and buried to within about a foot of the top. The letters are executed in relief, in bands sunk to the depth of the relief. These bands measure 86 cm. in length, and together 60 cm. in width. At the left of these bands is a space 14 cm. wide, at the right a space of 5 cm.: above the bands is a space of 4 cm., and below of 16 cm. The letters of the first line, however, measure only 52 cm. in length. Probably other letters, which once filled the remaining space in this first band, have been broken off; but I could not find trace of such letters. This first band is 11 cm. wide, and probably the other bands have the same width. Copy r 1

k M k p wa M *vU* .., *A(T(rov* f.,.... A c Cov/a A M 1A *r H s* ,, OI tne editor. (/cat) *Aau.ia.vov* (/cat) *iwavvov* N«/iujann«/ «

A name Bacrcros would seem more.. , ,,, .. v, x __w,,w (*KaL*) M7?/au,a Kcu *Ao-rovfiov.*

M H K I M A/ALXtfBtf natural than Ao-a-os, if it were not that ,,....,,111 *Holy Mary... of Assos and Damianos and Joannes* the proper division 01 syllables seems 11 _ *and Mckimas and Hassuoos!* to be observed in this inscription: compare Nos. 278, 336 and 353. M/aas is one of the forms of the Palmyrene-Nabataean name lDpD, in Safaitic DpD. Ao-o-ovySos is doubtless the Arabic Hasstib. The forms of the letters indicate that this inscription belongs approximately to the sixth century, and the fact that Arabic-speaking people frequented this region as early as 512 A.d. is shown by the trilingual inscription found at Zebed by Professor Sachau, No. 336 a below.

I believe that this panel is similar in purpose to that which bears inscription 337, and the Syriac inscriptions 22-24,

found at Zebed in a parapet described by Mr. Butler in Part II, p. 302 f., and discussed in detail by Dr. Littmann in Part IV, pp. 47-56. It is possible that these inscriptions were intended to show that certain parts of the buildings in which they were placed were associated in some way with the persons mentioned in the inscriptions. But I am inclined to think it more likely that the names upon these panels were placed in this prominent position before the eyes of the community merely for the sake of remembrance, very much as the names of distinguished scholars are carved on the walls of universities, of artists on art museums, of statesmen on public buildings, in our own times. In such communities as those of Mektebeh and Zebed in the early centuries such inscriptions might naturally take the form *Lord, remember so and so,* or *Holy Mary,* or *St. Sergius, remember these persons.* In the present inscription, then, I am inclined to supply *fiinjadrfrt, remember.* Possibly the verb was abbreviated, so that the letters Mn could stand for the imperative form at the end of the first line. Possibly the verb was contained in the inscription of one of the other panels in the same parapet, now lost. Consequently I believe that the present inscription may be translated as follows: *Holy Mary be mindful of Assos (?) and Damianos and Joannes and Mekimas and Hassnbos!*

On the other hand these names may be of persons for whom seats were placed opposite this part of the parapet. If so, I would understand the inscription to mean: *Holy Mary, bless us) These are the seats) of Assos, etc.* Or lastly we may read *'Ayiq. Mapuj.* and translate: *To Holy Mary: this is the work) of Assos, etc.* See Part IV, p. 56.

315. Mektebeh. On a block of basalt set up on end in a pile of stones, in front of five miserable kubbes. It looked like a small lintel; but if the cutting on one side was that of the under side of a lintel, as it appeared to be, the inscription was upside down when the stone was in place. The block is 1.10 m. long, 54 cm. wide and 43 cm. thick. In the center of its face is a disk or ring in relief, 44

cm. in diameter: if there was painting or carving within this ring, it has now disappeared. The letters are in relief, and are from 6 to 10 cm. high: they are rudely carved, irregular in size and shape, and NENBOH IHITOVB.

E I T owx (dSk) E O vTo V badly aligned. They have been much damaged, □ T o V Ovoa anc e reacnng *1S* uncertain. Copy of the editor.

The second part of the first line may be EwCCK. I have been unable to find in these letters, as they now appear, Greek words which seem to me certain. And it is possible that we have here Syriac words in Greek letters, as in two Syriac inscriptions found at Zebed, and published by Dr. Littmann in Part IV, Syriac Nos. 23 and 24. I believe that it is more probable, however, that the inscription is.Greek, but that it was so badly carved, and has been so badly damaged, that its original meaning is not clear. I would suggest that the letters on each side of the ring are to be read separately, and that the author intended to quote the words of Psalm xc, 1 f. If so, we should read as follows: + 'O *Ko.toi)kuv iv l3or)dei(q) Tov* 'T(»/»)iCttov, ecu? 07ce 77775 Tow BeoO *Tov ovpa.yov.* *He that divelleth in the) help of the Most High, unto the) shelter of the God of heaven shall he come)!*

Compare Nos. 207 and 267: see also Chapter 1, p. 16. For this use of «»s, compare Psalm XLI, 5 Tt SteXeucro/iai iv Two 0-/071/775 *0av/j.ao-Tfj; ew5 Tov Oikov Tov Seov.* The confusion between *im,* «5 and *iv* was the more natural to these people because all three might be represented by the Semitic preposition D.

316. Burdj SbInn Eh. On a block of basalt, like the pedestal of a statue or a small altar. It is about 3 feet high, and the top about a foot and a half square. All four sides have mouldings at top and bottom. The inscription is on the face of the die, and measures 40 cm. in length and 11 cm. in height. The letters are incised: they are regular in shape and well cut, but badly weathered. Copy of the editor.

I do not know what the character after the H signifies. Perhaps it is a Mh/pia...

..

cross, perhaps it is a P, perhaps it is merely to nil out space. I think the author meant to write Ma/n'a: *Mary.* 317. Resm Il Kubbar. Tomb. On a stone upon the ground about 50 yards south of a well, where there is a little hill and the ruins of an ancient building, probably a tomb. The place is about four miles south-southwest of Khanasir.

The stone is 1.11 m. long, 79 cm. wide and 21 cm. thick. In its face a plate is sunk, 92 cm. long and 61 wide, leaving a border of 9 or 10 cm. A small dovetail is rudely cut on the border, at the right and left sides of the plate. The letters are incised, the first ten lines filling the plate, and the eleventh occupying the border at the bottom. The whole stone is similar to that of No. 170, and perhaps served a similar purpose, that is, it may have been one of the panels inserted between the columns of the peripteros of a temple-tomb with a high basement, like the tomb of Eusebios and Antoninos at Hass.' If so, this particular panel was probably placed at one side of the entrance. The letters are irregular in size and shape, and badly aligned: for example, both the forms A and A are used for the letter alpha. The reading of the ninth and tenth lines is very uncertain. Copy of the editor.

Farewell, loved places! Thou joy of enemies, grief of children, expectation of the) aged, healer of troubles, anguish of the) rich, desire of the) wretched, with no respect of persons, making equal all, thee none may escape! An eternal dwelling has Thalabathos, son of Ausos, built) for himself and his) children and dependents. Be of good cheer, my) soul! No one is immortal!

The first word of this inscription, *xePeT* doubtless stands for *xaWTe ' /te Tne* however, may be singular, although the verb is plural. If so, then Tovos perhaps has the meaning here of *place of burial,* and *xatPT* may be a word of greeting, rather than of leave-taking as in most funerary inscriptions. I believe, however, that £i'Xe roVe is for *4'ikoiTottoi,* and should therefore be translated as above. In line 7, *fvylv* is for *jvyeiv.* in line 11, *ddpai* and *ovhk* are for *ddpo-ei*

and ouSeiV

Dr. Littmann tells me that the phrase *olK-qnjpiov aivviov, eternal dwelling-place,* has a counterpart in the Palmyrene NDy *D2, house of eternity,* which came to mean simply *tomb.* Also that *®aXa/3a9o;* is the Arabic name *Tha'labat,* and Aso-os the Nabataean "IKHN, Safaitic DN, Arabic *Aus. Tha'labat* seems to have been a favorite name among the ancient Arabs of Syria: three subtribes, for example, named Tha'labat (belonging to the Tai'), arc mentioned in Ibn Doreid, *Genealogisches Handbuch,* ed.Wustenfeld, p.228.

In the last line the author of the inscription seems to be addressing his own soul: the same words are found elsewhere in tomb-inscriptions, for example in No. 241: see the commentary on No. 10, p. 40 above.

318. Khanasir. Lintel, 579 (?) A.d. On the lintel of the entrance to the citadel: the lintel is broken into three parts. The main part is 2.22 m. long, 88 cm. high and 73 cm. thick. The inscription is in seven lines, which occupy a space 68 cm. high, leaving a blank space, 10 cm. high, at the top and bottom. The letters are 7 to 8 cm. high. In the center of the inscription is a large cross within a circle, which in turn is enclosed in a square, 69 cm. broad. A cross and eight or more letters, 5 to 6 cm. high, were carved above this square, and below the square probably eleven letters of the same height: in the circle, above the horizontal arm of the cross, is the word 'e/wovtj'x.

The right end of the lintel has been broken off, but the fragment remains near the main portion. It is 41 cm. long at the top, and 38 long at the bottom. It contains from two to five letters of each line, and, at the end of each line, a blank space which varies from oy2 to 35 cm. in width. Another portion of the lintel has been lost from the left end, and with it from one to four or more letters of each line. Copy by Dr. Littmann, compared with the original by the editor.

Published by Waddington, No. 1832. *C. I. G.* 8712. Sachau, *Reise,* p. *121.* Hartmann, in *Z. P. V.* XXIII (1900), p. 107.

Waddington read the first line Befjois rtys/3ao-iXcias o-vyxwJ*pvtiacr'-v-*Dr. Neubauer (Sachau, I.e.) reads: Beijoisx. /3. o-vyxoprjpao-iv, 770X15 *KoTapovo-va-a* #ctx. For the beginning of line 6 Waddington suggests _kox 877. The letters connected with the central square Dr. Neubauer reads as follows: t *'lr)o-ov;* X/oto-ros *vucf. 'Ep.avovrj.* Merd/cja *p(d)TWV* Ke(ds).

I believe that Waddington was quite right in thinking that the author of this inscription intended to write iambic trimeters. Also that the title of some high official has been lost from the beginning of line 5. If it were not for the meter I should suggest *varpC (ki)ov.* Compare Waddington 2110 and 2562 c. Perhaps we may read here *o-rpa. T(r)y)6v,* or *8ovk)oi* for SoO/co, (see Waddington 2122, 2194, 2293 a), or *npaT)ov.* In the main the meaning of this inscription is as follows: *By the gifts of his majesty* (i.e. *of the emperor) the) city, contemning the inroad of barbarians, sets up at its gates its benefactors, the) Savior Christ, her) gloriously victorious sovereigns, the) all-praiseworthy commander), the prefects of the praetorians, also (?) its most holy bishop, and the?) most glorious engineer, in the month Gorpieos, in the 806th (?) year, indiction 13.* t t *Jesus Christ, Emmanuel,* t *God over all.*

Obviously some mistake has been made in reading or recording the date of this inscription. For I think there can be no doubt that the date is reckoned according to the Seleucid era, like the other inscriptions of this region. See No. 319. But the 806th year of this era fell in the 3rd, not the 13th, of the indiction series. The simplest correction is that made by Dr. Neubauer, who has rendered the date: *Tov ?&' erous iv8i. y +.*

In this case, however, it must be assumed that at this time in Khanasir the year began with the month Gorpieos: see the commentary to Nos. 90 and 273. There is, moreover, a plain mark of abbreviation, /, after the letters INA. Of course the stonecutter may have made a mistake, either in putting in an I here where it did not belong, or in omitting an I from the figures of the date: in the latter case we might read *Tov ;«o' erous, ivh. iy'* in the 816th year, indiction 13, i. e. 504-505 A.d. But other explanations are possible. The ends of the G) in this inscription slant upward unusually far, and come very close together at the top. It is not impossible that sA was written, and that the stone-cutter, not recognizing the somewhat unusual sign for 900, mistook it for a long-horned 0). If so, we might read the date: *in the) month Gorpieos, of the go6th year, indiction 13,* i.e. September, 594 A.d. But the first figure in the date looks as much like ?, which sometimes has the form *S,* as like S. In that case the date is 890, i.e. the year which began in October, 578, and ended in September, 579 A.d. The 13th indiction began in September, 579 A.d. , and, consequently, in this one month the year 890 of the Seleucid era and the 13th year of the indiction series coincided. Therefore I believe the date of this inscription to be September, 579 A.d.

It is uncertain whether this lintel belonged originally to the citadel or not. It is not unnatural that this citadel was built or rebuilt shortly before the building of the city walls, inscriptions from which, dating from 604 A.d., are published below, Nos. 319, 324 and 325. But it is quite possible that this lintel was itself a part of the city walls, as Waddington supposed, and was carried to the acropolis at some later time, when a castle was built there after the city walls had been ruined. If so, it seems all the more probable that its date was not far from the end of the sixth century. And I myself can imagine much more readily a gateway such as this must have been, adorned with eight or more statues, placed in the plain atone of the entrances to the city, than upon this rough and irregular acropolis. Moreover, if 579 A.d. is really the date of this monument, then the *ivSogoTaTo? firjxaviKos* may be the same Isidoros who is mentioned in Nos. 305 and 306.

The mention of inroads of barbarians is interesting: this city must have been constantly exposed to attacks from the desert.

The words connected with the central square recall Romans ix, 5: *e$ 5v 6*

X010T09 To *Kara aapKa,* 6 *ov* cVl *irdvrwv* ©eos Kt., or Kphesians iv, 6. The phrase 6 *irdvrwv* ©to? also occurs in the liturgies, e.g. in the "Liturgy of St. James," Sw. pp. 244, 268, etc.

319. Khanasir. City Gate, 604 A.d. On the lintel of the north gate of the city, found on its face, half buried, just outside of the gateway. It is mentioned by Burton and Drake in *Unexplored Syria,* 11, p. 181. The lintel is 4.10 m. long, 93 cm. high and 70 cm. thick. The tops of the gates fitted into the bottom of the lintel at the back, the space cut out for them in the lintel being approximately 3.46 m. wide and 34 cm. deep. In this inset, at one end of the lintel, the socket to receive the upper pin of a gate is preserved: it is 17 cm. in diameter. Probably then, when the gates were closed, their backs were flush with the back of the lintel. If so the gates were 34 cm. thick, and the extreme width of the opening, between the two gates when opened wide, was 2.78 m.

The inscription is in four lines, executed in relief. The first six or seven letters of the first line have been erased, leaving a mutilated space of 49 cm. after the cross. The remaining portion of this first line is 2.55 m. in length, the letters *6l/2* cm. high. Immediately below the first line is a heavy torus moulding. The other lines of the inscription are in bands, about 13 cm. wide, sunk below the surface of the stone and separated from each other by a space of 2 or 3 cm. The second line, including the cross at its beginning, is 3.81, the third 3.83 m. long. The fourth line is 3.76 m. long; but between the word *7raTpiSos* and the date a space, 30 *l/i* cm. long, has been left blank, except that upon it a little dove-tail plate has been marked out in shallow, incised lines. The letters of the last three lines are from 9 to 10 cm. high. The third and fourth lines of the inscription are broken in the center by a large cross, 34 cm. in height and width: the arms of the cross are 2 cm. broad at their intersection and 4 cm. at the ends. Below the inscription is a blank space, 19 cm. high, on which two parallel lines, 12 cm. apart, have been incised, as if to form a fifth band: it may

be that the band included between these lines bore painted letters or an ornamental design of some sort. In the upper right-hand corner of the lintel, at the right of the torus moulding and above the end of the second line of the inscription, is the curious design shown in the accompanying photograph. It is 19 cm. high and 14 broad, and is incised upon the plain face of the stone in thin, shallow lines. When the lintel was in place it was doubtless inconspicuous, unless it was painted. I cannot explain its presence. Perhaps it had a religious or a magical significance, perhaps it was a mason's mark, or perhaps it was cut in mere idleness, without a definite purpose of any sort. The upper left corner of the lintel has been broken off, so that it is impossible to tell whether there was a similar design there or not. We found, however, a few similar designs elsewhere in this country, in particular on the rear wall of a house in the north center of the town of Der Sambil. They are not unlike some of the gnostic symbols. Copy by the editor, and a squeeze.

The emperor Phocas, in his short reign, made himself so generally hated throughout his empire, that it is not surprising to find his name erased from such a monument as this. His name was erased from at least one other monument in this same city, No. 324 below. Gregorios figures also in No. 325.

320. Khanasir. On a fragment of a moulded block, found by a native about a quarter of a mile south of the north gate. It seemed to be the right end of a lintel. The fragment was about 50 cm. long at the top. The letters, which are 10 cm. high, are executed in relief, in bands sunk below the surface and 13 cm. wide. Copy of the editor. -O N M X C T ay P
co T N A 9 t
*oi»/li me Tov (rravp(ov) of the cross
Ctous o', ivS. ff. the year 8—, indiction
p.+*

Compare Nos. 91, 328 and 331: also Chapter 1, p. 19 f.

321. Khanasir. On the lintel of a ruined building outside of the south wall of the city, about a quarter of a mile southeast of the citadel, and the same dis-

tance southwest of the gateway mentioned under No. 324. It faces southward. The building is now so ruined that it is difficult to determine its original plan or purpose. It seemed to me that there were originally two stories, in which there were three chambers, each measuring about 25feet by 1 o. The middle and eastern chambers of the upper story seemed to have entrances on the north, the western chamber on the west side; but these openings may have been windows and not doorways. The walls are of small, rough-hewn stones and, in their present form, are about 3 feet thick. I supposed that this was a tomb of some sort: it may have been a guardhouse outside of the walls. It has doubtless been rebuilt, perhaps in medieval times. See Part II, p. 300 f. Inscription 321.

The bottom of the lintel is now just above the ground. The whole block measures 1.60 by 0.60 m. On its face a plate, 1.42 by 0.45 m., is marked out by an incised line. In the center is a disk, 34 cm. in diameter, and formed by two concentric circles in relief, enclosing a broad-armed cross in relief: the cross has been hacked off. The letters are incised, and are very rough and irregular: those of the first line are 7, those of the last 5 cm. high. Near the lower left-hand corner a slot has been cut in the stone, 17 cm. long by 8 cm. high, as if for the string of a latch. But evidently this slot was made long after the lintel was finished, for the first four or five letters of the fifth line, and the bottoms of several letters at the beginning of the fourth line, have been cut away. Copy of the editor.

Published, in part, by Professor Hartmann in *Z. P. V.,* XXIII (1901), p. 108, and by M. J.-B. Chabot in *J. Asiat.,* Nov.-Dec. 1901, p. 442, D, e.

Instead of Ad(ra IIaTpi *Kal* Tiw ical *Ayuo Uvevfian,* the words *Harpl Kal Oiov Kal 'AyCov Hvev /naTos* have been carved. Perhaps the memory of the familiar phrase 'E *ovofian narpbs Kal Tlov Kal 'Aytov JlvevpaTos* may have caused the sudden change of case. See the inscription from Kefr Nabu published by M. V. Chapot in *B. C. H.,*

xxvi, p. 181: Adfa *Harpl K7) olov KTf ayLov* 7riuyxaT09. *'Aprjv.* After *ilvevftaTos,* instead of the words *vvv Kal d«,* which I think were intended here, the stone-cutter has carved volKAIAfjOl or riG) or rov or TIN. The first of these letters looks more like a N with the first leg omitted, than like an Y. Perhaps the author wrote NO IN for *vvv,* as he wrote *Oiov* for *Tlov* or 'ToS, and this may have confused the stone-cutter, if this was a different person from the one who composed the text, so that he reverted to the fourth word of his copy, and carved the fifth and sixth words a second time. Or the author may have wished to strike out *Oiov Kal 'AyCov nvevfiaTos* from the copy, and to write instead 'Tw *Kal 'Ayuo* ni/eu/xan; but, if so, *nvevpan* was not carved, and, instead of the incorrect forms, the words *vvv Kal aei,* required by the context, were omitted. However, the letters are so badly carved, and the stone so much weathered, that quite a different reading of the last three lines may perhaps be found.

The last line I cannot explain at all. At the end of the fourth line 1 seems certain: after these letters there may have been C, in smaller size; but perhaps there was nothing at all after l in this line. The first letter in the fifth line, after the hole, may be o or H: between the TT and the edge of the disk may be UJ, OV or IN, possibly OI or O. Below the disk there appear to have been from four to six letters, of smaller size, the first of which appears to have been T, the last Y; but I am not sure that there were letters here at all. After the disk, in this line, the first letter may be A, the fourth P or K, the sixth may be merely an accidental mark, the seventh may be A, the eighth and eleventh may be B.

I believe that the main part of the inscription is merely the "Gloria Patri." + Ad£a *Harpl Kal Tup Kal Ayiw Tlvevp. ari, vvv Kal* aei *Kal* eis Tov? aiawa?. *Afirjv.*
+ *Glory to Father and to Son and to Holy Spirit, now and ever and to the ages. Amen.*

See above, Chapter 1, p. 10.

322. Khanasir. City Gate (?). On three fragments of a large lintel, lying on the

ground near the east wall of the city, and several hundred yards east of the ruined building with vaulted chambers. The fragments are 77 cm. high and 53 thick. The first is 74 cm. long at the bottom, 61 at the top: the second is 2.27 m. long, the third 57 cm. long at the top and 65 at the bottom. The letters are in relief in a plate, 37 cm. wide, sunk in the surface below the torus moulding, leaving a border of about 4 cm. at the bottom and at the left end. The letters of the first line are 9 to 13 cm. high: those of the second line on the third fragment are 84 to 12 cm. high, those of the third line 4 to 8 cm. in height. Dr. Littmann's drawing of the third fragment shows that the border, at the bottom of the plate containing the inscription, has been cut away to within about a centimeter of the bottom of the stone, and at the right of the fragment there is a blank space, apparently 36 or 37 cm. high and about 24 cm. broad, reaching from the torus moulding to the bottom, and from the end of the inscription to the extreme end of the stone. I cannot tell whether this space represents a hole cut in the lintel, or a portion of the original surface of the stone which has been left blank for some reason. Copied by Dr. Littmann. The third fragment was published by M. Chabot, in *J. Asiat.,* 1901, p. 441, D, a.

I believe that the original form of this inscription was as follows: + Ayios 6 ®cds, aj-yios 'Icru /so?, ayios Aflayjaros, 6 o-rai/-
+ *p* a#ts sv iJ/Aos, *iXeqcrov* 17/ias. +

If so, we have here the trisagion, in the monophysite form: *Holy God, holy Mighty One), holy Immortal (One), crucified for us, have mercy upon us!*

See above, Chapter 1, p. 8f., and Inscription 6. I believe that at some later time, when some alterations were made in this lintel, a hole was cut in the right end of the stone, perhaps to support the end of a beam. In cutting this hole the last three letters of the first line, TAY, were destroyed. I believe that these were then recarved below the last of the remaining letters of the line in which they originally belonged. The character after the Y is perhaps a cross and not an

I. In order to carve these letters in relief it must have been necessary to cut back the surface of the original plate still deeper at this end, and, in doing so, the plate seems to have been extended into the lower border, thus providing room for a few letters, of smaller size, below the second line. These last letters probably contain a date: vhtos (for erous?) r)vain the) year 858. (546-547 A. D.)

This was probably the lintel of one of the gates in the east wall of the city.

323. Khanasir. On a corner stone with mouldings, like the cap of a pier, found near the east wall of the city, not far from No. 322. The block at present is 75 cm. long at the top, and 63 cm. long at the bottom. The lowest member is a broad fascia, 22 cm. wide. Above this is a bead moulding, then a splay-faced moulding, then a plain band 9 cm. wide. I judge from Dr. Littmann's drawing that the corner of the pier was on the left of the inscription, and that the block is broken on the right. The other side of the stone is 55 cm. long. The inscription is on the top band of the mouldings, in letters 6 cm. high. Copy of Dr. Littmann. OWPAANHOM h ' S fJ
The first and last letters are perhaps mere ornament. The fourth might be A, A or o: the eighth might be 9. Possibly this is a name, 'iwpSdvr)? M....: lordanes, son) of M 324. Khanasir. City Gate (?). On a block with mouldings on two adjacent sides, found lying upon the ground, about a hundred yards southeast of the building whose vaulted roof is still preserved, near where the south gate of the city stood. The block formed the corner of a course, probably the cap of the left pier of an arched gateway in the south wall of the city. The inscription is obviously complete at the left end, which is at the corner of the block, and may be the beginning of a longer document. I am inclined to believe, however, that it is complete in itself. The length of the block at the bottom is 1 m., its height 51 cm., its thickness 73 cm. The letters, 6 cm. high, are executed in relief, in bands, 8 cm. wide, sunk below the surface. The first and second lines of the inscription are

88 cm. long, the third 81. The stone is broken somewhat at the right end, so that perhaps two letters have been lost from the first two lines, three letters from the third. The first seven or eight letters of the first line have been completely erased. Below the inscription is a blank space, 44 cm. wide. See also the next inscription. Copy of the editor. Squeeze.

Published by M. Chabot in *J. Asiat.*, 1901, p. 442, D, c.

The name of the emperor,,. TONYC6B6C +, *rbu* rfotfTM) which wag j haye 2. YPrTHNKAINIKHTH *cvepyerrjv* /ecu racnrrfMi flacnXea,.., *e* T . /v *It* -1 J plied from Inscription 310.

3. BACIAAKYPI(tYAAI Kvpie wXafov. *v v 0 v*

No emperor had greater need + *Phocas, the mostpious benefactor andconqueror, (our) king, O Lord.. protect/* protection than this one, nor was any other name more thoroughly, not to say justly and properly, erased from the monuments. For no emperor was more cordially hated and loathed, throughout the whole empire.

325. Khanasir. City Gate. On a block with mouldings on two adjacent sides, like that of No. 324, and found upon the ground a few steps from it toward the east. The corner is on the right of the inscription. The mouldings of the two blocks are are somewhat different. In Mr. Butler's opinion these blocks could not have been placed in a continuous course; but they may have balanced each other at opposite ends of the same wall, or occupied corresponding places in the piers at each end of an arched gateway.

The present block is 1.02 m. long at the bottom, 58 cm. high and 70 cm. thick. The letters, 6 cm. high, are in relief, in bands, 8 cm. wide, sunk below the surface. The first line of the inscription has been completely erased. The third line is 87 cm. long. Below the inscription is a border, 3 cm. wide. The inscription is obviously complete at the right. Copy of the editor.

Published by M. Chabot in *J. Asiat.*, 1901, p. 441, D, b.

I believe that ABIM6NOC is a proper

name, and possibly there is concealed in it some name of Semitic origin. On the other hand, Dr. Littmann suggests 'A/SiXos, and recalls Waddington No. 2557 c. It would be interesting to know that Grcgorios, the "pious branch from a noble stock" mentioned in No. 319, came from the Tetrarchy of Abilene, a district of Coele-Syria not far to the northwest from Damascus. Perhaps, however, *a.pifievo;* contains the ending of some participle. The first line perhaps contained the name of Leontia, the wife of Phocas, and, if so, we might supply from

No. 319 the words Kcu *Aeovriav,* Tous *rjfiwv* 8eo"7r(6Yovs), or fat *XtovrLav, rjfitov Sea-rroivav* and *Leontia, our masters,* or and *Leontia, our mistress* (i.e. *empress*). In that case this inscription is practically a continuation of No. 324.

326. Khanasir. On a fragment of a block, with mouldings on two adjacent similar, and also the forms and size of the letters; but the dimensions of the blocks 327. Khanasir. On a large block of basalt, half buried in the ground, about a hundred yards north of the citadel. The stone is 1.93 m. long, 41 cm. high and 45 cm. thick. In the center is a circle in relief, 34 cm. in diameter. Within the circle are lines which suggest the letter B, 20 cm. tall and turned towards the left: I think, however, that these lines are not original. Probably there was here, originally, a cross in relief, which has been hacked off. The inscription measures 78 cm. in length on each side of the circle. The letters, 12 to 13 cm. high, are in high relief. Copy of the editor.

Published by Professor Sachau, *Reise,* p. 121.

OIKHAniCAM HKATAICXYN9
OIBOHeOCK«40 BHGHCOMAITITT
'Err! r oC, K(vpi)e, r/Xmcra, pr) Ka.Ta. icr/)(yvdtL,r)v In thee, O Lord, I put my trust: let me never be ets *Tov aluiva. ashamed.*

K(upio)? coi for)do;, ff(al) ov stj&jcto/jmu-(The) Lord (is) my helper, and I shall not fear: Tl It 0177W pot dvdpwno. what shall man do unt0 me?

Dr. R. Neubauer, whose rendering of

this inscription is given by Professor Sachau, recognized that each line of this inscription is a quotation from the Psalms. The passages quoted, however, are not Psalms xxiv (xxv), 2, and lv (lvi), 11, to which Dr. Neubauer refers; but Psalms xxx, 1, and cxvii, 6, are quoted here literally. See above, Chapter 1, p. 16 f.

Since seventeen letters are to be supplied at the end of the second line, the right half of the inscription must have been about 1.20 m. longer than at present. From the center of the circle, then, to the right end of the inscription was 2. 15 m. This is of course too long for the half of a lintel which was only 41 cm. high. Moreover the circle, or disk, is not even near the center of the inscription. It is probable therefore that there were two disks. The extreme length, then, between the two ends of the inscription was at least 3.72 m., which is still too long for a lintel of this height. I believe, therefore, that the present block was laid in a course above a true lintel, forming with other blocks a kind of over-lintel or door-cap. If so, the present block is probably unbroken. The block on the left then bore the first four letters of each line of the inscription, while the block on the right bore the last fifteen letters of the first and the last seventeen of the second line, and also the second disk. If this second disk was placed after the first four letters of each line on this block, the whole first line of the inscription was divided into groups of fifteen, fifteen, and eleven letters, the second line into groups of sixteen, fifteen, and thirteen letters. And if the centers of the two disks were placed above the inner faces of the jambs, the width of the opening was 1.40 m., a natural width for a doorway in this region.

328. Khanasir. Two fragments of a large lintel, which was originally composed of two or three pieces mortised together. The central portion is missing. Fragment A was the left end of the lintel: it was found on the ground about 15 yards north of the citadel and 50 yards west of No. 327, and was copied by the editor. It is 1.45 m. long, 66 cm. wide, and 29 cm. thick. In the right end a hole, shaped

like a dove-tail, is cut entirely through the stone, into which a corresponding projection on the next block was fitted. A photograph of this fragment is given in Part II, p. 296. Fragment B was the right end of the lintel: it was found near the other, and copied by Mr. Butler. Its extreme length is 1.10 m., and its width 66 cm.

The inscription was in two lines, at the top of the lintel. The letters, which vary from 4 to 7 cm. in height, were executed in relief below the surface, in bands *gl/2* cm. wide. The two lines of fragment A are 1.06 m. in length: the first line of fragment B is 42, the second 31 cm. long. Below the inscription is a rude grape-vine pattern, framed by an elongated bead and reel moulding, executed also in relief below the surface: this vine was returned and carried down the jambs.

The first fragment was published by Professor Hartmann, in *Z. P. V.,* xxin, p. 106.

A. B.

t Gntwctay — xxerr s- Omnoct«c 6MOYCtIAOYCKKATATH YMAl t *f'Evrw trravpw rov,* X(p«rr)e, Tt o-,.,. v + /« *thy cross, O Christ, my friends, ana pevos* rows *ip-oix;* tfn'Xou? #c(ai) *Kara* Ttj v */moi.* +

The first part of this inscription recalls Galatians vi, 14: 'E/xot 8c *p.r) ytvoiro Kavxaa-Oai el firf iv To)* TTavpq Tov *KvpCov* 17/xwj/ 'itjctoo Xpiorou, but I am unable to suggest any plausible reconstruction. The first letter of the first line of fragment B may be u: the other letters I believe are certain. Compare Nos. 91, 320 and 331: also the inscription quoted in Chapter 1, p. 19 f.

329. Khanasir. Graffito. On a block of basalt upon the ground, a few yards east of No. 328. The stone is 61 cm. long, 44 wide and 27 thick. There seem to have been three lines of inscription; but, if so, I was unable to decipher the first line. In the center of this line there seems to be a N, 5 cm. high, above which is a space of 8 cm. to the top of the stone, and below which is a space of 7 cm. to the second line: on each side of the N are two doubtful letters, as shown in the copy. The letters of the second line are

from 11 to 15 cm. high: below this line is a space of about 9 cm., containing the third line. Copy of the editor.

I am not sure whether there is a letter between the E and the 1. I a) N Uj IL A of the second line; but I think probably there is not. I should 2 EIAAANDC therefore read as follows: 'EXcwos, (o)uer/)aj'ds; 3. CYETP-N *Elanos, a veteran.* Perhaps the first line contained the name *'loxivv)rjs.* The name in the second line may be for AiXtcwds: Jerusalem was called AiXi'a, after its restoration under Hadrian. Possibly then we may read *John of Jerusalem, a veteran.* 330. Khanasir. Fragment, by the north wall of the city, about 50 yards west of the main gateway. The height of the stone is 1.03 m., its length at the bottom 60 cm., its average thickness 55 cm. It looks like the base of a statue, and if so the top was probably about 75 cm. square; but the sides are so damaged that it is impossible to make certain of this. Moreover, in the side on the left as one faces the inscription, near the bottom of the side, is a sort of socket, which suggests that this block was mortised into another, as e.g. in No. 328, and consequently it may have been the right end of a lintel. The inscription is certainly complete on the right side. The letters are in relief, in bands 13 to 15 cm. wide. Between the first and second lines is a band containing some sort of ornament, which looks like the end of a serpent, but which is probably intended to represent a vine. Below the last line is a band, 22 cm. wide, apparently blank. The first line of the inscription is 23*1/2,* the last 29 cm. long. Copy of the editor. I; ION WW Too little of this inscription is preserved to warrant even an 2' NHN *vr)V . r* 3. HCAC "ho-as attempt at reconstruction. I he first line suggests of course, *v &&* 4. A6NAC aevas.

fjLvrjfi eiov: monument, but also a host of other words. The second line suggests *eipyjvrjv; peace,* the third *Crfo- as; having lived,* the fourth *devds* for devaas. *perpetual.* 331. Khanasir. Two Fragments lying upon the ground near the center of the ruins, about a quarter of a mile northeast of the citadel. The face of each fragment is perfectly plain ex-

cept for the inscription: the back is un-squared, as if imbedded in a wall.
Fragment A is 60 cm. long, 43 high and 43 thick. The left end is blank: the in-scription begins 23 cm. from the left end of the block, and is 37 cm. long.

Fragment B is 62 cm. long at the top and 43 at the bottom: its width and thickness are the same as those of the other fragment. The last three letters, together with the cross, are 30 cm. in length: at the end of this line is a blank space of 20 cm., at the end of the first line a blank space of 40 cm. The letters are 8 to 9 cm. high. The two fragments are evidently the beginning A B and ending of an inscription, of which a por-t C T A Y O I C I tion, probably more than half, has been lost. n n H C r A C

Copied by Mr. Butler and the editor.
9 A A o N A r-r

The first letter in the second line of B + %Tavp oicn may be Z or I. For the text see No. 328. iKTrqr_ yas

Other inscriptions from Khanasir have 0ao tvS. y. + been published by Professor Hartmann in cross indiction j. t Z. P. V. Xxiii, p. 108, and by M. Chabot in J. Asiat. 1901, p. 442.

332. MU'ALLAK. Church, 606 A.d. Two fragments of the lintel of the south por-tal of the West Church. See Part II, p. 307. Fragment A is 1.17 m. long at the top and 0.39 at the bottom: the lower left corner is broken off, the first line of the inscription, however, remaining intact at the left: on the right side this fragment is broken in an almost per-pendicular line. Fragment B is 68 cm. long at the top and 38 at the bottom: on the left side the line of the break slants slightly towards the right from the top downward, so that between the two fragments about two letters more have been lost from the fifth than from the first line. The lintel was 72 cm. high. The inscription is in a plate, 67 cm. high. Above the main portion of the in-scription, but within the plate, there was, in the center, a disk containing a cross, and, on either side of this there appears to have been a cross and the letters X M r. These letters are 15 cm. high. The letters of the first three lines of the main inscription are 9 to gl/2 cm.

high, those of the fourth 7 /2, those of the fifth 7 cm. in height. Copy of the editor. *This gate (is) the Lord's: (the) righteous shall enter in it. Upon this rock I will build my church; and the gates of hell shall not prevail against it. This house of the holy father* (or *abbot*) *Baraps* (?) *was built through , most il-lustrious , indiction 10, in the pi8th year (being the) mason.* (606-607 A..D.)
On the letters X M r see the notes on No. 155.

The first line of this inscription is quoted from Psalm cxvii, 20: it is found not infrequently on lintels of ancient Syrian churches. Compare Waddington, Nos. i960, 1995 and 2413 a; *C. I. G.* 8930-8934 incl. See also above, Chap-ter 1, p. 17.

The second and third lines are from Matthew xvi, 18, and are particularly in-teresting as a direct quotation from the New Testament, such quotations being comparatively rare in these inscriptions. See, however, Chapter 1, pp. 9 f, and 17.

The name in the fourth line is very strange. Dr. Littmann was of the opin-ion that I should read Bapaoa/8/3d, gen-itive of *BapaftPas,* the Syriac *Barabba.* But all the letters of this inscription, ex-cept those mentioned below, seemed certain. I believe, therefore, that BA-PAYABBA is on the stone. Perhaps, how-ever, *Bapax Barach)* might be read.

The title *afivpp.* in line 4 would seem, from the doubling of the last letter, to be in the plural. But there is hardly room for more than one name, together with the article, before the adjective. Perhaps then the doubling of the last letter was intended to indicate the superlative de-gree; but I know of no other certain ex-ample of this. Moreover, this title is ap-plied commonly to persons of high rank. See Koch: *Die Byz. Beamtentitel,* p. 10 ff. Consequently one would expect the preposition cVl before the title, rather than 81a. However, compare *C. I. G.* 8640 and 8650.

The first three letters of the fifth line are quite uncertain: they look more like H C N. All but the top of the last figure of the date, A, has also been lost. This character, however, which is similar to

that in Inscription 319, I believe to be certain, and the date is further attested by the indiction year. This then is one of the few Syrian inscriptions dating from the seventh century of our era. It is in-teresting to note that extensive building was being undertaken at this time both here and at Khanasir.

333. MU'ALLAK. Lintel. On a broken lintel, lying upon the ground in the northern part of the town, a little east of the center, on the west slope of a mound on the south bank of the wadi. The face of the stone at present measures 1.25 by 0.44 m. It contains, besides the inscrip-tion, two disks in relief, each containing a cross, the first 41, the second 34 cm. in diameter. The stone is broken at both ends: at the left of the first part of the inscription, so that the first letter of the first line, but probably no other letter, has been lost: also through the VMEu t CYME right half of the second disk. The letters, NHCYI Uunhc DISK DISK which are incised, are from 6 to 10 cm. high. ocrew YIOCA -ru c 4. v c u c 4. c 4.U prlc NNHOC

Ihe first line of the first part of the in-scription is 32 y2 cm. long, the first line of vio rTMP7-t Svpofop vibs Amps, the second part, including the cross, 38 cm. in length. Copy of the editor.

One would naturally understand this to mean *Symeones, son of Georgis.* t *Symeones, son of Hanneos.* But rewpyis is apparently for *Tewpyios, Avisos* prob-ably for *Aiva.io,* the Semitic *Hannai.* Both Tewpyis and Afos, then, are nom-inative forms. It may be that *Zvfi(oiT);* was regarded as indeclinable, because, being pronounced *Symeonis,* it resem-bled the Syriac form.1 If so, then prob-ably Georgis and Hanneos were broth-ers, and we should translate the inscrip-tion: *Symeones son, Georgis. t Syme-ones' son, Hanneos.* 334. MU'ALLAK. Chapel(?). On a lintel lying upon the ground. The stone at present is 1.32 m. long, 45 cm. high and 33 cm. thick: it is broken at the left end. In the center of the original lintel was a square, enclos-ing a large cross, 38 cm. high and 35 cm. broad. In each upper corner of the square is a circle 4 cm. in diameter, and in the lower corners A and G); but the Q is on the left, the A on the right. From the 1See the commentary on No. 313. left side of this square to the farthest point on the line of the broken end of the stone is 31 cm.: on the right of the square the inscription occupies a space 66 cm. long, and appears to be complete. If then the square was originally in the center of the lintel and of the inscription, the lintel was originally 1.67 m. long and the first part of the inscription consisted of about twelve letters in each line. The lines on the right of the square seem to have been the continuation of the corresponding lines on the left. The letters, are 4 to 7 cm. high, and very badly carved: some of them are now most uncertain. Copied by Dr. Littmann.

At the end of the first line there 1. Matv-TovAnoYAoee seems to have been the name of viicOA KICATPAeKTI-CA. „ «„ some saint: *rov ayiov ....* MAPTVP Hntovtnhtic „ _____ Iapxk, EY1H VTTP The second part of the second line -EfhM APIAHrVNH looks a little like *iv* Or eVi *irerpq.* POVV AVTOV t ocTio-a: *in or on the) rock I built.*
See Matthew vii, 24 f.; xvi, 18; xxvii, 60. The third line seems to be *pdprvp Tovtwv* HTIC: *I was witness of these things).* Compare Luke xxiv, 48; Acts i, 8; ii, 32, etc. In the fourth line I am tempted to read *d.rrapxv) ei(x)y vnip-' avow of first-fruits in behalf of.* The rest of this line seems to have been blank. In the fifth and sixth lines we have Mapia, 17 *yvvr) avrovf: Mary, his wife,* t Apparently then this was the lintel of a chapel *paprvpiov)t* built in fulfillment of a vow.

335. MU'ALLAK. On a small fragment of a moulded block, at the extreme west of the ruins, near the hill, between the dry bed of the stream and the aqueduct which runs down from the hills. The space occupied by the letters is 28 cm. long and 7 cm. wide: the letters are *y2* cm. high. Copy of the editor. tAANIHA t Awtij'X. t *Daniel.*
The aqueduct of which I have spoken is a small conduit of stone, its channel being 20 cm. wide at the top, 9 at the bottom and io4 deep. In some places it seems to have been laid upon the

ground. There was no evidence that it was covered in any way. See Part II, p. 306. A few feet west of the present inscription is a block of basalt 62 cm. long, 43 thick, and 40 high, having in the center a rectangular hole, 30 cm. long, 20 wide, and 13 deep. In the bottom of the hole was a sort of socket, 3 cm. in diameter. In one side of the hole there was a small opening, through the stone, into a little cup carved in relief on the outside. Perhaps this was a benitier, like that found on the left pilaster of the church at Ksedjbeh. If not, it was doubtless a drinking-fountain, connected with the aqueduct. A socket for the basin of a drinking-fountain was found on a street in il-Barah, in the rear wall of a house: at the back was the hole for a water-pipe which led from some tank in the interior.

336. Zebed. Tomb. 337 A.D. On a handsome monument, consisting of a pedestal supporting a sarcophagus, on the hillside, ten or fifteen minutes' walk southwest of the city. There are no buildings near it. The monument is described and a photograph of it given in Part II, p. 299 f.: see also Part IV, p. 51 f. The die of the pedestal is about 8 feet high and 2.32 m. broad: at the top and bottom are simple splay-face mouldings. Originally it may have supported two sarcophagi, one of which has disappeared. The remaining one is narrow and lies east and west: its sides have been cut out in a regular curve, so that to one coming from the north, as we came, it looks like a huge crescent mounted upon a high pedestal, as if it were a monument of the Mohammedan conquerors. I think some Saracenic chieftain must have conceived this genial idea, to the glory of his cause and the discomfiture of the soul of the good Christian whose body once had rested here. At the foot of the south side is the cover of this sarcophagus, with four acro r 0 Tomb at Zebed. Inscr. 336. teria, but narrow and not cleanly cut.
The first line of the inscription begins on the west side of the monument, on the plain fascia above the splay-face moulding at the top of the pedestal, and is continued on the south side. On the

west side this line of the inscription is about 2.40 m. long, on the south side 1. 37 m.: its letters are *8l/2* to 9 cm. high. The second and third lines are below the moulding, and on the west side only: they are 2.17 m. in length, the letters 9 cm. high. All the letters are well cut and deep, and, with the exception of the last letter in the first line, they are all certain. Copy of the editor.

Published in part by M. Chabot, in *J. Asiat.,* Nov.-Dec. 1901, p. 441. See also Clermont-Ganneau, *Recueil,* VI, p. 40 f. and p. 401.

1. t 6YAOrHTOCO0OCCYNXPICTUJAY-TOYTOYCHMXiANAKOYI 2. tIAOKAA-IABACCOYBAIAKTUUNTOY 3. 9EOYMN-HC6HMAPUJNA CAIGOTOMOC + EvXoyrjros 6 Beos *crvv Xptarw avrov-erou? VX'* Hai/8(i)/cou t. IiXo/cata Baocrou, *f3aia* e'/c *Tcjv Tov* Bcou. *Mvrjcrd-fj* MapaWs, *Xidorofios.*
This inscription, though complete, and perfectly legible, is still somewhat obscure to me. The difficulties, of course, are only in the second line. Such a monument as this, standing apart from all others and in a most conspicuous place, visible from great distances, can hardly have been other than the tomb of some distinguished person. This person seems to be the Bassos mentioned in the inscription. I believe then that *(fnXoKaXiq.* is to be interpreted as a dative, used in much the same sense as *irpovoLq,* and so the equivalent of such phrases as e *vpovoias,* 8ia or *4k* O-ttoustjs, *i£* eVi/ieXeias, etc., which are common in these inscriptions. The adjective */3cuds* is frequent in metrical epitaphs in the sense of *small* or *little,* e. g. *$a.i6v (xpovov)* in *C. I. G.* 5172, *fia. i6v epyov* in *C. I. G.* 5649 h, *PaLr)v* x-*Ptv* in *C. I. G.* 5724; and, though primarily a poetical word, it is quite possible here in this sense. Lastly, the phrase *Tsv Tov ©coo,* which certainly recalls the very common *TMv Ih'uov* and the very familiar phrases in Athenian classical inscriptions like e *T&v Ttjs 0zov,* most probably means *from the moneys of God, i.e. from the treasury of the church.* I would therefore translate as follows: *Blessed be) God, with his Christ I In the) year 648, Xandikos 10th*

(i.e. April, 337 A. D.). *By the) desire of Bassos, in small fart also) from the funds) of God. May Maronas, the) stone-cutter, be remembered I*

By this I would understand that the tomb was built by Bassos or in his memory, with some assistance from the church treasury. But I know of no other example of a similar expenditure of church funds upon a tomb standing thus apart from any church building.

On the other hand, JnXoKaXi'a may be a proper name, the name of a daughter of Bassos: 4iXo#ca«a is known as the name of a city in Pontos, and tuXoKaXos is well attested as a man's name. The adjective ySaia, then, may mean a little (child),1 and c *rcov-TovSeov*, supplying *ixXeKTtov* or some such word, *one of God's elect*. If so, this line might be translated thus: *Philokalia, daughter) of Bassos, one of God's children is buried here)*, etc.

Phrases such as *p.vr)rdr) 6 Sctva, Xi#oro'/Aos* occur not infrequently in Syrian inscriptions: I found it, for example, in several inscriptions from the neighborhood of Kefr Nabu:2 compare also Clermont-Ganneau, *Recueil*, vi, p. 40 f.

On Bassos see above, No. 278, and on Maronas, Part IV, p. 51 f.

336 a. Zebed. Church, 512 A.D. On the lintel of the west portal of the church in the western part of the ruins. See Part II, p. 305. The inscription was found by Professor Sachau and published by him in the *Monatsberichte der Berl. Akademie*, 1881, p. 169 ff. See also *Zeitschr. d. Deutschen Morgenldnd. Gesellsch.,xxxv'*, pp. 345-352, and Sachau, *Reisein Syrien*, etc., p. 125 f. Lidzbarski: *Handbuch der nordsem. Epigraphik* 11, Taf. xliii, 10. I understand that the lintel has been carried to Aleppo. Professor Sachau describes the lintel as broken in three pieces, which together measure 3.04 m. in length, and are 66 cm. in height. In the center is a large disk in relief, the diameter of which is nearly as great as the height of the whole stone. The lintel is

'See *atriraxrlrj f3aujs* (AxKt'as) *avo: lovely from her infancy*, in *C. J. G.* 6268.

2 See also the notes on No. 314 above. ornamented with four mouldings, returned at each side, and reaching to a little above the center. Above and at each side of the mouldings is a broad, plain border. On the upper border at the left of the disk and on the left side-border is an inscription in Syriac. The main part of the Greek inscription is on the upper border at the right of the disk, and on the right side-border; but in the uppermost fascia of the mouldings, on both sides of the disk, is a single line of Greek letters. In the second fascia from the bottom is an Arabic inscription. This is the now famous "trilinguis zebedea."

The following is the text of the Greek inscription as given by Professor Sachau in the *Z. M. G.*, p. 350: ETOYC TKUJ W TOTTIOY AK E9EMAEOGI TU) MAPTYPION TOY AHOY CEPrIOY ETTI TOY TTEP
IWANNOY KAI ANNEOC POYKEOY (?) KAI CEPHC TP (or TTP)
EKTICYN CYMEUUN AMPAA HAIA AEOMTIC CATOPNINOC AZIZOC AZIZOC GEPHOY KAI AZIZOC MAPABAP KAOY (or MAPA BAPKA AI)

In the drawing which faces p. 190 of the *Monatsberichte*, I.e., the verb in the first line appears to be 6GMAOei, the name after ANNOC appears as BOYK60Y, the letters after AOMTIC are APXTT0C, though the TT may involve one or more other letters in ligature. The completion of 7rep(iooWoS), at the end of the second line, is made certain by the Syriac inscription: both the Syriac and the Arabic inscriptions contain the name *Mara*, mentioned in the last line of the Greek.

Dr. R. Neubauer, in a foot-note to p. 126 of Professor Sachau's *Reise*, reads this inscription as follows: *etous y«(x) ///(vos) Top)Triov Sk idep.eitodr) To fiapTvptov Tov dyiov Xepyiov ivi Tov irep(ioo'evTov)*
'iwdvvov tov Kal avvlo; Bovkcov 2,epyioiro(iT)ov.
"ektlo-cv 2,vp.eav Afipda 'HXia. *AecWis dpwv) 7rdX(e)crj?.*
SaTopiai'OS Afifo?, afifo? Xepyiov, Afifos Mdpa BdpKa vo(C).

I wish, however, to suggest a somewhat different reading for the last three lines, namely: *'Icodvvov Kal "Avveoq Fovkcov (or Bovkcov) /ecu Scpyis, irpeo-(3vTepoi),*
iKTiaav) avv %vp.ewv 1, A/xpaa, '*HXict-Aco(v)t; dpx(l)(dp)(vo);*
SaTopvlvos Afi.£os, Afi£os (%)pyiov Kal Afi£os Mapa BapKa, Zi(aKovoC).
Tn the) year 823, on the) 24-th of the) month Gorpiaios, this chapel of the holy Sergios was founded under the visiting presbyter Ioannes; and Anncos, son) of Boukcos, and Sergis, presbyters, built it) together zvith Symeon, Amraas and) Elias: also) Leontis, chief-of-virgins: also) Satorninos Azisos, Azizos son) of Sergios, and Azizos son) of Mara Barka, deacons. (September, 512 A.D.)

Perhaps, however, we should read after *Trpeo-/3vTepoL)* or *irpeofivTdpav)* as follows: *XaTopvlvos Af«.£os, Afi£os (S)ep-ytou Kal Afi£os Mapa BapKa, oi Ck T(o)v 'S.vp.ewv, 'Ap.paa,* '*HXt'a, Aeo(v)tis dpx(i)irdp)0(po)i: Satominos A 2120s*, etc., *of the tribe of Symeon, Amraas), E/ia(s), (a/so) Lcontis, chief-of-virgins.* See the facsimile published by Professor Sachau in the *MonatsbericJitc*. A *taTopvtlvos 'Afe% ov* is mentioned in an inscription from "Yedoudeh," published by M. Fossey in *B. C. H.*, xxi, p. 45, No. 24.

337. Zebed. Panel Of A Balustrade. On the border of a panel of the balustrade in the basilica described in Part II, p. 301 ff. See also Part IV, p. 47 ff.

This panel is at the southeast corner of the balustrade and faces southward. It is one meter long, and about 92 cm. in height, 18 cm. in thickness. The first part of the inscription is on the top border, and measures 95 cm. in length, including the cross: the letters are 3 to 4/2 cm. high. The second part is on the left border of the panel, near the top. It measures 28 cm. in length, and the letters are 3 cm. high. Its first, second, fourth and sixth letters are upright, while the third and fifth are turned on their sides, towards the right, so that they face downward. The third part is on the right border: it is 24 cm. long, and its letters 4 to y2 cm. high. The first two letters face downward, while the last two are upright. The letters are incised, rather rudely and irregularly. Copy of the editor.

For an interpretation of this t
CVMEWNOVANTILUXOV   --Zvpeovov
'vTihxov Xepyis.

M(a/3i'as) v(le), K(v/3i)e.

Panel, bearing Inscr. 337.

inscription see the commentary to No. 314. Three other panels in this balustrade bear inscriptions: the other inscriptions are in Syriac, however, one written in Syriac letters and two in Greek letters: see Part IV, I.e. *Of Symeon, son) of Antiockos. O*

Sergis J O Son of Mary, Lord!

338. Kasr Zebed. Fort, 326 A.d. On a lintel of basalt, found on the ground in the northern part of the ruins of what appears to have been a kind of fort. Both this and No. 339 were evidently lintels of gateways in the north wall of the courtyard mentioned in No. 340. See Part II, p. 300.

The lintel was 1.85 m. long, and 0.42 wide: it is broken at the right end. The inscription is complete. It is incised in a dove-tail plate in relief, which, without the dove-tails, measures 68 by 32 cm. At each side of the plate is a disk in relief, 27 cm. in diameter, consisting of a wreath, from which two ends of a ribbon hang down, and within which are two broad TOYCHAXYTT *Zotj. 'etovs vx', (Mvb?)* ,Tirep lines crossing diagonally. The words *Zotj,* and *'Tyia* are in the dove-tails. The letters of the inscription are 7 cm. high. Copy of the editor.

Both the inscription and the disks are pagan in general character. Compare No. 114. *'Avavecocrev* is for *aveveaxrev.* 339. Kasr Zebed. Same Fort, 326 A.d. On a broken lintel, similar to that of No. 338, and found on the ground 55 paces farther west. The lintel is broken at both ends; but the inscription is com *AyaOrf* Tvtj-*Zorj- 'Tyia.*

BcXXtov *AifSiavov, Tov rj-X (erovs),* /xt7j/(6s) *'Tirep(/3epe-TaLov)* 8'.

plete. The inscription is in a dovetail plate, which is in relief. Without the dove-tails the plate measures 85 cm. in length and 25 in width. At each side of the plate is a disk, 24 cm. in diameter, and similar to those described under No. 338. The letters are incised, and are 52

to 8 cm. high. Copy of the editor.

This lintel, like the foregoing, has nothing about it which is not pagan in character.

Good Fortune.' Life-' Health! (This is the work) of Bellichos, (son) of Libianos, in the 638th (year), (the) jth of (the) month Hyperberetaios. (October, 326 A.D.) 340. Kasr Zebed. Portal Of The Same Fort now broken in two pieces, lying about 20 feet east of a large pile of ruins. The larger piece lay upside down. The face of the lintel was perfectly plain except for the letters. These are incised, finely cut and regular, and about 9 cm. high. The u of zSiW, in the second line, has the form of two small letters o close together. The 5, of the' word e£ is cut in double lines, so that it has the appearance of being in relief. A few of the letters are joined together in ligatures. Copy of the editor. On a large lintel of basalt,

Inscription 340.

The word *iirevat* is for *iitaxvv, dveyipev* for *dvrjyeipev.* In the second line the author has written the article again, as if he intended to write another participle, instead of an indicative. The final v of *opio(v)* seems to have been omitted through carelessness, perhaps on account of the form To which precedes it.

This is doubtless the lintel of the fort, on the west side of the courtyard mentioned in the inscription. Its date is doubtless the same as that of Nos. 338 and 339, i.e. 326 A.d. It belongs then to the year after the "Peace of the Church" was proclaimed by Constantine. And this, perhaps, accounts for the fact that the formula Efs 0eo9 was prefixed to an inscription which otherwise seems wholly pagan in character.

341. Kasr Zebed. On a voussoir of an arch, lying about 75 yards east of a large pile of ruins. The stone is 46 cm. high: its face is 35 cm. broad at the top and 28 at the bottom. It seemed to belong next to the key-stone, which was found near by, and which was ornamented in some way, I think with a cross in a disk. The face of the present block is perfectly plain, except for the letters: these are incised, and neither well nor regularly

cut. The lines vary from 23 to *2%l/2* cm. in length, the letters from 6 to *8l/* cm. in height. Copy of the editor. EAtuK/CY e interpretation of this inscription is most uncertain; but I am in

M A P H N clined to read as follows: "EScuK(as) *evp.dp-qv tvap.4vjj; Thou hast given re* E Y 5 A *lief to her who prayed* (or *made a vow).* If this is correct, then *evp.dp7v* is

M E N H for *evp.dpei.av,* and the whole is an acknowledgment to the deity or to some saint, most probably to the Virgin Mary, on the part of some woman, that her prayers had been answered, her vow having been paid. On the other hand 6Sw/c(as) may be without an object, *o-v* at the end of the first line may be correct, and HAPHN may be for *Mapta.* Or the verb may be in the third person, and followed by a proper name, *evijapeviq* then being nominative. In this case we should read: *Eumaren* (or *Eumare f) gave this) in fulfillment of her vow.* 342. BA'ALBEK. Tower, 635 A.d. On a stone, now in the garden of the British School for Girls. The stone measures about 3 feet by 2, and is perfectly plain except for the inscription. It is said to have been found in 1895, in the north wall of the city.1 Copy of the editor.

Published, with notes by the Bishop of Salisbury, by M. Michel M. Alouf, in his *History of Baalbek,* 6th ed., Eng. Translation, 1898, p. 121 f. Clermont-Ganneau, *Etudes d'Archcologie Orientate,* II, 1897, P-J47Uspensky, *A. M. S.,* p. 5.

The letters ri are certainly an abbreviation 2 M Usoensky has Dro-K T 1 A n ¥ P *Kria-fia* irtfp(you) *ri,v ®(e)a, Dreviauon.* Ivi. uspensicy nas pro cYNGuriMA w *x sy* / posed yi(ferai). I he meaning of the KEAwNuN L, /v v 1- (erov9).

next word, *MaKeSaivcjv,* is not clear to I N A 9 T Z M A me: if it denotes the era, i.e. the Se-*The) building of (this) tower (took place) with the help* 1-1 i_i. ii. 1 i-.i 1 *of) Godin the year 047 of(the) Macedonians* (?), *indiction o.* leucid era, then the order of the words J' 'y +' J v w y . 1 U U 4. (635-636 A.D.) is most singular. However, the date itself can hardly be in doubt, or the nature of the building to which this inscription belonged. 343. BA'ALBEK. On a column recently dug up in the front garden of the Hotel Palmyra. The letters are rude, but clear.

Copy of the editor. AOC KXauSios *'Avdlcavos Mdyvov.*

Published by M. Alouf, *History of Baalbek,* p. 123. A N 6 I *Klaudios (son?) ofAnthion* a) N oc MATNOY

The Bishop of Salisbury3 suggests that uiVlfriv *Magnos.*

Klaudios was more probably a slave of "Anthion," and that the latter name is perhaps a mere barbarism for *'Apfuov.* 344. BA'ALBEK. Pedestal (for a statue?). On a hexagonal pedestal, apparently of marble, now serving as a part of a jamb in the doorway of a chamber in the Hotel Palmyra. In each face of the pedestal a bevelled plate is sunk, leaving a border about 5 cm. broad. The upper line of the bevel is *22l/2* cm. in length, the lower is 18 cm.: the die of the pedestal is 24 cm. high. The letters are about 2 cm. high, but well made and clear. The first line of the inscription, on the second, third and fifth faces, is on the bevel moulding: the rest of the inscription in each case is within the plate. On the fifth face are three or four letters, about twice the size of the others. One of these, S, M. Alouf found on the left border about opposite the middle of the die: I myself did not notice this letter. On the opposite side of the border is a T, and in the-lower right corner of the die an O. Half-way between the T and the O, half on the border and half on the bevel, there seems to be another o: I am not sure, however, whether this is a letter. I do not know the meaning of these letters, and I doubt if they have any connection with the inscription. Copied by the editor.

Published by M. Clermont-Ganneau, in *R. Arch.* 1884, IV, p. 278, No. 41; *Recueil,* I, p. 21, No. 41. Alouf, *History of Baalbek,* p. 123 ff.

1 M. Alouf, I.e. 2 This is shown by a cross-stroke through the I: the same cross-stroke is made in the *p* of *wvp(yov),* and in the S of 1V8. 3 Alouf,

History of Baalbek, I.e. 'Epdvio-cs *£K0eZv' fJ.4v* Ckci, »cal a/Sc (i.e. *avel).* fl KaX-s 17/Aepas eV7reo-ajv e£? *fj.eLpa.KLov* avevf-pa(v)Tos, airr)OTLa de(i)a Kevet.

Face i, in M. Alouf's publication, is as follows: XPONICCA9? MN? KIN A B. The Bishop of Salisbury has interpreted this as follows: *ixp6vi.res iXde/xev, iKtLva.* (for eWi/17) 8' 17, to which he has next joined Face 5: aXon'a xdXeiav *Keivel* In the third line on Face 3, M. Alouf gives NYP? Antoc, which is doubtless correct. In the first line of Face 5, I read the third letter from the end as P or 4: M. Alouf gives the last word in this line as XOA6IAN, which the Bishop of Salisbury considered to be for x0"

The meaning of this inscription is somewhat obscure as well as obscene; but I think it may be translated as follows: *Thou didst delay to come: stay there and farewell ave)! O thou who one fine day didst fall in with a boy, to thy sorrow, insatiate desire stirs the) bile!*

Perhaps this pedestal was made for a scurrilous caricature of an emperor or some other dignitary, who, for personal reasons, had disappointed the populace by not appearing in some expected pageant.

345. BA'ALBEK. On the base of a small and much-mutilated female bust, in the Hotel Palmyra. Copied by the editor. 6PWHCKAIAW7 Published by M. Clermont-Ganneau, in *R. Archeol.* 1884, IV, p. 278, No. 42: 7TTA IATPC6TTO I HC see aiso h;s *Recueil,* I, p. 21, No. 42. Alouf, *History of Baalbek,* Eng. translation, p. 123.

In the second line, M. Alouf gives TTA-IATOC, which is doubtless correct. 'Ep/As *Kal* Aju.7rX.iaT(o)s *eTroLr-fcrav).*

Hermes and Ampliatos made this statue).

346. Tell Nebi Mindo. Milestone (?), About 300 A.d. A base and part of a column was found in a field a short distance from Tell Nebi Mindo, on the east side of the road to Horns. The column is about a foot in diameter and what is left of it, together with the base, about 5 feet in height. The letters were badly carved,

and the surface of the stone has been much damaged. The natives said that the inscription had been copied, about a year before, by a foreigner, who had also made a squeeze. As our company was anxious to press on, I copied, for identification, the first two, the fourth, and the eleventh and twelfth lines. The whole inscription has been published by MM. Perdrizet and Fossey, from a copy made in 1896, in *B. C. H.,* Vol. xxi (1897), p. 6/f.: the text which follows is that given by these gentlemen.

Imp. Caes. Gaio Aurelio Valerio Diocletiano Invicto Aug. et Imp. Caes. Marco Aurelio Valerio Maximiano P. F. Invicto Aug. et Flavio Valerio Co(n)stantio et I Galerio Vale)rio Maximiano nobb. Caess.

To the emperor, Caesar, Gains Anrelius Valerius Diocletianus,the Unconquered, Augustus, and to the etnperor, Caesar, Marcus Anrelius Valerius Maximianus, the Devout, the Fortunate, the Unconquered, Augustus, and to Flavins Valerius Constantius, and to Galerius Valerius Maximianus, most noble Caesars.

The date of the inscription falls between 292 and 304 A.d. 347. Tell Nebi Mindo. Stele(?), 198 A.d.(?). On a fragment like the bottom of a stele or the pedestal of a statue, in the southwest side of the causeway, where the road to the hill, on which the modern village is built, crosses the stream-bed. At the bottom of the stone is a base-moulding, 28 cm. high, above which is a portion of a shaft or die, 33 cm. high, but broken at the top. The left end of the base-moulding has been broken off at the left corner of the shaft, the remaining portion being 63 cm. broad at the bottom. The stone is 30 cm. thick. The letters are rude and almost illegible.

Published by MM. Perdrizet and Fossey, in *B. C. H.* xxi, p. 67, No. 4, whose reading is as follows:

My own copy gives at the end of the third line 91, and in the 1.-A A O Y t fourth KM--lt; but I believe that the other reading is more correct.

2.-YA-AKAP6 3. XHN-N69H _AAOY4--_ YA-A *Kclt)' evxw .£vSr,K»,* too if (erous): 4" ' *in fulfillment of a vow set up this stele), in the year) 510. (198-199 A. D.?)*

There may have been one more figure in the date, in the units place, in which case the date might be as late as 208 A.d. 348. Tell Nebi Mindo. Stele. On a stone, evidently a fragment of a stele, in the southwest side of the causeway, about 4 feet east of the foregoing. The fragment, which seemed to be of whitish limestone, was 1.12 m. in length, 54 cm. in width, and 30 in thickness. The letters are well formed: those of the first two lines are 4 cm., the rest 4 cm. high. The third line, ¥o/3ios Kta.., is 50 cm. below the second. Copy of the editor.

Published by Conder in *P. E. F,* 1881, p. 168.

AYANAIOY

IA

In the year , //A of the month Audynaios. Wealthy is this tomb, since it hath received the pure body of Ammia, whom her country praises, a priestess of Prudence. (She was aged) 31 years.

A little farther along, towards the mill, in the opposite side of the same causeway, is another inscribed fragment which contains a few letters; but these seemed so illegible that I did not even try to decipher them.

Liiinuios(?),(sou)ofPhilippics (?), *physician ofAugustus* fo mutilated thev ire well (i. e. *of the emperor): Flavins Sakerdos, of Emisa, (set up Ul* DCCn mulllalea tneY are well *this statue of) his friend.* formed and clear. Copy of the editor.

Published by MM. Perdrizet and Fossey, in *B. C. II.* XXI, 1897, p. 66 f. Dussaud, in *R. Arch.* 1897, XXX, p. 355. Oppenheim and Lucas, in *Byz. Zeitschr.* 1905, p. 2o, No. 5.

For the first name Dr. Lucas proposed Auc*iwiov*: or possibly the name was *'Icodwrjv.* P.J*iilippikos* is perhaps a cognomen of this same person, not the father's name. Dr. Lucas translates *larpov* Se/Slao-roO): "kaiserlichen (?) Arzt." 350. Hama. Stele, in the narrow street called Sherkiyeh *(East Street)* by the natives, in the eastern part of the city. The + GpoiA stone had been lying in the street before a CYAOIT ruined

house. When I saw it, it had been HCAC TTOINHC built into a low wall on the north side of the street, near a street corner. It had been Qeotokx turned face inwards, doubtless on account of /TCONA the cross; but some of the people turned it rlWNK over for me to see. The stone was 1.38 m OCMAy + *Boundaries inviolable* (i.e. *boundaries of the sanctuary) of Our Lady, the Mother-of-God, and of the holy Kosmas and Damianos, bestowed by* AAMIA long, 31 cm. wide and 12 cm. thick. At NtfAG) the top was a large cross in relief, the hori-PC© zontal arm of which extended the full width of the stone. The stele was broken at the top, through the middle of the upper arm of the cross, and also at the bottom, through the twelfth line of the inscription. The letters are 7 to 8 cm. high, and of the forms common in the sixth century: they are well preserved, and, except in the last line, certain. Copy of the editor.

Published by M. Uspensky, *A. M. S.,* p. 55.

350 a. MA'ARRIT In-nu'man. On two fragments of a lintel or an architrave, built into the wall of the mosque, opposite to the entrance. The letters are large and well formed. My copy was not made directly from the stones, because there were many people in the court and about the mosque, and as the people in this town had shown themselves unusually fanatical it seemed unwise, when the fragments appeared to be of little importance, to give offense by writing down letters from the wall of the mosque. I therefore committed the letters to memory and wrote them down when outside. My copy, therefore, may not be accurate. FRAGMENT A. FRAGMENT B. NNAAN (or M or Nl) O OCKAI (or H)

The first of these fragments suggests the name re 1WS10 s, *Gennadios:* the second is obviously os *Kox.* 350 b. Khan Sebil. On a fragment, perhaps of a lintel, now built into the wall of a ruined modern house. The whole fragment measures 43 by 31 cm. The three AQ H lines of letters measure *gl/2, 8l/2* and 7 cm. respectively. Copy of the editor, A
I o I r

The first line suggests 'Aya#V) Ti?,- the second Atoye?. AIOIAY" 351. Isriyeh. Temple. On the north side of the temple, on the base of the third pilaster from the northeast corner. The hollow moulding carried across the face of the lowest member of the pilaster-base runs between the two lines of the inscription. See Part II, p. 76 f.

The letters are rudely but deeply cut. At the beginning of the first line is a space of *lift* cm. The three letters which follow occupy *l/2* cm. After these is a space, 41 cm. long, where no letters could be read. The next four letters of the drawing measure 30 cm. in length, and extend to the break in the stone. The second line measures 62 cm. to the beginning of the cross, which is immediately below the N of the line above. The cross and the two letters following measure 30 cm. in length, and are followed by a space of 17 cm. The N is 8 cm. high. Copy of the editor.

On the base of the next pilaster towards the west are IOP Nono... ,,.,. ,,,,

"j 'Q Arabic graffiti, and on the walls of the temple, on the west and south sides, near the ground, are other graffiti, some of which are very fresh. Some of these resemble TT or N or 3, and may perhaps be masons' marks, made by the original builders. But I am inclined to believe that these resemblances are purely accidental. And indeed I am not sure that the inscription given above is Greek after all. The rudeness of the letters indicates that they were not placed there by the builders of this over-handsome temple. On the other hand, the depth to which these letters were cut indicates that they are more than mere graffiti. The cross in the second line would seem to prove that this inscription was cut here by some Christian, a century or more after the temple was built. Doubtless this temple was used by the Christians, perhaps as a church. For the inner face of the walls is highly finished, and at the west end of the building are clear traces of Christian painting, consisting of crosses inscribed within circles, in deep red.

Isriyeh has no ancient building, except.the temple, of which even a small

portion remains standing. This temple, according to the modern natives, was used as a castle, doubtless by Mohammedans. Northeast of the temple are traces of a wall, which seems to have been part of a rectangular fortification. At one place enough of the wall remains to show its character: it was a strong wall, built of fine blocks of white limestone. Farther towards the northeast are traces of a wall like a city wall, within which are to be found here and there single fragments of building-stones, drums of columns, etc. In one place there is a small pile of such fragments. I believe that there was a small and not very important city here, which flourished about the time of Diocletian: about this time the temple was built, as Mr. Butler tells me. Doubtless on this little eminence by these wells in the desert there was an ancient shrine, and there, under the Roman empire, a handsome temple was erected. See Oestrup's description of the place, in his *Historisktopografiske Bidrag til Kendskabet til den syriske Oerken*, p. 79 ff. *Memoires de lAcad. Royale des Sciences et des Lettres de Danemark*, Copenhague, 1895.) 352. Palmyra, Temple. On the face of a bracket, on a column in the eastern portico of the "Temple of the Sun," near the northeast corner: the Greek part of a much mutilated bilingual inscription. The bracket is now about three feet above the roof of a modern dwelling. The body of the inscription is 34 cm. long, the letters occupying about the space of 1 cm. each. But the first line, being on a moulding above the rest, is somewhat longer than these: before the six extant letters in this line is a space of about 13, after these letters a space of about 32 cm.: the height of the fascia, on which the first line is carved, is 1.8 cm.: the height of the face of the bracket, below the mouldings, is 16 cm. The Palmyrene text is below the Greek: it is published by Dr. Littmann in Part IV, p. 59 f. The present text is from a copy by the editor.
! NUUNHHO 2. OXXAICOYAPC TTAAY-
HT6KAITOIC96 3. AIAONTAilAlUUNe!C
P0NCTTONA09C ( ) 4. AlOYMjATHPINX-
PYCASГAHNAPIWNPNKAITO ( ) 5.-AAK-

TECCAPAXPYCATAHPKKAITT( ) 6. AI-7K
C AAANIONICTHNT--AC( ) 7. AC-
NHNHГOPAMCNAAPГYPJOYAI--AN 8.-CK
ANK6NTOYCBTTTMHNOC
A clue to the restoration of at least the first two lines is furnished by the Palmyrene text, which is translated by Dr. Littmann as follows: *This is the portrait of Mokimii, the son of 'Ogailii, son of Phasdel, son of Taimai, who is called Hokkaishu, of the family ofZ()...., which was set up to him by the community* (?) *of all the Palmy renes at their own expense, because* (?) *he offered* (?) *to the house of their gods*

It seems evident from the accusative of the participle at the beginning of line 3 that the present inscription was composed in the familiar form: *the city, etc. set up) such an one* (i.e. his portrait), *who, etc.,* the verb *O.v4o-tj)o-zv* being usually omitted. Assuming then that about thirteen letters have been lost from the beginning of the first line, and thirty-two letters from the end, and employing the information given in the Palmyrene text, I would read the Greek as follows: 1. *Tav HaXfivpr) vcov r) (7r)dXis Mo/cei/AOi/ Tov OyaiXov Tov aaarjXov* 2. *Tov Oattrou, ape Vow* (t) *a aur re Kai Toi? #eois,* 3. *SiSoWa ef 18lwv eis to lepbv nrov8(eia) K* 4. *al (d)vfiiaTT)pi(a) xpvera e(i'), brjuapiaiv pv, Kai To* 5. — *XX Tecrcrapa xpvera erSrjpK, Kai ir* 6. *at K (T— aXXviov eis T-qv T ao* 7. *Xe vrv r/yopa(o-)p,(e)va apyvpiov Si av, ti/4* 8. *rf; #cal eva/storia(s) eve/cey, erovs /3ttt, p,rjvb The city ofthe Palmyrencs (set up this portrait of) Mokimos, son of Ogailos, son of Phasaelos, son ofHokkaisos, who was pleasing unto her and to the gods; for he gave, at his own expense, unto the temple (vessels) for libation and censers of gold, 13 (in number, valued at) 130 denarii, and bought of silver , for sake of honor and gratitude, in (the) year 382, in (the) month (70-71 A.D.)*

At least the hundreds figure in the date is certain, and this is important because it shows that the "Temple of the Sun" is at least as old as the first century of our era. See also Dr. Littmann's commentary in Part IV.
353. Palmyra, Altar, 178 A.d. On a little

altar now set at the west end of a modern grave in the southern part of the Mohammedan cemetery. The face of the altar on which the inscription is carved measures 26 cm. in height by 244 in breadth. The letters are 2 cm. high, and most of them are still clear. Copy of the editor, and a squeeze.

Published by Waddington, No. 2572. Clermont-Ganneau, *Recueil VI*, p. 31 f.; see also v, p. 1 77 £T. and p. 196.

V. 1.: At the beginning Waddington read All: the squeeze, however, shows clearly that there was but one iota. The two letters following appear to be both Y, and I believe they are so through the fault of the stone-cutter. In the third line Waddington read IOYAIOCC-YIC. In the sixth line Waddington gives IAIBAC: the first of these letters might possibly be a T, the second might be a A, but I think not a A, the third might well be a 9 or an O or C, the last might be any of the round letters.

The writer of this inscription evidently had very little idea of Greek syntax, or else the stone-cutter was extremely careless. 'Jnekevdepov has been carved for *aireke68epo;*, perhaps by assimilation to Taiov. A sigma, which was perhaps intended for *a-nekevOtpos*, has been added after *TaLov*, where it is obviously out of place. In line 6, Iaei/8a? and vios are in the nominative, instead of the genitive case. As to the name *laeibas*, see M. Clermont-Ganneau's notes: compare also an inscription published by MM. Dussaud and Macler, *Voyage au Safd*, p. 191, No. 70. M. Clermont-Ganneau renders the third and fourth lines as follows: *dv&rjKt ll(ov/3Xtos)* 'Iov'Xios *ve/jw? d7reev#epo(s) Vaiov* EiouXiov *Bdacrov.* 354. Palmyra, Grand Colonnade. On a single drum of a column standing alone on the north side of the grand colonnade, about 200 yards east 6IC9OCZOH 0f the temple at the west end of the colonnade. The drum is about 6

Els ©eo'?. *Zojj* feet high above the sand. The inscription, which is 3 feet above the sand, appears to be merely a graffito, roughly picked out with a metal *There is but)* .

one God Life' Point some sort, but the letters are well formed. The inscription measures 45 by 5 cm. Copy of the editor. It is most probable that this was written, not by a Christian, but by some Jewish traveler or resident of Palmyra. See above, p. 51 f. 355. Khan Il-abyad. On a plain block, without mouldings, lying face up on a pile of other stones, within the ruins of a Roman camp on the present road from Damascus to Palmyra, about 15 miles southwest of Karyaten: it is close inside the inner part of the double wall about the enclosure, on the northwest side and immediately west of that portion of this wall which is still standing. The stone itself is of white limestone, now quite yellowish on the surface, and measures 77 by 54*1/2* by 35 cm. The letters are 2.8 cm. high, well made, but not very regular or well aligned. I made no copy from the stone, but made a squeeze from which very good casts have been taken. The accompanying cut is from a photograph, taken by Mr. H. M. Huxley in 1900—1901.

Published in *C. I. L.* Ill, No. 6660, from a squeeze made by Professor Euting in 1883 and deciphered by M. Dressel. Also by Professor Buecheler in *Carmina Latina Epigraphica*, I, No. 296. By Messrs. Kalinka, Kubitschek and Heberdey, from a copy or squeeze made by Dr. Alois Musil in 1895, in the *Jahreshefte des Oesterreich. Arch. Inst.* Ill (1900), *Beiblatt*, p. 34 f. Also in *C. I. L.* Ill, No. 14161. An excellent drawing is published in the *Jahresheft d. Oesterreich. Arch. Inst.*, l.e.

In presenting the text of this inscription I have followed Professor Kalinka and his associates, whose restorations seem to me to be confirmed by my cast, except in those instances expressly mentioned below. I have, however,' adopted Professor Buecheler's restoration of the beginning of the first and third lines, which were rejected by Kalinka on the ground that they comprise more letters than the space seems to allow. But in the first place, since the upper left-hand corner of the stone has been broken off, and since the letters are not regular either in size or in

alignment, it is not possible to determine the number of letters at the beginning of the first lines with certainty. In the second place, the number of letters supplied by Buecheler in the first and third lines corresponds to the number of letters in similar parts of the other lines. For in the first six lines the letters *a, x, q, i* before *d,* r and_/are approximately in a perpendicular line: before these letters, in the lines as given below, there are thirteen, thirteen, thirteen, eleven, fifteen and twelve letters respectively. Moreover,

Buecheler's restorations in these two cases seem to supply satisfactory sense, text then is as follows:

Inscription 355.

The 9. Hospes, unde laetus itineris perage cursum, 10. et boni potitus actus cum laude caneto 11. magnanimi iudicis pace belloque nitentis, 12. quem praecor superos altiori gradu subnixum 13. talia dominis uel ardua condere casj-tra, 14. et natis gaudere decorantibus facta parentis.

In line 3 the reading *grauius turn,* proposed by Buecheler, is absolutely irreconcilable with the traces of letters in the cast: *gravius malum,* proposed by Mommsen, is possible, but I believe with Kalinka that there are distinct traces of double /. In line 5, the letters *bis* seem to me very doubtful, in view of the traces in the cast: *limitis huius,* suggested by Buecheler, is impossible: *limitis urbiumque,* proposed by Bormann, is perhaps possible, but gives no satisfactory sense: moreover, the letters *mu* seem to me certain. Line 6, *fide* seems also certain: *cultorum* agrees perfectly with the traces in the cast. Line 7, *caelestibus* agrees perfectly with the cast, and the reading which Kalinka bracketed, seems to me certain: *campos etsataparasti*and *campos hos itaparasti,* proposed by Mommsen and Buecheler, are impossible. Line 8, *Bacchique* agrees perfectly with the cast. Line 10, *potitus,* except the *s,* and *caneto* are, in my 4 opinion, sure. Line 11, *iudicis* alone fits the space and the traces of letters: *-ace belloque nitentis* I consider certain. In line 12 I feel sure only of *altior* and *subnixum,* and in line 13 only of

/ ardua c ere; but *castra* suits the traces of letters at the end of line 13 perfectly. Line 14, the ending *-tibus,* in *decorantibus,* is certain.

Kalinka, feeling that some verb is needed to govern the *campum* of the first line, suggests that possibly a preceding line has been lost. I believe, on the contrary, that the stone is complete, except for the upper left-hand corner, and I see no reason why *campum* and *castrum* should not be regarded as double accusatives with *reddidisti.* In lines 5 and 6 it seems to me that, if the present reading is correct, *urbis* must limit *custns,* and that *muro* must be regarded as parallel with *dominorum fide,* both being ablatives with *fortissimae:* in that case, *limitis,* unless it is considered an adjective form agreeing with *urbis,* is a genitive limiting *urbis.* I would therefore translate as follows:

"A plain that is dry indeed, and hateful enough to wayfarers, on account of its long wastes and its chances of death close at hand, for those whose lot is hunger, than which there is no graver ill,1 thou hast made, my lord, a camp, adorned with greatest splendor, O Silvinus, warden of a city of the high-road, most strong in its wall and in the protection of our masters revered in all the world: and thou hast contrived that it abound in water celestial, so that it may bear the yoke of Ceres and of Bacchus. Wherefore, O guest, with joy pursue thy way, and for benefit received sing with praise the doings of this great-hearted judge, who shines in peace and in war. I pray the gods above that he, taking a step still higher, may continue to found for xOr perhaps, where no graver ill besets. our masters such camps, arduous though they be, and that he may rejoice in children who add honor to their father s deeds."

On either side of the inscription is carved +, and below, on the left A, on the right u. Kalinka believes these symbols to be a later addition to the monument, and certainly, as he says, the character of the verses is wholly pagan, and such a document could hardly have been composed in Latin, in this locality, after the division of the empire. Most probably the monument belongs to the third or fourth century after Christ. At that time the road from Damascus to Palmyra was a very important one, and there was great need to provide stations where travelers might find both water and protection, even in times of peace, from brigands and from the uncontrollable Bedawin. That this plain is "dry indeed and hateful enough to wayfarers," except perhaps to those for whom it may have the fleeting charm of novelty, any one who has ever traveled this road will willingly testify. It was a good work which Silvinus and his laborers wrought, and they deserved a roseate eulogy, and the water which they provided must have had celestial properties, if they caused that arid desert to bring forth much corn or wine. Silvinus was doubtless a *dux limitis,* i.e. *commander of the border.* Such officials had also the title of *comes,* which occurs in this inscription, line 4: they also had jurisdiction as military judges over the soldiers under their command, and this fact doubtless accounts for the title *iudicis* in line 11

The vagaries of spelling, declension and of syntax may be passed over cheerfully: they are not worse than those of the Greek inscriptions in this land. As to the versification, the judgment of the editors of the *C. I. L.,* in, will doubtless satisfy most: "Carmen efficere studuit qui haec dictavit." At the same time, as Professor Kalinka has noted, there is at least this much regularity in the verse, that in the last two feet the verse accent coincides with the word accent.2
356. Dmer. Grave Stele, 166 A.D. In the southwestern part of the town, on a stone built into the left jamb of the entrance from the street to a courtyard. The stone seemed to be marble, and is upside down. The letters are 3 to 4 cm. high. Copied by Dr. Littmann and the editor.

Published by MM. Dussaud and Macler, *Voyage au Safd,* p. 209, No. 103.
MM. Dussaud and Macler read in the third line rauros Xcxoukov, which is quite possible. The same editors supply in the fifth line *(e)vp6poipo;.* Dr. Littmann's copy and mine agree, and

the reading seems fairly certain. But *Tvpopoipos* seems to me impossible. I am inclined, therefore, to emend the first letter to TT. Then *wp6p.oLpos* may stand for *irvpip.oi.po;,* and may mean *fire-fated.* I believe, however, in spite of the agreement of the copies, that the word must be *irvp6p.evo* or *irvpovpevos, burnt with fire.* 1 Th. Mommsen, in *Hermes,* xxiv, p. 266 f. : "Da jeder Jurisdiction nicht auf seine Offiziere, und noch weni *dux* auch *comes* ist, etc."... "Der Dux ist nicht bloss ger auf die etwa in seinem Sprengel cantonnirenden Kaiser in seinem Sprengel der Hochstcommandirende, sondern truppen." auch der rechte Richter fur den Soldaten der Grenz-2 Concerning *caneto,* in line 10, Kalinka says: "Caneto truppen seines Sprengels; jedoch erstreckt sich seine mechanische Erweiterung von cane nach caue—caueto." *"etovs lav', ZavhiKmi y* The,ast letter is vei7 uncertain: raiosSd(£)tixov£Te£wa if Z is correct, it is curious that the «(»)»'tC-three extant inscriptions of this sort /;/ *the year 477, Zandikos* from Dmer (cf. *C. I. G.* 4518 f. = Wad. *jrd, Gaios (son) of Seleukos,* 2562 h and i) all refer to boys who died *died ("god)* at the age of seventeen. All three in *sevciteenyears.* (April, 166 A. v.) Options fall within a period of 36 years. 357. Dmer. Temple, 245 A.d. On the east wall of the temple, between the two pilasters at the right of the portal. The first part, A, is in line with the first voussoir of the arch over the portal. On either side is a stone which contains on one end the continuation of the pilaster on that side, in the center an upright palm branch, and on the other end a rude imitation of a dove-tail, as if the inscription were in an ornamental plate to which these stones supplied the dove-tail ends. The stone on the right is a corner stone of the building. The stone which bears the second part of the inscription, B, is in the next lower course, and slightly further to the right than the stone containing A. The jamb of a mud brick doorway, 37 cm. thick, has been built against this inscription within the last few years, covering about 5 letters in the center of each line. The doorway

connects two compartments in the upper story of one of the modern houses built close against the east wall of the temple. The letters thus concealed, however, are known through the earlier copies of the inscription. The photograph given in Part II, p. 402, shows the east end of the temple and the modern houses, the inscription of course being hidden by the highest of the mud-brick walls. The stone of inscription A measures 168 by 76 cm. The letters, which are rudely and irregularly cut in the black basalt, are *$l/2* to 9 cm. high. Copy of the editor.
Published in *C. I. G.* 4516. Waddington, 2562 g. Cagnat, / *G. R.,* 1093.

V.l. Line 5: de Vidua, AXAAAC; Waddington, 'AeixaXas. Line 7: de Vidua, ANONΓAOPOYKAïΓAYPONO-CX; Franz, *vdov V. 6pov1 Kal* ;Waddington, *"veov Taotpov Kal Tdapov* 'Oao-at*dov.*

Waddington believed that A6IXAAAC was the name of a god. He quotes, however, the following note by M. de Vogue on this word: "La transcription naturelle de 'AeixaXas est fcDTl, mot tres-commun qui signifie *temple.* Dans l'inscription palmyrenienne No. 16 (Waddington, No. 2585), on le trouve £crit xbrri, avec suppression de la quiescente et rendu dans le texte grec par fads." M. de Vogu6 adds: "S'il s'agit, comme je le crois, d'un nom divin, etc. " But in my opinion a«xaXas in the present text is the Aramaic noun, for which the Greek word fads was an imperfect substitute. For I believe that signifies a building erected by, or for the use of, a religious association or brotherhood.

The name Aieos is the Arabic *Hani,* Safaitic Taw/oos or *Tavpos* is the Arabic *Gaur* or *Gahttr.* Oao-ixatfos is the Greek equivalent of the Nabataean rCCI: see, however, Dussaud et Macler, *Voyage au Safd,* p. 155, No. 20.
358. Dmer. Lintel of the western portal of the same temple. The whole lintel is about 18 feet long, or about the size of the lintel of the temple of Zeus at Kanawat. The letters are well formed and deep, but not perfectly aligned: they are 4 to 5 cm. high. Copy of the editor.

Published by Briinnow in *M. P. V.* 1899, 5, p. 91. See Clermont-Ganneau,

Recneil, IV, p. 122, No. 59. Cagnat, /. G. R. Ill, No. 1094. Dittenberger, *O. G. I. S.* No. 628.

In the first line Professor Briinnow read, after TOPWN the letters C--AOC: Dittenberger restored 2TaTiXtos, from SranXtou *"Aiavov* mentioned in an inscription from Der'at, dated between 260 and 268 A.d.1 1. YTT6PCWT-IACTWNKYPIW ATOPUUN CANNIANOC-TPATWPOTAPXOY 2. 6IAHCOYOKONT!--Ne6ACHNOCneCUJA---:UJTOTTIC-KTWNIAIWNKAT6YXHNAYTOY 3. --YC-UUOY/ KAITKNUUN 1. *'Tirep aonr)p* ias *Tov Kvpuay AvTOKpa.T6pov,* Mapo?s *'Avvt.av6s, rrpdrcop indp-ov,* 2. 1X175 *Ovokovtlcdv,* QeXcrefds, eVeo-(Kc) ua-tr (e) To emo"tvxioj' Ck *T5v l&Ccav* /car' *tvyyv avrov Kal* TCKPCDV. 3. etous ', /xTjfos A toou s'.

For the safety and victory of our lords and) emperors, Markos (?) Annianos, equerry of the prefect, (a soldier) of the troop of the Vocontii, from Thelsea, built the entablature at his own expense, in fulfillment of) a vow on the part) of himself and his) children, in the) year..., on the 6th of the) month Loos.

An equerry (strator) was properly one who saddled the horses of his superior officer and assisted his master to mount. Special attendants of this sort were in the train of emperors, but not of the prefects of senatorial provinces: for the latter this service was 1 *O. G. I. S.* 614. rendered by centurions or other military officers. Besides the duty of caring for the prefect's horses, moreover, these *stmtores* often had charge of certain other matters connected with the care of the horses of their troop. There were two troops of cavalry called "Ala Vocontiorum," one of which was stationed in Egypt in the second and third centuries of our era: doubtless this is the one meant. A town Thelsea is mentioned in the *Itinerarium Antonini*, as lying between Geroda, the modern Djerud, and Damascus: this is identified by Dr. H. Kiepert with the modern Khan il-Maiuliyeh.1 With regard to the date, I believe that the letters in Briinnow's copy, which both Cagnat and Dittenberger read as the date *va-'=o6*, i.e. 94-95 A.D. according to the Seleucid era,

really belong to the word eYov9. The date therefore has been lost, and it is much more probable that it was approximately the same as that of the preceding inscription, 245 A.D., and that the emperors referred to are Philip and his son. Then it is quite possible that the *Anniaiws* of this inscription is, in fact, the Statilios Ammianos of Dittenberger No. 614. 359. Dm£r. Tomb. In a cave northwest of the town, on the opposite side of the wadi. The cave contains a number of sarcophagi lying at odd angles to each other, and all nearly buried in pebbles and sand. Near the foot of one sarcophagus and at a slightly lower level, the top of a stone, which appears to be the side of another sarcophagus, is visible in the sand. On this stone the following letters are scratched: KA AA.

The natives say that there is no other writing in this or in the neighboring caves.

1 These notes are taken from Professor Dittenberger's commentary. CHAPTER V INSCRIPTIONS OF THE DJEBEL HAURAN 360. Sawara Il-kebireh. On the under side of a stone beam of the ceiling of a house. The stone is much, _, ,,,,,, _ r , ArA9HTYXH56NIACAOY Aya0T? *TvXy-Uevia.* blackened by smoke. Copy of the „«AW,,W *J rJ* POCCAOYPOY iaoupos *Zaovpov.* editor. *Good Fortune (attend us, and) hospitality! Saiiros, (son) of Saiiros.*

Dr. Littmann tells me that the name *taovpos* is probably the Safai'tic int, *Shahfir,* but that other equivalents are possible as well, such as "!?□, *Sa'iir.* 361. Sawara Il-kebireh. Church. On the lintel of the south portal of a church, known to the natives as "// *keniseh."* The letters are formed by broad, shallow lines, and were painted red. Copy of the editor.

Published by Waddington, No. 2537 c.

M. Waddington, in his commentary, speaks of a fish carved on __ a stone at the right of the door, which I did not see. Nor did I IYXE f BOH0EI see the leaves of the door, which are mentioned by M. Wadding

'if *TO)V* X(M7"7")c ton, and which he says were of stone. He found, fur-

thermore, + /8oi?'0«....

in another inscription, the Greek name of this place: "L'ancien *Jesus Christ,help(us)* . / nom de la locahte doit etre *zavapa*, dont nous avons rencontre" l'ethnique *Savapr)v6;* dans une inscription de Tharba (No. 2203, a)." 362. Ilhaiyat. Two fragments lying on the ground immediately before the ruined building which is situated a short distance southeast of the town. See Part II, p. 397 f. The inscription was enclosed originally in a dove-tail plate. A third fragment, or a separate block, containing the dove-tail at the left end, has disappeared. The two fragments which were found, however, contain the rest of the plate, and consequently the whole inscription, complete. Fragment A, which contains the first part of the inscription, is 67 cm. long, 46 high and 27 thick: fragment B is 70 cm. long, 46 high and 27 thick. The space occupied by the inscription, i.e. the space inside the plate when the stone was intact, measures 105 by 38 cm. The letters, which are in relief, are from *6l/2* to 9 cm. high (most of them are about 8 cm. high). Copy of the editor. FRAGMENT A.

I. A OMHAHC

This inscription is similar to, perhaps identical with, that published by Waddington, No. 2135, from "Deir-esch-Scha'ir." In his commentary M. Waddington relates that, according to Josephus,1 at the beginning of the revolt of the Jews, Agrippa II sent to Jerusalem to support the peace party two2 thou

At*ofirj8r); Ajaprfios,* eirapxo! /SacriXeiw? *fieydXov 'A-ypLirva, dirb* sand Cavalrymen from *0xUov* Auranitis, Batanaea and

Trachonitis, under the command of the hipparch Dareios and the strategos Philippos. From this I judge that the present inscription belongs to the period of the reign of Agrippa II, 50-100 A.d. , and is probably earlier than 66 A.d. See also below, Nos. 380, 404 and 428. The name *Dareios* occurs in Waddington, 2116, 2176 and 2227, etc.

Diomedes Dareios, eparch of King Agrippa (the) Great, erected (this building) from (the) foundations. 303. Il-haiyat. In the front wall of the building, in front of which No. 362 was found, just above the eastern pilaster of the arch and about 30 feet from the ground. Copy by the editor.

Published by Waddington, No. 2095.

There being spent for all the building-expenses from the sacred (funds) and (from the) common (fund) sixty thousand, Thaimos (son) of Manos and his sons gave three thousand denarii of the building-expenses, as an act of piety, out of their private (property).

The omissions in my copy of this inscription have been supplied from the copy of M. Waddington, who had himself lowered by ropes from the top of the wall, in order that he might be able to read the letters which can not be seen clearly from below.

After the word cf there is a design like a long leaf, occupying about the space of three letters. The word KYNOY is obviously for *Kolvov.* 1 *Bell.Jud.* 11, 17, 4.

-Or three thousand: see the edition of Niese.

On the names *Thaimos* and *Memos,* see Renan in *J. Asiat., yc,* xix, p. 8 f. and 7 f.: they appear to be the equivalents of the Arabic *Taint* and *Ma'u.* 364. Il-haiyat. the eastern window. The inscription is in a dove-tail plate formed by a moulding in relief. See Part II, p. 398, fig. 143. The space occupied by the inscription, inside the

In the facade of the same ruin, high up in the wall, just east of plate, measures 49 cm. in length by 42 cm. in height. The letters, which are incised, are 4 cm. high. Copied by Dr. Littmann and the editor.

Published by Porter, *Five Years in Damascus,* II, p. 39, and *Journal Am. Oriental Society,* V (1856), p. 183 ff., No. 2. Waddington, No. 2096.

In the fourth line the C after OIKOAO-MI-Twas evidently omitted by mistake. On the names *Mdvos* and *ftal'xos* see the preceding inscription and its commentary.

364a. Il-haiyat. "Sur une pierre employ-ee dans l'enceintc du meme Edifice" (i. e. the same as that of No. 364). Waddington, No. 2097. Published also

in the *Journal Am. Orient. Soe.,* v, 1856, p. 1836., No. 3.

Il/30/fXos *Avfiov Tu dew Tov Tavvp. rjhr)v* tSuuv *vnep Avjaov vlov dvedr-jKev. Proklos (son) of Auntos set up this (statue of) Ganymede (as an offering) to the god, at his own expense, in behalf of his son Aumos.*

The name As/aos has an Arabic equivalent *Aum.* 364b. Il-haiyat. "Dans la cour devant le meme Edifice, sur une pierre brisee par le haut." Waddington, No. 2098.

'O *Kiiva Tt)v 'AjpoSeiT7v if* i8iW *virep yAo-fid8r); dvya.Tpo; dveffrjKev. set up this (statue of) Aphrodite at his own expense, in behalf of (his) daughter Asmathe.*

The name *Ao-fidd-q* seems to be the Arabic *'Asimaf.* 364c. Il-haiyat. "Sur le pilier d'une arche, dans le souterrain de gauche du meme edifice." Waddington, No. 2099.

A/3i/3os *Kal tofio-dyri* crv/x/3ios *rrjv iiucrfp dveffrjKev. Habibos and Thomsakhc (his) wife set up this (statue of) Nike.*

Thomsakhe, the wife, was evidently not of sufficient importance to affect the number of the verb. The name A/81/809, or A/Ja/Jo?,1 is the Arabic *Habib,* a name "very common 1 Waddington, Nos. 2420 and 2520.

in pre-Islamic Arabia": Renan, in *J.Asi-at., ye,* xix, p. 7. Blau, in *Z. M. G.* xv, p. 447. Wetzstein, No. 75. On ®*op.o-dxr),* see Clermont-Ganneau in *Recueil* iv, p. 167 f. 364 c!. Il-haiyat. "A l'interieur du second etage de droit, sur-roANA9MA une pierre qui a servi a recharger la voute; inscription fruste et mal /iHMI-TAitfAr gravee." Waddington, No. 2100. acttanay

"On ne distingue que les mots To ivdOefia et ©uov." 9 A I M AI 9 365. Il-haiyat. Statue. On the base of a statue, found immediately north

Apve'Xaos Sa/SeuaavoS, e'f east of the same ruin-The APXAAOCCABINI-ANOY *Arckelaos (son) of Sabeinianos,* at Statue has been broken off *(his) own (expense).* below the knees, so that only the base, with the left foot and the bottom of the drapery, remains. See Part II, p. 418. Copy of the editor.

366. Il-haiyat. In a modern building east of the village, on the east side of the doorway. The stone itself measures 92 by 42 cm. The inscription is in a dove-tail plate: the space inside the plate, occupied by the inscription, is 62 by 36 cm. The letters are 4 to 5 cm. high. Copy by Dr. Littmann.

Published by Waddington, No. 2101.

On the name *Tkemos* see No. 363 f. : on *Aumos* No. 364 a. The names *Anamos, Sabaos* and *Hane*

I. 9EMoCAYM0VrVlol *Afyov y, viol 'Avdpov UfUm,* /, doubt,ess _ Ai'iyX. os *Aypnrov* o', *Avjjlos 'Aypinov Koli* ANAMovCABAOVr v ,0, the equivalents of zapaos e, «PtAi7ros Oo(i/))ow, 0c/ xos ANHAOZArPinoVA 0(8)ijpoi». the Arabicw'aw, AVMOCArPinoVKAl *Themos (son) of Aumos* 3, (the) sons of aMl an(*Hatl* CABAOCllAinOC *Anamos (son) of Sabaos* 3, *Hanelos* (?) (son) of nel. *Oderos* is *Agripa* 4, *Aumos (son) of Agripa* and *Sabaos* probablv for the OVMP0V9EMoCOV „ D,./ Jk , s. n, 7V /., v 3

HpQ 5, *Philipos (son) of Oderos, Themos (sou) of Safajtic, UdhajK*

The numbers after certain of these names perhaps signify that these persons contributed to some common undertaking in the proportion of these numbers, or owned so many parts of the finished work. For example, if the inscription refers to a tomb, built by these persons, and containing fifteen or seventeen sarcophagi, I would understand that Themos, son of Aumos, reserved for himself three of these, the sons of Anamos three, Hanelos four, Aumos and Sabaos five, Philipos and Themos, son of Oderos, each one. But see the commentary to Waddington, No. 2061: also Waddington 1908.

367. Il-haiyat. Lintel, 578 A.d. On a lintel in place in the north wall of a court-yard in the center of a complex of buildings. Waddington says that the stone has been cut down somewhat at each end, but that the inscription is intact. The inscription itself measures 232 cm. in length and about 30 in height. The letters are 8 cm. high. Copy by Dr. Littmann.

Published by Waddington, No. 2110.

f 1. Seos, *O(3o.vov,* eViT/3(o7ros), *Kal oXftavos Flavios Seos, (son) of Ol-banos, procurator, and* utoSi *l&icw eKTicrav Tt/v iracrav avkrjv dnb depe-Olbanos (his) son, at their own expense built the whole LsiV pXPl tyovi,* eVi Tov travv(-qp.ov) *'Aka.fji.ovv-court from foundations to top, under the all-praisc Sdpov, naTp(iKcov), iv eri voy* Ttjs eVapx(«"s) *worthy Alamundaros, patri-cian, in (the) year 473 of lv8. «x'. the province, indiction 11.* (578 A.D.)

For a further description of and full commentary on this inscription see Waddington 2110. The name *Seos* is probably from the Arabic *S/iai':* if so, Seos is probably for

Saios.

368. Il-haiyat. In the west wall of the same court, at the south side of the door. The whole inscription measures 88 by 37 cm. Copy of Dr. Littmann.

Published by Waddington No. 2111.

369. Shakka. On the street which runs westward along the south side of the kaisariyeh, on the north side of the street about 50 yards west of this build-ing.

The stone measures 01 by 26 by 16
KAT6YXHN   6ATTIAIO   Kar'dn'v
'EXm'8ios u 1 f +u A

A/ / t L cm.: it is broken at the right end.

v , Mcuopos (e/ca-. MAlOPOCv; Yioc '"
I he leaves are in "incised relief. ., ...,
, The letters, *K* cm. high, are very well *According to a vow: hlpidios , (son) of 'u 0 J Maior(the) centurion,* CUt' deai"
and re&ular-CPy f the editor.

It is not possible to say with certainty how long this stone was originally; but I am inclined to believe that all of the inscription has been preserved. The names *Elpidios* and *Maior* appear in Waddington Nos. 1929 and 2150.

370. Shakka. In the courtyard of a house in the southern part of the town, on a stone like a lintel, 1.32 m. long by about 26 cm. high. The inscription itself mea-sures 66 by 26 cm.: the letters

OvaXou   *Wpovdov,   Xaipdvov*
AXouaiov, *'Ofiao-epov* Za/8Sa*pov, if; i* Si *ojv,* To *pvrjpa.* are 4 cm. high. Copy of the editor.

For these names see especially Wad.

2203 a, found at Tarba, and Wad. 2455, found at el-Djrein and dated probably 221 A.b. OvaXo? is a Greek form for *IVa'l,* Apouaos for *Anuah,* Xaipafo? for *Khairdn,* Ofiao-epos probably for *Ubaisir,* Za/38afos for *Zabdan.* All these names are Arabic.

(This is) the monument (or tomb) of Wa-los (sou) of Aruaos, Khairanos (son) of Alaphaios (and) Obaseros (sou) of Zab-danos, (built) at their own (expense).

371. Shakka. At the east end of a grave in a field just east of the village. The grave stands alone in the field, the mound being faced on all sides with blocks of black basalt: at the west end of the grave is set a block containing an in-scription published by Waddington, No. 2145 c. The stone at the cast end looks as if it tdsS might have been the lintel of a small door or window. It has been bro-ken at its left end: the fragment which remains measures 77 by 18 by 16 cm. The letters, 4J/2 to 6 cm. high, are good and

Mohammedan grave: Inscr. 371 upright at the left end.

lairly regular. Copy of the editor.

This is evidently the latter part of an inscription j JCKAIANAMOC . ,,,,,,,,' » j u found by Waddington "dans une cour, and pub 2. MANoYKTUUN Xt hshed by him, No. 2140. rutting the two frag-ments 3. OIHCANTOMNHMA,,,,...., togeth-er, the whole inscription reads as fol-lows: Macraos /ecu *Avapos,* viol Yep-pavov, 4k Twv IhLoiv inoirjo-av To pvij-pa.

Masakhos and Anamos, sons of Ger-manos, at their own expense built this tomb (or monument).

The name Macmxos has in Arabic the form *Masik.* This document furnishes an interesting example of a mixture of nationalities in the names of a family. Both sons have purely Arabic names; but the father's name is Roman. Proba-bly the father had also an Arabic name, which is not given here: compare No. 373 below. The name *Germanos* is known among the modern Greeks at Jerusalem. Dr. Littmann tells me of a Greek monk called by that name. If the Germanos of this inscription was not an Arab himself, he must have given

his sons Arabic names according to the fashion of the country in which he lived, most probably because their mother was an Arab.

372. Shakka. In the wall of a house in the northeastern part of the village, just above and at the left of the doorway: the house faces the south. The inscription is incised in a dove-tail plate, which is in relief; but the letters are badly executed. Copy of the editor.

I do not know what sign or figure is in the fifth line, after the OIC. It is about one and a half times as large as the letters: it has the form of o or x, and appears to have been mutilated. Doubt-less, whatever it represented, it was in-tended merely to separate these two parts of the inscription. It may be that the author of this inscription intended to write an elegiac couplet; but, if so, he succeeded imperfectly.

373. Shakka. On the right side of a little window high up in the wall of a house which stands looking east in the north-ern part of the town. The stone is about a foot square. Copy of the editor.

Doubtless the missing name of Dio-genes was his original, Arabic name. Here then, as in No. 371, an Arabic fa-ther, who had adopted for himself a Greek or Roman name, gave native Arabic names to his children: in this case the names are both feminine, *Ruhailat* and *Ghauwaiya* name *'VovXd-drj* occurs in Waddington 1968.

1.
2.
3-
4-
5-

374. Shakka. In a house adjoining that of No. 373. The stone, face up, formed the bottom of a small closet or niche. It was broken at the bottom and at both sides, perhaps also at the top. It was covered

N«MH 'vttov, *yvvt,* with mud. but as j had thjs scraped away *Aioyevoy;, er(ov).* carefully as possible, I believe that I have *Namera (?), (daughter) of* CQpied ajj the jetters there wefe Qn the stQne *Philippos (and) uife of* The letters are in relief, fine and regular, and *Dio-genes, (aged) — years.* are about 5 cm.

high. Copy of the editor.

The name *Namera* may be the feminine form of *Nameros,* found in Wad. 1984. *Nameros,* however, is from the Arabic *namir=panthery* the feminine of which, in Arabic, would be *namirat:* in Greek the latter would be *Nap.epd.0r).* 375. Shakka. On a stone forming part of a raised dais in a modern dwelling, at the right of the door. The stone itself measures 60 by cm. A fine line is drawn between each two lines of the inscription. The letters are 4 cm. high, well formed and regular. The stone is cracked, the crack running perpendicularly through about the middle of the inscription. Copy of the editor.

The first verse of this epigram might well refer to Proklos Diadochos, who, to quote Christ's words,1 "for his learning, piety and wonder-working power had among his contemporaries an extraordinary, and to us hardly comprehensible, reputation." This Proklos died in 485 A.d., a date which would suit the present inscription very well. He was a Lycian by birth, studied at Alexandria, and came, while still a young man, to Athens, where he became the pupil and successor of Syrianos, the head of the school of the Neo-Platonists. His biographer, Marinos, says that he died at Athens, and was buried in the same tomb as Syrianos, near Mt. Lykabettos: that he left particular directions as to his funeral, and the following epitaph, written by himself:s *TlpoxXos eyw ye.vop. riv AiJ/aos ye'vos, ov Su/stad? ivdd8' dp.oL/3bv £rj; Qp&ie SiSacrf- caXi.*

Ewos 8' dp.foTcpov 08c (rwpara Sefaro Tvp./3o;-

aWe Be #cai «a»as xopo; eeis XeXaoi.

Once, at least, during his lifetime, this Proklos was forced to leave Athens in consequence of his antagonism to Christianity. Is it possible that after his death his body was not allowed to remain in Athens, but was removed by some pagan admirer to the far-away Hauran?3 The Shakka epigram, in its form and spirit, bears a faint re 1 *Griechische Literaturgeschichte,* 2nd edition, p. 694. 3 That Shakka itself was a Christian community, perhaps *2Ant/*

wbgia Palatina, VII, 341: *I, Proklos, was a Lycian* as early as 323 A.D., is shown by Waddington, 2158. See *by birth, whom Syrianos reared to be a successor in his teaching.* the commentary on No. 377 below.

This common tomb hath received the bodies of us both, and would that one place our souls alike might have. semblance to the epitaph quoted by Marinos. Or is the person celebrated in the present inscription another and a quite unknown Proklos? 376. Shakka. Before the door of the same house as that of No. 375. The inscription is 42 cm. in height and 19 cm. in width: the letters are 54 cm. high. Copy of the editor. *Masalemos* son of *Rabbos is* mentioned in an inscription found at "Nahite" (C. /. G. 4659, Wad. 2412 1), dated 385 A. d. Possibly Zenon! ZHN *Zrfvwv Pdftfiov,* was another son of the same Rabbos, and if so this WNP *er(o)v) K.* inscription must be of about the same date. In any ABBO *Zenon, (son) of* case Wetzstein's reading Pa/8/3ov, which Waddington V ET *Rabbos, (aged) 20* adopted in preference to the *'idov* of the Corpus, will K *years.* e conf;rme(j by the present inscription. *Rabbos* is a common name, appearing for example in the Safaitic inscriptions in the form Dl = *Rabb.* 377. Shakka. Stable (?), 361-362 (?) A.d. Lintel of a house in the northern part of the village. The house, which has a courtyard before it, faces the south. The stone is of plain black basalt. The letters are simple in form, but deeply carved: a few of them are now weathered and indistinct, but the rest are clear. Copy of the editor.

Published by Dussaud and Macler, *Voyage Arch.,* p. 145, No. 4.

I am not sure what the words *irpor. Twv* tt6PMlNOCHPAKAlOYnPOT/TLJN *Qepfiivov* really mean. I have followed in (JPMINOY2IAIU)NKTICNTUCTA this case the reading *irpvr(evw)* given by BAONKAITOYCAVOTPIKAINOYCT/T/n/TT MM Dussaud and Maclei, Waddington t *Sepp2vo;* 'Hpa/cXiou, *Trpyr(zvoiv* ?) *Tsv teppivov,* 2498 and 2499 contain the word *trpontvoiV, eg I8iav eKTio-ev* Tw *a-Tci/Bxov Kol* Tou? *8vo* Toikxivous, but in both these cases the word seems

er(ous) T(s) (dXews) T. t to refer to a church official. Here, how + *Pherminos, son of Heraklios, head of the house of* ever seems as if Only a family Or clan or *Pherminos, at* (his) own expense erected the stable and the faction of some sort were involved. *two rooms, in* (the) year of the city joo. + A *ardXov TTtpWkivov* is mentioned in

Waddington 2161, an inscription from this same town, dated in the year 568, doubtless according to the same era. The first editors of the present inscription, in commenting on this phrase, say: "II ne faut pas comprendre avec Waddington: une £curie munie d'un toit ayant de la pente de tous les cotes ce qui est absolument contraire aux habitudes architecturales si caracteri sees de la region comme une auberge, probablement une simple piece munie d'un diwan toutautour. Attenant devaient etre des ecuries." I am inclined to think, however, that the expression means a row of sheds enclosing a court, rather than a khan in the modern sense. My recollection is that at least in northern Syria the ancient inns had accommodations for people only: if there were stables, they were separate. I do not remember to have seen any ancient inn in the Hauran of which enough remained to give any idea of its original character. A noun *rpUXivos,* meaning *granary,* is quoted in Sophocles' *Lexicon* from Heron Jun. 168, 29. Doubtless there was an inn, however, near this "stable," perhaps the same as that for which the *o-Tafikov irtpUkivov* was built some three hundred years later.

The era of Shakka is not known with certainty. The dated inscriptions from this city are as follows: Wad. 2145: in the year of the city 71;1 Wad. 2158: in the year 263, indie. 15; No. 277: in the year of the city 300; Wad. 2159: in the year of the city 310, indie. 14, in the month April; Wad. 2161: in the year 568, indie. 3. The second of these is not reckoned according to the same era as the others, if Waddington's reading is correct. But if the number of the indiction is emended to IB, 12, instead of IE, 15, then the era will coincide with that of the rest. In that case the era must begin with the year 1-2 A.d., or with a year represented by the number 1-2 plus some multiple of 15. This year can not be earlier than 61-62 A.d., for otherwise Wad. 2158 would fall before 312 A.d. when the method of reckoning by indictions was established. Nor can this year be later than 61-62 A.d., for if So Wad. 2161 would be dated after the Arabic invasion. This I believe to be highly improbable, Waddington to the contrary notwithstanding. Only four other inscriptions are given by Waddington as dated after 637, viz. Nos. 1830, 1997, 2028, and 2413 a. No one of these, excepting No. 1830 (from Cyrrhus), is certain, and in one, No. 2028, the date assigned by Waddington is evidently incorrect. For the date given here is "in the month of May 12, ind. 3, of the year 539." This Waddington has reckoned according to the era of Bosra: the 539th year of this era began March 22nd, 644 A.d. But, as Waddington himself says, the third indiction began on the first of September of that same year. The 12th of May, 644, therefore, fell in the second, not in the third indiction. This date then can not be reckoned according to the era of Bosra, but might be reckoned according to an era which began in October, 61, or March, 62 A. d., although I do not know any event in this year in which such an era might have had its origin.

Two objections occur to me to the dating of these inscriptions according to an era beginning in 61-62 A.d. 1. I can hardly believe, as Waddington did, that Wad. 2145 is earlier than the end of the fourth century. This opinion, however, depends upon the meaning of *norvia vvpft* and XMr in 2145 c, lines 4 and 6, and upon the date at which the worship of the Virgin became prominent in the Syrian church, or rather in the Hauran. 1 In this inscription Waddington gives a second date P9'; but I believe these letters should be read ?0-
See Wetzstein, and Dussaud, p. 145 f. But 8 = 99 = fyi7/v. See Chapter I, p. 24.
2. The forms of the letters in Wad. 2158 and 2159, as we as ne contents of these inscriptions, are more appropriate to the

sixth than to the fourth century, at least if we may judge by the inscriptions of the northern districts of Syria. It is questionable, however, how early these letters may have appeared in the Hauran. These objections then are not conclusive. And the only other alternative would be to acknowledge two eras for Shakka, i.e. one, perhaps from 272 or 287 A.d., for Wad. 2145, and perhaps for No. 377 and Wad. 2158 also, and another for Wad. 2161. But this seems to me impossible, because in that case one era must have been reckoned from an event which occurred long before the other era ceased to be in use. Moreover Mommsen found an era for an inscription of Agrippa II from Aere (is-Sanamen), and also for a coin of Agrippa II, beginning with 61 A.d. See Mommsen, in *Wiener Nitmismatische Zeitschrift,* in, p. 451 ff. Also Mordtmann, in *Arch.-Epigraph. Mittheil. aus Oesterreich,* vm (1884), p. 189 f. Bursian, *Jahresberichie,* Supplementband 26, p. 179 f. I believe, therefore, that the era of Shakka began October 1st, 61 A.d. If so, then Wad. 2158 is dated October, 323-September, 324 A.d., Wad. 2159 is dated April, 371 A.d., Wad. 2161 is dated (September), 629 A.d. 378. Tarba. Column. On a drum of a column, now used as the right jamb of the doorway into another en *Tov Belva,* Trpeo-levr) *Xtftaorod) cosme* from the courtyard of *amMTTpaiTinyov),* ol dirb £0vovs voudScw, ,11 j 1.1 ,, the house now occupied by the ayv«as Xoptv. *q (This statue of) , legatus* Sallam. This house belongs *Augusti propraetor, (zvas erected by) those q* himsdf. cq1_ *of (the) nomad folk, on account of (his) uprightness* (?). umn drum was in the courtyard of his own house, and he had it dug up some little time ago. When it was seen by M. Waddington, it was upside down, so that he thought that the whole inscription might be found by digging the drum out. The first part of the inscription, however, was on another drum, which has disappeared. The inscription is 26 cm. long, and 35 cm. high. The letters are 4 cm. high. Copy by the editor.
Published by Waddington, No. 2203.

379. Tarba. On a stone in a low parapet on the roof immediately south of the foregoing. The stone, which is broken on the right and at the bottom, measures 36 cm. in length by 33 in height. The letters are about 5 cm. high. Copy by the editor.
Published by Burton and Drake, *Unexplored Syria,* Vol. II, Appendix, No. 138.
AY2ITO Avfi, *Tuv* Oo-sixou, u(I)6s Bd(/)8ov, c'»c This reading is, of course, OCAIAOY *Tsv tl&Uov otKo&6peo-v* very uncertain: the fragment Y6OCBOY may be part of a much longer KTON6IA *Auxi,ofthe(tribc)ofOsdilos,sonofBordos,* inscription. The name Av£i _OAOMC *at his own exPense built ithis)* occurs in Wad. 2006 and 2415, Aufi'Swpos in Wad. 1930, AvfiTo»(?) in Wad. 2037. OfSiXo? may be from the Semitic "l!fj? with Bd/580? is obviously the Arabic *Burd:* this name appears in Wad. 1990 and 2265: see also the commentary on No. 88 above.
I believe that, in the third line, the reading YOC is correct. If this is really for vios, it is a strange corruption, unless it is merely a mistake of the stonecutter. But perhaps some proper name was carved here, for example Tcos. so that the inscription read: Aufi Ts» OcrSiXov (kox) (r)eos Bo(p)8ov Ck Tov e£8iW O'ik oSopea _av 380. Mushennef. Temple or Temenos. Two fragments of what appears to have been the lintel of a gateway, now lying outside the wall near the middle of the north side of an ancient temenos. M. Waddington says of it: "Devant le temple, sur une pierre brisee en deux morceaux; l'inscription est encadree, avec un trait entre les lignes; la fin est fruste." The letters are 3 cm. high. Copy of Dr. Littmann.
Published by Wetzstein, No. 30. Waddington, No. 2211.
V.I., Wad., line 3: ɴATPIIOYONN--; line 4:--OAo Comonoiac.
'Tire/3 *o-arrrfplas KvpCov* yScunXciws '*Aypimra.* /ecu eVavoSou, /car' evijv, Ai6s *Kal Tra,Tp(q)ov* AftjvaL? (oSos *bpovo* 1 as *Tov Oxkov iucohop.* ijcrevj.

For the) safety of (our) lord King Agrippa, and (for his) return, according to a vow, (the) Synod of Concord erected this house of Zeus and of (the) Athena of (our) fathers.

This was probably the inscription of the lintel of the gateway in the north wall of the temenos within which a temple, or shrine, of Zeus and Athene was built in the reign of King Agrippa. See Part II, p. 346 ff. According to Waddington, this was Agrippa I: if so, the inscription dates probably from about the year 41 A.d. M. Waddington has also called attention to the importance of this inscription as showing that the kingdom of Aprippa extended at least as far as Mushennef.

380 a. Mushennef. The Same Temple. This inscription was not copied by any member of this expedition; but it is re-published here because of its intimate con nection with the other inscriptions and the buildings of this place. Waddington says that it was found be-side the preceding (No. 380=Wad. 2211). He says also: "Les lettres sont belles et l'inscription est encadree, avec un trait entre chaque ligne."

Published by Waddington, No. 2212. Wetzstein, No. 21. Cyril Graham, *Transact. Roy. Soc. Lit.,* VI, p. 280. Waddington's reading was collated and verified by Dr. Littmann.

"Les mots entre les crochets ont ete legerement marteles dans l'antiquite, mais sont parfaitement lisibles": Waddington. The date of this inscription is approximately 171 A.d. 381. Mushennef. The Same Temple. A stone face up in the debris, near the northwest corner of the temple, at the edge of the pool. The maximum length of the fragment is 82 cm., the height 46 cm. The letters of the first line are 4, those of the other lines 6 to 7 cm. high. Copy of Dr. Littmann.

The stone which contains this inscription is obviously a fragment of a handsome lintel. The name in the second line appears at first to be AoveiSos, the Greek form of the Arabic *'Aividh,* a name not uncommon in this region. This name occurs six or seven times in Waddington's inscriptions, and was

found by Dr. Littmann in a large number of the Safai'tic inscriptions in the desert immediately to the east. One Aoueidos, mentioned in Wad. 2413 b, erected at 'Akraba, a town about fifty miles northwest of Mushennef, in the time of one of the Agrippas, "the door-posts with their ornament, and the altar, to Zeus the Lord." Inscription No. 380 shows that there was a shrine of Zeus at Mushennef in the time of one of the Agrippas, and it might be thought that the inscription under consideration be-longed to this period also, and that per-haps the same 'Awldh was concerned in the adorning of the sanctuaries of Zeus at both Mushennef and 'Akraba. On the other hand, the design of this lintel and its mouldings are totally unlike any of the architectural remains of the Idumean kingdom in this district, and altogether such as would naturally be assigned to the age of the Antonines. In the second place this inscription ob-viously contained one of the common-est formulae of the Roman imperial in-scriptions, in which the name of an im-perial legate would naturally follow the «rt in the second line, while the name of the centurion in charge of the work would naturally follow the eeoTWTo? in the third. Lastly the letters of this in-scription correspond very closely, so far as can be judged from M. Waddington's publication, with those of No. 380 a= Wad. 2212, which belongs to the reign of Marcus Aurelius, and which gives the name, partially erased but still per-fectly legible, of Avidius Cassius the imperial legate, and also the name of Kyrinalios Gemellos a centurion. I be-lieve, therefore, that in the second line of the present inscription we should read: eVl Aove.8iou *Kaa-a-Cov Tov Xafi-irpoTCLTov virarLKov* as in No. 380 a, or, following the more common formula, e.g. in Wad. 2525, «'" Aouei8i'ov *Kaa-crCov Trpeo-fi.*

Inscr. 381. From a drawing. Scale 1: 10.

Sc/3. *ami(TTpa.rqyov.*

Now it is a singular fact that among all the many mistakes of orthography in these Greek inscriptions of Syria, while «i and are often interchanged, as for ex-

ample '*Avrwveivov* and vcooj?, both of which appear in No. 380 a, « for T rarely occurs, at least in inscriptions of this period. The best example which I have found is *i£ eiSiW,* found in No. 379 and also in an inscription from Habiba in the Hauran, dated 303 A.d. (Wad. 2514). Perhaps, however, in the case of the name Avidius the accent of the nominative may account for the lengthened form of the antepenult. Or possibly the other name, 'AovetSo? or 'AouiSos may have been confused with this one. But whatever may be the ex-planation of this irregularity, I believe that the second line must have contained the name of an imperial legate, and if so this can hardly be other than that of Avidius Cassius.

If, then, we may read in the second line the name and title of Avidius Cas-sius, and in the third line the name and title of a centurion, I think we may safe-ly conclude that Wad. No. 2214. con-tains the end of the inscription ,... AAIO-TYPCC r under discussion.

M. Waddington says of this inscrip-tion: "Fragment de linteau. Grandes, belles lettres; la deuxieme ligne a ete martel6e, et la lecture en est douteuse. " His description, therefore, agrees per-fectly with the description of the frag-ment found by Dr. Littmann. The forms of the letters also correspond. And if the inscription in Waddington's fragment was partially defaced, this would be a further indication that it originally re-ferred to Avidius Cassius and probably also to the third Gallic legion, for the names of this legate and of this legion were erased from many of the monu-ments in the empire, doubtless in conse-quence of the rebellion of Avidius Cas-sius, which took place about 175 A.d., and in which the third Gallic legion took part (see Waddington's commentary on Nos. 1845 and 2212). It may be said that the end of these two lines would hard-ly have been erased unless the begin-ning, containing the names themselves, had also been erased, and that it does not appear from Dr. Littmann's copy that any erasure in his fragment was no-ticed. It must be remembered, however, that the erasure in Waddington's fragment was so incomplete that the letters were read by him, although with some uncertainty, and also that it is characteristic of the inscriptions in Syria referring to Avidius Cassius that his name is not completely erased. M. Waddington, in his commentary on No. 2212, says: "Avidius Cassius jouissait d'une grande popularité en Syrie, ou le nom de Cassius ne reveillait que des souvenirs sympathiques; et, bien que les legions lui fussent hostiles, les populations s'etaient prononcees en sa faveur. On en trouve sur les monuments une preuve remarquable. Le senat l'avait declare ennemi de la patrie, et, selon l'usage en pareil cas, son nom devait etre efface de tous les monuments publics ou il avait ete gravé; or, tandis que les noms de Commode, de Maximin et d'autres princes sont effaces de maniere a ce qu'on ne puisse en lire une seule lettre, celui de Cassius n'est jamais martele que tres-legerement et pour la forme; on peut presque toujours le lire sans la moindre difnculte."

If, then, Waddington's fragment be added to that of Dr. Littmann, we shall have for the last three lines:
eniAOYIAIOYKACCIOY   ANTICTPA-TOY
tECTLJTOC lAAjOTYPCC-f
TAAAIKH

Then following as closely as possible the formulae given in Wad. 2525, 2528 and 2438, and supplying the name of the centurion from No. 380 a, I would read: 'Earl 'AoveiS iou *KacrcrCov, Trpecr/3.* 2e/8. dp Tiorpat *rjy)ov,* eeorcuros *KvpivakLov TepeWov,* «c (a)(Tov)T(d)/(xo)y y TaXA-i/d?.

It is of course most unusual not to find the abbreviation Xey. in such a phrase. There is, however, a somewhat similar omission in Wad. 2271: Meo-d/iapos (1), *imreix; Kvpi-qva'iKrjs), ydvo%* Nd/3as. Compare also Wad. 1929, 2212 and 2225, where only the title, *tKa.T6vTapxo;* or occurs, the name of the legion not being given at all.

If my reading of these lines is correct, the first line must necessarily have contained the name and titles of the emperor Marcus Aurelius. The second and third lines moreover consisted of forty letters each, and since the three remain-

ing letters of the first line have but two thirds of the height of these, we may conclude that about sixty letters in the first line would equal in total length the two lines following. Then since the first line projected beyond the others about the space of four letters at each end, we may conclude that this line consisted of about sixty-eight letters altogether, which I would supply from No. 380 a, reading the whole inscription as follows: 1. 'T7rep crwnjpias *Tov Kvpiov AvroKparopos* KaiVapos M. *Avp-qXiov 'Avrcjuetvon* Se/SaoroO, 2. *inl* AovetS i'ov Kacrcriou, *irpeafi.* SeS. di Tiorpa t *(yjy)ov,* 3. *ifecrT(i)To; KvpivaXiov TepeWov,* Ck (a)*(tov)tcl)p((o)* u *y'* 4. TaMi/a) s.
For the safety of our lord Emperor, Caesar, M(arcus) Aurelius Antoninus, Augustus, in (the administration of) Avidius Cassias, legatus Augusti pro praetorc, Kyrinalios Gemellos, centurion of (the) 3rd Gallic (legion), being in charge (of the work).
The date of this inscription is probably the same as that of the foregoing (No. 380 a), 171 A.d. The stone was probably the lintel of the temple built at that time.

381 a. Mushennef. This inscription was not found by the present expedition: it was found and published by Waddington, No. 2214, who says of TICTPA-6TOY jt; «Fragment de linteau. Grandes, belles lettres; la deuxieme ligne AA OTYPCC r a martej£e) et ja lecture en est douteuse." M. Waddington does not say in what part of the ruins the fragment was found.
Waddington's rendering of this inscription is as follows:
'Em *Tov Selves* npe(r/3-Se/8. *d.vTicrTpa(rtjyov), erous....*

In my opinion, however, this fragment belongs to No. 381, with which I have incorporated it.
382. Mushennef. The Same Temple. In a wall built of all kinds of fragments across the front of the portico of the temple. The stone is about 8 feet from the ground, and between the remains of the two columns of the portico. It was originally part of an entablature, similar to, but not identical with, the lower

member of the entablature of the present temple, as seen at the southwest angle shown in Part II, p. 349. Mr. Butler believes that it belonged to a colonnade inside the temenos wall. In that case, this colonnade was built some fifty years after the completion of the temenos wall under Marcus Aurelius (see Nos. 380 a and 381).
The stone is 190 cm. long by 40 high, and is cracked across near the center. The letter space is *iol/2* cm. high, and the letters 3 to 4 cm. Copy of Dr. Littmann.
1.---YHPO-A-E DYEYTYXDYCCEBA 2. DADM HCENAEAIAAYPM APK-YYA-- MWNDCAAEZAN
I-Seo *vrfpo* v 'A X e£dvSp ov, Eutvou?, Se/8aoTou, 2. OikoSd/xijcrei' 8c Sia *Avp.* Map«ou (X)aa/u,/iw0Si 'AXe£eu/ 8/30V.
1. *Severus Alexander, Felix, Augustus,* 2. *and built through Aur(elios) Markos Khaammon, (son) of Alexander.*
The name of the emperor can hardly be other than Severus Alexander (222-235 A.d.). The inscription, therefore, although only a fragment, still records the important facts that the structure, to which this piece of an architrave belonged, was erected between 222 and 235 A.d., by some person or corporation, who employed for the work someone whose name seems to have been Khaammon, and who was doubtless the architect or contractor. Since the inscription was on an architrave, and neither the beginning nor the end has been preserved, it is of course impossible to tell how long the inscription was originally. Judging, however, by the other inscriptions, which obviously belonged to this temple or its temenos, it would seem that the whole inscription was much longer than the extant fragment. Comparing then Wad. Nos. 2212, 2480 2114, 2213, 2456 and 2187, I would propose the following reconstruction, as conveying in a general way the probable tenor of the original: 1. *'Tirep rom)pta% Tov Kvpiov AirroKpaTopos,* Kawra/jos, *MdpKOV AiprjXtov %eovrjpoy* 'AXe favSpJou, EuruoCs, Sey8aorov, 2. 6 Scu/a Tov Stios (or To *Koivov rrj;* Ttoxcws) *eKTiatv To TrepiaTvkov* (?)

Oik *o86pr)a-v* Sc Sid *Avp.* Mapcou (X)aat/i(oi'os, *We£di 8pov. For the safety of our lord Emperor, Caesar, Marcus Aurelius Severus Alexander, Felix, Augustus, (son) of* (or *the community of the city) erected the colonnade, and built (it) through Aur(elios) Markos Khaammon, (son) of Alexander.*

The name *Khaammon* appears to be Arabic, a diminutive of *Ka'ammih.* 383. Mushennef. A block of stone found inside of the temple, apparently in its original place, immediately in front of a pier which supported the north side of the transverse arch of the cella. The interior of the temple is now filled to the level of the inscription with debris, soil and dung of sheep penned there. The stone is smoothdressed on the front and both sides. Its face measures 78 by 38 cm.: its thickness is about 33 cm. From the bottom of the lowest line to the bottom of the stone is 12 cm. The letters are 5 to 6 cm. high. Copy of. Dr. Littmann.

There is no other case of O-wsiko? *vopdhav* among 06OALUPOYCYN eeoScS/oot/, *o-w* the inscriptions of Syria, so far as I know, unless it Aikoy Noma *BUov vopdBatv.* be in Wad. 2112, a fragmentary inscription of the time of King Agrippa, where Waddington himself *Of Theodoros, syndic of nomads.* . restored o-r/jaттjyJo? *vopaSav.* The latter title occurs also in Wad. 2196, which belongs probably to the time of Hadrian: *idvdpxov, o-rpcvrqyov vopdSwv.* These two inscriptions, as well as the one under discussion, all are from places near each other, and all on the eastern slope of the mountains towards the desert. Doubtless, as Waddington in his commentary on No. 2196 suggests, these are titles of Arab shekhs who were recognized in some degree as vassals by the Roman Empire. 384. Mushennef. Stone upside down in the south wall of the weli, about an eighth of a mile north of the village. The stone is about 4 feet from the ground, on the right of the doorway. The inscription, which is in unusually deep, clear and regular letters, is contained in a rectangular plate sunk in the face of the stone and ornamented at each end with a design of acanthus (?) leaves in place of the usual

dove-tails. The whole stone meas 1. AIAIOCTIB6PPI ures 104 by 36 cm., 2. NOCT6CCAPA the plate 55 by 31 3. AfΓKYPTOW cm.: the letters are 4. NHMION6AYT 4 to 4/2 cm. high. 5. WT-TOIHCN Copied by Dr. Litt mann. Inscr. 384. From a photograph of the stone. A *tessararius* was a

AiXio? *TiieppLVO;,* recro-a/3a(/3io?) ey. y' *Kvp(jvdiKrj;),* To *fivqfjuov* eavnu soldier who received *iTTOLT)o-v.* and distributed the *Aelius Tiberrinns, tessararius of (the) jrd Cyrenaic legion, made this monument* watchword from the (or *tomb) for himself.* commander. 385. Mushennef. In the interior of the ruined mosque. Copy by Waddington, verified by Dr. Littmann.

Published by Waddington, No. 2229.
BA96AOCMAN
OYMANOCY6IOC
ONHMA9HC
OYHPOYBOCPH
NH
The name *Ovqp.adr)* is apparently Arabic, from 'Unaimat, diminutive of Anamat.* 386. Tafha. On a stone lying face up in the ruins immediately northwest of the church. The stone itself measures 112 by 39 cm., and is 22)4 cm. thick. The inscription is in a dove-tail plate, the inside measurements of which are 64)4 by 21) cm. The lines are separated by bands in relief.
Both plate and inscription are in relief. The letters are 3 to 4 cm. high. Copy of the editor
Published by Waddington, No. 2168.
The name ESeos is perhaps the Arabic
Adz. AAEIANAPOCEACOY
OIKOAOMOCEVNOUUN
TNAVTOVnATPIAIC
(frAOTIMHOAMENOCOl
KOAOMHC
Alexandros (son) of Edeos, builder, in devoted service for his country (or *contributing through love for his country), built (this).* 387. Tafha. On the uppermost of three inscribed blocks placed one above the other, the lowest forming a lintel in the front, i.e. the south side, of the last row of buildings on the north side of the town. Doubtless none of these blocks is in its original place; but

probably this and the following belong together. The houses were probably built by a colony of Druzes, who are said to have settled here, but to have moved away about twenty years ago on account of a plague which broke out among them.

The uppermost block measures 108 by 34 cm. The inscription is incised within a dove-tail plate formed by raised bands: the space occupied by the inscription is 93 cm. long. The letters are 44 to 6 cm. high, irregular and somewhat crude, as if the workman found difficulty in carving letters in the hard basalt. Copied by Dr. Littmann and the editor.

The syllable *pa* in 'Apipd8ri; is supplied from No. 389 below: doubtless, like the sec *By provision of Alexandros, the eunuch of the household) of Kerzilauos, and Maximos of (the tribe of) Arimathe, and Taurinos (sou) of Sammulanos.* ond *v* in *tvvoxxov* it was omitted through the carelessness of the stone-cutter: *pipdd-q* is doubtless the Greek equivalent of *ar-Rimat).* The mixture of Greco-Roman and Arabic names in this and in the two following inscriptions is interesting. *Kerzilanos* and *Sammulanos* are both Arabic names, the former probably from *Kurzul;* both are diminutives or hypocoristica,[1] *Sammulanos* uniting in itself two kinds of diminutive formation.[2]

The present inscription and No. 388 seem to belong together and to form one document.
388. Tafha. On the second of the three inscribed blocks mentioned under No. 387. The block itself measures 99 by 34 cm. The inscription is incised in a rude dove-tail plate formed by raised bands: the space within the plate, occupied by the inscription, is 78 cm. long. The carving is still cruder than that of No. 387. The letters are 4 to 6 cm. high. Copied by Dr. Littmann and the editor.
!Part IV, p. 127 f. 2Part IV, p. 219.
See the preceding inscription and its commentary. Maximos is probably the same person as the Mafi/ios 'A/na'? of No. 387: in the one case his tribe, here his father is mentioned. The name *A.fx-*

fao-o;
seems to be an
Arabic diminutive in a rare form,1 perhaps from *Hafs:* Bapos is the common Arabic name *Bakr.*
and of Maximos (son) of Sauphanios, and Haphp/iasos (son) of Aumos, of the (clan) of Bakhros, this house was renetved. 389. Tafha. On the lowest of the three inscribed blocks mentioned under No. 387. The inscription, incised on a plain surface, is 137 cm. long: the stone itself is about 25 cm. longer, and is 25 cm. high. The letters are well formed, regular and clear. Copied by Dr. Littmann and the editor.

I believe that this inscription re 1. 0YNOYXOCTXNKP 'o ewoSxo? *Twv Kep-*fers to the same persons as No. 387.
2. ZIAANOYKAIMAIIMOCAN *Xdvov Kal* Mafias Maximos, son of Anamos, was
3. AMOYAPIMA9HC *Avdp.ov Apip-dd-q.* perhaps a grandfather of Maximos, *The eunuch of the (household) of Kcrzilanos and Maximos son of Sauphanios,* mentioned in *(son) of Anamos of AHmathe.* No. 388. The name *Anamos* is of course the Greek form of *An1 am* for the other names see the notes to No. 387 f. 390. Tafha. A fragment, containing the latter part of an inscription, in the ruins at the foot, on the west side, of a low wall about 20 feet west of the tower which stands at the northwest corner of the church. The stone measures 30 cm. at the top, 41 at the bottom, is 37 cm. high, and 32 cm. thick: it seems to be broken at the top and at the left end. The inscription, excepting the last line, is incised on a plate in relief, with rectangular projections instead of dove-tails at the ends: the last line is immediately below the plate. The letters are 4 cm. high. Copy of the editor.
Published by Dussaud and Macler, *Voyage au Safd,* p. 149, No. 14.

After the letters 90Y in line 1 there may be UU or OI, instead of O. After the A in line 3 there appears to be a mark of abbreviation. The name Moyvto? in line 4 is the Arabic and Safaitic *Mughiii.* 1 See Part IV, p. 219. (Addendum to p. 128.) 2 See also Nos. 366, 371, 427,435. 391. Tafha. House (?). Lintel of a doorway facing west, in the northeast corner

of the town. The whole design X(/ hot6s) M(api'as), A (ai) n. (?) js *2gy2* cm SqUare: it was originally well cut arid deep; but it is now badly weathered and covered with lichen. *Christ son) of Mary, Alpha and Omega.*
Except for this ornamental design, the lintel is perfectly plain; but it is larger than most of the lintels of this region, and the stone is better dressed: the whole doorway is of exceptionally fine masonry. Copy of the editor.
392. Shehba. On a lintel, now serving as the lintel of a modern house, on the north side of the street, about a hundred yards west of the hexastyle temple. This lintel is doubtless in its original place; but I was unable to discover the original character of the building. Waddington says that the whole stone is 2.50 m. long. The inscription is in a dove-tail plate, formed by a band *2/2* cm. broad. The space within the plate measures 1422 by 37 cm. The letters are exceptionally handsome, and are perfectly preserved. The first four lines are each 5 cm. high, the fifth line 7, the sixth, which is on the lower border of the plate, 2 cm. This sixth line is repeated in substance in the dove-tail of the right end. Copy of the editor.
Published in *C. I. C,* 4601. Waddington, No. 2071. Ewing, in *P. E. .F.,* 1895, p. 354, No. 185. /. *G. R.* Ill, 1195.

Inscr. 392, showing the entrance to the modern house, and the right jamb of the original doorway with an ancient arch before it.

In Waddington's opinion this inscription is to be dated 177 or 178 A.d., Cornmodus having received the title *Augustus* in 177, and Martius Verus having returned to Rome early in 179 when he was consul for the second time. See Waddington's interesting commentary on the persons mentioned here and on the Sixteenth Legion. The name AiXa/xos is doubtless the Arabic *'Ailam,* Aa/3cuos the Arabic and Safai'tic *Dhahbau.* On the title *stmtegos* see Waddington's commentary: compare also No. 150.
392 a. Shehba. On a bracket on the east side of the portal of a large ancient building, on the south side of the main

street, nearly opposite the hexastyle temple. The building is marked B in the plan on p. 376 of Part II. The bracket, which is about 8 feet from the ground, is now within a modern structure, built against the ancient facade and upon the pavement of the ancient street. Two other brackets may be seen in the same facade, further towards the east. The portal, which is 8 feet wide and about 12 feet high, stands across a modern passage which leads southwards from the hexastyle temple. There is a smaller doorway in the same facade, about 25 feet east of the inscribed bracket, which doubtless belonged to the same building.
Published by Waddington, No. 2073
393. Shehba. ing the roof of a dark stable, into which one enters from a courtyard near where No. 402 was found. The inscription is on the middle drum of the column as it now stands, and is upside down. The height of the inscription is 85 cm.: the first line is 50 cm. long, the eighth 63. The letters are 5 to 6 cm. high, and well aligned. Copy of the editor.

Published by Professor Briinnow in *M. P. V.,* 1899, p. 85, No. 48. By Professor Domaszewski in *R. M.* 1899, p. 159 f.

Iulio Prisco, v(iro) (e)m(inentissimo), fratri et patruo d(ominorum) n(ostrorum) Philipporum Aug(ustorum), et praef(ecto) praet(orii), rect(o)riq(ue) Orientis, Trebonius Sossianus, p(rimus) p(ilus), domo Col(onia) Hel(iupoli) (?), devotus numini maiestatiq(ue) eorum.
To Julius Priscus, vir eminentissimus, brother and uncle of our lords Philippi Augusti, and praefectus praetorii, and rector of the East, Trebonius Sossianus, primus pilus, of the Colonia Heliopolir (Ba'albek?), who was devoted to their will and majesty.
I. 2.
3 4 5-
6.
I. G. R. Ill, 1198. The text given here is from Waddington.
Column-drum. On a column, about 2 feet in diameter, support
The title *vir eminentissimas* indicates

that the bearer belonged to the highest equestrian order. This column belonged originally perhaps to the peripteral building to which No. 392 a belonged. Doubtless the drum above that which bears the present inscription had a bracket on which stood a statue or bust of Julius Priscus. See the very interesting commentary on this inscription by Professor Domaszewski.

394. Shehba. On a drum of a column inside of the courtyard where No. 402 was found, close to the north wall near the entrance. The diameter of the drum is 56 cm.: the total height of the inscription is 55, the length of the first line 39 cm. The letters are 5 to 6 cm. high. lX0" *Kal evdewov* Copy Qf the editor. *dpeTrjs KpeLTTova,* Aoukio? *Ptopavos, Tov eve pyeTr/v.*

I. 2.

XONKAITTA
CHCENeEUUOY
APETHCKPEITTO
NA

(this statue of) his benefactor, Lukios Romanos (set up).

Doubtless the drum which originally stood above this one, bore a bracket and a statue, and below the bracket the beginning of this inscription. Perhaps the letters ENGEUJOY compose an adjective formed by combining the words *iv&§* and adding a termination. I suppose, then, that the whole phrase: *irdo-r); evdewov aperr? KpeiTTova,* must signify: *master oj;* i.e. *possessed of, every divine virtue.* Compare the similar phrases in Nos. 319 and 340.

395. Shehba. On a stone in the wall of a modern house, at the right side of the door, about 100 yards south of the hexastyle temple. The stone measures 69 by 35 cm. The inscription is incised on a perfectly plain surface. The letters are 2 to 4 cm. high, irregular, but well preserved. Copy by the editor, and a squeeze.

Published by Waddington, No. 2072. Porter, *Five Years in Damascus,* II, p. 79.

The form *itrfieXoofievcou* is obviously for *eVi/ueXov/xeVtw.* Concerning Shehba-Philippopolis, and the emperor Philippus Arabs, see Waddington's

commentary on this inscription, Wad. 2072. Marrinos or Mareinos was the father of the elder Philip. See No. 400 a. The date of this inscription must fall between 247 A.d., when Philip received the title *Augustus,* and 249 A.d., when he died.

396. Shehba. Philippeion. On the bracket at the east side of the portal of a temple-like structure, called by Mr. Butler the "Philippeion." See Part II, pp. 376 and 380 f. The bracket is right-lined, and has, in general, the form of a small pedestal for a statue or bust, like many of those at Palmyra. Lines 1 and 2 of the inscription are on i-9 Lu ®e the face of the die, which is about 32 cm. wide: 2. MAP6INW *Mapdvco* the third line is on the moulding at the bottom 3-JOCYTTA « wa «&. of the bracket, which was originally 44 cm. ....'. *To (the memory of the) divine Mareinos, os,* wide, but of which only 25 cm. now remain,, ,, t., , ,,.,. *J u 'consular (legate), (set up this statue).* the left corner having been broken off. About four letters, therefore, have been lost from the beginning of the third line. Except for these four missing letters, the inscription is complete. Copy by the editor.

Published by Waddington, No. 2076 a. / *G. R.* Ill, No. 1200.

On Mareinos see the preceding inscription. Waddington says that the letter before OC in the third line was T or r.

397. Shehba. Philippeion. On the bracket at the west side of the portal of the en "Philippeion ": the bracketis badly broken at vi./ all four corners. Doubtless the inscription is 2. 61 NO) *Mapjeww f u7raTiKos* (?). similar to, if not the same as that of the corres ' ponding bracket (No.396). Copy by the editor.

Published by Waddington, No. 2076 b. /. *G. R.* Ill, No. 1200.

See the preceding inscription.

398. Shehba. Philippeion. Fragment built into the wall which fills up the portal on the north side of the same building as the two preceding inscriptions. It is in the fourth tier from the door-sill, the second stone from the east jamb. When seen by Waddington, this fragment was "Aupres de la porte de ce

meme temple."

The face of the stone measures 92 by 43 cm., and is perfectly plain, i.e. without mouldings or ornament, except for the inscription. The letters are 7 to 8 cm. high, and of fairly good form; but they are now badly weathered. Copy by the editor.

Published in *C. I. G.* 4587. Waddington, No. 2074 b. / *G. R.* Ill, 1197.

1. lclAITTTTOYCCBB In the third line, after TTAAriC or TTAArie, there are 2.-- AYPHA ANTLONINOC marks on the stone which may be letters, perhaps AOC or 3-TTAAriC Aw/ or NB6; but these marks are very faint and uncertain, so that I believe that they are accidental, and that the last line consists simply of the word IleXayis or *UeXdyie.*

This fragment doubtless belongs with the following, No. 398 a, which was found by Waddington, and combined by him with this one in his publication, No. 2074.

This inscription'doubtless refers to statues placed in the "Philippeion." I suppose IleXayis to be for IleXayios.

399. Shehba. Philippeion. Three fragments, A, B, and c, of the same inscription. Fragment A was found in the wall which fills up the portal of the "Philippeion," in the fourth tier from the sill, between the east jamb and the stone which contains

No. 08. This fragment is set on its right end, with its head to 1. XONTOYIP ov 6.

wards the west. It measures 62 cm. in length by *Kj* in height, 2. NCYNBION... and, except for the inscription, the face of the stone is perfectly 3. lOC TTAAri. plain, like that of No. 398. From the top of the stone to the inscription is 7 cm.: the inscription itself measures 29 cm. in height: from the bottom of the inscription to the bottom of the stone is 21 cm. : the letters are *$l/2* to 7 cm. high. It is unlikely, therefore, that the inscription consisted originally of more than three lines. The letters are of fairly good form, but are badly weathered. Copy of the editor.

Fragment B was found in situ, inside the "Philippeion," on the face of one of the piers which support the arches over the

niches on the east side, 1. XWTATONT-
TA r the first pier from the front: the inscribed stone is the third from 2. NT-
PYtUUNIAN r the present ground level.
The inscription is *6k* cm. long and 3.
ZOCAOYKHNA, *r* 24 cm. high: it begins
nearly at the top of the stone, and from
the bottom of the inscription to the bottom of the stone is 28 cm. The letters are
5 to *6l/2* cm. high. Copy of the editor.

Fragment c was found on the ground
inside the "Philippeion,"

I. OYTTPAITUUPIOS.,,,, *r* ,,, *c i r* immediately below fragment B. 1 he length
01 the hrst line is 71 cm., the height of
the whole inscription 29 cm. The inscrip
tion apparently began at the top of the
stone; but it is not possible to be certain
of this, since the stone is broken at the
top. From the bottom of the inscription
to the bottom of the stone is 15 cm. The
letters are *6V2* cm. high, and of good
form. Copy of the editor.

These fragments, placed together in
the order B, A, C, are as follows: 1. XU-
UTATONTTA XONTOYIPOYTTPAITWPIOY
2. NTPYtUUNIAN NCYNBIONAYTOY 3.
ZOCAOYKHNA IOCTTAAriC

From Nos. 400, 401 a, and 401 b it
seems quite certain that the name of
Julius Priscus should be restored in the
first line, and from Nos. 398 and 400 a
it seems equally certain that the name of
Aurelius Antoninus should be restored
in the last line. The reading then will be:

B AC 1. 'oviov HpeloKOv, Tov ioar-
rarov 67rapov Tov lepov npairwpLov,
2. TpvfwvLav 77 v, crvvftiov avrov, 3.
AiprjX. 'AvravZ(i)o;, SovKrjvdpios,
IleXayis.

(*These statues of*) *Julius Priscus, the
most excellent prefect of the sacred
praetorian guard, and (of) Tryphoniane,
his wife Aurelius Antoninus, Pelagis,
duccuarius, (set up).*

Doubtless this inscription was on the
front of the bases of the three niches
on the east side of the building, immediately below the bottom of the niches
themselves, and running across the piers
between them. Since there were three
niches, it is probable that there was also
a statue of Priscus' son, to whom No.
401a refers. If so, then the words /cat
Tov hdva, viov amov, feat may be sup-

plied for the lacuna in line 2.
400. Shehba. Philippeion. Stone at the
right corner of the present entrance to
the "Philippeion," which is in the west
side at the northwest corner of the building. This wall is of modern construction, built to replace the ancient wall,
which has tumbled down. The stone is
upside down, in the third course above
an ancient pavement. The thickness of
the stone is about 44 cm., and its face,
which is perfectly plain except for the
inscription, measures 102 by 54 cm. A
straight piece, 9 cm. wide, has been
chipped from the face of the stone at the
left end, all the way down. Also, at the
lower left corner, and inside the piece
just mentioned, another flake, 17 cm.
wide and 19 to 24 cm. high, has been
chipped out. At the upper right corner a
small triangle has been broken off, and
the lower right corner is badly weathered. The letters are fairly good at the
beginning, but smaller and of somewhat
different form in the last two or three
lines. Most of the letters are about 5 cm.
high. Copy of the editor. *These statues
of) the masters of the world, Marci Julii
Philippi, Angus ti, and our lady, Severa
Augusta, and the most excellent prefect
of the sacred praetorian guard, Julius
Priscus, Claudius Aurelius Tiberius,
ducenarius, dikaiodotes lord justice) of
this city of most illustrious men, being
promoted by them, set up).*
This inscription was probably below the
niche opposite the entrance.
400 a. Shehba. "Sur une pierre d£-
tachee, pres du petit temple carre mais
de l'autre cote de la voie antique. Grandes lettres mal gravees, semblables a
celles du numero precedent (Nos. 398
and 398 a); l'inscription est incomplete
a droite." Waddington, No. 2075. /. G.
R. in, No. 1199. 1 ONMAPI.... M. 'ovCov
Maplvov, This statue of) Marcus Julius
2. ©ONTTATPA 0ebv irarepa rov 2e/
8acrroC, Marinus, divine father of Au-
gus 3. AYPHA-ANTU).... Avprpio%)
'Avrwvivos, tus, Aurelius Antoninus,
ducena 4. AOYKHNAPIO hovK-qvdpio9.
rius, set up). 401. Shehba. In the wall
of a house, above the roof of the first
story, a short distance west of the
"Philippeion." Copy of the editor. _,,

The name 'PovSeav is probably another
1. PDYAEuNDC PovSewvos Ajvtjpov ....
Arabic double-diminutive, from *Ru-
daik,* 2. NHMaY *Of Rudeon (son) of
Anemos.* .... *r* ,,,.,..
the diminutive of *Radk,* with the
diminutive termination -*mv.* If so, the
original name was *Rudaihdn* or *Rudaihdn,* which in Greek should have been
both written and pronounced
'PovSaioiu, not 'PouSewv. The same
confusion of vowels seems to have tak-
en place in the name A os, which I suppose to be for the Arabic *An1 am.2* Perhaps, however, *pvr)pov* should be read.
On this roof was a torso of a winged figure in relief, about three quarters of life
size. The figure appeared to be that of a
Nike, flying sideways, probably with a
wreath in the outstretched hands. Head
and bust were gone, and I think also the
feet.
1 Like *Sfi/ifuvXavoi:* see No. 387.
2 See Nos. 366, 371, 389, etc. A name
Avt/ios, however, is found in Wad.
2053 d, 2412 f and 2412 h.
401 a. Shehba. "Sur une console dans
le mur, aupres du carrefour antique, entre le passage voute et la maison du
scheikh." Waddington No. 2077. C-J-
G4602. /. G. R. in, 1201.
I found this inscription and compared
Waddington's copy with it, but made no
copy myself.

Toy *Selva* ..., 'loi»X *Lov Hpeicr* kov,
Tou i£owrd toi/j indpov Mecro iroj Ta/
Aias, *vibv d_cjpov, f* 7rdi?, Sid 'iovxlov
MaXou, *f3ov(euTov),* Ouv8lkov Ko.1
c7ri/AeXi7Tou, *p,(vrjp,rf;)-(dpiv).* This
statue of) 1, youthful son of Julius
Priscus, the most excellent governor of
Mesopotamia, the city erected, through
Iulios Malkhos, councilor, syndic and
superintendent, for (his) remembrance.

On the persons mentioned in this inscription see Waddington's commentary to No. 2077. See also No. 399
above. Julius Priscus is probably the
brother of the emperor Philip, to whom,
at one time, the emperor entrusted the
command of the troops in Syria, and
whose exactions led to the revolt under
Iotapianos.1 The senator Iulios Malkhos
is probably the same as Iulios Sentios
Malkhos mentioned in No. 395.

401 b. Shehba. "Sur une autre console, a cote de la precedente." Waddington, No. 2078. C. I. G. 4603. /. G. R. in, 1202.

I found this inscription and compared Waddington's copy with it, but made no copy myself.

Top *8elva, 'lovXCovTlpeia-Kov, Tov owraTou iirdpov* Mco-07roTa/iias, *viov,* Kacrcrto? *Tei/Ao#£os, dnb f3(ev)f(i. Kia.piov) nereiTop, Tov dwpou, p.(yrjp. t);) (dpiv).* (This statiteof) youthful son of Julius Priscus, the most excellent governor of Mesopotamia, Kassios Teimothcos, beneficiarius and afterwards petitor, erected for (his) remembrance.

See the commentary on the preceding inscription.

402. Shehba. Altar. On a small altar in a modern courtyard, into which one enters after passing through the portal men Aa/3105, *.ypdp.ov, dvedrjKev.* tioned under No. "3Q2 a and turning to the right. CArM

The height of the altar is 72 cm.: its top AMOV Darios, (son) of Agmamos, set up (this altar) s lV2 em. square. The die is 20 cm. high, and 17 broad. The first four lines of the inscription are on the face of the die, while the fifth line is on the lowest fascia of the mouldings, so that it is 12 cm. below the fourth line. The letters are slightly over 4 cm. high. Copy by the editor.

Published by Professor Briinnow in M. P. V., 1899, P-86, No. 51.

On the name Aaos, the Arabic '*Agmam*, see Part IV, p. 219 (addendum to p. 118).

403. Shehba. Church, 552 A.d. In a house at the south side of the court w here No. 402 was found. The inscription is on the soffit of an arch, about 3 feet 1 Waddington, I.e. Zosimus, I, iy-20. Compare also No. 393. See, however, Waddington's objections, in his commentary. above the present floor. Total height of the inscription 47 cm.: length 73 cm. The letters of the first line are iol/2 cm. high, those of the fourth line 5 cm., those of the fifth 6 cm. Copy of the editor.

Published by Professor Briinnow in M. P. V., 1899, p. 86, No. 50.

5

I think that the Y, in line 4, was intended as a correction of the preceding letter, C, carved there by mistake.

Probably the arch which bears this inscription was one of the lower arches over the side aisle of a basilical church, such, for example, as that shown in the lower photograph on p. 409 of Part II.

404. Kan Aw At. In a wall facing the north, a few steps northeast of the "Medresseh": the inscription is upside down, about 10 feet from the 1. Okaiiap ground. The wall, into which this fragment has been built, seemed 2 AErEI to be of quite recent construction. The fragment itself measures 3. EX1 2 2g cm. te ietters are 8 cm. high. Copy of the editor.

This is a small part of what is perhaps the most important inscription in the Hauran. It has been described and published by Cyril Graham, Transact. Roy. Soc. Lit., VI, Nos. 23 and 24, and by Waddington, No. 2329. Also in /. G. R. in, 1223. Waddington says of it: "Sur deux assises separees et employees dans la construction d'un edifice, qui parait avoir ete une eglise. Cet edifice se trouve a droite de la voie pavee antique qui monte vers le batiment, que les habitants appellent le *medresse*. Les lettres sont belles; celles des deux premieres lignes sont plus grandes que les autres. " Waddington's text of the inscription is as follows:

A. Bgutixcus '*Ay pCirva; jioKai(rap /cat (fLkopw p.ouo;* Xeyei-0r)pt,d&ovs *KaTaxrTci* creco?

B. *Ovk* oT8' oVos *pXP1, vv* Xa#diTs *Koi iv* 7roXXoi? *Ts a)pa; pepecriv ivf-fxokev r* ai'Tts e *Xev v* Z1?' ow5 *vore y* King Agrippa, Friend of Caesar and Friend of Rome, says: from (your) beast-like condition / know not how, lying hid until now, and lurking in holes in many parts of the country had, or at least never wholly

See Waddington's very interesting commentary on this inscription.

405. Kanawat. Base Of A Statue. A stone in the front wall of a house on the west side of one of the principal streets in the north part of the village, a little west of the stream. The inscription is

contained in a dove-tail plate, sunk in the face of the stone. The stone is 63 cm. long at the top, 70 cm. at the bottom, and 40 cm. high. It is broken at the right end, so that perhaps half of the inscription is lost: at the left, however, the stone is complete. The dove-tail measures 29 and 6 cm. in height, by 9 cm. in length, and extends to within 1 y2 cm. of the left edge of the stone. The letters are incised, and are from 4 to 4y2 cm. high. Copied by Dr. Littmann and the editor.

Published by Professor Brunnow in M. P. V. 1899, No. 45, p. 84. I. G. R. Ill, No. 1230.

1. r. *Tle(Tp)uviov,* roiou *vlov,* (?) 2. *Lckowsov,* YipovS Xey(iaij/os) 3. 8' *2. kv0(ikj;) irpivKiira yarepov, iirl* 4. '*IouX(iov) HdTopveivov, _irpea-/ 3(evrov)* S/S(aoroC) 5. *avTMTTp(arqyov),* '*S.eirjvol* 6. Tt?5 *lepa;* 7rXa.Teia? *ayvcL()* 7. a? X"/31" (This statue of) G(aius) Petronius, G(aius' son), Secundus, of Brond(isium?), (second) centurion of the second line (of the first cohort? in the 4th Scythian legion, under Julius Satoruinus, legatus Augusti pro praetore, the people of Si' (erected), in recognition of (his services in connection with) the sacred square.

Julius Saturninus was imperial legate of Syria under Severus Alexander (222235 A.d.). Compare Waddington 2309, 2309 a and 2524. The fourth Scythian legion is mentioned in Waddington 2407 and 2714: the *tu-qvoi* or *tmvoL* in Waddington 2367 (from Si') and 2418 (from " Rimet-el-Lohf"). The letters BPONA probably denote Petronius' native town: perhaps the adjective should be read *Bpov8co-tvof,* for *Bpevrealvov, of Brundusium.* For the ending of line 3 Professor Brunnow suggests *vf' r)yep,oviq;* but I believe the last extant letter to be C, before which I believe there are traces of a small and cramped Y. For the ending of line 5 Professor Brunnow suggests *irpa.yp.aTc.vTaL,* and for the ending of line 6 dyeia? which I have adopted: for the latter see Waddington 2530.

406. Kanawat. Over a niche, now to be seen in a courtyard in the northern part

of the town. The first line is 68 cm. long, the second 116. The letters of the first line are 4 cm. high, of the second 10 cm. Copied by Dr. Littmann and the editor.

The second line was published by Porter, and by Waddington, No. 2359. The whole inscription has been published by Dussaud and Macler, *Mission*, p. 245 (647), No. 18. Also in / *G. R. Ill*, No. 1227. The wall, which contains this niche, was at one time covered with stucco, and this doubtless concealed the first line when Porter and Waddington made their copies.

Inscr. 405. From a drawing. Scale 1:io.

A. 6TOYCIAKYPIOYC6
B. AYIONIMAKAPI
"Erovs *ia KvpCov owjpov. Avfjovi. fia.Ka.pi. In the 11th year of(our) lord Sevcrus ?). To blessed Auxon.*

Doubtless the Severus here referred to is Septimius Severus: if so, the date given in the first line, A, is 203 A.d. But I doubt whether this line and the second, B, belong together. The upper stone looks like a part of the cap of a large pier, roughly cut to fit inscriptions 46 A and B. this piace Consequently its inscription is but a fragment of a line originally much longer than B. 407-411. Kanawat. Temple Ob Helios (?). This is a small peripteral temple, of which the cella is now completely ruined, about a quarter of a mile northwest of the town, on the road to 'Atil. See Part II, p. 354 ff. From the rather uncertain evidence of one of the inscriptions, No. 407, it appears to have been a temple of Helios.

407. The inscription is on the east face of the die of the pedestal, just above the base moulding, of the first column at the south end of the outer row of columns on the east side of the temple. Probably there was another column in this same row, still further south, bringing the corner column of this row into line with the columns of the south side. The columns at the west end of the temple also bear inscriptions; but these are on the inner side of the pedestals, on or above the cap moulding. The face of the die is 93 cm. wide, and the space above the top

of the base moulding, to the joint between the lower and the middle stones which form the pedestal, is 12 cm. high. The space which contains the inscription, therefore, is 93 by 12 cm. The inscription itself is 85 cm. long, the letters are from 3 to 5 cm. high. Copied by Dr. Littmann, Mr. Huxley and the editor.

Published in *C. I. G.* 4605. Waddington, No. 2333.

V.I., at the end of the first line: Buckingham, TO.... IAI IOY; Seetzen, TOY. IAI.. AIOY; Waddington, TOYTA--" AIOY; Berggren, TON NAONTOYHAIOY. 6e/8xpT7S *scdpov* Tov vaoi' 'HXiou e#c *Twv IBitov, evrefH5)v, dv0r)Kev. Thcbanes, son of SitJiros, in devout service erected at his own expense this temple of Helios.*

The reading of the first line is unfortunately most uncertain. Waddington renders the line:.... eySai? *XLdpov* Too Ta. . *yaiov* 00 But I am inclined to believe that Berg gren saw this pedestal in better condition than most of his successors, and hence I have followed his reading in the main. The question, however, whether this was really a temple of Helios — and this is of course the most important question of all— must be left for the present unsettled.

408. At the west end of the temple, on the east side of the pedestal of the fourth column from the north, corresponding to the two following (Nos. 409 and 410). The inscription is contained in a single line, in the place occupied by the upper lines of the corresponding inscriptions, while the letters are of the same size as those of the lower lines. The first letter A stood 75 cm. from the beginning of the original space: the extant part of the inscription is 30 cm. in length, the total length of the original space 1.21 m. (see below, No. 410). The letters are *y2* cm. high. Copied by Dr. Littmann and the editor.

Published in *C. I. G.* 4606. Waddington, No. 2334. Burton and Drake, No. 74.

A9OYANA0....

Cloov a.va6r)fLCL. An offering, set up by son of (?).... athos.
Waddington suggests *Maixddov.* 409. At the west end of the temple, on the east side of the pedestal of the third col-

umn from the north, corresponding to the preceding inscription, No. 408. The A of the first line stood 40 cm. from the beginning of the original space; but both the left and the right corners of the pedestal on this side are now broken off. The space occupied by the upper line is 8 cm. in height, the letters themselves 6-7 cm. high: the letters of the lower line are 3-4 cm. high. Copied by Dr. Littmann and the editor.

Published in *C. I. G.* 4606. Waddington, No. 2335. Burton and Drake, No. 74.

AIJIA0.... evcreT/s *Kol £cAdaT/3is* COPAB UUPAB..... *devout and patriotic, erected t/iis).*

With this inscription compare Waddington 2580 (Palmyra). But see also, for a somewhat different phrase which would perhaps be equally admissible here, Waddington, No. 2339 ff. (Kanawat). It is curious to note that the letters of this fragmentary inscription would help to supply the missing portion of the famous Agrippa inscription (Waddington 2329= No. 404 above): BcurtXcvs 'AypiWas *fyikoKaicrap* kai tiAOpw/zaios Aeyei *Kt.* But the letters of this fragment differ both in size and in form from those just quoted, and in any case it is of course inherently improbable that the stones which had once borne Agrippa's proclamation were afterwards made into pedestals for the columns at the back of this little temple. 410. At the west end of the temple, on the inner or east side of the pedestal of the second column from the north, corresponding to the AO.IxeTTCCOYA Ms)xTMi preceding inscriptions, Nos. 2-'AIUJN6YC6BIACXA & TM X«l. 408 and 409 The Upper *Erected by.... los, son of Khettesos, at his own expense, for sake* line is just above the cap *fPtety* moulding, the lower line on the highest band of the moulding itself. Both of the inside corners of the pedestal are broken off. The remaining portion of the upper line of the inscription measures 67.5 cm. in length: the remaining part of the lower line is 3 cm. shorter on the right. The space occupied by this inscription was originally 23.5 cm. longer towards the left, and 29 cm. towards the right.

The corresponding space on the west side of the pedestal measures 121.5 cm. The space of the lower line is about 1 cm. longer at each end than that of the upper line. The letters are 5 and *2XA* cm-high. Copied by Dr. Littmann and the editor.

Published in *C. I. G.* 4606. Waddington, No. 2336. Burton and Drake, No. 74.

410 a. This inscription was copied and published by Waddington, No. 2337: he says that it was found "Sur un fragment d'une base renversee, a cote des precedentes. L'inscription est complete a droite." I did not see this monument. 1 aXos SaXa/ota-*a/os, son of Salatnanes, together* 2. vov crvv Tw inS Koiuo)VTjcra;. *with his son, erected this f).*

Salamanes is a good Arabic name, *Salman:* kindred forms occur in Safaitic. See also above, p. 124 f.

410 b. One other inscription, reported by Seetzen alone, seems to have belonged to this same temple. It is published in *C. I. G.* No. 4606, together with three of the inscriptions published above (Nos. 408, 409 and 410), as if all four formed one continuous document. Possibly this fragment contains the name of some god, other than Helios, who was worshipped in this temple. iAN6NOC0UUYABPOY:.... evfa(/i)o/ os 0w YABPOY6. 411. At the south side of the temple, on the top of the plinth below the pedestal of the column which was fourth or fifth from the east. The pedestal, if in place, would cover the inscription. The top of the plinth at present measures 121 by 95 cm.: the inscription measures 80 cm. in length, and begins 41 cm. from the left edge of the stone. I think, however, that the plinth was originally somewhat larger than this block in its present condition. For in a drawing which Dr. Littmann made for me of one of the pedestals of this temple, the length of the plinth is given as 130 cm. If, then, some 10 cm. is lacking from the plinth in question, there was room originally for one more *Riifimis.* letter at the right, viz. I or Y. The letters are very large and well formed: P is 14 cm. high, $ 21 cm., and the rest 9 to 12 cm. Copied by Dr. Littmann, Mr. Hux-

ley and the editor.

Published by Waddington, No. 2338.

, „ r Waddington read 'Yov6&ve. Perhaps some stone-cutter POYtINO *Vov4uvo; /* 1 amused himself cutting his name here, while the building was in process of construction.

No other inscriptions, belonging to this temple, are known. I found, however, on the east side of the pedestal of the only column still standing on the south side, a small dove-tail plate in relief, which I believe to have contained an inscription in incised letters. But, although I worked over it for several hours, I was unable to read a single letter with sufficient certainty to make it worth recording.

412. Kanawat. A small, irregularly shaped fragment, found in a rude stone fence about 30 yards east of the "Temple of Helios" (Nos. 407 ff). The fragment is *Sy2* cm. long at the bottom, and 30 cm. high at the highest point. The letters are in simple relief, and about 12 cm. in height. Copied by Dr. Littmann and the editor. e I C 0 H «f T *Lo-07 was erected.* 413. Kanawat. Temple. Before the temple of Zeus, immediately south of the seraya. The stone, which bears this inscription, was the plinth below the base of the column on the left of the entrance: recently it was split up, on planes parallel with the face, into four slabs, of which the first has fallen forward and turned face about. See the photograph on p. 352 of Part II. The face of this slab measures 1.44 by 0.34 m., the space occupied by the inscription 43 cm. in length, by 32 in height. The letters, which are in relief, are 4 to 5 cm. high, and are well preserved. Copied by Dr. Littmann and the editor.

Published by Wetzstein, No. 189. Rey, p. 139. Waddington, 2340. Also by Wright and Souter, from a copy by Ewing, in *P. E. F.* 1895, p. 271.

413 a. Kanawat. Same Temple. "au temple situe au midi de l'edifice qu'on appelle le Serai: sur la base de la colonne de droite. Inscription tres-bien conserved." Waddington, No. 2339. Wetzstein, No. 188. Rey, p. 140. IIou7rXto9 A1X10? repiai'09 *$ovevrij;, HovirXiov Alkiov* tii7r7rau uios, *Tsv J±evvd8r);,*

fioTifirjxdixevoi Ail /Acyiara) *i T5v ihi-wv evcre/3iv dvearrjcrcv. Puplios Ailios Germanos, councilor, son of Puplios Ailios Philippos, of the (clan?) of Bennathe, in devotedservice to Zeus most-high, at his own expense, in piety set up (this column).*

A modern stone fence is built against this column base, so that the inscription is now concealed from view.

It would be interesting to know what god is called here Zeus Mey«rros. Doubtless it was the chief god of this place. Perhaps it was Ba'al Samin, whose great temple at the neighboring Si', which was obviously the seat of a most important cult, shows that this god was the object of very special veneration in this region. See Part II, p. 334 ff., and Part IV, p. 85 ff. The name of the tribe, *Bevvddr),* is probably akin to the Safaitic *r12.* 414. Kanawat. Built into the east wall of a house in the western part of the town. The inscription is in relief, in a dove-tail plate formed by bands 2 in relief. Copy of the editor. 3

Published by Waddington, No. 2344.

V.l. Waddington gives in line 2: TAIPHAOY, in line 3: 6YCBIAC.

Line 4, after the letters x APIN, was left blank originally. As M. Waddington remarks, the omega in this inscription has the form H: the inscription, therefore, is probably not later than the first or second century A.d. But compare No. 418, which has U).

The names are apparently Arabic: Xaaos *Faip-qXov* would be in Safaitic NTi? p HDJD. On names such as 7NTj?, see Part IV, p. 122.

415. Kanawat. On the base of a column in the seraya. The space occupied by the; inscription measures 39 by 10 cm. The letters are 4 to 5 cm. high. Copy of Dr. Littmann. 6KTUJNIAIUU e'#c *Tuv Islwv*

N *at his (or their) own expense* 416. Kanawat. Before the door of a house near the seraya, and said to have been brought from there.' The stone is broken on the right: its maximum length is 44 cm., its height 38. Copy of Dr. Littmann.

417. Kan Aw At. Fragment in the street

leading to the seraya, and said to have been brought from there. The total height of the fragment is 17 cm., of the letter space 11 y2: the length of the fragment is 21 cm. The letters are 3 cm. high. Copy of Dr. Littmann. *Rufus, (son) of , and , (soft?) of Banathos,.. built*

"Petit autel bris6 par le bas et gisant sur le bord du chemin, entre le medresse et le deuxieme moulin. Inscription mal gravee et fruste." Waddington, No. 2343.

In line 3, *yyvpQy* is doubtless a solecism for *avijyei.pev,* as *This holy altar a (man) of Kenatha set up, saved from, to savior gods, (being cured?) of (his) sickness,* Waddington assumed. In Kea *Rufus. 07)v6sl* Waddington believed the ancient name of Kanawat to be found. I cannot explain line 5: perhaps this contained the name of a village, belonging to Kanatha, where Rufus lived. In lines 8 and 9 I am tempted to restore *x-PLV*

418. Kanawat. In a courtyard, a short distance northwest of the "medresseh." The whole stone measures 85 by 36 cm. The inscription is in a dove-tail plate, the space inside of which, occupied by the inscription, is 32 cm. long and 34 high. The letters are 5 cm. high. Copy of Dr. Littmann.

Published by Burton and Drake, No. 84. Also by Professor Briinnow in *M. P. V.,* 1899, p. 85, No. 46.

Xa.Gui/x.09 *YtaprfKov,* evcre/Sei'as *dpiv,* Ck *Toiv* ιxc *Khaamtnos (sou) of Ghearelos,for sake of piety, at his own expense.*

Inscr. 418. From a drawing.

Compare No. 414. Professor Briinnow gives *Xadp,o.* 1 Properly Kamft/ ras: see Wad. 2216 and 2331 a. See also Waddington's commentary on No. 2329.

419. Kanawat. Above the lintel of a courtyard, in the northwestern part of the town. The inscription is in the upper left-hand corner of a fairly large block, the face of which is otherwise perfectly plain. It is probable, therefore, that the block which originally adjoined this one on the left contained a part of the inscription, possibly also the block or blocks above. Copy of the editor.

Published by Waddington, No. 2347. V.I., line 1: TYAON, Waddington.

If Waddington's reading of the first line is correct, his text of this line should doubtless be accepted, To *8io-tvov: this distylos (i.e. these twin columns?).* Compare the following inscription (419 a).

419 a. Kanawat. Column. "Sur un fragment de colonne, tombe dans le ravin qui longe la ville, pres de la maison du scheikh." "Copie de M. Wetzstein, No. 193." Waddington. No. 2347 a.

XiXio? O... Xto? To *Siotvxov K TOiV Islcjv avedrjKtv. Silios O... lios set up this bicolumnar (monument) at his own expense.*

This inscription is possibly the same as *C. I. G.* 4615.

420. Kanawat. On a broken stone in a field on the east side of the stream, a short distance north of the bridge. The stone is 1.54 m. long, 42 cm. high, and 32 cm. thick. The inscription is in a dove-tail plate, the space within which measures 54 by 26 cm. The letters are 62 cm. high, well formed and well preserved. Copy of Dr. Littmann.

Published by MM. Dussaud and Macler, *Mission,* p. 245, No. 16. *I. G. R.* Ill, No. 1233.

421. Kanawat. Altar. A small octagonal altar, in a house a short distance northwest of the bridge, and now used as a pillar supporting an arbor. The height 78 cm. The face, which bears the inscription, measures 50 by 11 cm.

The letters, which are 2 to 3 cm. high, are of fairly good form, but are badly aligned. Copy of the editor.

Published by Waddington, No. 2348.

The second o in the second line is carved on the next face of the column on the right.

The name Movai/ceiSai'o? is a double diminutive, like Sa/x/iovXai'os in No. 387: it is from *Munaikidh,* the diminutive of *Munkidh,* with the diminutive termination *-an.* 422. Kanawat. In a wall in the northern part of the town. The stone is about one meter long, and 40 cm. wide: it has been built into the wall upside down. The inscription is on the upper left-hand corner of the stone, so that it is probable

that the first part of the inscription was on the stone which originally adjoined this on the left, as in the case of No. 419. The rest of the stone is blank. The letters are 5 cm. high. Copied by Dr. Littmann and the editor.

Published by Waddington, No. 2353. Also by MM. Dussaud and Macler, *Mission,* p. 245, No. 17. INTirOCMIN-NIOCnAK Ioriyo? MiVi/cos nAK.

V.l. The first letter might be H or n.

The inscription appears to be complete at the right end, but there was doubtless the beginning of another line on the other stone, completing the word which begins with Tok. In Waddington's copy, the first letter has the form I: see No. 122.

423. Kanawat. Tomb. "Au-dessus de la porte d'une maison, dans un encadrement." Waddington, No. 2354. Waddington's text was compared with the original by Dr. Littmann. 1. BAAPOCCI9POYTOY 2. KAIEMMICANOY-TOM 3. NHMEIONEKTUN *Badros, (son) of Sithros, who (is) also Hemmisanos, built this monument* 4. IAIWNETTOIHCEN V.l., line 1: BAAAPOC, Dr. Littmann.

Both *Badr* and *Si?rare* Arabic names. The name E/u./uo-ai'os is probably the Safaitic DDri: there are also Arabic names from the root DDI"!. Consequently I believe that E/A/xio-afo? has nothing to do with *'Eiiurqv6$=ofEmesa,* i.e. *of Horns.* 424. Kanawat. Tomb. Above the door of a house. The inscription is in a dove-tail plate: the letters are in relief. Copy by Dr. Littmann.

Published in *C. I. G.* 4567 (wrongly assigned to Zorava). Waddington, No. 2356. Burton and Drake, No. 83.

Possibly *Zavanos* is the Arabic *Sanam.* But perhaps the second C in line i is due to a mistake: if so, the name in line 2 is doubtless *kvaAn'am.* See Nos. 366, 389, etc.

1. 2. 3 *Klaudios, (son) of Sanamos, (built) this monument* (or *tomb).* 425. Kanawat. Tomb. Over a window beside a door, in the northwestern part of the town. The inscription is incised in a plate with rudimentary dove-tails at the ends. The plate itself is in relief, and measures 39 cm. in length by 31 in height. The dove-tails are 7 cm. long.

The upper right-hand corner of the stone is somewhat broken; but the raised plate with its inscription is intact. The letters are 32 to 4 cm. in height, and rather rude, but perfectly legible. I could find no trace of letters beyond the plate: the H, which stands at the end of the last line, evidently belongs to the line above. Copy of Dr. Littmann.

Inscr. 425. From a drawing. Scale i: 10.

XcuXov Xaaerou *Tov* Seeipov To *fj. vTffj.clov*. *Khailos (son) of Khasetos, (son) of Seeiros, his monument.*

The name XalXos occurs in Waddington, 2140, but refers there apparently to another person. *Xdo-eros* occurs in Waddington 2298 and 2544. The person mentioned in No. 2544 (Umm iz-Zetun), who may possibly be the same as the father of XcuXo? of Kanawat, seems to have lived in the time of the emperor Decius (249-251 A. d.). Moreover, the name may indicate a connection with the family of the *XaoeTrfvot* (Waddington 2393, 2396, 2397 and 2547). I do not believe, however, that there is any necessary connection between the *Xaa-crrfvoL* and the tribe of *Azd* The originals of the names in the present inscription are doubtless *Khail, Kasit* and *Sa'ir.* 426. Kanawat. Fragment, probably a part of the top moulding of a pier, lying before the door of a house in the western part of the town. The length of the fragment is 38, its height 20 cm. The letters are 4 to *y2* cm. high. Copy of Dr. Littmann.

AITKNON *Kox Tekvov and child* or possibly *and (of their) children* 427. Kanawat. Two fragments in the east wall of a vineyard, about a mile north of Kanawat. The larger fragment is used as a lintel, being laid face down over the 1 Wad. 2393, commentary. entrance gate. The last two or three letters of each line of this fragment are partly concealed by the stone on which the right end rests. The other fragment, containing the last three letters of the first three lines and a blank space at the end of the fourth line, is the lowest stone in the southern jamb, facing northwards. The two fragments give the whole inscription complete.

The inscription was in a plate sunk in the face of the stone, i cm. deep. Three lines at the end form a rude dove-tail. The first fragment measures, inside the plate, 94 by 31 cm., the second about 20 by 31. The letters are 4 cm. high. Copy of the editor.

I.   CAM90C0KAIYB0YA0CAN Sa/AC0os, *0 Ko.1* Evvxo?, *Samethos, who (is) also Eubu*

It is difficult to avoid the conviction that *0$ trarpcoa)* should be read at the end of line 3 and the beginning of line 4. I believe, however, that nAnnuu was actually on the stone: these letters were not covered in any way, and there is no suggestion of any uncertainty in my copy. But there may have been great similarity between *irdmrb)* and *Trarpwa)* in the original writing, and the stone-cutter may have made a mistake. In that case we should translate: *Samethos... built this tmver... for the god of his fathers, for sake of piety.*

The name EuySouAos may be a translation of the Semitic name Sa/ieos. For, as Dr. Littmann tells mc, there is in Arabic a verb *shamata,* meaning *to say "God bless you"* for example to one who sneezes. If so, the name would show that sometimes the people who assumed Greek or Roman names were still conscious of the significance of their original Semitic names. On the name Ava/ xos see No. 366, etc.

427 a. 'atil. Temple, 151 A.d. "Sur l'ante de gauche du temple corinthien; inscription complete et tres-bien conservee. La raeme inscription etait repetee sur l'autre ante, mais il n'en reste que la moitie' de droite." Waddington, No. 2372. *C. I. G.* 4608. /. *G. R.* in, 1237.

This inscription is now hidden by the modern walls which have been built against the ancient front of the temple, so that only the first few letters can be seen. See Part II, p. 343 ft, Fig. 121.

'*Tirep* trcuTTj/Dia? *Kvpiov* Kaura/aos '*Avrwvelvov* Se/SacTToS Eucrej8oC(s), OvaSSxo?   *Ma0eiov   Tov* Ova(S)877X01; ras 7ra/3aora8a.? *nai* «adV(i)a *Kox* Tx *iirdvoi avrwv* eVicrrvXia *Kal* /aXi'(a)s *ix Tw(v) 18lwi iTrorjaev,* erows 18' '*Avrtoveu/ov* K(aura/so)5. *For the safety of (our) lord*

Caesar Antoninus Augustus Pius, Uaddelos (son) of Matheios the (son) of Uaddelos made the portico and colonncttes and the entablature upon them and (the) niches (?) at his own expense, in (the) 14th year of Antoninus Caesar. (151 A.D.) los, (son) of Anamos, built this tower at his own expense to his divine grandfather (?), for sake of piety.

All the parts of the temple mentioned in this inscription are shown in the photograph of the similar temple given in Part II, p. 346, and in the restoration of both temples n p. 345

The names *Wadd'el* and *Mattai* are both common in Safaitic.

427 b. Si, Statue. "Sur une base trouvee devant le temple, a droite de la porte; le pied de la statue etait encore adherent a la base. Inscription tres-bien conservee. " Waddington, No. 2364. /. *G. R.* in, 1243. This inscription is said to be now in the Louvre.

BaJfriXeZ '*HpwSei Kvpio* 'O/SauraTo? SadSou *iQyjKa Tov dvBpidvTa* reus e/tal? *hairdvaAJ;.* To King Herod (my) lord I, Obaisatos (son) of Saodos, set up this statue at my own expense.

The names *Obaishat* and *SiVd* are common in Safaitic.

428. Si', Lintel (?). Three fragments of a lintel or architrave, two of which, the first and third, found by this expedition near the middle of the great court of the temple. A squeeze was made of the first fragment, containing the first 20 letters of the first line and the first 19 of the second and third. This fragment, measured along the first line of the inscription, is 83 cm. long. The inscription is at the bottom, incised on three fasciae, each of which is between 5 and 6 cm. high. The letters are from 4 to /2 cm. high.

Published by Waddington, No. 2365. Wright and Souter, in *P. E. F.* 1895, P-272-/ *G. R.* in, 1244.

Inscr. 428. Cast from a squeeze.

The whole inscription is published by Waddington as follows: 1. ETTIBAII AEXlIMErAAOYArPinnA(J)l   AOKAI-IAPOXEYIEBOYIKAItIAOP.QM A 2. OY-TOYEKBAZI-
AEIlIMErAAOYArPinnAJ)IAOKAI-IAPOIEYIEBOYZKAI..

3.   AOPilMAlOY
A4APEYIAnEAEYeEPOIKA-
IArPinTTAIYIOIANEeHKAN
'E7Ti /Sao-tXtw? *peydXov* 'AypiWa,
to«aio-a/30s, *Under (the) great king
Agrippa, Friend-of-Caesar, Evcrefiovs
Kal Siop(o(j.a 1 ov, Tov e'/c /3acriXe
&)S Pius, Friend-of-Pome, the (son) of
(the) great king peydkov ypLmra,
iikoKalo-apo;, Eucre/SoO? Kal Agrippa, Friend-of-Caesar, Pius, Friend-of-
Rome, 4i Kop(opaiov, (fapev; di-
rekevdzpos Kal yplir-Aphareus a freed-
man and Agrippa his son erected 7ras
ino? av£8r)Kav. (this).*

The date of this inscription falls between 50 and 100 A.d. It is uncertain
to what building this inscription refers.
See Part II, p. 322. A full description of
the temples and sacred precinct at Si'
will appear in the publications of the
Princeton Archaeological Expedition of
1905.

428 a. Si', Statue. "Sur un piedestal,
trouve devant le temple; l'inscription
est dans un encadrement de forme particuliere." Waddington, No. 2366.

'O *Srjftos, 6 Toi* 'OySaicrT/vttii/,
*eTeLp.noev M.aet)(adov Moaieoov
vneooLKoSofirjo-avTL To iepov, aperijs
re Kal eucre/Seta? apiv. The people of
the Obaisenoi honored (with this statue)
Malcikhathos (son) of Moaieros, who
built in their behalf ("i) this temple, for
(his) virtue and piety.*

The form *vwepoiKohop-rjo-avri.* is
doubtless for *vnepoLKoSoiMijo-avra:*
possibly the word means *built higher ox
enlarged.* Compare *Corpus Inscr. Sem.,*
11, 164, and Part II, P-335-See also Part
IV, p. 85 ff.

428 b. Si, Statue. "Sur une base encore
en place sur le parvis du temple. Lettres
de 3 centimetres." Waddington No.
2367. *'Zeeirjvwv To Kolvov a vedrjKav
MaXctaJa Avaov Tov* Moaiepou, on
Kareo-Keva o"as *To £ep6i'? Kal Tov
wepl avro navra Koajfjuov. The community of Seeienoi set up (this statue) to
Maleikhathos (son) of Ausos the (son) of
Moaieros, because thou hast equipped
the temple and (furnished) all the ornament about it.*

Compare the preceding inscription and
its commentary; also the commentary to

Waddington 2367.

429. Si. Stone lying on the top of a heap
of other blocks, about thirty feet southeast of the main portal of the temple.
This stone is 51 cm. high by 27 wide:
it was originally part of a wall, for it is
smoothly dressed only on the face, and
partially dressed on the sides for about
6 inches back from the face. The letters
are from 3 to 5 cm. high. Copy by the
editor.

Published by Wright and Souter,
from a copy by the Rev. W. Ewing, in *P.
E. F.* 1895, p. 273, No. 140.

I have been unable to decipher this
inscription: it seemed hopeless to the
first editors also.

430. Si', Stele, found lying face down
on a modern wall, which runs down the
center of the ancient pavement between
the inner, i.e. the westernmost, and the
central gateways. The bottom

I. MACA

Mao-axos So8atov e'7roiei *pvrjp r) s
x-PLV Masachos, (son) of Sodaio made
(this) for sake of memory.* of the stele
has been broken off: what remains is
from 65 to 75 cm. long, 24 cm. broad
across the lower part, and 24 cm. thick.
The upper part contained originally a
figure in relief, about 30 cm. high. The
figure is from the waist up, and is doubtless that of a man; but it has been battered off almost completely. Above the
head appear marks like the letters Y Y.
Below the figure are the mutilated remains of the first four lines of an inscription. The letters are about 4 cm.
high, and rather rude. Copy of the editor.

The name Mao-aos is akin to the Arabic *Mdsik:* SoSeuo? is perhaps *Sa'dai.*

A similar stele, a little larger and better perserved, lies about 40 feet down
the hill from the pavement, on the north
side, about opposite the other; but it was
not possible for me, with the time and
force at my disposal, to move the second stele so that I could see its face.

431. Sr. Temple Gate. On the east face
of the north jamb of the northernmost of
the three arches of the easternmost gateway across the sacred road to the tem-
ple.1 Two stones one above the other,
forming part of a pilaster, bear the in-

scription. See Part II, p. 361 ff. The total height of these two stones is 89 cm.
The original width of the pilaster was
about 40 cm., but a strip has been broken off the left side, leaving but 26 cm.
of width measured above the first line,
and 30 above the fourth. The first line
of the inscription is 22 J/2 cm. long, the
fourth line 25. It follows,

Right side of northernmost portal of
gateway at Si', looking west.

therefore, that two or three letters may
have been lost from the beginning of
some of the lines, one or two letters
from the others. The letters are 6 cm.
high, and fairly well carved. Copy of the
editor.

Published by Mordtmann in *Arch.-
Epigr. Mitth. aus Oesterr.,* VIII, p. 184,
from copies of Dr. Schroeder and M.
Loytved. Clermont-Ganneau in *R. A.,*
3e, IV, p. 270; *Recueil* I, p. 12, No. n.

There may be an Y at the end of the
third line, and in any case one would
naturally read *tv(x)v(v)* in the fourth; but
the A in this line is certain.

432. Si, The Same Gateway. Three fragments of what appears to have been an
architrave, found in the ruins of the
easternmost triple gate. This architrave
had at the top a vine ornament, below
which are handsome egg-and-dart and
bead 1 Marked A in the plan on p. 335
of Part II. mouldings. The center is occupied by a heavy meander pattern,
having heads or masks in the open
spaces. Below the meander is another
bead moulding, a plain fascia, and, at
the bottom of all, the inscription, incised
on a flat band, in exceedingly handsome
letters, *8l/2* cm. high, and perfectly
sharp still.

Fragment A was found in front of the
northernmost of the three gateways, on
the east side: it is 76 cm. long. Fragment
B is 34 4 cm. long, and fits on the left
of fragment A. These two fragments are
shown together in the photograph.

Fragment c was found in the gateway, with its face close against the inside of the north jamb: it could be
moved only far enough to see the letters. In the meander was a face, evidently male, with handsome features.
Copies of the editor. The fragments,

placed together in the order B, A, C, are as follows: nYAoNeKTHNIAIiIN *Tov nvkov Ik Twv ihuav*

Perhaps, if the words *ai dvpat* in the preceding inscription refer to the whole gateway and not merely to the doors themselves, we might suppose that the inscription on the jamb was merely an abridgment, placed on a level with the people's eyes, of the inscription on the architrave, which was doubtless at a considerable height. If so, the latter might perhaps be restored, after the model of the inscriptions from the temple of Zeus at Kanawat, as follows:

'IouXios 'Hpa«Xiros. /)iXorijU. 7jcraju.evo5 Au *MeyCo-rco, Tov Ttvxov Ik Twv Ibicjv _eKTt,oev. Iulios Heraklitos in devoted service to Most Mighty Zeus erected this gateway at his own expense.*

But this of course is purely hypothetical. Another fragment, which seems to be part of the same architrave, and has, like the other fragment, a face enclosed within the meander pattern, shows traces at the bottom of seven or eight letters, which seem to have been erased intentionally. These traces suggest the letters YAA-u--. But I could read nothing here with certainty. See the upper photograph on p. 364 of Part II.

432 a. Sr. "Sur une corniche ornee de pampres et brisee en deux morceaux. " Waddington, No. 2368. Wright and Souter, in *P. E. E.* 1895, p. 272, No. 138 f.

Maix«os Avtrov *Tov Moaiepov. Maleikhathos (sou) of Ausos the (son) of Moaieros.*

See Part IV, p. 85 ff.

Fragment No. i of architrave of gateway at Si'.

432 tx SI'. "Sur une autre corniche pareille, en deux morceaux." Waddington, No. 2369. *P. E. E.* 1895, p. 272, No. 137.

MaXetaos M *oaie'pov. Maleikhathos (son) of Moaieros.* 432 c. Suweda. Stone in a pier between two arches of a portico of a house, recently built, in the northern part of the town. The stone measures 85 by 36 cm. The inscription is in a dove-tail plate, the space within which is 62 cm. long by 28 cm. high.

The letters are *3l/2* to 5 cm. high. Copy of Dr. Littmann.

Published by Savignac, from a copy by PP. Jaussen and Wittner, in *R. Bid/.,* 1905, p. 95, No. 8.

T, c, *Under the oversight of Lukios, centurion.*

Inscr. 432 c. From a drawing. Scale i: 10. *6 J'*

Coc. Rufinus, who seems to have been a legate of Arabia, is mentioned also in an inscription in Der'at, Waddington 2070 c 432 d. Suweda. Statue. In the seraya, on the base of the statue of a man.

,, The face of the stone, on which the in XAAinoC XaXi7ros *Ooa.iva.Tov.* scription is cut, measures o by 12 cm. OAAINATOY *Khalipos (son) of Odaiuatvs. _,.., _,. , ..,*

The letters of the first line are 6 cm. high, those of the second 4 cm. Copy by Dr. Littmann.

Published by Briinnow, in *M. P. V.* 1899, p. 83, No. 41.

The name *0&a.maXos= Udhainat* was a very ancient and honorable one in Suweda. See Waddington 2320 and the commentary to Waddington 2308. *Khalipos* is probably akin to the Safai'tic *Khalaf.* 432 e. Busr Il-hariri. On the second pilaster from the south, on the east side of a building-just southwest of a large pool, in the northern part zt77? Ooeoo? o oidao-Kaos, frap.

b r l 2. Daiaa:kaadc: of the town. COPV of the editor. *May Odedos the teacher live, may he live!* 3. ZHCH

Published by Waddington, No. 2472.

V.I., line 1: Zhchdaeadc, Waddington.

Waddington No. 2474 is on two stones, one above the other, at the right of, and in the second and third course above, the pilaster on which is the inscription just described. Waddington says of both these inscriptions that they were found "dans la petite eglise." But I think it is obvious that they are not in their original places. Certainly the second belonged originally in a tomb. Perhaps the present inscription was written by some pupil, who wished his teacher well enough, after he was dead. In any case I believe that the verb *live* here

refers to the life beyond the grave.

The name oSeSos is probably the Safaitic *Hadaid,* diminutive of *Hadd:* compare the name ASSos, Waddington 2115, etc.

432 f. Busr Il-harirl Inside the wall in which the preceding inscription was found, on a stone now a step in a rude stair which leads southward to the roof of a building, perhaps originally a tomb or columbarium. The stone is 68 cm. long, 142 high, and 28 thick. The letters are 8 to 9 cm. high. Copy of the editor. TTTTOYTAI.... iX.t7T7rovTa :... . *of Philippos the* 432 g. ZOR'AH. Bath, 222-235 A·D·Stone now used as the lintel of a small doorway in a wall at the northwest corner of a building, perhaps a medieval khan, just west of the tower. Waddington says that this was a mosque, the tower a minaret. The stone is perfectly plain and rectangular: it is 1. 65 m. long at the top, 1.83 at the bottom, 36 cm. high and 40 cm. thick. Evidently it was originally a lintel. The right end has been lost: what remains is broken a little at the upper right and left corners. The letters are *l/2* cm. high. Copy of the editor.

Published by Cyril Graham, *Transact. Royal Soc. Lit.,v,* p. 290. *C.I. G.* 4562. Wad. 2480. /. *G. R.* Ill, 1155.

1. ArAGH TYXH 2. YnPCUUTHPIACK-AINIKHCTOYKYPIOYHMUUNAYTOK 3. AYPHAIOY660YHPOYA YYCBOYCEYTYX 4. KWMIACZOPAOYHNWNKTICCANTO-BAAANIONIA

V.l. Waddington gives, in line 3, AYPHAIOYCOYHPOY, and in line 4, 6KTICAN; but the letters 6 and CC, in these places, are marked as certain in my copy, and can be seen distinctly in the photograph.

A y a 6 y T v x 7). 'Twep crawij/ Jtas Kal vei/ojs *Tov Kvpiov rp-oiv* AvtokpdYo/aos, Kaurapos, Map/covJ *Aip-qkiov (tyeovrfpov A* XefdvSpo v, *Eucrc/ Sous, Evrvxovs, SefiacrTov, oi dnb p,r)Tpo /ctu/nias Zopaovrfvwv eKTiao-)av To ftakavetov* i8iais Saaai?.

Good Fortune.. For the safety and success of our lord and emperor, Caesar, Marcus Aurelius Severus Alexander, Pius, Felix, Augustus, those of the) metrokomia of the) Zoraouenoi built

this bath at their own expense.

The name *AXegdvh'pov* was erased from the stone in antiquity. Severus Alexander was emperor from 222 to 235 A.d. The form *Zopaovrjvuv* in this inscription is important because it indicates the true form of the ancient name of this place. See Part IV, p. 205.

433. ZOR'AH. Tomb (?). On the north side of a wall, at the left side of an arch, just north of the tower which is near the northwest corner of the same building. The stone is built into this wall upside down, about twelve feet from the ground. The in *I* scription is in a simple dove-tail plate formed by mouldings in very low relief. The plate measures 89 by 34 cm. inside the mouldings. The top line of the inscription seems to have been carved on the stone after the rest of the inscription was finished. It was carved partly on the upper moulding, and never had full room, even if the letters extended to the very top of the stone: it has since been so battered as to be almost completely effaced. The letters are 4 to *8l/2* cm. high. Copy of the editor.

Published by Cyril Graham, *Transact. Royal Soc. Lit.*, VI, p. 289. *C. I. G.* 4571. Wad. 2486. Mordtmann in *R. M.* 1872, p. 146. *I. G. R.* Ill, 1057.

irpivKLiros ey(twvos y
TaXXt/cs, OLKoSofirjcra Tois c/xot? T
&kvois Ztosgjp(a) Kal Aiofiij8(ei) /cat
ApaKovrCco Kal KXauSiaya)
OIKOAOMHCATOIC6MOIC *Kal* !«
TKNOICZHNOAWPKAI) *of the) princeps of the 3rd* AIOMHAHCKAIAPAKONTI-WKAI *Gallic Legion, I built for my children, Zenodoros and* MH *Diomedes and Drakontios and Klaudianos and Ge-*
T7 /

V.l. In the last two lines Waddington gives Aiomhahkaiapaioniikai, Kaayaia NuuKAireT--UJIAOtPHC. Richter *(C. I. G.)* gives OMHAHK Ap KAI, rT PHC. In the fourth line Waddington gives Zhnoawpw. 434. ZOR'AH. A plain stone in the south wall of the tower at the northwest corh ner of the same building, behind a column. The 1- letters are at the extreme left end of the stone, so 2. KA60 2 Xeo-....

z . that it is evident that this block pre-

serves only the 3. WNTHN 3 «vti)v. r *3* right end of an inscription, the rest of which was on the block which originally adjoined this one on the left. The whole stone measures 1.12 by 0.38 m.: the third line of the inscriDtion is 42 cm. in length. Copy of the editor.

Published by Waddington, No. 2489.

The last letter of the second line might be 9.

435. ZOR'AH. Tomb. Stone on the left of the lintel over the entrance to the vestibule of the same building, on the west side. The stone is ornamented with a dove-tail plate, formed by mouldings in relief, which contains the inscription. A similar block, which also contains an inscription in a dove-tail plate, is placed above the lintel of this same vestibule, and another at the right of the lintel. The plates at the right and left of the lintel about fill the faces of the blocks on which they are carved: the plate above the lintel is somewhat narrower, and the block which it occupies is much longer than the other blocks. All three are now placed upside down. On all three, in the angles formed by the dove-tails, are to be seen the remains of a coating of plaster, which had a fine, smooth, white surface. On the stone over the lintel this plaster was one centimeter thick. There is, however, no trace of plaster on the plates themselves, and in one case, No. 436, the letters of the inscription show traces of red pigment.

This stone measures 1.09 by 0.50 m.: the plate, including the dove-tails, is 1. 03 m. long, and inside the mouldings measures 64 by 38 cm. Most of the letters are 3 cm. high; but the first two or three letters are 5 cm. high. Copy of the editor.

The last two letters of line 5 are beyond the moulding of the plate.

Theodoros was probably another son of Aurelios Azizos, and died before the others built their monument. The name Afiɛos, the Arabic *'Azi2*, is found in No. 336 a; *Avapos*, the Arabic *An'am*, in Nos. 366, 371, 389, etc.

436. ZOR'AH. Stone above the lintel over the entrance to the vestibule of the same building, on the west side. The inscription is in a dove-tail plate, similar

to that of the foregoing (see above, No. 435). In this case the mouldings of the plate are in relief, *6l/2* cm. high. The space within the plate measures 63 by 27 cm. The letters are *.l/2* cm. high, and were at one time painted red. The inscription seems to have been intentionally erased. At any rate only traces of some of the letters remain. I think, however, that more can be read than I was able to make out in the time at my disposal. Copy of the editor. 1. KXau8io(s) K ta 2. *viol* 3 4. e(/CTi)crav ra *i*-(?) 5. S(wus 8)aj7ra(fai) s (?) 437. ZOR'AH. Tomb. Stone, similar to the foregoing, at the right of the lintel over the entrance to the vestibule of the same building, on the west side. The inscription is incised in a dove-tail plate formed by bands in relief. The whole stone 5 6 7 8 9 10 11 *For himself and (his) family Aineias built (this) splendid monument, having the renown of a great* exNOY *pedition, and furthermore having crossed (?) (the) un* TOYNEKAOITA-MENEC9AATTOPOI *failing Indus, none of (his) own brothers having stretched* OEOCEIAETICAIN HC *out (their) hands to him. Therefore may God grant him good; but if any one shares praise so unusual(l), may he give to this one sorrows.* CKAINHCMETEXEIAArEATWAE-ACTW

V.I., line 3: AYAOCEXWHITTA, Richter; KYAOCEX OPA, Burckhardt.

Line 5: OCAEITEAHIACINAONAOITON. Richter: YnOCAEnEAHIAT-TNaONAt9ITON. Burckhardt.

Line 11: 10 HTuET, Burckhardt: Richter does not give this line. For other readings see the *C. I. G.* 4563: these other readings have been omitted here, because in these places my own copy seemed to me certain.

The interpretation of this inscription proposed here is at least questionable. In the second hexameter TreS'o-a? might perhaps be emended to 77178170-05, or to *neXo-as* for *7reX. ao-as: having drawn near to*, or to *irepr-jcra: having crossed.* The Indus referred to may have been some stream not far from Zor'ah. The first six letters of the last line are very uncertain: the first might be any letter. Kaibel's text has, in the third verse, n-oj&s 8e 7ri'aicm' 8d/Liov *df0LTOi,* in the fifth and sixth, *aivrj; KeTTTocrvvr)jf /xerexei.* 437 a. ZOR'AH. Church Of St. George, 515 A. d. "Au-dessus de la porte de l'eglise Saint-George, a sa place originaire. L'inscription est tresbien conservee; de chaque cote, il y a une croix et des pampres, et sur le mur a cote, une croix, A et *n* et deux grappes de raisin." Waddington, No. 2498. Cyril Graham, *Transact.*, p. 305. *C. I. G.* 8627. Stokes, in *Con tent p. Review,* xxxvn, 1880, p. 979. Dittenberger, *O. G. I. S.* No. 610.

Inscription 437 a.

(7!4w) has become a house of God which once was) a lodging-place of demons: saving light hath shitted where darkness covered: where (once were) idols' sacrifices, now (are) choirs of angels, and where God was provoked to wrath, now God is propitiated. A certain man, Christ-loving, the primate Joannes, Diomedes' son, at his own expense, as a gift to God, made offering of (this) noble structure,placing herein the revered relic of (the) holy martyr Georgios, the gloriously victorious, who appeared to him, Joannes, and not in sleep, but manifestly, in (indiction) p, in (the) year 410. (515 A.D.) 438. ZOR'AH. Stone in a wall, a short distance west of the building described under No. 432 g. The whole stone measures 1.76 by 0.31 m. The first four letters are 36 cm. long, the last eight 55 cm. inscr. 438. From a drawing. Scale i: 20. In the center is a plain disk, about 25 cm. in diameter. The letters are 8 to 9 cm. high. Copy of Dr. Littmann.

Published by Waddington, No. 2502.

V.I., line 2: NECIACIA, Waddington.

+ 'H *ayia. MapCa.* + *Mapdi.* Neorcuna. The second line, as Waddington says, is obscure. Perhaps *Mapdi* is for *Mapff-q,* Neorao-ia for *'Avaaraaia.* I should then read: + *Holy Mary.* + *Martha. Anastasia.* INDICES TO PART ABBREVIATIONS

A. M. S. Th. Uspensky: *Archaeological Monuments of Syria (Archeologitcheskie Pamatniki Sirii), Sofia,* 1902 (Publications of the Russian Archaeological Institute in Constantinople, Vii, 1-2).

B. C. H. *Bulletin de Correspondence Hellenique.*

Burton and Drake: *Unexplored Syria,* London, Tinsley Brothers, 1872.

C. I. G. *Corpus Inscriptionum Graecarum.*

C. I. L. *Corpus Inscriptionum Latinarum.*

Clermont-Ganneau. See *Etudes* and *Recueil. Comptes Rend us.* Academic des Inscriptions et BellesLettres: *Comptes Rendus.*

Dussaud and Macler. See *Voyage* and *Mission. Epigr. Gr.* Kaibel: *Epigrammata Graeca ex lapidibus conlecta. Etudes.* Ch. Clermont-Ganneau: *Etudes d'Archeologic Orientale.*

I. G. R. *Inscriptiones Graecac ad res Romanas pertinentes,* edited by Cagnat and Lafaye.

J. Asiat. *Journal Asiatique.*

Migne: *Patrologiae Cursus Completus. Mission.* Dussaud et Macler: *Mission dans les Regions desertiques de la Syrie Moyenne,* Paris, Leroux, 1903= *Nouvelles Archives des Missions scientifiques,* Tome X.

M. P. V. *Mittheilungen und Nachrichten des Deutschen Palaestina-Vereins.*

O. G. I. S. *Orientis Graeci Inscriptiones Selectae,* ed. Dittenberger, Leipzig, Hirzcl, 1903-5.

P. E. F. *Quarterly Statements of the Palestine Exploration Fund. Princeton Arch. Exped. Publications of the Princeton University Archaeological Expedition to Syria in 19041905,* Leyden, Late E. J. Brill, 1907.

R. Bibl. *Revue Biblique. Recueil.* Ch. Clermont-Ganneau: *Recueil d'Archeologie Orientale.*

R. E. G. *Revue des Etudes Grecques. Reise.* E. Sachau: *Reisc in Syrien und Mesopotamien,* Leipzig, Brockhaus, 1883.

R. M. *Rheinisches Museum.* Sachau. See *Reise.*

S. C. Marquis de Vogue: *La Syrie Centrale,* Paris, Baudry, 1865-1877.

Swainson: *The Greek Liturgies,* Cambridge, The University Press, 1884. de Vogue. See S. C. *Voyage.* Dussaud et Macler: *Voyage Archeologique au Sofa et dans le Djebel ed-Dritz,* Paris, Leroux, 1901.

Wad. Waddington: *Inscriptions Grecques et Latines de la Syrie,* Paris, Didot, 1870= Le Bas: *Voyage Archeologique,* Tome III.

Wetzstein: "Ausgewiihlte griechische und latcinische Inschriften, gesammelt auf Reisen in den Trachonen und urn das Haurangebirge," in *Abhandlungen der Akademie der Wissenschaften zu Berlin,* 1863, p. 255 ff.

Z. D. M. G. and Z. M. G. *Zeitschrift der Deutschen MorgenlSndischen Gesellschaft.*

Z. D. P. V. *Zeitschrift des Deutschen Palaestina-Vereins.*

Lightning Source UK Ltd.
Milton Keynes UK
UKOW022111201212

203971UK00010B/444/P